VANCE VIBRATIONS—FEATUR

ted. Mr. Daughety found
ad a new "student" when
ecting mouse dropped
sh class (via
l pipes).

NOVEMBER, 1971

Death By A Cheeseburger

It has been said that when a person dies an unnatural death, his
spirit forever haunts the place of
his doom. Therefore, my spirit will
forever haunt the Vance High School
Cafeteria. day, November 2, started as
day for me.   I slept
ced to skip break-
d study hal

oo
fro
a
e don
you
sider
have

Down

n Bulloc

DEATH BY CHEESEBURGER
HIGH SCHOOL JOURNALISM
IN THE 1990s AND BEYOND

Death By Cheeseburger:
The name and the staff

This book takes its name from a 1971 incident at Vance Senior High School in Henderson, N.C. The school newspaper was shut down that fall based on three student articles. One, "Death By A Cheeseburger," was a satirical tale of the death of the writer after eating a cafeteria cheeseburger. The newspaper was closed, the adviser let go, a novice hired to teach English and journalism — without the student paper.

That story is a microcosm of some discoveries made while researching this book — stories of untrained teachers thrown into advising roles, innocuous stories becoming major controversies, the daily tensions and, as the novice teacher found, the ultimate exhilaration of publishing a student newspaper.

Death By Cheeseburger was conceived and guided by Alice Bonner and Judith Hines. The book was edited by Carol Knopes, copy-edited by Jacqueline Blais and designed and produced by Richard Curtis. Informational graphics were by Jeff Dionise.

Editorial contributors were: Zita Arocha, Gelareh Asayesh, Mike Brodie, Sara Cormeny, Louis Freedberg, Jon Funabiki, Leonard Hall, Retha Hill, Joel Kaplan, Anne Lewis, Shinji Morokuma, Sheila Owens, Michael E. Phelps, Adam Clayton Powell III, Larry Sanders, Mark Thalhimer, Craig W. Trygstad, Ed Wiley III.

Photographers were: Jim Brown, Mike Clemmer, Richard Dole, Steven M. Falk, Rick Friedman, John Glenn, Acey Harper, Joe Kennedy, Ernie Leyba, Scott Maclay, M.L. Miller, David Rees, Jeff Reinking, Barbara Ries, Bob Riha Jr., Shawn Spence, Karen Tam, Bruce Zake and John Zich.

FREE PRESS. FREE SPEECH. FREE SPIRIT.

DEATH BY CHEESEBURGER
HIGH SCHOOL JOURNALISM
IN THE 1990s AND BEYOND

First Amendment

Congress shall make no law
respecting an establishment
of religion, or prohibiting
the free exercise thereof; or abridging the
freedom of speech, or of the press; or the
right of the people
peaceably to assemble,
and to petition the Government for a
redress of grievances.

A publication of
The Freedom Forum
February 1994

Death by cheeseburger / The Freedom Forum — 1st ed.

"The Freedom Forum"
Includes index.
ISBN 0-9640284-0-9 (pbk).
1. Journalism — high school. 2. First Amendment.
I. The Freedom Forum (Arlington, Va.) II. Title.
Manufactured in the United States of America
10   9   8   7   6   5   4   3   2   1

A high school without a newspaper is a poorer school indeed

Growing up in South Dakota during the Depression, I had to work at a succession of after-school jobs to help out my family, but I still found time to serve as editor of the Alpena High School newspaper, *The Echo*. I had held a delivery route and worked in the composing room of my hometown weekly, but *The Echo* gave me my first newsroom experience and the beginning of a lifetime in journalism.

Fifty years later, high school journalism is still one of the best experiences a young person can have. That is why we published *Death By Cheeseburger: High School Journalism in the 1990s and Beyond*.

We at The Freedom Forum believe that the values of free press, free speech and free spirit are best learned early. Secondary education is enriched by the application of those lessons in putting out a school newspaper.

A few students usually gain the direct benefits of learning to report, write, edit and manage time and resources among other skills that are fundamental to the production of a newspaper. But the entire school is better for having a vehicle of expression, a means to exchange ideas, to raise issues and even to provoke controversy. These lessons of free expression and of a society based on free flow of information are the essence of our democracy in the USA. A high school without a newspaper is a poorer school indeed.

Death By Cheeseburger is our best assessment of the state of scholastic journalism in the 1990s. Here you will read about those who succeed and those who struggle to keep journalism alive in our schools. And, regrettably, you will read about those who have given up.

We think you will enjoy the adventures and anecdotes and be enlightened by some of the realities. Most important, we hope you will be left with a renewed appreciation of the value of newspapers in the institutions we trust to train our future citizens.

Allen H. Neuharth
Chairman
The Freedom Forum

Seattle: Teresa Tamura of *The Seattle Times* and student Jean Sim edit photos for The Urban Newspaper Workshop.

St Louis: Mary Beth Tinker, who, in the 1960s, battled for school freedom all the way to the Supreme Court.

Detroit: (l-r) Students Floren Ansong, Jacqueline M. Taylor, Tracie Etheridge, Jabari J. Dew with adviser Mary B. Hines and *Detroit Free Press* coordinator Michele Vernon-Chesley.

Fairfax County, Va.: Carol Lange teaches Intensive Journalistic Writing.

Our goal: Putting high school journalism back in spotlight

During the first week of my high school journalism class in Jackson, Miss., I turned to my best friend David Thomas and asked, "Do you mean they pay you to do this?"

It seemed too good to be true: discovering something you loved that brought a paycheck as well. Until that day, I thought such a dream was reserved for centerfielders of the New York Yankees.

High school journalism has inspired and ignited thousands of careers, thanks largely to hard-working journalism teachers like mine, Richard L. Vinson and Mary Tom Bradley.

But times are changing. High school journalism is being threatened by budget shortages, community indifference, poor teacher training and occasional outright hostility from school administrators. In this increasingly complex Information Age, high school journalism is too important to ignore or minimize. That is why The Freedom Forum produced this first comprehensive report in 20 years on high school journalism.

Death By Cheeseburger: High School Journalism in the 1990s and Beyond is a book committed to the idea that all high school students deserve vehicles of expression and communication. This idea is at the core of The Freedom Forum's mission of free press, free speech and free spirit.

We dedicate *Death By Cheeseburger* to all high school journalism teachers, who endure countless obstacles to give young people their first glimpse at the joys of journalism and the practical importance of the First Amendment.

Charles L. Overby
President and CEO
The Freedom Forum

"Whosoever would overthrow the liberty of a nation must begin by subduing freeness of speech"

By John Seigenthaler
Chairman
The Freedom Forum
First Amendment Center

The nation's newspaper editors, always fearful of legal restraints on their First Amendment liberties, knew they had lost their most loyal judicial advocate when U.S. Supreme Court Justice William Brennan retired on July 20, 1990.

A wave of laudatory editorials flooded their opinion pages in the wake of Brennan's departure, acknowledging, praising and thanking him for his unflinching fidelity to the First Amendment in the face of legal attacks on freedom of the press.

There was an irony in those opinion columns. Slightly more than two years earlier many of the editorialists who praised Brennan's free press record as he retired had deserted him to sing the praises of other members of the Court as they handed down a precedent-altering press-censorship ruling from which he dissented with eloquence and passion.

The story of the Hazelwood East High School journalism case, in which Brennan wrote a stinging dissent, joined by Justices Thurgood Marshall and Harry Blackmun, is well-told in Chapter Seven of *Death By Cheeseburger.*

Many of the editors who rushed to embrace what one newspaper called "the mature logic" of the Court's majority opinion, written by Justice Byron White, have since told me they had not bothered to read Brennan's dissent.

Because this case, *Hazelwood School District vs. Kuhlmeier,* dramatically changed the law of the land and drastically reversed the way school officials view the high school press, Brennan's little-read dissent is worth emphasizing here.

The school board for Hazelwood East High had affirmatively promised in writing at the outset of the school year that "school sponsored publications will not restrict free expression or diverse viewpoints … , " Brennan noted.

That promise notwithstanding, said the Justice, the school principal, "without prior consultation or explanation, excised six articles — comprising two full pages" of the school newspaper, the *Spectrum.*

"He did so," said Brennan, "not because any of the articles would 'materially and substantially interfere with the requirements of appropriate discipline,' but simply because he considered two of the six [articles] 'inappropriate, personal, insensitive and unsuitable' for student consumption."

Brennan declared: "In my view the principal broke more than just a promise. He violated the First Amendment's prohibitions against censorship of any student expression that neither disrupts the classwork nor invades the rights of others … ."

The principal, said Brennan, did not fulfill the school board policy of discussing his censorship with student journalists before he shredded six articles in the paper because he objected to some content in two of them. One of the "offensive" articles dealt with teen pregnancy; the other with divorce.

Nor, the Justice continued, did the principal consider other less oppressive options — deleting or adding words to the articles, or rearranging the layout of the two pages so that the four inoffensive articles he also killed might have been published.

Justice Brennan decried the "brutal manner" with which the principal acted—and the court majority's approval of that brutality.

"Such unthinking contempt for individual rights is intolerable from any state official," Brennan said.

Note that the Justice correctly identifies the principal as a "state official."

None of the editorials I read that embraced the censorship posture of the Supreme Court in *Hazelwood* — and the endorsements came from newspapers large and small — noted Brennan's dissent.

Many editors who rushed to endorse the press censorship in *Hazelwood* have since defended it with the same sort of "mature logic" that guided Justice White in crushing high school press freedom.

I recite here some of that logic, published and spoken by journalists in *Hazelwood's* aftermath:

"Kids who want to be journalists must learn to crawl before they run."

"Teenagers simply don't have the experience to write about such serious subjects as pregnancy and divorce."

"Our schools have become jungles of permissiveness ... If students — even student editors — can defy administrations and principals, there will be anarchy in the classrooms."

" ... An irresponsible teenage editor with a newspaper in his hands can be more dangerous to a school administrator trying to keep order than a student with a gun or drugs in his hands."

"The school administration is the publisher of the newspaper and has the same right to censor the student editor as my publisher has to censor me — and I am 55 years old. The student editors should grow up."

I am sad to say that attitudes that drive such comments are identical to expressions I heard 20 years ago when Jack Nelson wrote *Captive Voices* — a book that recounted the findings of a commission that reported on the state of high school journalism in 1974. I was a member of that commission, which was a project of the Robert F. Kennedy Memorial.

There are cases of outrageous censorship documented here. They are horror stories — gripping to read, oppressive to think about, offensive to the First Amendment.

Justice Brennan, of course, made the seminal point in his dissent: The school administrator is a state official, not a newspaper publisher. He is paid by tax dollars to run a school, not to censor newspapers. The First Amendment bars state officials from the business of censorship.

As Brennan pointed out in his dissent, the 1969 Supreme Court decision *Tinker vs. Des Moines* acknowledged that students may not engage in speech that "materially and substantially interferes with other requirements of appropriate discipline."

No, students may not engage in conduct that disrupts the good order of the school. But beyond that their *Tinker* rights should remain inviolate, as Justice Brennan, the champion of editors, both professional and student, has consistently declared.

When I talk to my old friends from professional journalism, it hurts to hear them talk about the immaturity, inability and lack of knowledge and talent of today's youth.

The truth is that this generation of young people has been saddled by "mature" generations' difficult issues — AIDS and drugs and violence and sexual promiscuity and single-parent homes — problems unprecedented in the nation's history.

The suggestion that they are immature and lacking in knowledge would be laughable were it not ludicrous.

The truth is that among every generation of teen editors there has been clear evidence of remarkable maturity and talent.

The classic story that appeals to me has to do with a teenage editor who was a dropout, his formal education completed by the time he was 14. He had planned to go to Harvard, this student journalist, but his father died and so he became what we would call an intern, what they called in his day an "apprentice," to his brother who owned a newspaper in Boston.

The older brother thought his father had not adequately disciplined the young journalist and made life miserable for him. But he did give him the opportunity to work in every department of the newspaper — from the reporting, writing and editorializing to the production of it.

It was a rewarding experience for that young journalist. He was 14 when he came to the paper. And he found there a career that was to aid him throughout his life.

If you review his work at that early age you conclude that he was far more talented than his older brother. In many ways, he accomplished more with that newspaper than the brother. Still later, he moved out of Massachusetts and founded his own publication in Philadelphia.

Now, the tone of this Boston newspaper his brother owned was largely anti-establishment. It challenged authority. It criticized and satirized the policies and the politics and the administration of most of the institutions in Boston. It was very tough, for example, on education as a system, particularly higher education and more particularly on Harvard.

Much of what was published was satire. Some of the most biting examples of it ultimately led the older brother to a period of imprisonment because he had offended the Boston authorities.

The young intern, by that time 16, was about to become the temporary publisher of the newspaper.

And he was up to it. He knew all there was to know about the operation of the paper.

His brother was taken into custody, held without bail, taken before a court of law without an indictment, thrown into jail without a trial.

The offending article for which he was jailed would be considered today a mild gibe. The authorities thought it a high affront. The story had to do with pirates who were preying on ships near the Massachusetts coast. It included this sentence: "We are advised that the government of Massachusetts is fitting out a ship to go after the pirates … " And it named the ship's captain, and said, "it is thought he will be on his way sometime this month, weather permitting it."

The words teased and needled the government that had decided to wait a month to pursue the pirates. It is not clear what role the 16-year-old apprentice of the *New England Courant* actually had in the production of the story, but his knowledge of the newspaper's operation gave him certain knowledge of it.

It was on a June day in 1722 that this 16-year-old was called to give evidence against his older brother, whom he had come to despise. It might have been a temptation to testify against him. But he held his tongue.

Later he wrote about it:

"I, too, was taken up and examined before the council at 16 … but though I did not give them any satisfaction, they contented themselves with admonishing me and then they dismissed me."

"I had the management of the paper," he later wrote.

During the first week of his brother's imprisonment, he wrote much of the paper's content, edited and printed it and helped distribute it.

While his brother was in solitary confinement, he continued to run the paper. He later said, "during my brother's confinement, I wrote a good deal. I resented his imprisonment, notwithstanding our private differences, but now I had management of the paper and I made bold to give our rulers some rubs which my brother took very kindly to but which others considered or read and considered me to be a young genius with a turn toward libeling and satire."

Sixteen years old, and he had his own paper.

After three weeks, the Governor, failing to get the legislature to pass an ex-post-facto law that would declare the *Courant* "seditious and scandalous," released his brother.

In a few months, however, the unrepentant newspaper once more had him in trouble with the authorities. He became a fugitive.

The older brother designated his younger brother to become, officially, the manager and the operator of the *New England Courant.*

That teenage editor-publisher, of course, was Benjamin Franklin.

Those who know of his early career will recall the series of essays he wrote and published under the byline "Silence Dogood." There were 14 of them that attacked virtually every sacred institution in the Boston society and every revered aspect of the Massachusetts Bay Colony culture.

He also reprinted the arguments on press freedom that previously had been published in Great Britain under the name "Cato." They included these words: "This sacred privilege of free speech is so essential to free governments that the security of property and freedom of speech always go together. Whosoever would overthrow the liberty of a nation must begin by subduing freeness of speech."

I have no doubt that the same editors — not to mention the Supreme Court Justices — who deny rights to student editors would have found Ben Franklin immature, irresponsible, insensitive and intrusive of the privacy of others. His paper included examples of bad grammar, occasionally bad spelling and, often, bad taste. Unlike the student editors in *Hazelwood,* his paper was judged by the judges of his day to be disruptive.

Having considered the work of the high school press from *Tinker* to *Hazelwood* and from *Captive Voices* to *Death By Cheeseburger,* no one could square the present plight of high school editors with the language of the First Amendment.

And it is impossible to understand how high school administrators, Supreme Court Justices or editors of daily newspapers can square the censorship of student newspapers with the history of the country, the writings of Thomas Jefferson and James Madison — or the work of young Benjamin Franklin.

Justice Brennan, the best friend a free press ever had, deserved the support of the nation's newspaper editors in *Hazelwood.* And so did the student journalists.

Contents

Maurice Hill combines parenting his son, Maurice Jr., with producing videos at Paul Robeson High School in Chicago.

Lori Mathews, right, a reporter for the *Detroit Free Press,* also is a mentor to high school student Darlene Harper, left.

California State student Justino Aguila learned about journalism from a visiting *L.A. Times* staffer.

Jessica Roman studies video journalism at Middle College High School in Queens, N.Y.

H.L. Hall, adviser of the journalism program at Kirkwood (Mo.) High School, with colleagues Debra Shrout, left, and Nancy Menchhofer, center.

DEATH BY CHEESEBURGER
HIGH SCHOOL JOURNALISM
IN THE 1990s AND BEYOND

Imagine a time, centuries from now, when archaeologists and anthropologists discover a trove of high school newspapers representing the United States in the 1990s. The scientists might well be delighted by the richness and idiosyncrasies of the find, yet perplexed by the differences and the inconsistencies.

For in the absence of any other vehicle, the high school newspaper offers the voice of America's young people within their own time: It chronicles the condition of scholastic life: the hopes, fears and gripes of students, their victories and their failures, and the teen-driven triage that determines who is "in" or "out" or just plain overlooked.

From the magnificent to the murky and the mundane, the newspapers that serve the nation's high schools and their students form a touchstone, interpreting and connecting a generation that most often is overlooked by the professional media.

These young people are groping for answers to what a high school newspaper is supposed to be. What is its mission? For whom is it written? What should it cover? The answers to these questions determine the content of a newspaper.

A Freedom Forum content analysis of newspapers from 233 high schools across the country shows the vast range of the high school press:

• March 10, 1993: Stuyvesant High School's *The Spectator* in New York City brags that seniors Irwin Lin and Martin Fisch advanced to the finals in the prestigious annual Westinghouse Science Talent Search, and that 33 others made it as far as the semifinals.

• Feb. 5, 1993: Chapman High School's *The Dickinsonian* in Chapman, Kan., reports on the Future Farmers of America's annual Sweetheart competition. The story says six young women competed by sawing and nailing wooden boards, catching eggs in paper cups and diapering pigs. The winner will be named at the upcoming Sweetheart Dance.

• Feb. 12, 1993: Lakewood High School's *The Lakewood Times* in Lakewood, Ohio, tells of a plan to install surveillance cameras in the school's cafeteria to stop fights. The story says some students think the $15,000 plan is a waste of money and that campus officials don't "trust us enough."

• March 12, 1993: Newton North High School's *Newtonite* in Newtonville, Mass., reports a student was stabbed during a fight and that the suspected assailant was charged with assault with a dangerous weapon. The newspaper also has an editorial condemning violence.

• April 9, 1993: City High School's *Little Hawk* in Iowa City, Iowa, chronicles the nation's sometimes violent debate over abortion in a feature story. A companion piece asks students whether the recent murder of an abortion doctor by a pro-life activist is justified. They all say no.

Do these subjects reflect the interests of students, the whims of the young journalists or the fiats of the school? To be sure, there is plenty of the humdrum of student life. In our analysis, school-related events and news account for 37 percent of the typical high school newspaper. After this comes sports news, editorials and a sprinkling of other subjects (fiction, cartoons, etc.).

Entertainment reviews, school surveys, and pro-

Chapter 1

Magnificent, murky and mundane: What's in today's high school newspapers?

1

files of students are popular, but after that the issues that most frequently appear in the high school press are racial prejudice and race relations, drug and alcohol use, family issues, college, and an array of sex-related issues, including AIDS and safe sex.

Some student newspapers cover changes in the class schedule, others examine the changes in the American family. Some cover the parking policy, others write about the prevalence of sexually transmitted diseases.

What students are telling us

The Nov. 30, 1992, headline in *The Fourth Estate* of Bartlesville (Okla.) High School reads: "Lost souls: Teens search for new hope." The story reports the statistical chances for the Class of '93: They stand a 40 percent chance of being a partner in a pregnancy, a 65 percent chance of becoming regular users of alcohol, a 25 percent chance of being abused at home, a 25 percent chance of living in poverty. An opinion piece says: "*It is time we fight teen pregnancy like we fight drug abuse; with education, in all grades, where it is needed.*"

Megan Stacy writes in *The Gavel*, Holmes High School, San Antonio, Texas, on Dec. 18, 1992: "*… sometimes, I think television has stolen my heart away. Taken it and wrapped it up in a thick covering of cable cords and steel. Taken it from me willingly and turned it into stone … . TV has made today's kids indifferent to death. But, I never thought it would happen to me.*"

Some teen journalists can jab. Consider this October 1992 editorial by Lalayafe Manning from the *Panther Press* at Chicago's DuSable High School: "*While there are gang bangers, drug dealers and thugs still causing havoc around the school, innocent people who come to school to learn and get an education every day … are being harassed for 'wrong doing.' These students are being harassed not only by the school staff but are 'running scared' from the violence that is persistent and getting worse… . A staff person can come in the lunchroom and harass a person about a two-day-old issue and disturb a person's lunch in the process, while the gang bangers are still in the hallways harassing students in class, making wild noises, just being a nuisance. NOBODY is stopping them! My question is when does it stop? So I'm asking you students, how do you feel about this injustice? And Mr. Mingo [the principal], what are you going to do about it?*"

Some teen journalists can surprise us. The Dec. 9, 1992, opinion section of the *Westlake Featherduster* at Westlake High School in Austin, Texas, includes this story by Daniel Fu:

"*I looked at the scrumptious curve of her luscious thigh and the soft flesh of her breasts and heaved a sigh of contentment. She would be around for a long time … .*" The subject: Thanksgiving turkey.

Some print outspoken opinions. "'Yo Nigga!' — THINK About What You're Saying," reads the headline from a Dec. 22, 1992, editorial deploring the use of the word "nigger" among blacks, published in *The Ellington Express* at Duke Ellington School of the Arts in Washington, D.C.

Or, from "The Consequences of The Los Angeles Riots," by Reyna de la Cruz in the *Pathfinder*, John C. Fremont High School, Los Angeles, in June 1992:

"*Many say the riots were an excuse for juvenile delinquents to destroy and destruct property. However, for those who live in South Central L.A. the riots were simply a way of expressing the frustration that many people have lived with for many years.*

"*As a young person living in South Central, I question things such as 'Why [are] judicial systems … created to help the people fail? How can the people who took articles like milk be criticized so severely when there are congressmen bouncing checks and sitting at home living their daily lives as if they never committed a crime … . As for those who so very coldly judge South Central L.A. all I can say is 'Not everything is like Beverly Hills 90210.'*"

Like their professional brethren, some high school journalists grapple with the toughest issues in journalism. The *Beak 'n Eye*, the student newspaper at West High School in Davenport, Iowa, developed an in-depth report for a Dec. 18, 1992, issue called: "Gays Under Attack." The package looked at discrimination against gays, local and school policies, and whether one is born gay or chooses to become gay. Sidebars told the story of a sophomore at a local high school who is gay and featured a local support group for gay youth.

In an editorial titled "Homosexuals deserve our respect," Brendan Roberts, the editor in chief, describes some of the challenges the staff faced in reporting the package.

"*The stories were extremely tough to write and finding gays to interview was difficult … . Our in-depth reporters also faced the ridicule of others in order to get their story. It took courage to write about homosexuality despite the public attitude. How much courage? When one reporter interviewed a West High counselor about gay support groups, he asked if she was a 'member of that group' because she was writing [about] such a 'forbidden' topic.*"

Some high school newspapers in our survey run intensely personal stories. They are all the more powerful because they use the personal to lend meaning to the universal — quoting students who were in gangs, students who became pregnant, students who had abortions, and students who are gay or who have gay parents.

"*I was there sweating and thinking about my little innocent baby inside me. Maybe it was crying, or sensing it was about to die … . Maybe it was my fault for*

At a glance

DuSable High School
Chicago, Ill.

<u>Principal:</u> Charles E. Mingo.
<u>Number of students:</u> 1,399 ('92-93).
<u>Ethnic breakdown:</u> 100% black.
<u>Publication adviser:</u> Lucia Podraza.
<u>Newspaper:</u> *Panther Press*, 1,600-1,800 circulation, tabloid, 12 pages average; $350/issue annual budget; published 7 times a year.
<u>Revenue sources:</u> $4,300 from student fees and principal's funds.
<u>Staff:</u> 53 (26 of whom are journalism class students).
<u>Computers:</u> Mac IIsi with scanner, laser printer, Tandy for word processing (for '93-94, have purchased 10 IBMs, will use Aldus PageMaker).
<u>Software:</u> Aldus PageMaker, Claris MacWrite.
<u>Offered for credit:</u> English elective, though students can also work on paper as an extracurricular activity.
<u>Other publication activities:</u> Yearbook, done by adults; literary magazine, extracurricular.

Sean Jensen, left, and Elizabeth Del Pino were part of a group of high school students who reviewed 233 school newspapers in summer 1993.

Our analysis: 12 students, 233 papers from 32 states

The Freedom Forum High School Newspaper content analysis was conducted by a group of 12 students during the summer of 1993. Newspapers from 233 high schools in 32 states and the District of Columbia were reviewed for types of stories, size, amount of advertising, and subjects in photos.

A listing of student newspapers analyzed is in the appendix.

Surveyors were chosen for their journalism experience. Most worked on their high school newspapers or independent student papers. Many were participants in the 1993 Howard University Multicultural High School Journalism Workshop. Students from Thomas Jefferson High School for Science and Technology in Fairfax County, Va., were from the Intensive Journalistic Writing class.

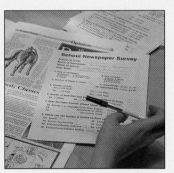

Jeanell Benjamin is a 1993 graduate of Bowie High School in Bowie, Md., where she wrote for the *Pacesetter.* She attends Morgan State University.

Chakesha Bowman is a senior at H.D. Woodson High School in Washington, D.C., where she is managing editor of *The Insider.*

Suzanne Coyle is a 1993 graduate of Thomas Jefferson High School for Science and Technology in Fairfax County, Va., where she was an Intensive Journalistic Writing student. She attends Virginia Polytechnic Institute and State University.

Elizabeth Del Pino is a senior at Montgomery Blair High School in Silver Spring, Md., where she writes for *The Silver Chips.* She is also on the staff of

Young D.C., the metropolitan Washington newspaper by and about teenagers.

Jeff Fishman, a 1993 graduate of Winston Churchill High School in Potomac, Md., is the former managing editor of *Young D.C.* He attends Brandeis University.

Jonathan "Chip" Goines, a senior at Thomas Jefferson High School for Science and Technology in Fairfax County, Va., writes for *tjToday* and also is a reporter for *Young D.C.*

Marianne Jacoub is a junior at Paul VI High School in Fairfax, Va., and news editor of *Panther Press.*

Michael Janssen is a 1993 graduate of Thomas Jefferson High School for Science and Technology in Fairfax County, Va., where he was feature editor of *tjToday.* He attends Wake Forest University.

Sean Jensen is a senior at Mount Vernon High School in Alexandria, Va., and sports editor of *Young D.C.* He participated in the 1993 Washington Association of Black Journalists Workshop.

Suzanne Newby, a senior at St. Andrew's Episcopal School in Bethesda, Md., was a 1993 summer intern at The Freedom Forum.

Marisa Stubbs, a senior at Oxon Hill High School in Oxon Hill, Md., is the editorial page editor of *The Searchlight.*

Mina Trudeau, a 1993 graduate of Thomas Jefferson High School for Science and Technology in Fairfax County, Va., attends Hampshire College.

S C H O O L   N E W S P A P E R
SURVEY RESULTS

Most newspapers are tabloid size:

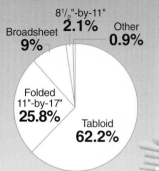

- 8½"-by-11" **2.1%**
- Broadsheet **9%**
- Other **0.9%**
- Folded 11"-by-17" **25.8%**
- Tabloid **62.2%**

Few use color

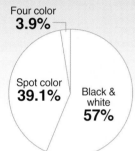

- Four color **3.9%**
- Spot color **39.1%**
- Black & white **57%**

Average: 12 pages

Average of all papers	Those with advertising
12.47 pages	**13.09** pages

Types of content

Avg. number of stories per issue:

School events/news	**11.04**
Sports	**6.36**
Editorials	**5.27**
Letters	**1.00**
Editorial cartoons	**0.68**
Fiction/poetry	**0.50**
Cartoon strips	**0.32**

Percent of all papers with item:

School events/news	**100%**
Sports	**96%**
Editorials	**96%**
Letters	**49%**
Editorial cartoons	**41%**
Cartoon strips	**18%**
Fiction/poetry	**15%**

School news leads content

Percent of all stories:

School events/news	**37%**
Sports	**21%**
Editorials	**18%**
Letters	**4%**
Fiction/poetry	**2%**
Editorial cartoons	**2%**
Cartoon strips	**1%**
Other	**15%**

Percent of papers that have:

- World/national news **42%**
- Community news **63%**

Nine out of 10 papers carry advertising ...

- No **10.2%**
- Yes **89.8%**

...but few offer classifieds

- Yes **10.5%**
- No **89.5%**

Most ads are small

Average number of ads per issue (all papers):

- 1/8 page **10**
- 1/4 page **2**
- 1/2 page **0.5**
- Full page **0.2**

Who appears in photos?

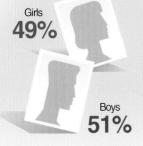

- Girls **49%**
- Boys **51%**

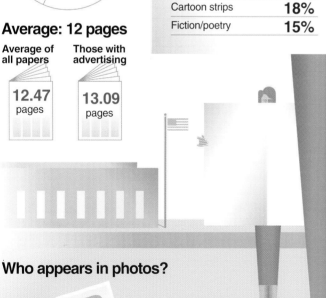
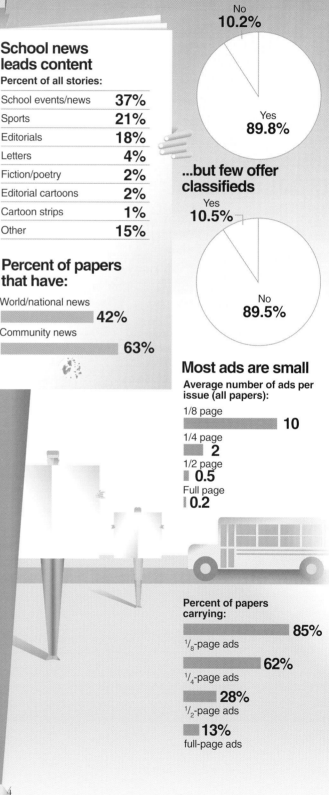

Percent of papers carrying:

- **85%** ⅛-page ads
- **62%** ¼-page ads
- **28%** ½-page ads
- **13%** full-page ads

4

SURVEY RESULTS

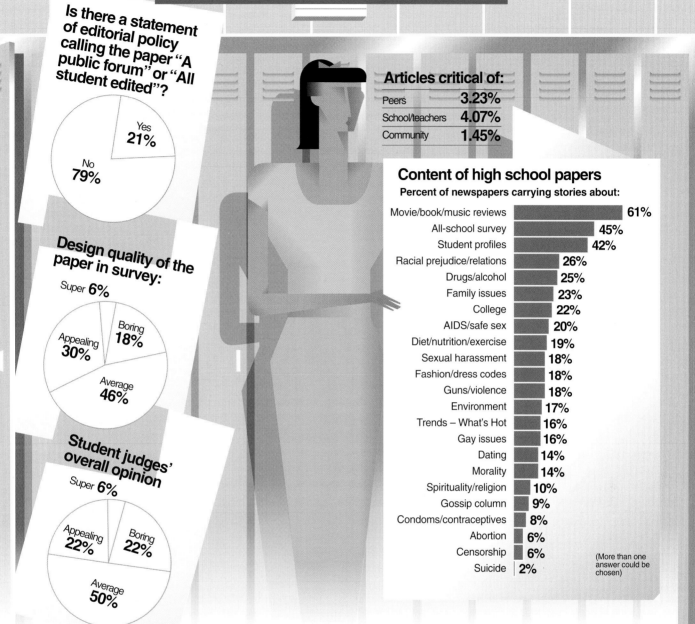

Is there a statement of editorial policy calling the paper "A public forum" or "All student edited"?

- Yes 21%
- No 79%

Design quality of the paper in survey:

- Super 6%
- Boring 18%
- Appealing 30%
- Average 46%

Student judges' overall opinion

- Super 6%
- Appealing 22%
- Boring 22%
- Average 50%

Articles critical of:

Peers	3.23%
School/teachers	4.07%
Community	1.45%

Content of high school papers
Percent of newspapers carrying stories about:

Movie/book/music reviews	61%
All-school survey	45%
Student profiles	42%
Racial prejudice/relations	26%
Drugs/alcohol	25%
Family issues	23%
College	22%
AIDS/safe sex	20%
Diet/nutrition/exercise	19%
Sexual harassment	18%
Fashion/dress codes	18%
Guns/violence	18%
Environment	17%
Trends – What's Hot	16%
Gay issues	16%
Dating	14%
Morality	14%
Spirituality/religion	10%
Gossip column	9%
Condoms/contraceptives	8%
Abortion	6%
Censorship	6%
Suicide	2%

(More than one answer could be chosen)

Impact of color on design opinion

The use of color — both spot and four color — had a direct impact on opinions concerning the appeal of the design of the newspaper. Those newspapers that used color received higher marks in both the Appealing and Super categories. How the papers rated for design:

	Black & white	Spot color	Four color
Boring	21%	14%	11%
Average	53%	38%	11%
Appealing	21%	42%	45%
Super	5%	6%	33%

Impact of color on overall opinion

Although the use of color positively affected opinion about the paper's design, it did not carry through into the overall opinion of the papers. In fact, the papers with four color that were rated Super in design failed to show up Super overall. How the papers rated overall:

	Black & white	Spot color	Four color
Boring	26%	17%	11%
Average	52%	47%	45%
Appealing	18%	28%	44%
Super	4%	8%	0%

Impact of general content on overall opinion

Papers with world/national news tend to influence opinion more positively than those with community news.

	World/national news		Community news	
	Yes	No	Yes	No
Boring	13%	29%	17%	29%
Average	48%	52%	47%	58%
Appealing	31%	15%	29%	11%
Super	8%	4%	7%	2%

Source: Computer analysis by L&D Information Services, 1993

not being strong enough to face the problem and have my baby instead of getting rid of it." — Yanina Gomez, on the abortion she had at the age of 15, as told in the November 1992 issue of *The Rainbow,* the student newspaper at Bell Multicultural High School, Washington, D.C.

In writing about the issues in their lives, some high school newspapers make few distinctions between the personal and the public realm. The result is a more intimate account of their readers' lives.

Consider a spring 1993 issue of *Train Of Thought,* the news journal at Benjamin Banneker Academic High School in Washington, D.C.

The front page is devoted to President Bill Clinton's inauguration and the District of Columbia's quest for statehood. Inside, movie reviews and stories on high school clubs share space with essays and poems on a broad range of topics:

• Dorian Baucum, on "good" and "bad" hair: *"It is a symptom of a problem that has divided Black America for decades … . Subconsciously, the young women that approached me saw 'good' hair as hair with a texture closer to that of Europeans … . 'Bad' hair to them was anything African, anything kinky, anything nappy."*

• Daphne Jones' journal entry describes how her family came home from a trip to find their home trashed by vandals: *"I noticed the graffiti on the far wall of the living room … . Mom read it aloud: 'The next time I'll hang your a—, KKK Power.' "*

• LaShawn Howell, describing an encounter on the bus home from school: *"The ski-masked boy stood up over Tony as though he was going to jack him up right there on the bus. The whole back of the bus had gotten quiet, as everyone looked on. The ski-masked boy sat down and continued his insults. All the while his hand was in his pocket. The girl beside me cringed, and I sent a silent prayer to God, hoping that the ski-masked boy didn't have a gun.*

Tony's friends, Oliver and Eric, sat by trying to act like they didn't know Tony. … Tony sat there, his eyes swimming with tears, as he tried to ignore the boy." [Tony lives, but gets roughed up and loses his Walkman.] *" 'Nice guys finish last, they say.' "*

Sadly, these young journalists also must reckon with death. Sometimes the world of young people seems to be crashing down all around them — accidents, homicides and suicides are the three top causes of deaths among people in the 15-24 age group. More high school newspapers are forced to develop policies on how to handle student deaths and suicides. For some teens, writing becomes a way to cope with death.

"On Monday June 1, 1992, my brother died at the Washington Hospital Center at 6:17 a.m.," writes Brenda Stanback in early winter 1993. She is a reporter for *Brighter Days* at M.M. Washington Career High School, Washington, D.C.

"Martin was shot on Lamont St. N.W. over eleven times all over his body. My brother was twenty-one years old … . Sometimes I still cry when I think about my brother … . Sometimes I just go in my room and write ten letters to God! Sometimes more. It just doesn't make any sense that so many young teens are being killed today for materialistic objects, a girl or a boy, or sometimes for even looking at someone the wrong way. The world today is so crazy."

Measuring success

But these examples don't mean that every campus newspaper represents a paragon of outstanding, or even good, journalism. In truth, the old-fashioned bell curve is very much in play. A journalistic critique of the high school press would

At a glance

James Bowie High School
Austin, Texas

<u>Principal:</u> Kent Ewing.

<u>Publication adviser:</u> John McCartney.

<u>Newspaper:</u> *The Lone Star Dispatch;* monthly; tabloid; 4,000 circulation, including through local grocery stores; 28 pages average; annual budget: $20,000.

<u>Revenue sources:</u> A school district "free newspaper fund"; $6,400 - $11,000 from advertising; yearbook profits.

<u>Staff:</u> 9 in class, 40 free-lancers.

<u>Computers:</u> IBM PC 25s, 3 Mac IIsis, one Dell 386.

<u>Software:</u> Aldus PageMaker, Aldus Freehand, WordPerfect, MS Word, Adobe Photoshop, Adobe Illustrator.

<u>Offered for credit:</u> General elective.

<u>Other publication activities:</u> Yearbook for general elective; literary magazine produced by yearbook students as extracurricular activity.

be no different from a critique of any group of newspapers in this country. The criteria are the same. Do stories have more than one source? Do they illustrate the impact of an event on those primarily affected? Are they balanced? Are they thoroughly reported? Are they well-organized? Are they well-written? Do they parrot the sources or maintain a healthy skepticism? Are they reader-friendly?

High school journalism is subject to the same pitfalls as professional journalism. In schools, as in society, some newspapers do better than others at avoiding those pitfalls. Some newspapers are excellent, most are average, and some poor. Just how many belong in each category depends on who's doing the grading and what standards are applied.

When The Freedom Forum, as a part of this survey, asked a dozen teenage journalists to rate 233 newspapers, they concluded:
- 6 percent were "super."
- 22 percent were "appealing."
- 50 percent were "average."
- 22 percent of the newspapers were "boring."

"This activity has been somewhat disheartening," says Michael Janssen, a 1993 graduate of Thomas Jefferson High School for Science and Technology in Fairfax County, Va. "I really haven't seen many decent examples of high-profile journalism."

Here's what Marisa Stubbs, a senior at Oxon Hill High School in Oxon Hill, Md., says about the exciting newspapers:

"The newspapers that were enjoyable covered a variety of topics and issues, not just 'bubble gum' issues. They were controversial and aroused opinions, and maybe dissension, not just agreement or the label 'goodie-two-shoes.'"

Suzanne Coyle, a 1993 graduate of Thomas Jefferson High School for Science and Technology in Fairfax County, Va., describes the average papers:

"The average papers ... are the ones that have nothing that particularly stands out. They have the same articles in all of the papers — dances, football games, parking lot problems, and a few feature articles on topics such as gays in the military, vegetarianism or abortion. They aren't necessarily bad, but they aren't that great either."

Here's what Suzanne Newby, a senior at St. Andrew's Episcopal School in Bethesda, Md., says about boring newspapers:

"One flaw in the 'bad' newspapers is poor layout. The articles were crammed together and hard to follow. The second thing I noticed ... was their concentration on pointless issues like prom and homecoming."

You might take the opinions of these teen analysts with a grain of salt: Each brought his or her own prejudices to the table. Naturally, they reflect the confidence and brashness of youth, the angst of

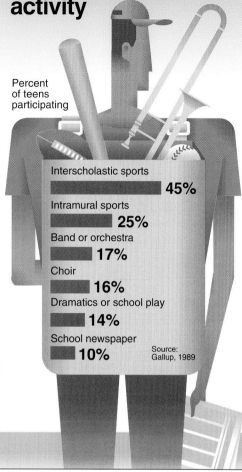

How school newspapers rank as an extracurricular activity

Percent of teens participating

Interscholastic sports **45%**

Intramural sports **25%**

Band or orchestra **17%**

Choir **16%**

Dramatics or school play **14%**

School newspaper **10%**

Source: Gallup, 1989

Looking back

"Though there was a high school paper, I was actually involved in a newspaper outside of school. I started working at *Black News*, a weekly community newspaper in Brooklyn, when I was 16, and became the assistant editor. I also sold the paper, and it was a wonderful experience to do that, to see it getting out in the community. I did go on to college as a pre-med student, and only took one journalism class there. But I went to graduate school in journalism and here I am now."

Addie M. Rimmer is the assistant managing editor of the Long Beach (Calif.) Press-Telegram. *She is a 1970 graduate of George W. Wingate High School in Brooklyn, N.Y.*

a developing generation. But they also reflect a demand for more sophisticated student journalism, student newspapers that provide an accurate mirror of our times and a road map to help plot a course for our future.

Putting out high school PR ...

Our collection of high school newspapers reveals a lot about the life of America's teenagers. But in some ways, they hide the truth and plant false ideas about the important issues of the day. That leads us to some of the Great Mysteries for our archaeologist friend to ponder.

Why do some teen journalists push the envelope of expression, while others practice safe journalism and fill their newspapers with what Suzanne Newby calls "pointless issues"?

Who ultimately decides what gets into the newspaper? Why are some subjects taboo?

Why do most student newspapers portray their schools as almost exclusively white? A close look at the photographs will demonstrate this point. The exceptions: schools in inner cities or in regions with large ethnic minority and immigrant populations.

Why do so many newspapers have just a handful of young writers and photographers listed in the staff box? Who decides who can participate, who can't, and who will simply be ignored?

The answers to these questions may well come to our scientist in the next chapters, when we ask two central questions:

Who teaches America's students the craft of journalism? And how do they teach that most fundamental American right, the right of free speech?

Putting out a high school weekly

In 1986, four years after taking over as journalism adviser at Narbonne High School in Harbor City, Calif., Alison Rittger made a gutsy decision. She doubled the publishing schedule of *The Green & Gold,* Narbonne's newspaper. Since then it has come out weekly, more than 30 times in a year.

"It seemed like the best way to be realistic about making mistakes and improving," says Rittger. Because students always put a deadline off as long as possible, she figured, why not just make that deadline come more frequently? "As we try to perfect our skills, there is always next week to improve."

The payoff seems worth it. There is a certain status to handing out a newspaper to a waiting line of students outside the journalism classroom every Friday morning. When Thursday night is game night for one of the athletic teams at Narbonne, *The Green & Gold* staff works late and the scores and stories appear in the next morning's newspaper.

While a weekly schedule does not allow the luxury of many in-depth articles, staffers do extensive reporting on topics they consider important, says Rittger. What may be missing in depth is made up for in currency, she points out.

Each year Rittger gives the staff the choice of weekly or biweekly publication. "They always choose the weekly schedule," she says. The process is easier now, thanks to computerization of design and composition. "We have our own photo lab here. We do our own halftones, our own graphics."

The paper goes to 2,000 students plus a number of home-delivery subscribers, most of them parents. The annual cost of printing is about $10,000. Aggressive advertising sales bring in $4,000. The student body contributes the rest from the sale of activity cards and other fundraisers.

The Green & Gold prints four to eight pages a week. One price of frequent publication is competing for national awards against monthly newspapers that have much more time to develop stories, graph-

ics and photos. Each year Rittger's students plan a special 16-page issue that they submit to competitions. The paper usually places in the top 10 in "best of show" competitions.

Narbonne High School has a magnet math/science program, drawing students from all over Los Angeles to Harbor City. "Ours is not a wealthy neighborhood. We have one of the biggest Hispanic gangs in the area. But we have a lot of motivated students," says Rittger.

She recruits constantly to keep a representative racial balance on the staff. In the 1993-'94 school year, *The Green & Gold's* editor in chief is Japanese, with three black editors, a Hispanic, and many Asian-Americans. "We're always looking around and seeing how we stack up," she says. "We don't pretend that race isn't an issue."

Revisiting a high school newspaper

In 1979, Gelareh Asayesh graduated from Chapel Hill High School, a few miles from the University of North Carolina. In 1993, she returned to see how the journalism program was faring. Here is her story.

Long after the last class has ended, the students on *The Proconian* staff are coming and going in the halls of Chapel Hill High School. It is a Thursday in late April — production day.

In the journalism room, Ted Kaplan is cutting and pasting pages with exquisite care, a paper bag spilling bottles of rubber cement onto a table at his side. The paper's adviser, Don LaCoste, is grading papers in the teachers' lounge. He periodically strolls into the computer lab where Noah Kotch, the 18-year-old editor, sits typing at the keyboard of a computer. A couple of ads won't fit, and the story on the search for a new principal had to be updated five minutes ago.

Noah Kotch, 1993 editor of *The Proconian*, felt strongly about the paper's independence.

Familiar territory for anyone who has worked on a high school newspaper. *The Proconian* is typical of many high schools where the editor, staff and adviser are trying to hammer out policy, learn journalism, and put out a paper all at the same time.

For 67 years, *The Proconian's* mission has been to detail the pros and cons of the school. That's how it got its name. In my time here, *The Proconian* put the emphasis on things like ski trips, foreign exchange students and the prom. There was more excitement in the hallways than there was in the newspaper — such as the mysterious streaker who did a flit through the courtyard one year.

These days, however, there is more "con" to *The Proconian.*

The staff of *The Proconian* today writes about multiculturalism, sexual harassment and condoms in the schools. The paper exposed a grade gap between black and white students. That report led to a school system panel to study the issue. It reported on students who rejected nomination to the National Honor Society, placing the criteria for membership under scrutiny. It closely tracked the search for a new principal, questioning the need for secrecy and the delay in hiring a new administrator.

Acting Principal Marguerite Peebles often calls the editor, Noah, in to talk about stories that trouble her. Earlier in the year, she addressed the journalism class about what she believed was proper to print.

There are tensions between Noah and adviser LaCoste, about the direction the paper should go in and the role the adviser should play. (LaCoste: "I think Noah thinks my only role is to let them in and out of the building." Noah: "I have very strong opinions about the independence of the paper.")

Noah has a role model that would not have occurred to the Class of '79: *The New York Times.* He reads it daily. But there is some debate about Noah's view of the *Times.* That is where some of the conflict comes.

The staff overruled Noah when he wanted to endorse political candidates.

LaCoste sometimes shows teachers or administrators copies of stories before they are published. "I ride this fine line between being loyal to (the staff) and loyal to the adult part of running the school." LaCoste pulled a story written in German because he felt most students wouldn't be able to read it. He also cut the phrase "whup-ass" from another story.

When he became editor, Noah set an aggressive editorial policy, trying to live up to the traditional press role of watchdog. He emphasized hard news while adding trendy features like a column on the popular TV show *Beverly Hills 90210.* He cut out club news and awards listings, disdaining them as "fluff." He doubled the length of the paper and added an Op-Ed page.

Opinions about *The Proconian* vary widely. Says Noah, "We're a real paper. We write about school politics, school policy.... We're using the power of the press like real newspapers do."

Adviser LaCoste: "I think the paper needs to be more representative of the entire student body. It should be read more."

Wendy Nichols, 17: "I always read it. A lot of people say *The Proconian* is too focused on the bad parts of the school, on negative things, on anything controversial. But I think that's really good."

Quana Mitchell, 16: "They need to stop printing that thing. It's just a waste of paper. They tell you if a white person is playing hockey. They don't tell you a black person can sing. They need to put in stuff black people do for a change."

Todd Mesibov, 17, co-sports editor: "I think we've totally missed the mark on the mission of a regular high school paper.... We're so fixated on becoming a 'real' paper and trying to expose 'real' issues that we've completely alienated the student body from our news pages."

Amy Evans, 18, staff writer: "The news puts me to sleep. It's journalism but I personally think the newspaper has not done the school a service."

Noah defends *The Proconian's* stance. "We're doing what real newspapers do," he says. "Real newspapers in many ways push agendas and push ideas and have an editorial policy that's somewhat reflected in the articles." Looking over his year as editor, Noah says, "simply the fact that students have some clout is in itself important."

Contest judges' opinions on student newspapers' evolution

Four of the best-known judges in national high school journalism competitions talk about how student newspapers are evolving:

Ron Clemons, who advises the student newspaper at Truman High School in Independence, Mo., has judged hundreds of student newspapers for state and national organizations during the past 20 years.

During that time he has seen student newspapers come full circle — from aggressive, sometimes sensationalized reporting in the rebellious '70s to tamer school-oriented news in the '80s to a more in-depth handling of sensitive social issues in the '90s.

"I think they are coming back to issues they did cover 20 years ago. There are a lot of stories about sexual problems of teenagers, about violence in the schools . . . feature stories dealing with death, suicide and really sensitive issues."

The difference, according to Clemons, is that "in the '70s kids were very active and there was rebellion and they questioned things . . . but now it's more of a quiet rebellion and they are asking a lot of questions and wanting to know why."

Teenagers also are writing more than in the past about school policies. "They are questioning dress codes and what the administration is doing both in editorials and news stories," Clemons says.

Generally, he says, today's teen journalists are more responsible, especially on newspapers where the adviser has a good understanding of press freedom and ethics.

"Whereas in the '70s they might get off on a tangent, today they are really thinking through issues," Clemons says.

Kathy Lawrence, director of Student Publications and Scholastic Media Programs at the University of Alabama, for 15 years has judged student newspapers in her state and some national contests.

"I think papers now are starting to take a look at issues that are on the minds of teenagers as opposed to what you used to think of as school news, which was homecoming, football games, new teachers, PTA announcements, principal columns or interviews with the principal.

"Fifteen years ago, I don't think drugs would be covered much in high schools and if it was covered, it was covered in a preachy way," Lawrence says. "Today you will find some student newspapers that are interview-

Above: H.L. Hall with colleagues Debra Shrout, left, and Nancy Menchhofer of Kirkwood (Mo.) High School's journalism program. Hall says student newspapers are doing a better job of localizing national and world stories.

Left: Kathy Lawrence of the University of Alabama thinks student newspapers are covering more topical issues.

ing students who have been through drug rehab, and doing interviews with people outside the school about the scope of the problem and what people are doing about it."

Candace Perkins, newspaper adviser at St. Charles High School in St. Charles, Ill., began critiquing student papers in the mid-1970s.

She says at schools where administrators respect First Amendment freedoms, today's student journalists are much more likely to write about formerly taboo subjects.

"I can't imagine in the '70s someone writ-

ing about how to put on a condom. And that is not a rare topic today," says Perkins.

The biggest difference between student newspapers 20 years ago and today, she says, is that "more of the good ones look beyond their school campus to other things that affect them — be it AIDS, drugs, stress in the home, parental divorce or homelessness."

Another change over the last 20 years is that student journalists now tend to localize national and international topics just like community newspapers, according to H.L. Hall, adviser at Kirkwood High School in Kirkwood, Mo., who has critiqued more than 600 student newspapers.

"When an earthquake hit San Francisco four years ago, our student paper ran a major story on that because we had students and parents who were out there on a bus and students with relatives out there."

He says that 20 years ago student newspapers also were dealing with controversial issues, "but not on the broad scope you are seeing today."

"Death By A Cheeseburger," a feature about that perennial favorite, cafeteria food, was not pleasing to administrators.

We ask so much of our nation's high school journalism advisers.

The best of them become teachers, cheerleaders, mentors and First Amendment advocates for our young people. Through the teaching of journalism, they impart valuable skills — clear thinking, researching, writing — that students will use for the rest of their lives in whatever profession they choose. They demonstrate the power of teamwork and the glory of achievement when they successfully marshal the talent and enthusiasm of teenagers to produce a newspaper. They nudge, they challenge and, yes, they bully their charges to succeed in school today so that they can succeed in society tomorrow. And through this process, they give young people a chance to report news and express ideas to a larger public — a hands-on lesson on the role the First Amendment plays in America.

"A good journalism teacher is enthusiastic, has good people skills and a good nose for what's going on around the school," says Kathy McAdams, a journalism professor at the University of Maryland and, until recently, the executive director of the Maryland Scholastic Press Association. "But most importantly, good teachers are project conscious. They want to start something, finish it, hold it up and be proud of it."

On the other hand, maybe we don't demand enough from these teachers and the system that produces and supports them.

The truth is, the world of high school journalism instruction resembles a factory in which many of the assembly lines clank with problems, shortcomings and dangers. Some teachers are so poorly pre-pared that they teach journalism in name only. From state to state, the standards by which teachers are certified as qualified to teach the subject vary wildly, or don't exist at all. Standards for what constitutes good curriculum are uneven, too. Censorship clashes in some schools put many a teacher's neck on the chopping block and warp his or her students' understanding of the First Amendment.

Interviews with newspaper advisers and experts across the country elicit complaints of puny budgets, poor equipment and indifferent administrators.

"It's difficult to be a journalism adviser," says Ed Sullivan, director of the Columbia Scholastic Press Association. "You are not given the time, support, or resources to do the job, and you are exposed to an enormous amount of anger and outrage."

The pity is that bad instruction could cause more damage than none at all. The students are shortchanged and tune out the news media. The school gets a lousy newspaper. The profession misses an opportunity to recruit new talent. The role of the press is poorly conveyed to young people, which is a tragedy for a nation that was forged on the hearth of free expression. We should be worried about the condition of the factory. Unless the assembly lines are overhauled, the factory will continue to manufacture missed opportunities. But who will be first to call in quality control inspectors?

All we want is R-E-S-P-E-C-T

The most passionate critics of the current situation are the teachers who care about journalism and continue to teach it despite the hard work and frus-

Chapter 2

Those who can: Thrills and spills on the way to publication

11

tration. They contend that in the educational world, journalism is given a back seat compared with English, history, science and other disciplines.

Ask Melanie Nunn, the adviser at Henry Ford High School, an inner-city school in Detroit.

By 1993, Nunn's students had acquired three laptops. Before that, her 16 students would write their stories for *The Trojan Star* in longhand. In the past, the students had access to one computer, which was kept in a locked closet. They would share it for word processing. There still is no camera equipment, so Nunn and another faculty member take pictures.

Even more discouraging is the tendency of some school counselors to steer functionally illiterate students into her course just to fill up the students' class schedules. The message she feels she gets from the school administration is that "they don't value journalism."

Nunn, who has an English degree from Kentucky State University, had vague recollections of working on her high school yearbook and newspaper when she began advising *The Trojan Star* in 1986.

She has worked to fill that void. She picked up some instruction in news writing and layout from an editor at the *Detroit Free Press,* which publishes and distributes the student paper as a page in a special high school edition. Three years after she began advising, Nunn was picked for a Knight Foundation fellowship for high school journalism teachers at Michigan State University. She applied for the fellowship, she says, because "I realized I was kind of stumbling in the dark, and since some of my students were seriously interested in careers in journalism, I had to know more of what I was doing if I was going to give them a good start."

The 42-year-old teacher thinks the effort is worth it. The students get out the paper and learn some valuable lessons in the process. The pain of hard work and the pride of accomplishment draw teacher and students tightly together.

"I get a lot more emotionally involved with my newspaper students," Nunn says. "They come and tell me their problems, and there are a lot of tears."

"She's like a mother and counselor," says Jeneil Johnson, 17, of Nunn. "She's given me the initiative to continue when I wanted to throw my notebook at the wall and give up."

Nunn's story is part of the lore of high school journalism. It's the story of the dedicated teacher who feels undermined by a system that shoves journalism into academic limbo. In the academic world, journalism gets snubbed.

Teacher training

Listen to Carol Danks tell how she became the adviser of *The Colonel* at Roosevelt High School in Kent, Ohio, in 1981.

"The adviser had decided she didn't want to do it again and she approached me while I was on bathroom duty," recalls Danks, talking in her typical rapid-fire speech. "The adviser and the principal were looking for someone willing to say yes — and I was it."

Danks had no experience in the field. Her college degree was in English. But she took up the challenge, and she has stayed with it ever since. Sometimes the most incidental moments in life turn out to be the most significant. For Danks, being stopped that day was a blessing.

"The summer before I was supposed to start teaching journalism I hooked up with a longtime newspaper adviser in a neighboring town," she says. "She became my mentor. I picked her brain and we talked and talked during the summer. I called her a lot that first year."

Danks' story is not unusual. Because of a lack of qualified, well-trained journalism instructors, schools frequently "volunteer" individuals with no background, experience or even inclination for the job. This reinforces the perception that high school journalism is not a serious subject.

For many teachers, the last time they worked on a publication was back in their own high school days — 40 percent of journalism teachers worked on a high school publication, such as a newspaper, yearbook or magazine.

In New York state, for example, where journalism teachers aren't required to be certified, it's not uncommon for teachers without a remote connection to journalism to advise the student newspaper, according to C. Marshall Matlock, director of scholastic journalism at the S.I. Newhouse School of Public Communications at Syracuse University.

"A few years back, a biology teacher was the journalism teacher and adviser at a major high school on Long Island," he says.

This is not meant to knock science teachers. But when almost one-half of the nation's journalism teachers start teaching the subject after being "volunteered," it means that many learn journalistic principles and newspaper production techniques on the job, as they go along. Would biology teachers accept that kind of a situation? Would parents accept that of their children's biology teachers?

To catch up, most neophytes turn to a combination of textbooks and workbooks and seek out advice and materials from other teachers. They attend conferences during the school year and summer workshops for journalism advisers where they can pick up instruction in news writing, photography, the First Amendment and desktop publishing.

That's how Danks built her own program, borrowing ideas from textbooks, other teachers and her own creativity. She even took a photography class and a course for high school newspaper advisers at Kent State University.

"I think my kids view me as demanding," says Danks. "I hope they view me as somebody who makes them think about what they are doing, somebody who will listen to them and let them make decisions. But one thing I say to them over and over again is, 'I will not let you embarrass yourselves in print.' And that's my major job — to teach them responsible journalism."

Who will teach the teachers?

Some experts attribute the shortage of college-trained high school journalism teachers to the small number of colleges offering majors in journalism education. Over the last 10 years some campuses have stopped offering bachelor's degrees in journalism education because of budget cutbacks, a lack of demand and other reasons.

"It's surprising how many schools of education

Carol Danks, an English teacher drafted by chance in 1981 to advise *The Colonel* at Roosevelt High School in Kent, Ohio, developed her own training program and signed on for a journalism teaching career.

and schools of journalism don't seem to feel a need to work on teacher training programs," says John Butler, an associate professor of journalism at the University of Northern Iowa.

Mary Sparks, past president of the Association of Schools of Journalism and Mass Communication and associate professor of mass communications at Texas Woman's University, complains that training people to teach high school journalism is "not a priority" for most colleges of journalism. "They feel their main job is to train people to be professional journalists," she says, "and they are also driven by the numbers."

Sparks recalls vividly a remark made by a journalism professor that reflects the lack of importance given to training journalism teachers: "I had a student who wanted to be a high school teacher and [the faculty member] said, 'Oh, what a shame,' " Sparks says.

Some campuses have joined with state scholastic associations to fill the demand for teacher training through summer workshops. Typically, these workshops cover newspaper advising, news writing, photography, desktop publishing, business management and First Amendment issues.

• More than 50 colleges and universities offer summer workshops in newspaper and yearbook advising for high school teachers.

• Some colleges and universities offer credit that counts toward a degree in journalism or state certification to teach journalism. For example, the University of Iowa offers one-week and three-day summer workshops.

• State and national scholastic press associations also offer sessions for newspaper advisers during conferences held throughout the school year. At annual conferences of the Journalism Education Association (JEA), a professional organization that represents about 1,600 journalism educators, participants can attend dozens of training sessions.

A conviction that well-trained teachers enhance the prestige of high school journalism programs prompted the Dow Jones Newspaper Fund in 1993 to revive a grant program that enables teachers to attend summer workshops.

Training in the newsroom

Helping to train teachers is an idea catching on among newspaper industry executives as well, especially as a long-term strategy to attract new readers.

Until Karen Flowers, the newspaper adviser at Irmo High School near Columbia, S.C., participated in a two-week internship at her local newspaper, *The State,* in 1989 she "didn't feel confident about teaching journalism."

An English teacher since 1970, she started teaching journalism two years later, in 1972. Flowers was able to teach students "how to write the stories, but

I couldn't make the stories real to them because they weren't real to me."

She shadowed *The State's* court reporter, wrote a feature article about a nursing program, and worked on the copy desk on the very night an airplane crashed in Sioux City, Iowa.

"I should have been paying them instead of them paying me," says Flowers, who received a $1,000 stipend and some graduate-level college credit as part of the internship. She picked up many news tips she is able to pass on to her students. Among them: Sometimes a reporter goes out to report on a story and comes back with a different one.

The highlight of her internship was seeing her name in print. "I had always told my students that seeing their byline in the paper is a thrill," Flowers says. Now she knows it from firsthand experience.

Certification hodgepodge

State departments of education impose certification requirements to ensure that teachers are qualified to teach a subject (journalism or English, for example) because they have completed a certain number of college courses in that area.

Educators view teaching certificates as a way to maintain high teaching standards.

Fewer than one-third of the nation's high school journalism teachers hold state certificates to teach journalism. But this figure is misleading because certification requirements for teaching journalism vary from state to state. Only a few have stringent standards.

In the summer of 1993, Marilyn Weaver, coordinator of the journalism education sequence at Ball State University, surveyed states to find out what the course work requirements are for teaching journalism. She found that nearly half the states do not require any journalism courses for high school journalism educators.

Moreover, even in states with high standards for requirements, there are many ways around certification. "All types of emergency permits are available," she says.

No state requires any kind of certification for teachers who only advise publications. Advisers who don't have a class and thus are not in violation of any state mandates for people who teach journalism are often left out of the discussion on required qualifications.

This jumble reflects not only the ambivalence with which the academic world views journalism, but also the debate over whether certification is a worthwhile system. While many educators believe widespread adoption of certification requirements will enhance the prestige of high school journalism and ensure teachers are well-trained, others believe strict standards will prevent some good teachers, who lack college course work in journalism, from

> "It's surprising how many schools of education and schools of journalism don't seem to feel a need to work on teacher training programs."
>
> John Butler

Karen Flowers, the newspaper adviser at Irmo High School near Columbia, S.C., was an intern at her local newspaper. "I should have been paying them instead of them paying me."

advising student newspapers.

In reality, if school systems decided to hire only certified teachers to teach journalism, there wouldn't be enough to go around. Consequently, even in states with moderate and strict certification requirements, there are ways to skirt the rules.

"In Indiana, a principal will call the state and say, 'I haven't been able to hire a journalism teacher this year and I need a waiver so that one of my faculty members can teach the course,' " according to Weaver. The waiver is usually approved.

Another sleight of hand: Carol Danks is not state certified, so officials at Roosevelt High School in Kent, Ohio, changed her course's name from "Journalism II" to the less academic-sounding "Newspaper Production." "The new name satisfied everyone at the state Department of Education," she says.

Given the problems that can arise when states establish stringent certification standards, some scholastic media experts favor a moderate benchmark. The Columbia Scholastic Press Association (CSPA), for example, has endorsed the concept of 15 semester credit hours in journalism for teachers.

The Journalism Education Association (JEA) has developed its own certification program for members — the Certified Journalism Educator and Master Journalism Educator (CJE/MJE).

Teachers with formal college training in journalism as well as those who have learned on the job can qualify for JEA certification, which is only a professional endorsement and is not recognized by state departments of education.

"The program shows that we want to be looked on as a bona fide profession," says H.L. Hall, a Mis-souri teacher who helped develop JEA's certification programs. "It also tells college admissions officers and state departments of education that we want strong academic courses, and you can't do that if you don't have qualified teachers."

Creating a curriculum

From the moment he started his job as adviser to the student newspaper at Asheville (N.C.) High School in 1991, Calvin Hall's mind was set on getting the first issue to the printer.

His teacher at a summer workshop for journalism advisers had urged Hall and his classmates to produce a newspaper as soon after school started as possible. Hall was hired as a beginning teacher with a bachelor's degree in English, some graduate work and an internship at the *Wilmington* (N.C.) *Morning Star.* He knew his principal also was anxiously awaiting the first issue of *The Cougar Chronicle.*

Unfortunately for the novice teacher, only one of his eight journalism students had worked on the school newspaper before. Worse yet, most of the students had signed up for his course as an arts elective. That year, he produced five issues of *The Cougar Chronicle.* There were successes: The newspaper won recognition from the North Carolina Scholastic Press Association.

Hall's second year as adviser brought its own challenges. The class was larger with 15 students, but only two of them had experience. Hall spent at least 10 extra hours a week working one-on-one with the students on their articles. Between teaching the students the basics of news writing, design and computer production, Hall would not have time to

Calvin Hall, left, with Stefan Weir, '93-'94 student newspaper editor at Asheville (N.C.) High School.

complicated by two factors: the way high schools give students credits and the way colleges accept student credits.

School systems usually choose one of four ways to deal with high school journalism courses:

• Extracurricular status with no credit

• Elective credit outside the basic requirements for graduation

• English credit, but not as a replacement for a required English course

• English credit, as a replacement for a required English course.

But many colleges will not accept journalism as a basic English credit, no matter what is decided at the high school level. And because there is little uniformity in the content and quality of journalism and/or newspaper production courses, there is little chance for a nationwide change in the situation as it stands today.

In the same way, the emphasis at most schools on newspaper production rather than on journalism as an academic subject makes it difficult for states to develop curriculum guidelines for journalism.

Some state-issued journalism curriculum guidelines are so general that teachers can't rely on them to develop lesson plans. In the absence of state-level guidelines, school systems often develop their own. Some teachers admit they don't even know if state or local guidelines exist.

Unable to rely on a nationally recognized, basic curriculum for high school journalism, most teachers use a patchwork of materials — textbooks, workbooks, ideas borrowed from other advisers and inventions of their own.

J.A. Rios, for example, teaches English and journalism at Natalia High School, a predominantly Hispanic school in a small farming community near San Antonio, Texas. Rios teaches interviewing skills by having students interview each other, faculty members, and community leaders. He also invites the editors, publishers and photographers of two

teach them about First Amendment issues until March, seven months into the school year — not an ideal situation.

Now his goal is to offer two journalism classes, one in newspaper production for experienced students and another in the basics for new students. "It's a more effective way to do it," he says. "That way the older, more experienced kids won't be bored, and the new students will be getting the structure and background they need."

Hall's experience is hardly unique among high school journalism educators. It reflects the widely accepted notion that journalistic writing and principles can be taught on an "as you go" basis as part of a newspaper production class.

This attitude is also reflected in the way high schools award credit for journalism. Among American high schools that offer journalism classes, only 13 percent give English credit.

Giving academic credit for journalism courses is

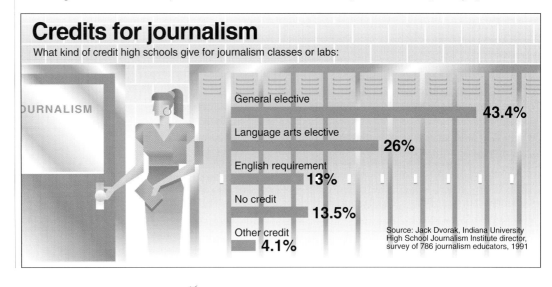

Credits for journalism

What kind of credit high schools give for journalism classes or labs:

General elective — **43.4%**

Language arts elective — **26%**

English requirement — **13%**

No credit — **13.5%**

Other credit — **4.1%**

Source: Jack Dvorak, Indiana University High School Journalism Institute director, survey of 786 journalism educators, 1991

local newspapers to visit his classroom and become mentor-advisers to his students. Every year, his students visit journalism programs at large, inner-city schools and a newspaper plant in San Antonio.

Making it fit

Jack Kennedy, journalism adviser at City High School in Iowa City, Iowa, and chairman of the JEA's curriculum development commission, says every teacher's curriculum is highly individualized because "the ultimate goal is not to prepare students for a test but to produce a publication. Each publication has its own needs and goals, and the curriculum has to be adapted to fit that."

Those who teach journalism basics and produce a newspaper during the same class "probably are relying on an old text and materials they can photocopy, magazines, bits and pieces of things from journalism guidebooks," believes Tom Rolnicki, executive director of the National Scholastic Press Association and co-author of the textbook *Scholastic Journalism* published by Iowa State University Press.

A 1992 survey of 525 JEA members reveals that 18 percent use a textbook to teach students about press rights, 25 percent rely on materials from the Student Press Law Center, a non-profit organization that provides free advice to student publications on First Amendment issues, 13 percent use handouts from several sources, and 11 percent rely on newspaper articles. Based on the survey findings, "it appears to me that most of the teachers have some kind of textbook, probably more than one, but they are not tied to it closely. They might use a chapter for certain things and then move on," according to Kennedy.

The most popular, comprehensive high school journalism textbooks usually have chapters on different types of news writing, reporting, interviewing, editing, headline writing, page makeup and design, photojournalism, business management, advertising, and student press rights. Most teachers cover some but not all of these areas, especially in schools where journalism basics are taught as part of a production class.

Also popular among teachers are specialty textbooks that deal with just one aspect of newspaper production such as writing, editing, or desktop publishing.

Recently published general texts tend to de-emphasize the history and theory of mass communications in favor of a more practical, hands-on approach to producing student publications. Modern journalism textbooks also stress student press rights and responsibilities to a much greater extent than do older textbooks. And some are responding to the fast-paced technological changes affecting the news industry by including sections on desktop publishing, electronic media, story packaging and

careers in journalism.

For example, in response to the demand for more sophisticated information on free press/free speech issues, the next edition of Rolnicki's *Scholastic Journalism* (first published in 1950) will include a chapter on journalistic ethics.

"We feel the student press is becoming more professional and serious about their work as an outgrowth of the *Hazelwood* decision," explains Rolnicki. *Hazelwood* is the 1988 U.S. Supreme Court decision that gives administrators greater latitude to control what gets printed in a school newspaper.

Some textbooks and teachers also are beginning to focus on the need for a multicultural curriculum to deal with the needs of racially and ethnically diverse schools and communities. The aim is to improve school newspaper coverage of the student populations within the schools and to improve recruiting of minority students into journalism classes. "Kids who see themselves in the paper will later see themselves on the paper," says the University of Iowa's Mary Arnold, who has spearheaded JEA's efforts in this area.

Journalism needs a new image

So, it's tough to fight an old image. Far too many educators and administrators rank journalism with metal shop, rather than Shakespeare. At worst, it's viewed as a dumping ground for hard-to-handle students.

In the current wave of educational reforms, one of the ways officials are deciding what's good and what's bad is by determining what skills the students acquire from taking a course or subject. In the jargon of educationese, this is called "educational outcomes."

Whatever official label is attached to this trend toward mastery of skills rather than facts, journalism education is a natural fit. Journalism provides a hands-on, skills-building approach. Producing a newspaper in a high school setting develops writing, analytical and self-presentation skills. As any student journalist can document, bringing out a regular newspaper is an intensive lesson in seeing a project through from start to finish — something usually missing in history, calculus or chemistry classes. And students who work on the school paper get immediate feedback from teachers, peers and the community.

Molly Clemons, a longtime high school newspaper adviser who is vice principal at Truman High School in Independence, Mo., analyzed how high school journalism programs would satisfy 11 outcomes developed by an Illinois school district. "All the outcomes could be met through a journalism class," she says. "For example, the outcomes on knowing how to analyze [information] and knowing about wellness and health could be met by a stu-

"We feel the student press is becoming more professional and serious about their work as an outgrowth of the *Hazelwood* decision."

Tom Rolnicki

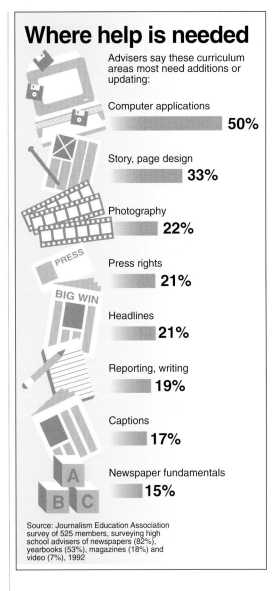

Where help is needed

Advisers say these curriculum areas most need additions or updating:

Computer applications
50%

Story, page design
33%

Photography
22%

Press rights
21%

Headlines
21%

Reporting, writing
19%

Captions
17%

Newspaper fundamentals
15%

Source: Journalism Education Association survey of 525 members, surveying high school advisers of newspapers (82%), yearbooks (53%), magazines (18%) and video (7%), 1992

Why *Death By Cheeseburger?*

Thank Kay Phillips. In 1972 Phillips became the adviser of the Viking *at Vance Senior High in Henderson. Following years of on-the-job training, she earned a master's in journalism and a doctorate in education at the University of North Carolina. In the 1993-94 school year, she returned as adviser to the* Viking, *bringing her enthusiasm and devotion back to where it all started.*

"In this position we need someone to teach English and journalism, but we don't need that student newspaper."

The administrator's words in my initial job interview struck me as unusual. "Won't that be like having someone teach home economics without students going near the stove?" I asked.

He vaguely mentioned "problems with the paper," but I wanted this job teaching English at Vance Senior High, so I dropped the question.

As it turned out, the administration had discontinued the newspaper the year before — in 1971. The English/journalism teacher, a former professional newspaperman, did not have his contract renewed. Administrative dissatisfaction with the student newspaper had arisen over three articles: "Death By A Cheeseburger," a feature about that perennial favorite, cafeteria food; an article about an assistant principal; and a news story containing a school administrator's unflattering comment about the community.

In response to the cafeteria story, the school dietitian threatened a lawsuit. The article about the assistant principal was considered disrespectful, particularly a reference to him as the "curly-headed dragon." And, reacting to the final story, the administrator denied a comment attributed to him that the average county citizen was incapable of understanding results of an education survey.

Angry administrators shut down the student newspaper after only two issues.

Into that situation I came. My only experience was as a high school sports writer and college news editor. I had no knowledge of student press rights or of the application of the First Amendment. I was told that if we produced a paper at all, we must print it on the school's duplicator machine and submit all material for prior review by an eight-member publications board.

Under those restrictions the students produced six issues that year. But we also took two major steps forward. First, in March three students and I attended the Southern Interscholastic Press Association convention at the University of South Carolina in Columbia. Second, in June the same group went to the North Carolina Scholastic Press Association workshop at the University of North Carolina at

dent doing an in-depth study of AIDS or of skin cancer in teenagers. The outcome on critical thinking might be met by a series of editorials or columns. Journalism could meet virtually any outcome a state would come out with."

In California, the Journalism Educators Association is developing a statewide journalism curriculum. Part of its work is to convince administrators that journalism is an important subject for high school students. Katharine Swan, an adviser at Mission High School in San Francisco, says the move toward outcome-based education is good news. "Journalism has always been outcome based. We have a product. The product is what makes the program so viable and exciting for the kids. That's the nature of journalism. When the kids learn the skills, they use them. I've had lots of kids get jobs because they learned to use computers in my classes. They write better. That transfers to college and beyond,"

Chapel Hill.

At those two meetings we learned the basics of the 1969 Supreme Court decision in *Tinker vs. Des Moines Independent Community School District,* knowledge that set the stage for me to request and gain freedom from the constraints of the first year.

Other problems lurked in the wings. At a school that was 60 percent black, our staff had two black and 18 white members. Furthermore, two students, dissatisfied with the watered-down content of the official newspaper, produced an underground paper and were suspended for 10 days.

Also, although we were now free to be printed outside the school building, our local newspaper, which was changing from hot lead to offset production, could only print us as a broadsheet — a thin four pages filled with many short articles and bumping headlines in a circus design. From judging received that first year, we knew many areas on which to work, but design problems seemed insurmountable.

Because the teacher was learning with the students, progress was slow and painful. Every year we attended every workshop and conference — North Carolina Scholastic Press Association, University of North Carolina, Chapel Hill, and the Southern Interscholastic Press Association at the University of South Carolina — that we could afford. We couldn't afford the Columbia Scholastic Press Association at Columbia University, but we sent our newspapers to them for critiquing. That meant three or four critiques a year, along with training in writing and design.

By 1976, the local newspaper was able to offer us tabloid printing, and we could design a much better package. We were entering contests without embarrassment. Thanks to a continued high level of enthusiasm along with a strong push to recruit black staff members and to include all student interests in the newspaper's content, we gradually became an award-winning publication. We began covering the classroom walls with certificates and plaques.

Today I know most of the unpleasantness of my initiation into journalism teaching and student newspaper advising could have been avoided had someone realized I needed training to do the job. That's why I have become the Johnny Appleseed of teacher training in North Carolina.

I started on a crusade for teacher certification through the University of North Carolina at Chapel Hill back in 1983. The payoff may finally be near. We have been negotiating with the state Department of Public Instruction, and the chances are good that they will officially recommend — and be willing to pay for — four graduate-level courses for all high school journalism teachers.

The future looks bright. After refusing to advise the newspaper last year in protest over the absence

of even one computer, I am back in the thick of things. We have computers. I've started a brand new course in broadcasting. Nine of the 34 students in my beginning and advanced classes are black — not good enough in a school that is 60 percent minority, but enough black students are turning up now "because my friend told me this is a good course" that I know diversity will continue to improve. That's certainly an aim of mine.

Another win at the state level has come after a hard fight to get journalism added to the list of mostly math and science courses students may take to qualify for the North Carolina Scholars program. Students who follow the Scholars course receive a special seal on their diploma. It should change par-

When Kay Phillips was hired as a journalism adviser, she was told, "We don't need that student newspaper." One article, lamenting cafeteria food, was especially displeasing. It was called, "Death By A Cheeseburger."

ents' view that journalism is not the thing to urge their children to study.

Jack Dvorak: Spreading the word

In 1968, Jack Dvorak was in Oklahoma City, a tenderfoot high school English teacher with an age-old problem: how to teach writing. For him, writing was a labor of love. For his young charges, it was moan-and-groan drudgery.

Salvation came that year cloaked as a journalism course no one else wanted to teach. To Dvorak's surprise, the course sparked his students' fire for self-expression. They not only wrote, but they also learned discipline, organization, responsibility and rigor. "I loved it," Dvorak says. "Journalism offers kids a tremendous way to learn the language and use the language in a way that's meaningful to them."

His students made Dvorak a believer in the teaching power of journalism. He's been living, preaching and studying it ever since.

He lived journalism as a reporter for *The Kansas City Star, The Kansas City Times* and the *Columbia Missourian.*

He preached it as a journalism professor and workshop director at the University of Iowa, Northeast Missouri State University and Indiana University.

He studied it as the author or co-author of more than 30 scholarly articles and papers, many of them on youth journalism, including a 1991 study of 786 journalism educators. And his latest book, written with Laurence Lain and Tom Dickson, *Journalism Kids Do Better: What Research Tells Us About High*

School Journalism in the 1990s, is scheduled to be published in 1994.

"Here at Indiana, Jack's run just a marvelous summer workshop, which attracts on the order of 700 high school students each year for yearbook and newspaper instruction," says Trevor Brown, dean of the Indiana University School of Journalism. "Most would agree that it is one of the premier workshops in the country." Enrollment in Dvorak's workshop has risen each year.

"The job of teaching journalism so often is shifted to a young, naive teacher who didn't want a pink slip. That's how I got into it," he says, noting that fewer than one-third of journalism teachers are state-certified to teach journalism. "If that happened to math or science, there would be an uproar from parents." Because of the critical need for qualified advisers and instructors, his institute trains teachers, too.

"Kids 16 or 17 know so much more about life than I did in 1962," says Dvorak. "It's not funny. They face more pressures. They grow up faster. They're more guarded, worried about crime, AIDS, crack, split families, broken homes. High school educators have to be so much more than I was."

Dvorak speaks to students, educators and administrators across the USA to sell them on his conviction: that a vigorous and vibrant scholastic press not only makes students better scholars, but it also makes for better citizens.

"Life will continue to become more complex. Maybe student journalism is one of the ways they can come to grips with it," says Dvorak, "They can

write about it, talk about it. The newspaper can become the agenda center of the school."

Encountering barriers

Dena Sadoski Nahm's journalism program at Columbian High School in Tiffin, Ohio, has grown from a single class to a full complement of beginning and advanced journalism courses. It took her 18 years to build the program, but the future is in doubt following a year of battles with the principal over what her students are allowed to print in *The Tiffinian.*

Dena Nahm was 20 years old, fresh out of college with a major in English and a minor in journalism, when she began teaching at the high school in 1975. She was assigned four English classes, plus a combination English literature/newspaper production class for seniors. Nahm prepared for the task by reading a journalism textbook, interviewing the former adviser about the offset printing process used at the school and meeting with the journalism students for one week before school started.

You can guess what happened.

"It was almost physically impossible to teach them the course of study in English, let alone try to teach them the basics of journalism," recalls Nahm.

"At some point I resorted to just teaching them what they absolutely had to know and trying to get the paper out. I didn't have time to cover freedom of the press issues that first year. And there was a lot of fluff in the paper. Of eight pages, five would be features on the prom, clubs, hayrides."

During her second year at the school, Nahm received permission to teach journalism as a separate class that covered the basics of news writing and libel law, as well as producing the newspaper.

Tired of having to train a brand new group of students to produce the newspaper every year, Nahm asked to add an independent study class for returning students who wanted just to work on producing the newspaper.

And in 1991 she developed and implemented an Intensive Journalistic Writing class after attending the Dow Jones Newspaper Fund's IJW summer program.

The Tiffinian has won more than a dozen state journalism awards, and some of her students have gone on to major in journalism and pursue careers in the field. She had never had any interference from the school administration.

But in early 1993 Nahm began to clash with a new principal over what subjects her students were allowed to write about in the newspaper. The students ran a column on teen sexual activity and condoms and planned another story on AIDS.

Principal John Frye told Nahm that student journalists could not write about teen sexual activity or condoms because "standards in our community don't uphold public discussion in newspapers, particularly student publications, relative to those subjects."

"They decided they couldn't write about AIDS and not talk about sex," Nahm says. "They were so upset. Some of the kids were crying." Months later, the story on AIDS ran after much discussion between Nahm and her students.

Frye says he's often caught between the First Amendment rights of student journalists and the wishes of the local school board that hired him and also approves the journalism adviser's contract. Frye says his school board reflects the politically and religiously conservative nature of the Tiffin communi-

When teachers first thought of getting involved in scholastic JOURNALISM

After assignment by administrator
43.1%

In high school
20.9%

After teaching something else
17.9%

In college
15.2%

Before high school
2.9%

Source: Jack Dvorak, Indiana University High School Journalism Institute director, survey of 786 journalism educators, 1991

ty. "There's a real fine line," he says, "between leadership and censorship."

"A newspaper is a small business with advertisers who underwrite the cost of the publication, and if the newspaper violates the standard that is acceptable in your community, then you go out of business. I don't view that as censorship."

Frye adds that if the school's newspaper adviser were to routinely allow students to print articles that violate community standards, then "I suspect I'm looking for a new sponsor."

In her performance evaluation, the principal noted that Nahm needed to be "cognizant of district and community attitudes and standards in the publication of 'controversial or sensitive' subject matters."

In addition to these clashes, Nahm has had other pressures. Because she lacks advanced computers (the school's equipment budget has been reduced), students design and lay out the newspaper using traditional paste-up techniques with scissors and wax.

Four computers used for word processing and a rectangular table used for layout and production are crammed into a 10-by-13 foot room behind her classroom. Even that was taken away at the end of

the 1992-93 school year. She will now have equipment stored at the back of her classroom.

The equipment shortage, problems with censorship and a school reorganization plan to incorporate ninth graders into the high school will jeopardize Nahm's hope to teach journalism full time.

"If I didn't work as hard, would anyone realize it or care?" she asks wistfully, a touch of sadness in her voice. "When I'm in my classroom, I'm fine, and when I focus on how I feel about the kids and teaching I could be here forever. But when I focus on the externals, it's difficult."

All is not smooth sailing

Tony Gomez is a rare type among high school journalism teachers. The winner of a distinguished adviser award from the Dow Jones Newspaper Fund, he has experience and an academic background in journalism. Before earning a bachelor's degree in journalism education with minors in English and physical education from Northern Arizona University, he was a sports writer for his high school and college newspapers.

Gomez earned Certified Journalism Educator and Master Journalism Educator certificates from the JEA. "It means something to the kids and parents when you have a journalism teacher who is really qualified and that helps the program," he says.

During his last eight years at Tucson's Amphitheater High School — a racially and ethnically mixed city school — Gomez' students won numerous state and national writing awards at journalism conferences. The *Desert Gazette* is a winner, too, including the National Scholastic Press Association's All-American award for its news content and design, a George Gallup award and a Silver Crown award from the Columbia Scholastic Press Association — all top honors among high school newspapers.

In the past, his students have exposed drug use at school, problems with the fire alarm system, gun-toting gang members on campus, and faculty members' disregard of a school policy that prohibits drinking or eating in hallways and classrooms.

But all has not been smooth sailing for 43-year-old Gomez. Getting kids to sign up for the newspaper class is difficult, he says, because the school system offers only elective credit for the class. "The students have so many graduation requirements to fulfill that they don't have time to take journalism." The largest newspaper staff he ever had was 18 students. His most recent newspaper class started with 13 students but dwindled to seven by year's end.

A lack of adequate facilities and equipment makes the job of producing the award-winning newspaper challenging. His class has six computers, but students must use the school's computer lab, often after hours, to write stories and design the paper. The school photo lab is far from the computer lab and the classroom. And during one year, when there was no telephone in Gomez' classroom, students scurried about the school searching for a phone to do interviews.

Gomez attributes his success as a journalism adviser to this: "I let my students go with the flow. I let them explore anything they come up with that they think is newsworthy. I don't hold them back. And I'm not afraid to stand up for what I'm trying to teach them."

In 1992-93, however, Gomez quit as adviser for the newspaper, although he kept teaching a basic journalism class. He decided to take a one-year break from advising mainly because of battles with the previous administration.

Gomez returned to advising in the 1993-94 school year to teach "kids that they have rights, and they have a voice, and that if they find things they are not satisfied with, then journalism is an avenue they have for seeking to make changes for the better."

Sometimes, when he feels down, he recalls small incidents that mean a lot to him. Like the time, a few years ago, when one of Gomez' freshmen journalism students participated in the feature writing contest at a national journalism convention and won second place. "As he was going up to get his certificate, I asked him, 'Why do you think you did so well?' He said to me, 'Mr. Gomez, everything you taught me in the class I used.' That made me feel so good."

A new kind of journalism

Inside Carol Lange's sunny classroom in a suburban Virginia high school near Washington, D.C., students are engaged in a lively discussion of Nora Ephron's satiric essay, *How to Write a Newsmagazine Cover Story.*

In her article, Ephron tells wanna-be writers without knowledge of the "facts, talent or imagination" that they can become newsmagazine cover story writers by following her six easy rules. Among them: Find a subject that's been covered to death by the media and imitate the writing style of a press release.

As they comment on the piece, students toss out recent examples of what Ephron is talking about: newsmagazine stories on cult leader David Koresh, the return of bell-bottom pants and Boris Yeltsin's political struggles. Later, the discussion turns to Ephron's use of the rhetorical writing style called "classification," as well as examples of trashy publications, and whether a gay newspaper should have been banned from a local public library.

Lange's class, which combines elements of traditional English literature and journalism, is a new kind of journalism course called Intensive Journalis-

Certification

How to get certified by the Journalism Education Association

DEADLINE TODAY

Certified Journalism Educator (CJE)

■ **Must have:** Valid state teaching certificate

■ **To qualify:** Journalism training from: College major or minor in journalism or mass communication or 18 semester credits in journalism

or

Proof of at least 5 years' journalism teaching/advising and pass a 2¹/₂-hour, 20-question JEA test

■ **Fee:** $50 for JEA members; $85 for non-members

Master Journalism Educator (MJE)

■ **Must have:** CJE status; 7 years journalism teaching or advising; letter of endorsement from principal or superintendent who has observed the teacher; proof of participation in journalism activities on local, state, regional or national levels

■ **To qualify:** Must pass a 2¹/₂-hour written test and submit a preapproved project, paper or teaching unit

■ **Fee:** $75 for JEA members; $110 for non-members

Source: Journalism Education Association

tic Writing, an honors level course for which most students receive English credit. This is a journalism course that does not produce a newspaper.

Begun in 1988 by the Dow Jones Newspaper Fund, its aim is twofold: to give high school journalism academic status and to attract promising young writers to journalism. "The idea is to have a college-level journalism composition course that will challenge students," says Lange, who teaches four IJW courses to 87 students at the Thomas Jefferson High School for Science and Technology in Fairfax County, Va.

Because of its academic content, school systems are more likely to give English credit for an IJW course than they would for a newspaper production class, according to Tom Engleman, an administrator in the School of Communications and Theatre at Temple University who headed the Dow Jones Newspaper Fund for 23 years.

By 1992 approximately 100 teachers had been trained. That year some 500 high school students were enrolled in IJW. College-bound students who enroll in the course have the option of taking the College Board's Advanced Placement English Language and Composition Exam. If they pass, they often receive college-level English credit and/or exemption from taking a beginning English course

IJW's aim is to bridge the gap between journalism and the traditional English curriculum.

Teachers do this by teaching students clear, concise journalistic writing combined with analysis of contemporary and classic fiction and non-fiction.

Carol Lange teaches Advanced Placement English Language and Composition at Thomas Jefferson High School for Science and Technology in Fairfax County, Va. She uses journalism to teach composition skills, incorporating Intensive Journalistic Writing.

an individual IJW curriculum:

• Judy Cole, an English teacher at Billings Senior High in Montana, thought up a novel way of teaching John Steinbeck's *Of Mice and Men* using journalistic writing. She arranged for her class to visit a senior citizen's center, interview someone who had survived the Great Depression and write a personality profile.

• Dena Sadoski Nahm, who teaches an IJW class at Columbian High School in Tiffin, Ohio, has her students keep a journal in which they jot down daily observations and comments on their writing style.

• Lange's students write profiles of incoming freshmen for guidance counselors.

While IJW teachers are enthusiastic about the advanced writing course, convincing budget-conscious school officials to let them teach it may not be easy because most prefer to fund a traditional journalism class that produces a newspaper.

"Some teachers taught it for one or two years," says Lange, "and they found they couldn't sustain it because of budget cuts, or personnel cuts or because there weren't sufficient numbers of students willing to take an advanced placement class."

Despite the positive results so far, some experts caution that IJW will not catch on in a big way. "It's an excellent model," says Ed Sullivan, director of the Columbia Scholastic Press Association, "but it will never get widespread application ... because, while most schools will accept a skills-based class as a means to produce a better quality school paper, they will not generally pay for an academic-oriented class."

But even those no longer teaching IJW have managed to incorporate some elements into their traditional journalism and English classes. Says Lange, "Most of us who teach this class believe that what is valuable to students is what they take with them and apply as they go on to college and work."

The strength of IJW is its intense focus on the writing process, says Tom Engleman, who developed the IJW workshops when he was executive director of the Dow Jones Newspaper Fund.

"Writing is a skill you will take with you to any career," he says. "And the beauty of journalistic writing is that you take a complex thought and you synthesize it into something that's readily understandable."

Scholastic press associations

Friday night, 8 p.m., the first night of a press convention weekend in Long Beach, Calif. In the Sheraton Inn's Centennial B meeting room, the noise is getting intense. Two hundred teenagers are here. They could be out walking up and down Ocean Boulevard or primping for the student dance that's starting about now.

Instead, they are bustling about at the News-

Unlike traditional English classes where students write for their teachers' eyes only, IJW students are expected to try to publish what they have written. And research is done not only in the library. Students observe and do interviews in addition to other forms of research.

In IJW, students are taught the similarities between journalism and English: Editorial writing is like the argumentative/persuasive essay; news writing is informative; feature writing includes narration, expression, exposition and description.

Ron Bennett, who taught at Bonneville High School, a rural school in eastern Idaho, says that in 1991, 90 percent of his IJW students "passed" the Advanced Placement exam, compared with about 67 percent of his English students.

Nationally, in 1991, 64.7 percent of students in IJW classes got a 3 or above on the Advanced Placement exam, compared to a passing rate of 61.6 percent among students enrolled in English.

Beyond the basics, each teacher is free to develop

Certified teachers protect students' rights

Mary Anne Siefkes, who wrote the following article in favor of teacher certification, taught and advised newspapers and yearbooks for 18 years at four schools, all in Kansas. She teaches at Newton High School in Newton, Kansas. She is certified to teach journalism and English by the Kansas Department of Education and has a CJE certificate from the Journalism Education Association.

Thirty years ago, most student newspapers were filled with gossip columns and editorials about school spirit. Today, student journalists are writing about gangs, suicide, homosexuality, drug use, teen pregnancy — the issues of their age. The best of student newspapers inform and influence the entire school community, including adults. As their newspapers have become more professional, there is a greater need for better qualified journalism teachers and advisers.

Legal issues governing high school publications are intricate, and court decisions from *Tinker* to *Hazelwood* have determined what students can do and say in school. How can a teacher with little or no training help students stay within legal boundaries and, at the same time, encourage students to use their rights to a free press?

Part of a journalism adviser's job is to protect press rights. When I first began advising a high school newspaper, an administrator and I were talking about the kinds of appropriate topics for the newspaper. The administrator hinted the board of education did not have to continue funding. But I knew that was an empty threat. I had taken a course in advising high school publications and learned that school districts couldn't stop funding a newspaper because the content wasn't agreeable. If I hadn't been trained, I would have been censored. True, that was pre-*Hazelwood*, but it seems to me all the more important to know your rights these days.

Admittedly, no one needs a government license to start a newspaper in the United States (it just takes money) and reporters do not need a license. But in Kansas, I do need a certificate to teach journalism, just as other teachers are required to be certified to teach their subjects.

Sometimes I'm asked, "Why do I teach journalism?" And I say, "I want young people to know their rights under the First Amendment, so they would defend themselves if someone tried to take those rights away." I was surprised when someone once replied, "Then why don't you teach social studies?" The answer is, I want my students to experience these rights, to have a hands-on learning experience rather than just study the theory of it.

Many administrators understand that having certified journalism teachers is a protection. Trained teachers know the boundaries of the law and can keep a school district out of a lawsuit.

Certification is not a matter of elitism or status. It is a matter of being qualified for an important profession and having others recognize that you are qualified. Teaching journalism is not a hobby or a lark. It is not something my colleagues or I take lightly. It is a challenging, rewarding, frustrating, energizing, time-consuming profession.

High school newspapers strive for professionalism. Students need a knowledgeable and certified teacher to guide them.

Wait a minute ... You're telling me I need a license?

Helen F. Smith has been the journalism adviser at Newton North High School in Newtonville, Mass., since 1973. She is co-author of Student Newspapers: Managing the Business Side *and has edited five books for the Columbia Scholastic Press Association. Since 1986, she has been a board member of the Columbia Scholastic Press Advisers Association.*

I certainly agree that all journalism teachers need respect and credibility in their schools. But I believe that state mandates would prevent some good teachers from beginning publications projects with their students. These teachers need help learning newspaper skills. Why impose a specific number of college semester hours as a barrier?

By the time a teacher completes a program, several high school classes might have graduated without a newspaper. A supportive, professional education program can bridge the gap for teachers who have just started advising, and provide new information for experienced advisers who want to update their skills. Certification standards could stifle diversity, rather than promote respect for differences. Encouraging teachers to learn newspaper skills is far more helpful than emphasizing differences in status and privilege between teachers who are certified and teachers who are not.

Furthermore, I am seriously concerned about the First Amendment implications of certification. As a newspaper adviser, I consider myself to be a journalist as well as a teacher. The First Amendment applies to every publication, not just *The New York Times*. Similarly, no teachers of journalism, and, for that matter, no interested members of the commercial press willing to take the time to help students on a part-time basis, should find a government barrier in the way. Since journalists in this country need no licenses to practice, teachers of journalism deserve the same absence of restrictions, the same freedom to participate in any forum. The more voices, the more diversity, the better. If a business teacher, a French teacher, a math teacher, or a special-ed teacher wants to advise a newspaper, I think that's terrific. I've seen it happen. These teachers have been enthusiastic and effective.

I think adopting certification in states that currently lack it could lead to negative results. For instance, it would be all too easy for a school administrator to shut a newspaper down or to avoid helping a fledgling venture if there is no "appropriately certified" teacher on the staff. Hiring someone for the sole purpose of teaching journalism is, sad to say, very unlikely in school systems that already have cut programs to the bone. What about extracurricular newspapers? Would teachers who work with students after school, voluntarily or with a token stipend, have to get a government imprimatur to do so? It takes time to build a program, and many programs begin on an extracurricular basis.

Certification can hamper teachers of integrity who want to work on school publications out of interest, goodwill, and the desire to learn along with their students.

Journalism education teaching requirements

Requirements for teaching high school journalism, by state:

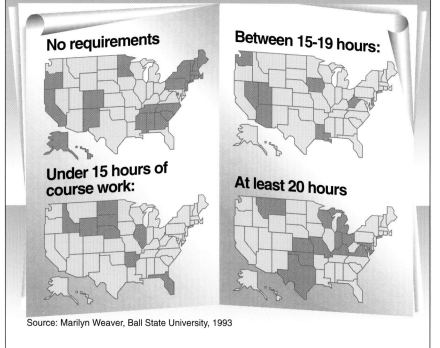

No requirements

Between 15-19 hours:

Under 15 hours of course work:

At least 20 hours

Source: Marilyn Weaver, Ball State University, 1993

paper Swap Shop, a regular event at every national convention sponsored by the Journalism Education Association and National Scholastic Press Association. Price of Swap Shop admission: multiple copies of their school newspaper.

Here they trade copy for copy with newspaper staffers from other schools. Sooner or later, groups of eight or nine form around tables. With little direction, they flip through the pages of their newspapers, one by one, describing staffing, coverage, funding, design techniques and problems. Questions and suggestions shoot back and forth. Students leave the session with their arms filled with sample newspapers, and their heads and notebooks filled with ideas for improving their own publications.

If all state, regional and national scholastic press associations were equally well organized and funded, and if there was enough money to allow every newspaper staffer and adviser to take advantage of the services they offer, then high school newspapers in the United States would soar.

Overall, though, associations' reach among schools is spotty, and many of their budgets are in jeopardy. And until the late 1980s, when a few associations made special efforts to change the complexion of their memberships, minority students and advisers were rarities at their get-togethers. Association directors themselves point out this is still true in too many cases.

At the grass roots

The strongest of these associations — Iowa, Florida, Michigan, South Carolina, Indiana, Texas and Kansas are most often mentioned by their colleagues — do a professional job of guiding inexperienced advisers and students toward the best of high school journalism.

John Hudnall, executive director of the Kansas Scholastic Press Association, worries, though, about the school deprived of association help. "Our state press associations are as fragmented as the schools they serve," he says. "In some states we see vibrant, involved active leadership supported by a major state institution. In others, we see secretarial help running the press associations. Even our most actively involved press associations are hampered by a lack of adequate funding.

"My primary concern is the excessively high percentage of poor quality programs that exist nationwide," says Hudnall. "We spend a great deal of effort on the 10 percent that we can take pride in and tend to neglect the other 90 percent … . In my 25 years with scholastic journalism, we have failed to raise that standard."

In an informal survey of 32 state press associations, not one reported more than half of eligible school newspapers had paid memberships. More typical was a 20 to 25 percent newspaper membership among eligible schools.

There are more than 80 state and regional press associations. Many states have more than one — Missouri has seven; California, six. More than two-thirds are run from college campuses.

The college connection

Along with providing office and funds for a faculty member to work part time directing a scholastic press association, universities sponsor dozens of press days, summer workshops and conferences.

Through college programs, high school teachers and students may study newspaper writing, reporting, editing, photography and press law. First-time advisers can take crash courses in how to publish a newspaper — absent a nervous breakdown. Desktop publishing courses are everywhere; students can't get enough training on electronic layout systems. Furthermore, colleges get to strut their stuff. Summer workshop attendees often are impressed at this first extended time on a college campus. Many want to return for four years.

Regional groups, like the Southern Interscholastic Press Association and the Great Lakes Interscholastic Press Association, cover several states. A few cities — New York, Chicago and Louisville among them — have established their own associations, where local problems and opportunities can be addressed.

The Scholastic Journalism Division of AEJMC — the association of university journalism professors — represents the high school press at the university level.

More than 100 Scholastic Journalism Division members serve as advocates and resource people for the high school press, usually in their own states.

Many have been — a few still are — high school journalism advisers.

The group presents its only annual award to an individual or group for achievement in bringing diversity to high school journalism. The award, today called the Robert P. Knight Multicultural Recruitment Award, was named for a highly respected University of Missouri journalism educator who devoted his career to journalism opportunities for minority youth.

Cutbacks, cutbacks, cutbacks

Greetings and best wishes for a happy and productive New Year. This is the first, and only, NCSPA (North Carolina Scholastic Press Association) newsletter you will receive during the 1992-93 school year. Whereas in the past we have produced two or three issues each year, the present economic health of NCSPA and the University of North Carolina at Chapel Hill has forced us to consolidate everything into a single issue.

This newsletter article, written by the part-time director of NCSPA, also told of the lack of funding for the graduate assistant who usually would be available to help the director. Only intercession by UNC School of Journalism's Dean Richard Cole provided a temporary substitute to produce the single newsletter.

On the other side of the country, Oregon State University has closed its journalism department. Carla Harris taught there and was director of the Northwest Scholastic Press. She began running the organization on a part-time basis out of the Student Media Department. "I will retire within the next six years," says Harris. "Since the OSU journalism department is now gone, I don't know where future NWSP leadership will come from."

Most universities, public and private, suffered severe budgets cuts during the 1990s recession. The help they have given to scholastic press associations has often been generous but, in most cases, less than a top priority. Today, as one budget reduction follows another, high school journalism associations are often high on the cut list.

There is little optimism among association executives about expansion of their services in the near future. They honor the "exceptional young men and young women out there" and "the oases of caring" at some high schools, as Jay Berman, a board member of the California Scholastic Press Association puts it, but they are not expecting any quick turnaround in the budgets at either the college or high school level.

On the national scene

The four national scholastic journalism organizations in the United States have been helping students and advisers for more than 60 years. They are the Columbia Scholastic Press Association, Journalism Education Association, National Scholastic Press Association, and Quill and Scroll. Through good times and bad, through wars and recessions, up and down the roller coaster of curriculum reform, these associations have been a motivational resource and advocate for publications at schools that could afford membership.

Each has developed its own character and specialties. But there is a surprising level of cooperation among the four groups. Despite natural competition for membership, contest entries, evaluation submissions, conventions and workshops, the four attend each other's meetings and report on each other's activities.

Often the same newspapers show up among the winners of different national contests, indicating that some newspapers can afford to participate in more than one of the Big Four. Membership figures, though, make it clear that the great majority of schools in the United States have no opportunity to get help from any national scholastic press association.

As with the state associations, these are not easy times for the Big Four. In fact, their longevity allows them to look back at alarming drops in school participation that may reflect both the demographics and the economy of the country.

In 1965, Quill and Scroll had 3,454 active schools, inducting 32,662 new student honorees.

In 1993, Quill and Scroll had 1,614 schools, inducting 10,435 students.

To some extent this parallels the drop in the total number of students in U.S. schools over that time. However, Q&S Executive Director Richard Johns says it also reflects a decline in the number of student newspapers in urban schools.

The Columbia Scholastic Press Association has gone up and down — from 2,300 members in 1982,

up to 2,974 in 1989,

down to 2,200 in 1991,

and up to 2,317 in 1993.

Director Ed Sullivan blames the 1991 dip on the economy and says the worst may be behind them. "When schools have a little bit more slack in their budgets, they'll spend on something like this," says Sullivan. "High school journalism has always been a Johnny-come-lately at the budget table — the last one to pick at the crumbs when times are good, the first one to be turned away when they're not."

Columbia Scholastic Press Association
Established in 1925
Location: Columbia University, New York City
Telephone: 212-854-9400
1993 membership: 2,317 school publications, including 839 newspapers
Membership fee: Ranges between $81 to $91 per publication annually (for high schools)

CSPA offers critiques of school newspapers, a series of contests and awards, CSPA-sponsored textbooks, fall regional conferences and a national conference in New York each spring that has become an annual high point in journalism education.

Student Press Review is CSPA's quarterly periodical. An affiliated organization, the Columbia Scholastic Press Advisers Association, serves journalism teachers who guide CSPA-member publications.

Journalism Education Association
Established in 1924
Location: Kansas State University, Manhattan, Kansas
Telephone: 913-532-5532
1993 membership: 1,598 journalism advisers
Membership fee: $35

Because it belongs to the teachers who guide student newspaper staffs, JEA tends to address matters of policy more directly than the other national associations, such as certification of journalism teachers, relations with school administrators, student press rights and credit for journalism courses.

JEA collaborates with the National Scholastic Press Association to present two national conventions each year — one in the East, one in the West. In recent years both organizations have developed programs to bring more young people and advisers of color into the membership, onto directing boards and committees, and to the conventions. JEA also runs a summer journalism advisers institute.

JEA sponsors competitions, publishes a magazine and newsletter, and runs the only general "bookstore" of publications on all scholastic journalism topics — a service other associations have tried and dropped over the years, though each of the others sells its own publications.

National Scholastic Press Association
Established 1921
Telephone: 612-625-8335
Location: University of Minnesota, Minneapolis
1993 membership: About 2,000 publication staffs, including 900 newspapers
Membership fee (with critique): $99
Membership fee (without critique): $49

When the National Scholastic Press Association and CSPA began, NSPA was considered the organization for the Midwest and West Coast, CSPA for the East Coast. The perception may remain, but membership rolls prove otherwise. Both organizations represent all 50 states today.

NSPA offers critiques, contests, summer workshops and two national conferences each year. Also, NSPA has introduced a two-tiered membership fee to allow publications to join at reduced cost if they're willing to forego a critique; an annual multicultural award for improvement of the diversity of the staff and content of newspapers; a trendy new tabloid newsletter; and membership for video news media and video yearbooks.

Quill and Scroll
Established 1926
Location: University of Iowa, Iowa City
Telephone: 319-335-5795
1993 total charter membership: 13,507 in 50 states and 41 foreign countries
Schools inducting honorees in 1993: 1,614
Membership fee (one-time charter fee): $30
Membership fee (new student): $10

Quill and Scroll is an international honorary society for high school journalists, founded "to encourage and recognize individual student achievement in journalism and scholastic publication." Schools, rather than publications, become charter members. Once a Quill and Scroll charter is granted to a school, it is considered a member forever — even if the school closes. If they meet grade and performance criteria, students at chartered schools may become individual members in their junior or senior years.

Quill and Scroll has no annual dues, no conventions or workshops. In addition to its role as honorary society, its programs concentrate on in-depth critiques of school newspapers and writing, photo and yearbook contests. Its magazine, *Quill & Scroll*, goes to all members.

A sampling on the state level
Florida Scholastic Press Association
Location: University of Florida, Gainesville
Telephone: 904-392-0460
Membership: 450 total school publications; 150 newspaper members out of 529 eligible schools
Membership fee: $15
Staff: Part-time director, paid by the university; two or three paid undergraduates working 10-20 hours per week; several volunteer undergraduate and graduate students

Julie Dodd, executive director of the Florida Scholastic Press Association, operates in a state packed with vibrant, successful commercial newspapers, and says many of the high schools follow suit. "Some of the top high school newspapers in the country are in Florida," she says.

Working out of the University of Florida in Gainesville, Dodd's office serves seven districts throughout the state. Each fall, about 3,500 to 4,000 students attend district conferences. A statewide spring convention pulls in more than 1,000 participants. One teacher and one student from each district make up the board of FSPA.

Many of the daily newspapers in Florida support their high schools. Smaller ones may print the high school newspaper; larger ones may provide mentors or scholarships to summer workshops or may sponsor writing competitions and awards programs.

Kansas Scholastic Press Association
Location: University of Kansas, Lawrence
Telephone: 913-864-0605
Membership: 240 total school publications; 82 newspaper members out of 356 eligible schools
Membership fee: $25 per adviser
Staff: Part-time director (salary for association work paid for by association), two part-time undergraduates

Contests, and lots of them, are the organizing theme of the Kansas Scholastic Press Association. Most state contests revolve around previously published material. But each February, KSPA students compete on the spot in full-day sessions held at six sites throughout Kansas. Semifinalists go to a statewide competition in April.

John Hudnall, executive director, says the contests are successful at drawing small schools into the association. " 'We're not good enough,' they protest at first," he says, "but I tell them, 'That's why you do it — to find out what your strengths and weaknesses are.' Once they attend the first time, they'll be back."

Almost one-third of Kansas high schools have fewer than 75 students. "By far the majority of the advisers for these schools know next to nothing about journalism," Hudnall says. "I visited one small school where the teacher took me back into her makeshift room — within a few minutes tears were in her eyes. She cried throughout our 30-minute talk, about the lack of facilities, financial resources, support. There she is, sitting in the middle of a dust storm, burdened by unreasonable expectations, with no help available."

Hudnall's philosophy is to take the association's services to these small schools. In recent years KSPA has added conferences on the Western and Eastern borders of the state along with the traditional large session in central Kansas. "We started the two (new) conferences so participants wouldn't need to drive eight hours from the Colorado border to a conference in Manhattan."

Nothing seems to fit the typical mold in Kansas. "I thought I'd seen everything," says Hudnall. "We have coaches as advisers. We even have a principal

as an adviser. Three years ago, though, the secretary of the Board of Education in Uniontown (pop. 250) started a high school newspaper there. She had worked on the town newspaper. She works one hour a day at the high school. They joined KSPA two years ago, entered the contest for small schools, and won the sweepstakes. They'll be back every year: 'I wouldn't miss this,' she says."

KSPA's publication membership has risen from 206 to 240 since 1990.

Interscholastic League Press Conference
Location: University of Texas, Austin
Telephone: 512-471-5883
Membership: 400 total school publications; 200 newspaper members out of 1,451 eligible schools
Membership fee: $25
Staff: Part-time director, secretary, two part-time undergraduate assistants

The Interscholastic League Press Conference started as an independent organization in the 1920s, but soon came under the protective arm of the University Interscholastic League, serving all Texas public schools in academics, sports, music, journalism, speech and drama.

Bobby Hawthorne has been the director of ILPC since 1977, coming from a variety of professional reporting and editing assignments at the *Tyler* (Texas) *Courier-Times-Telegraph*.

The unusual Texas hierarchy of the Interscholastic League suits Hawthorne just fine. "I get a lot of pleasure knowing football pays some of my bills," he says. "The League pays for our housing, telephones, duplication, auditing, and I get at least a full tabloid page free in the *Leaguer* newsletter, which goes to every high school in Texas eight times a school year."

It doesn't hurt journalism's cause that Hawthorne is also the managing editor of that newsletter. He writes an iconoclastic column for each issue, presenting his views on student press rights and often critical comments on the Texas state school administration in wry, pointed humor.

Money from the Interscholastic League allows Hawthorne to mount a spring convention that brings in top scholastic journalism experts from across the nation. "It's as good as the national conventions," he says, pointing out that attendance is close to 2,000 every year.

Hawthorne is not totally upbeat about high school journalism in Texas. The state education director has proposed a new back-to-basics curriculum to be applied to the current six-period day in Texas high schools, leaving room for only one elective in a student's entire high school career. "This would be devastating for journalism and all electives — music, speech, art," he says.

In addition, he strongly opposes site-based management, which is supposed to allow the administration, faculty and parents to oversee each school without "downtown" interference. That kind of approach, he says, is being taken over by "imperial administrator" principals who are protecting their own turf and muzzling school newspapers.

Washington Journalism Education Association
Location: Seattle, Wash.
Telephone: 206-784-9167
Membership: 157
Membership fee: $20

WJEA represents a different kind of state organization from those on university campuses. Like about 20 others, it is an independent group of journalism advisers with close ties to JEA. Its offerings for advisers and students are similar to state scholastic press associations — conferences, contests, critiques, a newsletter, special days led by professionals from *The Seattle Times* and *The* (Spokane) *Spokesman-Review.*

Lu Flannery, who has served as treasurer and whose home has been WJEA's "central office" for 12 years, says, "We've never considered anything else than being independent. We are picking up the slack because the university doesn't have courses that are absolutely pertinent to what advisers need. We step in when an adviser with no experience has been given the job of advising the newspaper and offer our help in any way we can. We give them a crash course through our summer workshop. It's been a lifesaver for many. Any of our members will serve as a mentor to an adviser in need of help."

Accepting the value of diversity, even articulating its importance, has far surpassed any success in having diversity in student newspapers.

Chapter 3

"Sometimes I feel like I don't fit in"

Honors student Amanda Washington, a junior at Omaha's North High School, took journalism in 1993 at the urging of friends, but had no plans to work toward a staff position on the newspaper. She felt that journalism at North High was "a white thing, a clique. Sometimes I feel like I don't fit in."

This "white thing," this "clique" thing, this sense of alienation that some students of color have about their high school newspapers and journalism in general, crops up at one school after another across the United States. It forms a barrier that divides students and weakens the role a newspaper can play in the school.

The words from *Captive Voices* still apply. It is still too often true that "school newspapers generally are dominated by college-bound middle or upper class students, with those of low income or of a vocational bent participating in minimal numbers." This results in "an elitism that excludes cultural and ethnic minorities as well as racial minorities."

There is a sense among young people of color that the school newspaper does not belong to them, nor do they belong on its staff. Newspaper insiders and outsiders will need to cross this barrier of cultural mistrust many times before they can make it disappear.

Thomas Harvey, the principal at North High School, sees the problem. Black students are often keenly sensitive to criticism of their written work, he says, thinking, "'What I write will be laughed at. What I write will not be looked at in the same light as that of other students.'"

"Traditionally, the journalism program looks for people who are good writers, students who are cre- ative. Many of our students coming from this community have not been exposed to things that journalism looks for."

His solutions:
• Begin with ninth graders. Give them access to computers.
• Get rid of "general English" courses and teach academic English.
• Require course work to be done on computers. Harvey believes computerized spell-checking and the absence of concern about penmanship can eliminate apprehension about red marks on papers, making black students more comfortable working with language and expression. And, in the end, more black students will find their way to the monthly student newspaper, *The North Star.*

The newspaper is not the only thing Harvey is changing at North High. Before the mid-1980s, the school had an ungainly appearance; fences surrounded the athletic field in the front of the school — symbolically cutting off the school from the surrounding neighborhood. In the 1970s, when mandatory desegregation offered an escape route, many of the brightest black students fled to the better-financed, traditionally white schools across town.

When Harvey arrived, he moved the athletic field to the side, improving the appearance of the school. He also led a campaign to make North High a magnet school. He vowed to give every student access to a computer. Result: North High has won praise as one of the best schools in the nation (*Redbook,* April 1992) and acknowledgment as a school on the cutting edge of technology (*Newsweek,* Feb. 15, 1993).

Solid communications education and a strong newspaper are primary weapons in Harvey's campaign to establish racial balance and understanding at his school. North High continues to lose black students as families leave the neighborhood even while white students stream in — bused past the surrounding turbulence — to take advantage of the school's academic superiority.

The demographics of the school in the 1992-93 school year are 63 percent white, 37 percent minority. Principal Harvey has pledged to have a minority staff on the newspaper that reflects the school population by 1996.

"For us there is a lot of integrity at stake in being able to say this paper represents the entire school," says Mike Krainak, the journalism adviser.

Krainak is pleased at the recent increase of minority staffers on the newspaper — from eight in 1992-93 to 12 in 1993-94. Harvey and Krainak are also encouraged that students of color have claimed many of the major editorial positions on the newspaper, providing models to attract other minority students. In the 1992-1993 school year, Anna Chan, a Chinese American, was editor in chief; Sephera Rosas, a Hispanic, was associate editor; Maher Jafari, an Arab American, was managing editor of the school magazine (an insert in the newspaper); and Zedeka Poindexter, an African American, was sports editor. A white student, Jennifer Sloderbeck, was news editor.

Krainak believes a good part of the improvement in numbers comes directly from the implementation of Harvey's prescription for change. He says that most freshmen and sophomores are now writing on computers in English classes and, as a result, more are following up with journalism or creative writing courses, the only classes that allow them to keep writing on computers. "As more minorities get through that program and feeder system, we'll get more of them," he says.

Uncommon commitment

Patsy Procuro is one adviser who measured the work to be done to achieve diversity, and then did it. In 1986, when he arrived to teach journalism at Arthur Hill High School in Saginaw, Mich., he found about half the student body was invisible — at least in the pages of the school newspaper. Black and Latino students, who made up nearly 50 percent of the school, rarely appeared in *The Arthur Hill News,* a broadsheet published every three weeks. Back then, it was produced by an all-white staff.

"When I first got here, the staff was covering rock concerts and the Pep Club. Nobody was covering R&B concerts," says Procuro. "Nobody was covering the Black Studies Club or the Latino Action Club."

Procuro immediately began a vigorous campaign to recruit minority students for the newspaper. He made his pitch to the three 10th grade English classes he was teaching. He encouraged all students to join the paper, but issued special appeals to the minority students. He enlisted counselors and other teachers to help him find interested students.

"You're not going to have a variety of coverage if the newspaper staff doesn't reflect the population of the school," says Procuro. "If half your students are minority kids, you should try to have a staff that reflects that. That's just being sensible. It seems unnatural to have it any other way."

Arthur Hill High became one of the few American high schools where students have the double advantages of a rich racial and ethnic mix as well as a strong school newspaper from which to learn about one another. What had been a divisive factor in the school's makeup became an educational asset.

Recruiting minority students to school journalism is a touchy proposition. Many minority students, accustomed to seeing inadequate coverage of their groups in adult media, avoid participation in school media, viewing them as alien if not hostile to their interests.

Procuro says his efforts to bring diversity to Arthur Hill High's newspaper were resisted by white and minority students alike. Whites balked at what they considered "special treatment" in Procuro's extra efforts to recruit black and Latino staffers. Many of the minority students demurred when nudged to sign up.

"I don't think a lot of minority kids saw journalism as an opportunity, when in fact it is a better opportunity than a lot of other fields," Procuro says. Yet he prevailed. The staff consistently includes 30 to 40 percent minority students. Minority students held key editorial positions, including photo editor and entertainment editor during the 1992-93 school year.

At schools where fewer than half the students are from minority groups, the greatest change regarding diversity appears to be in increased recognition of its importance. For although educators and administrators might find bringing minority students into the staffs and pages of their newspapers too daunting, most acknowledge it as an important goal.

Accepting the value of diversity, even articulating its importance, has far surpassed any success in actually having diversity in student newspapers. And, some cynics might say, the talking sometimes seems to substitute for the doing.

Still segregated

At the other extreme are schools populated by mostly minority-group students, often found in large and socially ailing cities. According to a 1988 study by the National School Boards Association, close to one-third of all black youngsters attend schools that are at least 90 percent minority. Another third attend schools with populations that are 50 to 89 percent minority. The same study shows that Hispanic students are significantly more segregated than black students.

These segregated urban schools are likely to have weak, infrequently published newspapers if any at all. Procuro, for example, said he deliberately chose Arthur Hill High School after leaving Saginaw High School in 1986, where he had taught English and journalism for 12 years, because Saginaw High "was moving toward phasing out its journalism program and I wanted to teach journalism." Saginaw High is a predominantly black school.

Washington, D.C., a city with a 96 percent minority public school population — mostly black with rapidly growing Hispanic representation — was a premier example of such a school district when reporter Retha Hill took a year off from *The Washington Post* to evaluate and shore up journalism in the high schools of the nation's capital.

The 1974 *Captive Voices* report declared Washington, D.C., a city "with a predominantly black population and an overwhelmingly black public school population" where "school journalism, with few exceptions, is dying."

In 1992, when Hill went into that system to take stock, it was nearly time to write the obituary. Hill, serving a one-year stint as a journalist in residence on a grant from The Freedom Forum, found a glowing ember here and there but rarely a spark of inspired, regularly published, free and open student news and expression. Despite the efforts of a group of supportive local journalists and a network of high school journalism advisers, only three of Washington's public high schools published more than three issues of their newspapers per year.

Hill worked through the 1992-93 school year to administer emergency life-saving support, but correcting the corrosive effects of more than two decades of neglect and abandonment would take more than one dedicated reporter on a 12-month assignment.

"What I found when I came in was a system with a lot of potential, but some disorganization," says Hill. "The schools that really needed help and attention weren't getting it. Basically, what I had to do was pull together a lot of different elements.

"All the teachers talked about the need for more money to buy equipment, to buy cameras, to buy film, to purchase all the little essentials. More important than resources was the need for training. Teachers and students needed and still need to learn to use their computers in the most cost-efficient and creative way.

"Many of the teachers needed professionals to spend time with them, to make sure they were on

Retha Hill took a year off from *The Washington Post* to help high school journalism in Washington, D.C.

the right track. Some were new, and needed to learn journalism. Some had been there longer, but they didn't have enough students, or felt they had no attention from the administration and professionals. They knew how to put a newspaper together, but they felt adrift."

No miracles have taken place because of Hill's temporary presence. A few schools published a little more often (one produced eight newspapers for the first time); a few published less often. But she was able to devote full time to school newspapers as a "personal advocate," as she puts it. Hill organized several workshops and an end-of-year conference attended by 92 students and advisers from across the city. A new awards program selected the year's top adviser, top student and a variety of bests in writing, photography and design. During Hill's year among them, D.C. advisers began planning a citywide interscholastic press association.

Hill feels she has been able to give journalism teachers and students some of the attention they needed. "I could go over and speak to classes. Really excite students about the newspaper. Give them confidence in their ability to write for the newspaper, and tell them how much fun it is. Recruit new students to staff and energize those already in journalism classes.

"I let teachers know they were not out there alone. If they needed something, it was possible to get it. Some teachers were so used to being told no that they had kind of given up. So they would do without a camera for two years, or without a software package for a year, just waiting and waiting

Racial, ethnic mix in high schools

% of:	All students	Journalists	Advisers
White	72.6	80.6	90.0
Hispanic	10.0	6.5	2.1
African American	10.0	5.6	1.2
Asian American	4.6	5.3	1.5
Native American	1.6	1.0	1.0
Other/no answer	1.0	1.0	4.6

Source: Journalism Education Association survey of 525 members, surveying high school advisers of newspapers (82%), yearbooks (54%), magazines (18%) and video (7%). May not add up to 100% due to rounding. 1992

and waiting for it to come."

"I think that the real test will be this coming year [1993-94]. They're starting on a really good foot. We've got backup mentors for the schools: younger people, more black professionals, more men."

Losing newspapers

Despite the potential of cities like Washington, D.C., that receive outside help, the plight of journalism in segregated urban schools has changed too little since *Captive Voices*. Barbara Hines, a Howard University journalism professor, has worked with high school journalism since 1969. "Unless you work on attracting minorities at an early age, you don't generate the interest or passion for the profession that people in other disciplines have already discovered," she says. "For example, those in the sciences have begun to identify young kids, particularly in the inner city. That had been an untapped talent." But, "by and large, there are very few [college]

From left: Denver journalism adviser Matthew Spampinato with students Rendell Draper and Randy Hollines. "I know people are reading my words," says Randy.

journalism programs that target youngsters."

According to Hines, there is a strong conviction among some educators that minority-group students are well-represented in high school journalism. "A lot depends on what part of the country you're in," Hines says. "The response has been uneven because there are parts of the country where it is not a problem." For example, as a member of the first Journalism Education Association diversity committee in 1986, she had difficulty persuading colleagues in San Francisco or the Southwest that a shortage of minorities in high school journalism exists. Colleagues from those areas said they see more Asian and Latino students than white students.

Building a multicultural newspaper

At Thomas Jefferson High School in Denver, photographs of the city's street scenes adorn the walls of the media room, pictures soon to be shifted to make room for the second award in two years for *The Thomas Jefferson Journal*.

In another nearby room, the monthly newspaper's staff of black, white and Latino students is feverishly working to produce the final issue of the school year.

Both the awards and the ethnic diversity of the staff are sources of pride for journalism adviser Matthew Spampinato. Building a multicultural newspaper has been one of his top priorities since 1990, when he started advising.

"TJ has a history of being a very Anglo school," Spampinato says. "The newsroom was always predominantly white, predicated on G.P.A. [grade point average] and tightknit."

Denver, a good example of major cities of the American West in its mixture of racial and ethnic populations, nonetheless is more a mosaic than a melting pot — black, brown and white citizens each claiming their own neighborhoods. Thomas Jefferson High School, located in a middle-class section of the city, has been enriched by students from all over the city since Denver began busing for diversity in the early 1970s.

"I don't think you can have diversity [in the newspaper] unless you have a diverse staff," he says. Still, *The Thomas Jefferson Journal* has a ways to go before it reflects the true mix of the school's 40 percent white, 40 percent black, 15 percent Latino students and five percent students from other minority groups.

Spampinato has recruited Latino and African-American students. He tries to teach diversity as an element in good journalism. He recognizes that curiosity, determination, thoroughness and other traits of a good journalist do not necessarily translate into top academic achievement.

"We try to stay away from G.P.A. students. We

don't go with the kids with the [A average]," he says. "You have to start by just making the reporters aware that something is happening. If you have been in my class, you know how to report. Now go cover it."

One black senior, Randy Hollines, recruited from a creative writing class, never considered a career in media. But he has come to appreciate the power of the press. "There's a lot of tension here and I wanted to make a difference," he says, referring to his piece criticizing the school's curriculum as too Eurocentric. "I feel like I have at least done my part. It's one thing to have a discussion, but now I know people are reading my words."

Murky reflections

Why have so many high school administrators and teachers missed the opportunities that the school newspaper offers as an educational vehicle for better understanding? There are too few who see the value of a strong student media to help students thrive in the crucible of diversity.

Too often teenagers who are not white look into their student newspapers and find little or nothing that reflects them, their culture, their values, their heritage. They can only surmise that they are unimportant and that there is no place in the media for their kind — either in the coverage or in the newsrooms. And when students think that way, everyone loses.

Wherever high schools are not encouraging the airing and disarming of prejudices, the broadening of minds, the expression that is essential to eradicating the old ills of superior/inferior thinking, they are failing the students, no matter how high the academic achievement they might boast.

A dirty word

How severe is the feeling of alienation from newspapers among black students? Consider West Philadelphia High School, where students in an experimental journalism program for minority students scoff at the profession's label. "Don't call us journalists," they insist. What they do is "expression," insist members of Carol Merrill's English class who produce QWest, a community newspaper covering their neighborhoods.

To the students, their 12-page quarterly tabloid is not a newspaper at all for it does what newspapers, as they know them, cannot or will not do. It takes the time and effort to put faces on the people of West Philadelphia. The stories are written by those who live in the neighborhood. The writers look like and live like the people they write about, and they experience the same joys and pains.

Nearly all, 99 percent, of the students are black, and nearly half are from families living below the poverty level. The school virtually had no newspa-

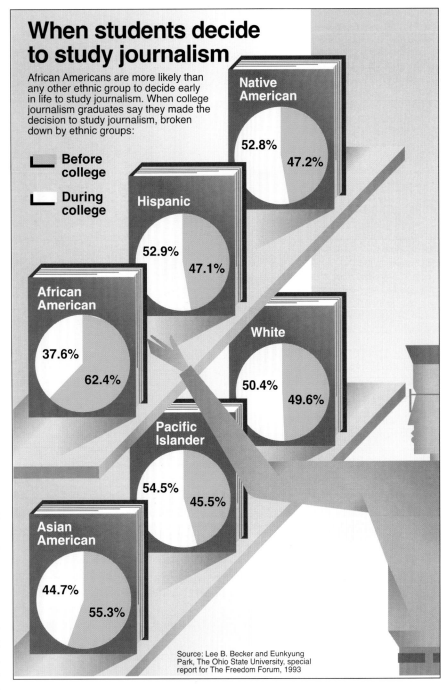

When students decide to study journalism

African Americans are more likely than any other ethnic group to decide early in life to study journalism. When college journalism graduates say they made the decision to study journalism, broken down by ethnic groups:

- Before college
- During college

Native American
52.8%
47.2%

Hispanic
52.9%
47.1%

African American
37.6%
62.4%

White
50.4%
49.6%

Pacific Islander
54.5%
45.5%

Asian American
44.7%
55.3%

Source: Lee B. Becker and Eunkyung Park, The Ohio State University, special report for The Freedom Forum, 1993

per — it published sporadically if at all — until Eleanor Novek, a former journalist, came on the scene in the fall of 1991. Novek brought the idea of a community newspaper to the school as her doctoral project for the University of Pennsylvania's Annenberg School for Communication. After Novek finished her research for the doctorate in June 1993, she turned over the project to Merrill, but continues as a consultant.

Her students, says Novek, "see the media as a monolith." Their community is sensationalized by the media. Still, says Novek, many of her students go about the job of reporting as if they are on a mission. Lamont Richardson, a junior, talks excitedly about an interview with a police officer who walks a

From left: West Philadelphia High School student Antoina Robinson, teacher Carol Merrill, consultant Eleanor Novek and student Lamont Richardson checking out an issue of *QWest,* a community newspaper produced by an English class.

beat. He has meticulously organized questions, anticipating logical follow-ups.

"My writing has voice, don't you think?" Antoina Robinson demands, gesturing toward her computer screen, as she animatedly describes her interview with an 85-year-old West Philly High graduate who recalled sneaking out of the schoolyard to buy sausages from a cart at recess.

QWest, a play on the name of the high school and "quest," is published under the auspices of the West Philadelphia Improvement Corps. It costs $350 to $425 to publish and deliver 3,000 copies of each edition for faculty, students and the community. The students use 18 computers donated through a grant.

The students select the story ideas, choose their interviews, handle the layout and even decide on distribution sites. They pick the cover story and critique each edition carefully after publication. Among the topics in recent issues of *QWest:* Afrocentric education, safe sex, rap music, teen suicide, premarital pregnancy, and sources of scholarship money.

"This English class was different from most," Eric Thompson, a sophomore, writes in one edition of *QWest.* "Instead of just reading books and writing about it, we had a chance to interview people in the community on subjects that we picked ourselves. We had visitors such as Acel Moore, a Pulitzer Prize-winning African-American journalist from *The Philadelphia Inquirer,* and Elmer Smith, a columnist at the *Philadelphia Daily News* [who graduated from West Philadelphia High School himself]. We went on field trips to learn about the journalism business — [to] both *The Philadelphia Inquirer,* the city's largest paper, and *The Philadelphia Tribune,* the oldest black-owned newspaper in the country."

Merrill sees the students "beginning to like the idea of seeing their work come out in print. They

are receiving a lot of positive feedback from family members, students and people in the community. Many of them, after they complete one story, are eager to do the work and get another one in."

Novek says she and Merrill do not emphasize the similarity of the students' work to television or big-newspaper reporters, instead encouraging the importance of serving their community.

"We let them know everybody has a story to tell, everybody is a human being. We push the idea that since we're all in this together, there are things that threaten us and please us that we all need to have information on and dialogue about," Novek says. "We tell them they should find issues that are important to them and the people around them, no matter what their career."

"I'm pretty encouraged, with one exception," says Novek. "The young people are growing and beginning to appreciate the things we are doing, but the school seems not to want to provide the necessary resources. Getting support from the community is difficult. I'm looking for local newspapers and television to get more involved. There have been a lot of promises, but not much cash. Individual people within the profession have been supportive, but everyone seems to be advising us to sell ads, and that's not what this is all about."

Instead, she says, a more reasonable kind of support might mean $5 to catch a cab home each time they have to stay late because many reside in unsafe neighborhoods. It could come in the form of child care for those with young children. Or a small stipend might help a promising candidate who needs to hold down a fast-food job after school.

On the road

Far from the asphalt and alleyways of Philadelphia, students in some of Alabama's most rural counties were gearing up in the spring of 1993 to launch community news coverage through their high school journalism programs.

University of Alabama administrators Kathy Lawrence and Robin Lambert set out on a long trip from Tuscaloosa to Coffeeville, in a remote southwest corner of the state. A community newspaper might be just what it would take to finally gain Coffeeville and its school some respect.

Coffeeville High is the doormat of its district, according to students in Jeannie Hackworth's social studies class who met with Lawrence and Lambert. Its football team is a winner — regional champions, in fact, as are boys' and girls' track — but the town is small, rural, 70 percent black, and poor.

The dark soil that gives the region its "blackbelt" label produces corn, cotton and pine trees. Coffeeville's main industry is "wood pulping," cutting and hauling trees to sawmills for lumber and paper — hardly prosperous work. Three-fourths of the

town's students qualify for the reduced-price or free lunch program.

"We're just like any other school," says one student. "Everybody tries to look over us just because we're small, but we're as good as anybody else."

Indeed, Coffeeville and kindred communities are an overlooked part of the solution to the problem of diversity in journalism, in the views of Lambert, assistant director of the University of Alabama's Program for Rural Services, and Lawrence, the program's director of student publications.

Lambert believes the community high school newspapers will fill a news vacuum produced by the absence of rural newspapers and serve as a vehicle for change in school and community. As student journalists illuminate concerns of their neighborhoods, they will be inspired to change what happens in the schools as well.

"There are a lot of people out there who have views," says Sean Franks, a student at Oakman High, a stop on another Lambert and Lawrence trek. Oakman, in the northwest part of the state, is a predominantly white community in the coal-mining Appalachia region — and just as poor. The average family income in Oakman is $16,908, and 32.1 percent of the families live below the poverty level, according to the Census Bureau.

Oakman High students want a newspaper so they can tell their community the findings of water quality testing projects they are conducting in chemistry class. At another rural school, students and teachers plan a living history project, to tell their community's story in a regular historical section of the paper.

As Sean Franks puts it, "It makes a big difference whether you get to share your views or not."

Above: Ozzie Pugh, left, and Fred Fluker, 11th graders at Coffeeville (Ala.) High School, where the athletic teams are winners but the school is in need of a student newspaper.

Left: Fluker, left, and Pugh, right, walk down a road near their hometown, located in a rural part of Alabama.

Sugar Beet

In Garden City, Kan., even as the city's and the school's populations have grown more Hispanic and Asian, the newspaper continues as largely a preserve of the white students.

Published every two weeks, Garden City High's newspaper retains the name adopted in 1910. The name *Sugar Beet* commemorates the town's first cash crop, although the crop left town in 1955.

The Mexican-American population remained a small, non-Anglo group in the town. Then, in 1980, a large meat-processing plant was built, attracting a group of new immigrants, mostly Central Americans and Southeast Asians, who came to work for the meat packers.

From 1980 to 1990, the town grew by one-third to 24,000. The new residents, who made Finney County the fastest growing county in Kansas during that decade, also wrought profound changes in the school system. The senior class of 1993 at the high school has 309 students, the freshman class, 480. Furthermore, "In two or three years, the really big classes will be coming in," says Rich Patton, the principal. About 150 students receive some English as a Second Language services and many more need them in order to gain spoken or written fluency in English, Patton says.

In many ways, says journalism teacher Monte Moser, this is an ideal school paper — good equipment and lots of freedom for the students.

However, while the journalism classes attract a range of socioeconomic groups, from "headbangers to superpreps," as Moser puts it, what they do not attract is a range of racial diversity. In a school that is approximately 28 percent Hispanic and nine percent Southeast Asian, the journalism and newspaper classes, with a total of 50 students, have only two Hispanics between them and no Asians.

Each year, says Moser, the demographics of the few non-Anglo students change slightly, but during his 11 years as newspaper adviser at Garden City High School, the percentage of non-Anglos in Journalism I and on the *Sugar Beet* has not increased.

Kristen Tate, editor of the *Sugar Beet,* and Laura Gilbert, editorial page editor, say that they would "definitely" like to see more Hispanics and Asians on the school paper. When asked about coverage of Hispanic and Asian interests, Kristen says that space keeps them from reporting on all activities in each issue. Also, students tend to cover what they're familiar with, which doesn't necessarily include clubs with mostly minority students, like La Familia, a school club for Hispanic students.

Tuan "Tony" Cao Le spends some of his spare time working on the *Sugar Beet* doing page layout — to learn as much as he can about computers — although he is not enrolled in journalism. Troubled by the lack of communication between ethnic groups, Tony decided last year to do something about it: Every day he ate at a different table in the cafeteria.

"I sat with a group of guys with almost no English, only Spanish. We couldn't talk much, but they were so happy to be talked to. Afterwards for a while in the halls they would see me and say, 'What's happening?' They couldn't even understand what I said in reply, but they were reaching out."

Hispanic students, whether first- or third-generation in the United States, say that they read the school paper. But they complain about the lack of coverage of issues that concern them — the soccer team, which is heavily Hispanic, and festivals and events like Cinco de Mayo that attract Hispanics.

Why don't they write for the paper? Some, like Gabriela Santana, hold jobs after school that are as important to them as anything they do in school. "Right now," says Gabriela, "we're paying off a trailer lot we bought. You know, my parents need all the help they can get from me and my brother," which is why she works after school at the grocery store. Many of the boys are involved in sports, basketball, football and wrestling in addition to soccer, which also take up considerable after-school hours.

Even more compelling than these reasons, though, is the feeling that they are not really a part of the school. Hispanic students, especially first-generation in the United States, share a culture of "outside looking in," as Jesus Hernandez, Spanish teacher and faculty adviser of La Familia, puts it. "It's a difficult, complicated issue," he says. The comment, "It's for them and not for us," comes up often as Hernandez' characterization of the attitudes of Hispanic students to school activities.

Flor Banda, a 15-year-old freshman, expresses this feeling when she says, "I've been told by the ninth-grade principal that we should express our culture. And when we do we always get into trouble. They don't let us wear the clothes that we want. Right away they think it's gang-related."

The barriers remain

The news on diversity in scholastic journalism in the 1990s is that there is much to celebrate but even more to decry. Concern for racial and ethnic inclusiveness is more evident than ever in high school journalism circles — just as among their professional counterparts. Yet there is little evidence that the barriers are falling.

Many advisers and journalism teachers appear to have taken a do-or-die attitude, and some of them are experiencing success in making a place for minority students on their school publications. Quite a few view the problem of exclusivity as significant, but are unable to find a prescription for change. Wherever teachers and students are along this continuum of broadening the reach of high school newspapers, much remains to be done.

Year after year, classes of young people march out of high schools with diplomas certifying their preparedness to take on the challenges of adult life in an ever-changing society.

Their preparedness, if measured against the realities reported in our daily media, would be found wanting. The world outside the high school and the one those students are leaving forever could be brought closer together if educators viewed school media as powerful instruments of learning. There is too little evidence that secondary education decision-makers value journalism, much less journalism that reflects the nation's diversity.

Too many adolescents continue to attend high schools where they are in a dominant majority. Where that majority is white, they have a greater chance of benefiting from a journalism program than their counterparts graduating from predominantly black or Hispanic schools. But again, when that majority is white, they have a lesser chance of benefiting from an inclusive and interracially respectful publication.

The American Society of Newspaper Editors' long-heralded goal to achieve diversity on professional newspaper staffs on a par with diversity in the population by the year 2000 is no longer viewed as realistic. Even as its noble goal drifts further from credibility, ASNE and other journalism organizations show too few signs that they recognize the vital importance of a strong high school press in their futures.

Racial reconciliation in America is not a reality, and many would agree that it seems to diminish with time as a realistic expectation. In a 1993 survey on racial attitudes in America commissioned by the Anti-Defamation League, 31 percent of the people 18 to 30 years old responded with answers indicating strong prejudice, compared with 23 percent of 30 to 49 year olds.

To deny youth the opportunity to confront the issues of increasing racial and ethnic divisions while they are still in the safety of the learning environment does not just avoid the problem. It makes it worse.

"Where are the black faces?"

Marcia Kovas teaches journalism and advises The Review *newspaper staff at James Whitcomb Riley High School, South Bend, Ind. The Review has received the George H. Gallup award for three consecutive years, '91, '92 and '93. She received her Master Journalism Educator certificate from the JEA and the Daghlian Award for Outstanding Teaching of High School English from Indiana University. She is a frequent speaker at national and state journalism conventions, a judge for Quill and Scroll, and a member of the faculty at the High School Journalism Institute at*

Indiana University. She also has served on the board of directors for the Indiana High School Press Association. This is reprinted from the Fall 1992 C:JET (Communication: Journalism Education Today, a magazine published by JEA).

"Where are the black faces?"

A friend of mine, who is a black teacher, taught me a lesson with that comment about a photo opinion column appearing in *The Review* at James Whitcomb Riley High School in South Bend, Ind.

What appeared to me to be a selection based on random sampling, to her appeared a slight. Riley is an inner-city urban school with a minority enrollment of 30 percent. And, with that comment, I realized that including minority interests in *The Review* would come about only through a conscious effort.

My staff, like many others, was predominantly white, and our paper reflected the interests and concerns of the middle-class culture. Perhaps without realizing it, my editors had alienated many of our readers by ignoring their interests and concerns in our coverage.

I also realized my white staff could never improve on this front solo. We needed direct input from the kids we had ignored. I honestly don't believe white high school reporters can cover the gamut of minority interests credibly. We needed to bolster our ranks and the diversity of our staff to do the job.

The Review staff has come a long way since those early years: Not only does our photo opinion column feature faces of every color, but the staff also

Marcia Kovas, a journalism teacher and adviser at James Whitcomb Riley High School in Indiana, has 10 tips on how to bring diversity to school newspapers. She is talking here with Racquel Gooden, diversity editor of the student newspaper.

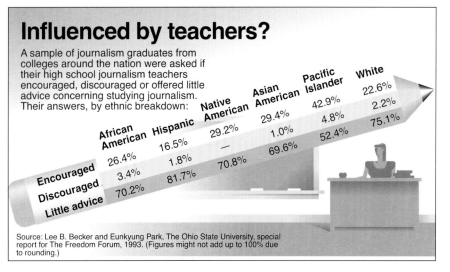

Influenced by teachers?

A sample of journalism graduates from colleges around the nation were asked if their high school journalism teachers encouraged, discouraged or offered little advice concerning studying journalism. Their answers, by ethnic breakdown:

	African American	Hispanic	Native American	Asian American	Pacific Islander	White
Encouraged	26.4%	16.5%	29.2%	29.4%	42.9%	22.6%
Discouraged	3.4%	1.8%	—	1.0%	4.8%	2.2%
Little advice	70.2%	81.7%	70.8%	69.6%	52.4%	75.1%

Source: Lee B. Becker and Eunkyung Park, The Ohio State University, special report for The Freedom Forum, 1993. (Figures might not add up to 100% due to rounding.)

reflects the diversity in our school. Minority coverage is no longer an afterthought, but a top priority for the staff.

Here's how:

1. Encourage a "Diversity is Special" mentality. Encourage your staff to seek out and explore the differences between cultures in their reporting. Fostering curiosity and awareness pays off. Several years ago two staffers (one black, one white) became buddies and decided to spend a week at each other's homes.

The adventure in the "other world" became the focus of a double-truck spread. Sara tried black-eyed peas for supper and Chiquita learned to "air guitar" to heavy metal music. The essence of their report, though, was more profound: "We're more the same than we are different," they discovered.

This year *The Review* ran a point-counterpoint standing column that explored the fairness of minority scholarships, the importance of including black history in the curriculum, and the problems of gang-related violence in the schools.

With outspoken minority staffers on board, class discussions often inspire story ideas.

In helping students respect their differences, be sure to give each group fair play in the staff room. At *The Review,* students have hummed along to everything from Ice-T to Amy Grant, learned beat box [making drumming-like noises with your mouth] and admired dreadlocks as well as tails and spikes.

2. Banish all cliques and become comrades in arms. When the overriding goal of the entire staff is a great newspaper, differences tend to fall aside. After several late sessions at deadline in the staff room, and after several "great" issues are produced, your staff will find a great deal of common ground. They'll share tears and headaches, food fights and Mac bugs, and pretty soon they'll become the best of buddies as well.

Ultimately, on *The Review,* the staffers who are

alienated or ignored are the do-nothings, no matter who they are. It is the hard workers who earn respect and top positions on the staff.

3. Create an atmosphere where sincerity and open-mindedness are valued. Encourage your staffers to enjoy and acknowledge their differences. But, as my feature editor last year put it, don't single minority students out with over "friendliness" because it is perceived as insincere. The best bet for making a diverse staff work, she thought, was to encourage staffers to treat each other as equals. And the advantage of working on a multicultural staff is the opportunity to learn about another culture first-hand.

"We talked about everything from comparing the types of shampoo and deodorant we use to comparing our cultural and philosophical views. I've learned more about alternative cultures from people on the staff than I could in any book," she said.

4. Encourage students to become advocates for their interests. Create a sense of mission among your minority staffers in covering topics of concern to them. Make them aware that the interests of the majority will, by the nature of the beast, get covered; but not so for theirs. Minority staffers have a vested interest in producing articles with a cultural bent, and they have the insight to cover them well.

At one point, a very strong fundamental Christian staff reporter doubted her future in the media, for fear she did not "fit in." At the time, many dishonest evangelical television ministers were falling prey to media scrutiny, and she feared all fundamentalists were getting a bad rap. I pointed out to her that for this very reason she should join the press corps to cover religious topics objectively. She went on to become editor in chief of her college newspaper, and now covers religion for a large metropolitan daily.

5. Use diverse talent in creative ways. Several years ago I recruited a talented editor to assist in the production of our *Wildcats on the Prowl* entertainment supplement to *The Review.* He was interested in and committed to the paper, but couldn't get the hang of straight news writing. He enjoyed creative writing, and rather than pressure him to change his style, I encouraged him to create an ongoing fiction column which would, through its narrative and dialogue, critique a black fashion fad or trend in each issue. Thus was born "Homie, Bart and E.," the story of three fictitious students at Riley High School. Our readers loved the column, and best yet, we didn't discourage or alienate a talented writer who had much to offer the staff.

To diversify our publication, and thus our input from staff, we've created a game page, a comics page, top 10 lists, candid photo pages and special reviews and features, aside from our standard fare. And in doing so, we've provided a forum for new talent.

6. Encourage writers to tell their own stories. Some of the best first-person feature stories have come from minority and non-traditional staffers who have told their own stories. Last year one of my beginning journalism students won a state-level award for describing her struggles as a teenage mom.

A young athlete described her wrenching emotional ordeal of facing open heart surgery as a junior in high school, and another staffer shared her sadness and bitterness after being betrayed by a boyfriend who date-raped her.

And soon after the nomination hearings of Supreme Court Justice Clarence Thomas when the issue of sexual harassment riveted the entire country, a young woman staffer described her own particular ordeal, and relayed how her complaints to management served only to get her fired. That column went on to win a national award from Quill and Scroll.

The first-person format allows novice staffers to try their hand at writing richly detailed pieces with strong reader appeal. And, as in developing any skill, success breeds success, and motivation and commitment to the staff.

7. Help your writers turn their anger into ideas. Let those students who feel disenfranchised find a forum for their opinions on your staff. With your guidance, they will be able to voice constructive alternatives to the status quo, and inspire real changes in your school and community.

Several years ago, two female staffers who enjoyed dressing in the "punk" style came to class irate. They were convinced that the security guards had accosted them only because their hair was spiked and their jackets were leather.

I suggested that rather than arguing, they objectively examine the guards' treatment of students based on dress in an article for the paper. The staffers, delighted and inspired, took the idea a step further. They set up five typical scenarios in which a student may encounter an authority figure: walking in the halls without a pass, sitting on the lawn during school hours, talking loudly in a library, playing with squirt guns in the mall, and carrying a soft drink into a clothing store.

On the first week of the investigation, the girls dressed in "preppie" attire: wore their hair in ponytails, donned penny loafers, clean jeans and crew neck sweaters. They enacted each of the five scenarios, and found that their behavior went largely unnoticed by those in authority. Not so the next week. Dressed "all out" as punkers, the reporters were verbally chastised each time.

The reporters detailed their experiences in the best read double-truck spread of the 1987-88 school year. They went on to win a Gold Key from Quill and Scroll. They were thrilled with the reader

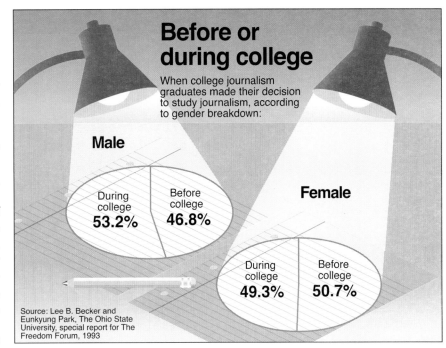

Before or during college

When college journalism graduates made their decision to study journalism, according to gender breakdown:

Male

During college 53.2%

Before college 46.8%

Female

During college 49.3%

Before college 50.7%

Source: Lee B. Becker and Eunkyung Park, The Ohio State University, special report for The Freedom Forum, 1993

response and the knowledge that they did "make a difference."

8. Don't just search in Honors English. It's a myth that only those from the honors track will succeed in your journalism program. Sure, it's great when they do join, but I've found that many of my "standouts" have been on the regular track. Honors kids often have many other activities which demand their attention and, as often as not, journalism just isn't their top priority.

And minority kids, too often, aren't placed on the higher track. Several years ago one of my shy regular English students wrote a provoking and thoughtful piece on her experiences with discrimination. I spotted superior verbal talent, and not only prompted her to try Honors English the next year, but I also convinced her that she would be an excellent editor. And she proved me right on both counts.

Scour the photography, graphic arts, drawing, keyboarding and marketing classes as well for new talent. Students who excel in these areas will be a boon for your newspaper staff. And don't forget to send out recruits to the junior high, middle and elementary schools in your neighborhood. One of my best feature writers admitted she joined up only because she was inspired by a recruiting talk back in sixth grade.

9. Make sure your minority staff is represented on your editorial board and voting boards. Ensure that your minority staffers have a say in all aspects of running the publication by reserving them a seat on your governing board.

It's the nature of the beast that they are bound to see things differently from your majority staffers, and you need their input to best serve your readers.

"Homie, Bart and E." would not have stood a chance if my white editors had voted alone on it. They didn't understand the humor or the dialect, and felt the space wasted. But our black readers loved it, and when we worked the names of Riley students and athletes into the plot, it became one of the biggest draws of new readership.

Minority perspective is essential in determining how to cover sensitive issues. My feature editor, who sat on the board, set me straight when she spoke out against using the tags, "who is white ..." and "who is black ..." as identifiers. And having minority members on the board helped provide direction in determining how to cover the sensitive topic of gang violence in the school.

10. Help minority staff to excel in your program and beyond. It's important to do more than pay lip service to wanting the involvement of minorities on your staff. You need to be their advocate as well. Minority students will begin to enroll in publications classes when they see the long-term benefits. Seek out minority scholarships to journalism workshops, and keep a sharp eye out for college journalism scholarships geared to minorities.

Several years ago a talented, but insecure, His-panic student joined *The Review* as a photographer. His work revealed talent, and he demonstrated a great desire to learn all he could and improve. And, in all fairness, he wanted to know what lay ahead of him if he gave his best. He set his sights on, and won, the $28,000 Foellinger Scholarship to study journalism at Indiana University. In the interim, he won national, regional and state-level awards.

While I couldn't give him guarantees, I did let him know what opportunities lay ahead, and assured him I would work with him.

Making minority and non-traditional students feel "at home" on your staff may be easier than you think. All students want their teachers and peers to respect them, recognize them for hard work, and help them to succeed. In our early days of diversifying, *The Review* staff worked hard to change students' perception that we were an elitist staff. We changed our coverage, sought diverse input, and implemented many non-traditional approaches. And now that the word's gotten out, minority students see *The Review* as a place where differences are valued. They see that all staffers can succeed, and yes, success does breed success.

A radiant newspaper

Frank Rivera should not be one of his city's top journalism teachers, at least not by conventional standards. His school system is financially strapped and the Northwest Washington, D.C., neighborhood surrounding Bell Multicultural High School, where Rivera has taught since 1981, is wretchedly poor.

The school has no gym or cafeteria and the classrooms are bursting at the seams with an overflow of Hispanic, African, Chinese, Vietnamese and African-American students who pour out of the nearby brownstones and tenements to walk the glass-strewn sidewalks to its safety.

Bell has a harrowing history. In the spring of 1993, it barely escaped being closed by Washington's money-starved school system. Also that year, until his capture, a serial killer stalked the neighborhood streets for weeks randomly shooting people, often in daylight.

In the midst of this destruction and despair, there is a rainbow. Actually, *The Rainbow,* Bell Multicultural High School's student newspaper. In a brightly lit fourth floor classroom, a dozen students, all new Americans from as far away as El Salvador and Ghana, publish the award-winning monthly.

In the process, they give voice to a community accustomed to being ignored. They rallied the community to save the school, smashed stereotypes (including the students' insecurity about their command of English) and pushed the envelope about as far as anyone in the scholastic press is willing to go these days. Abortion. Homosexuality. Sex. D.C. public schools. All are fodder for *The Rainbow.*

"I want the paper to be real visible in the building, as the backbone of the school," says Rivera. Students look forward to publication day and teachers incorporate the newspaper into their lessons.

Quite a change from a few years earlier when Rivera faced the same problems — money, time and support — that plague most inner-city high school journalism programs. As chairman of the English department with a full class load, Frank Rivera was a novice when it came to journalism, but a veteran when it came to motivating kids. In January 1990, *The Rainbow's* first issue was published.

"The kids take their cue from the teacher," says Rivera, who spends long hours working with *The Rainbow* staff. His energy, enthusiasm and commitment rub off. "Sure," he says, "you come in after school. You come in on weekends."

Just as Rivera's program was getting organized, other journalism teachers and a group of professional journalists pressed the school system to get Bell a computer and a printing budget. The paper now has one computer.

Since *The Rainbow* began, Rivera has sought help from professionals — a free-lance community news reporter, a magazine editor who used her ties in the community to fund the first issue, and an illustrator who designed the paper's masthead.

Lola Demma, the newspaper's mentor, agrees that putting in extra hours as deadlines approach is important, but she adds, "Frank is a good teacher to start with." She says professional journalists work with him because he's always open to ideas. "A lot of people, especially when they've been good in their own profession for many years, don't want someone coming in to tell them there's a better way. Frank never minds admitting he doesn't know. For the sake of the students' learning, he is willing to take advice and learn."

When asked to dream about what he would like for his program, Rivera sighs and lists money for darkroom material, a guaranteed budget to publish at least 10 issues a year, a second computer, more training in layout and design. But lack of money won't stop the program from expanding, he says, ever confident that the money, like everything else, will come from somewhere.

Working to make change

When diversity was a low priority, The Newspaper Fund was working alone to change the complexion of high school journalism. In 1968, The Newspaper Fund (later renamed Dow Jones Newspaper Fund) held the first summer workshop for minority high school students interested in journalism.

In 1993, the program marked its 25th anniversary with 31 workshops, partially paid for by DJNF, and an additional 31 workshops sponsored by others — newspapers or universities. Many of these were started with encouragement and money from the fund. That means that more than 1,000 minority students got an intensive baptism in journalism in one summer.

"The purpose of the workshops," says Tom Engleman, "is to identify and encourage talented students." Engleman was executive director of the Dow Jones Newspaper Fund for 23 years before joining Temple University's School of Communications and Theatre in 1992. "Once the workshops are over, the real work begins — college scholarships, good counseling by teachers and professionals, internships, etc. There's no secret to any of this. It's simple. If a young person receives sincere encouragement from adults [teachers, newspaper reporters and editors], he or she will be most likely to pursue a newspaper career. We all go where we're wanted."

Wanda Lloyd, now a senior editor at *USA TODAY,* is one who reaped multiple benefits when

At a glance

The Media Academy at
John C. Fremont High School
Oakland, Calif.

Principal: Robert Duran.

Number of students: 150 in the
Media Academy program.

Publication adviser: Steve
O'Donoghue.

Newspaper: *The Green & Gold*,
1,700 circulation, tabloid published every three weeks; 8-12
pages average; $6,000-$7,000
annual budget.

Revenue sources: $800-$1,500 a
year in advertising, not put toward
publishing costs; State of California, Oakland Redevelopment
Agency and school district.

Staff: 26.

Computers: IBM clones.

Software: PageMaker, FreeHand,
MS Word.

Offered for credit: English elective.

Other publication activities:
Magazine; video and radio documentaries.

the fund first started its minority programs. At Savannah State College, she attended a high school conference for minorities — a precursor to the summer workshop — in the mid-1960s. She was one of six students who took part in a minority teachers' workshop at Savannah State in 1967. And she was awarded a copy-editing internship in 1970, with training at Temple University and on-the-job practice at *The Providence Journal-Bulletin.*

Before joining *USA TODAY,* Lloyd was with *The Washington Post.* She is one of the many journalists who discovered and developed their love of journalism through the Dow Jones Newspaper Fund programs. Today she is on the board of the Dow Jones Newspaper Fund.

Finding the talent

Evelyn Hernandez is assistant metro editor at New York Newsday. *She is a past president and board member of the National Association of Hispanic Journalists. This article was excerpted from "Kerner Plus 25," a report prepared by Unity '94 whose members include the Asian American Journalists Association, National Association of Black Journalists, National Association of Hispanic Journalists and Native American Journalists Association.*

Whenever I'm invited to speak to high school or college students about journalism, I always ask the same question: How many of you have a relative or even an acquaintance who is a journalist?

Usually, at least one of the white students will raise his or her hand. In the dozen years that I've been asking that question, however, only one minority student has said she knew a journalist.

"Well, if you didn't know a journalist before, you do now," I tell them, and then I hand out my business card.

Experience tells us that too many young Latino, black, Asian and Native-American students know very little about journalists or journalism and that they do not get the opportunity to learn about us during those crucial years when they are determining what to do with the rest of their lives.

Indeed, an editor's search for a reporter from a minority community really should start at least eight years sooner than it usually does. The editor and news organization should take steps early on to ensure that Latinos, blacks, Asians and Native Americans at the high school and college levels are welcome to work on their school newspapers; that the high school or college does, in fact, have a newspaper or broadcast program; and that colleges, high schools and elementary schools are teaching minority students the basic skills — reading, writing and arithmetic — that all young people need to go into journalism or any other profession.

Offering hands-on journalism experience as early

as possible is key to engaging a youngster in the news business for life. There is no need to reinvent the wheel. Many programs already provide fine models that others can build on and expand. What is desperately needed is more of everything — more high school and college newspapers, writing contests, journalism days and workshops, internships, scholarships, mentor programs, job fairs and a better way of tracking talented young people so we do not lose them as they make their way through high school, college and that all-important first job.

There are many things the news industry can do to fire up young people of color about journalism. The industry can start by urging local news operations to adopt a school or school district and help produce a newspaper or broadcast there. With budget cutbacks, too many high schools, particularly in neighborhoods with high concentrations of minority students, are losing their journalism programs.

The industry must also provide intensive training workshops that produce a newspaper or broadcast, such as the Dow Jones Newspaper Fund's High School Journalism Workshops for Minorities, where students spend two weeks learning what journalism is, interacting with professional journalists and, most importantly, producing a newspaper. Yet often these workshops, intended to be paid for only partly by the Newspaper Fund, struggle to find additional funding from other news organizations and participation from professional journalists.

The industry also must provide its own news professionals to go into high schools and colleges and talk about diversity in the newsroom and in the news. If young people see that diversity is valued in the professional workplace, they are more likely to start practicing it while still in school. Visiting professionals can emphasize the advantage of including minorities on the staff of high school and college newspapers and broadcast. Helping to make sure that faculty members steer students of all ethnic backgrounds to these student productions would benefit the industry's recruiting efforts.

When strangers meet

At 6:00 a.m. on April 23, 1993, 40 students from The Media Academy at John C. Fremont High School piled onto a bus in Oakland, Calif. Twelve tiring hours later they arrived in Long Beach to attend the weekend-long convention of the Journalism Education Association (teachers and advisers) and the National Scholastic Press Association.

Their experiences went beyond the usual excitement and fatigue symptomatic of national gatherings of teenagers with similar interests. They were black, Hispanic and Asian-American students from a magnet communications school, and they were a large portion of the tiny group integrating a meeting of more than 1,000 white people.

"They live in a neighborhood that is almost 100 percent non-white," says Steve O'Donoghue, the adviser, who expressed some surprise at the level of discomfort they felt. He asked them to write about their experiences when they got back.

Their words illustrate the nuances of understanding/misunderstanding that are today's challenges of diversity:

I think Fremont students are not used to being around so many whites, and whites are not used to being with Fremont people. What I don't like about the convention is that I walked out of there without making a new friend. We all tend to stick together without making much effort in talking to others. The closest I got to meeting a new person was during my interviewing session, where we were forced to interview someone we didn't know. That was nice.

— Ming Chiu

I felt a little uncomfortable in the convention. Maybe because I wasn't used to being around so many white people. I didn't let this get to me. Overall, the convention was great. The sessions were informative and interesting. They really motivated me to become a journalist.

— Gabriela Garcia

The National High School Convention was a great experience for me because I actually got to meet great designers, editors and writers. ... Coming to the convention was great because I felt honored to represent my race there. ... I really recommend that more ethnic schools attend the next convention.

— Chio Saelee

On the weekend of the 24th, the joint classes of the Media Academy embarked on a journey that forever altered the lives of those who attended. ... The dance, for the most part, was OK, but when Fremont showed up, then everything sprung to life. Although the music was a little different from what we're used to here in Oakland, Fremont students showed class and flexibility by staying on the floor all night long.

— Raul Lago

[A Fremont girl] said they were riding in the elevator. Some Caucasian girls stepped in and started talking to her, everything's cool. But she stated that as soon as she turned around and talked to her friend in Spanish, the girls ignored her. Prompting a racial incident? Maybe. While I don't agree their reaction was proper, I also don't think it was racially motivated. More like the uneducated reaction. We have to understand this probably was the first time they've heard fluent Spanish outside their Spanish for beginners class. Don't get me wrong. I know racism exists. I know. But we can't cry wolf every time some white guy looks at us funny. It just isn't right. (Do I sound like an Oreo yet?)

My solution to this problem is so simple it's brilliant. It goes back to U.O.P [the University of Pacific summer journalism workshop]. Make us work together, with someone facilitating of course. Help us break the ice and become familiar with each other so that there's a line of respect (just like The Media Academy).

— Esteban Duenas

Not only did I have a great time, but I also learned a lot in just a couple of hours compared to two years of learning at school.

— Phuong Ngo

The thing that I learned was that racism is alive and strong, you can add color to black and white photos, Los Angeles has a lot of problems, and never again go on a bus ride.

— Elizabeth Morrison

Dedicated at an early age

George Curry was in the eighth grade when he decided what he wanted to do with his life.

The eldest of four children growing up in a Tuscaloosa, Ala., housing project in the 1950s, he would read the local daily, watch the way it covered the black community, and long to make a difference.

"I hated my hometown newspaper," recalls Curry. *"The Tuscaloosa News* was very segregated. The classified ads were segregated. The only time you saw black people in the paper was when they were arrested for allegedly committing a crime or for playing sports.

"I knew there was more to life than that. I thought there was another story to tell and I wanted to tell it."

Fast-forward to January 1993. Curry, 46, is named editor in chief of *EMERGE*, a national news magazine geared to black America. The position is the latest stage in a distinguished journalism career. He was New York bureau chief and Washington correspondent for the *Chicago Tribune,* and a reporter with the *St. Louis Post-Dispatch* and *Sports Illustrated.*

But his resume does not capture what Curry considers his most significant journalistic achievement — helping minority teenagers get into journalism.

Those efforts began in 1977, when Curry was on the *Post-Dispatch.* He helped to start a workshop where minority high school students in St. Louis could learn about newspapers from professionals.

As Curry's career progressed, he established similar urban journalism workshops in Chicago, New York and Washington. Working with local chapters of the National Association of Black Journalists, Curry brought together journalism professionals and students. The pros became mentors, providing high school and college-age students with reporting and

Magazine editor George Curry sets the highest standards for hundreds of minority students who attend the journalism workshops he helped to develop.

writing experience.

Curry's workshops generally run for seven consecutive Saturdays during the school year. During the first three to four weeks, the focus is on writing: hard news stories, features, Q & A's, simulated news conferences. Then students interested in print journalism work closely with local newspaper professionals, and those who prefer broadcast work with TV or radio professionals.

Print students produce a newspaper; broadcast students produce a newscast. At the conclusion, there is a graduation ceremony where the students show off their finished products to family and friends.

A tough, no-nonsense reporter and editor, Curry's workshops reflect his personality. He establishes the tone in the first meeting: He sets high standards for *all* journalists — teenagers included — and nothing less than maximum effort is tolerated. And he makes it clear that he expects more, not less, of his students who are minorities.

"A lot of kids just haven't been challenged. That's why I use the technique I do," Curry says. "Just because a kid happens to be the best writer in his class doesn't mean he's a good writer. If students are taught that their writing is outstanding when it's not, it does them a great disservice in the long run. If you don't challenge kids, you're underestimating what they can accomplish."

Over the years, Curry estimates he has worked with more than 600 students. Even more impressive than the number is the lasting impact he has had on them. The achievement Curry is proudest of — "the payoff" he calls it — is that many of his former students, now professionals, started journalism workshops of their own.

Mark Russell is one such student. Now an assistant city editor at *The Boston Globe,* Russell was a

high school senior when he participated in Curry's St. Louis workshop in 1980. Nine years later, as a reporter with *The* (Cleveland) *Plain Dealer,* he started his own workshop.

"George planted the seed," Russell says. "When I was in his workshop his mantra was, 'Give something back.' He was so serious about journalism, so committed, that I respected him right away. I knew that as soon as I established myself in the field I would start my own workshop."

Russell says the students nicknamed Curry "The Ayatollah."

"George could be *very* demanding. I think he reveled in playing the role of the heavy. I think a lot of people were taken aback by what he demanded of high school kids. He demanded that we read the paper, that we use correct English, that we be precise writers, that we be informed and ask intelligent questions. … He was relentless in his quest to make you better."

Indeed, Curry has earned a reputation as a master motivator: a tough teacher who will resort to any tactic — intimidation, embarrassment, harsh language — to get students to maximize their potential. Alternately charming and critical, he has the unique ability to challenge students without offending them, to drive them to the brink of frustration then rebuild their confidence with a few choice words of praise.

"Not everybody can get away with what I do," he says with a mischievous grin. "Some people have a kinder, gentler approach. This is what works for me. Yes, I'm tough on kids. Because I believe in them. When I'm tough and they do a good job, I go out of my way to praise them. And when I do praise them, they know I mean it.

"If you can't take the kind of treatment I'm going to give you, and I'm volunteering my time and obviously care about you and love you, what's going to happen when somebody who hates you treats you like that?

"That really goes to the whole core of my teaching technique. I get in their faces early because I care about them. I know they're going to need this tenacity to become successful. They're going to have to learn to deal with it, so why not start now?"

Kevin Pollard, a reporter with *The* (Nashville) *Tennessean,* recalls the first time he saw Curry in action. It was 1988, and Pollard, then with *The Hartford Courant,* sought Curry's advice on how to get a minority journalism workshop started in Hartford. Curry simply invited Pollard to New York to observe the first day of his workshop.

What he saw was vintage Curry.

"He really read those kids the riot act," recalls Pollard with a laugh. "And I really admired his style. Not just his teaching technique, but his use of humor. If you're going to be hard on kids, you have to be able to make them laugh, too. George does that. The thing is, while they're laughing, they're learning."

Pollard, who calls Curry "a major influence," not only started the workshop in Hartford, but established one in Nashville as well.

When it comes to relating to students, Curry's greatest asset may be his enthusiasm. George Curry *loves* journalism.

"I can take [students] behind the scenes. I can talk about going to the Vatican and meeting the Pope. I can talk about covering Ronald Reagan, Jesse Jackson, George Bush, Bill Clinton.

"I can introduce them to an exciting world that they know nothing about. I can share emotional experiences with them. I can share the excitement of being a journalist and convey that."

Raised in poverty in rural Alabama, Curry is an excellent role model for youngsters from disadvantaged backgrounds because he has been there. Thus, when Curry talks to students about overcoming obstacles and working hard to be the best, his message rings true.

"I'm 46 years old, and this is what I'm proudest of. It's not about winning awards — I've won a lot of awards. It's not about flying on Air Force One, it's not about going to the White House or meeting the Pope.

"This is by far the most rewarding thing I've done. And I don't really see it as an accomplishment for me. This is what I'm supposed to do. This what my mama did. This is what my coaches did. This is what my high school counselor did. I didn't have a choice. It's the way I was brought up. People around me were like this.

"And if they weren't, who knows where I'd be today?"

Reaching Native American students

In 1988, the dean of University Outreach asked Shiela Reaves, a journalism faculty member at the University of Wisconsin-Madison, "Why don't we bring in minority kids to use our computers in the summer, when they're available?"

Reaves wanted to take the idea one step further: "Why don't we bring people who are never reached — Native-American students?"

Thus was born the Native American summer workshop, which for five years has brought 12 to 15 young people from the Great Lakes region to spend a week learning journalism and putting out a newspaper, *The Messenger.*

The workshop is exclusively for Native-American teenagers. "We're reaching a lot of reservation kids," says Reaves. "Because of the distinct tribal nature of their culture, they're going to be attracted to programs that have a tribal nature. If they know they're going to be with Indian students and teach-

ers, they'll be more inclined to come."

The response has been enthusiastic. In fact, Reaves is upset that they turn away two applicants for every one accepted each summer. Unlike many similar workshops, students can return for one, two or three summers to keep honing their skills.

The Native American Journalists Association cosponsors the workshop. Paul DeMain, president of NAJA, has been director since the workshop's beginning. Reaves is co-director and a large number of Native-American journalists serve as faculty, coming from mainstream newspapers such as *The Dallas Morning News* and *The (Portland) Oregonian* as well as Indian newspapers, including *Menominee Tribal News* in Keshena, Wis., and *The Circle* at the American Indian Center in Minneapolis.

"Our goal is to teach journalism in a cultural setting," says Reaves. This means bringing in Indian artists and historians, as well as taking students to visit places that will enrich their sense of Indian culture.

The workshop is also about breaking down some of the cultural barriers experienced by Native Americans. There is strong emphasis on interviewing and teaching students how to ask questions, getting past some of their traditional reluctance to intrude on others' privacy.

"The workshop has been geared to the need to incubate more Native-American journalists," says DeMain. "Newspapers are looking to hire them. A good Native-American journalist can pick and choose where he wants to go. We also need to fulfill tribal newspaper needs. One of their goals is to get better coverage of what goes on on their reserves."

The majority of workshop participants come from traditional reservations. In 1993, one student came from Milwaukee, one from Madison, and 11 from reservations, including the smallest tribe in Wisconsin, Stockbridge-Munsee, a part of the Mohicans.

"Next year we're graduating one of the first students to go through this program. Michelle Greendeer will finish at the University of Wisconsin," says DeMain. He says Michelle is a top-notch student who may go on to law school, but is already being recruited by newspapers.

47

We begin with what students want to question, tell each other, tell the world — as troubling as that may be for adults to hear...

On this cold January morning, a yawning quiet cloaks the main newsroom of the *Detroit Free Press*. It's not quite 10 o'clock. By AM-newspaper standards, the deadline for tomorrow's edition is an eternity away.

As the minutes and hours flash by, the news budget will begin to fill out as reporters and editors fire up their computers, phones and faxes. Mark Thompson and Susan Bennett will file on the Bush administration's threatened military strike against Iraq. Michael Betzold will analyze a proposal to increase Michigan's sales tax. Debra Adams will cover elections at the Detroit school board meeting. There's snow on the ground, and though she doesn't know it now, reporter Lori Mathews will cover the big storm set to sweep into the city tonight and close schools the next morning.

But right this minute, Tracie Etheridge isn't concerned about Iraq, sales taxes, the school board or snow. The 16-year-old Murray-Wright High School student is fretting about her own particular problem as she stares into the unblinking screen of a computer monitor on the *Free Press* copy desk. She's struggling to write a good headline.

Brian Jarrell, a fellow student in her high school journalism class, has written a first-person account of gang life. Tracie likes the way Brian, in just a few paragraphs, manages to describe some of the differences among gangs, why kids get involved and, most important, why they shouldn't. "Whatever the reasons for joining a gang, you must always remember that gang life is very dangerous," Brian writes. "I have a bullet wound to prove it."

Brian's story will be published in the special *Free Press* high school edition. Thinking back to the lesson she got from *Free Press* staffer Matt Fiorito, Tracie wants the headline for Brian's story to "catch the readers' attention and give them an idea of what the story is about." The two-column, 36-point Roman, two-line headline called for on the page dummy won't give her very much space to play with. Nor does she have much time. After much hemming, hawing and pecking on her keyboard, Tracie settles on this:

> **Ex-gang member**
> **warns of danger**

The headline works, Tracie is pleased. Punching up the next story onto the screen, she starts work on another headline. Tracie Etheridge is on her way to a career in journalism.

What newspapers *are* doing

Tracie Etheridge and her classmates in Mary B. Hines' journalism class are part of the *Detroit Free Press* High School Journalism Program. In off-deadline times, students and teachers use the newsroom's computers to edit and do layout. *Free Press* editors offer guidance to teachers and students alike. And when the work is done, the *Free Press* high school edition contains a page of news from several of the participating schools. The project directly involves up to 400 students a year and puts newspapers (free of charge) into the hands of 75,000 others. In the process, it grows journalists.

While most newspapers do nothing for local high school journalism, there are a few that have made an effort to work with teen journalists.

Chapter 4

Good news, bad news: Newspapers' investment in local high school journalism

David Hawpe, editor of *The* (Louisville) *Courier-Journal*, says, "Given the primary importance of high school as a journalism career entry point, not nearly enough is being done. One summer workshop a year doesn't do it. ... I think it has to involve more people in a bigger, more sustained commitment. It happens too seldom because it's a lot of trouble."

Hawpe puts his money where his mouth is. *The Courier-Journal* has taken over the journalism instruction and production of the school newspaper at a local girls' school. The newspaper cosponsors three Urban Journalism Workshops each summer, then sends the best students to a national workshop at Northwestern University. It also follows up with internships once they're in college.

Other newspapers helping high schools:

• Lorraine Eaton, high school editor at *The Virginian-Pilot & The Ledger-Star* in Norfolk, Va., recruits and trains teen correspondents — more than 100 so far.

• Don Williamson, an editorial columnist at *The Seattle Times,* runs a summer workshop for minority students with the help of newsroom colleagues.

• Rick Senften, assistant city editor at *The Repository* in Canton, Ohio, works with high school journalism students and gets their news published in a special page called *The Student Times.*

• George Ramos, a columnist with the *Los Angeles Times,* visits schools to talk up journalism among young people.

• Diane McFarlin, executive editor of the *Sarasota Herald-Tribune* in Florida, set up a summer training program for high school advisers.

• Loren Ghiglione, editor of *The News* in Southbridge, Mass., has a standing offer to help every school newspaper in his community.

• The Poynter Institute for Media Studies and the *St. Petersburg Times* work with 16 local high schools in Florida.

Why they get involved

Schools these days may have the trappings of a plush university, journalism labs outfitted with computers, newspaper advisers with a real zest for journalism and students dreaming about Harvard or Howard. Other schools may have the barbed-wire feel of a juvenile hall, a couple of hand-me-down typewriters as the total equipment, teachers who don't have a clue about how to put out a high school newspaper and students who are struggling with life and death situations among family and friends every day. This is the way high schools are these days. This is what the newspaper industry must work with.

There are five reasons for community newspapers to get involved with high school newspapers:

• To bolster schools and to rescue journalism programs threatened by budget cuts, indifference, censorship and poorly trained advisers.

• To recruit young talent — especially ethnic minorities — into the profession. After all, more than half of today's newspaper professionals trace their start to an experience with high school newspapers.

• To connect with young people, their thoughts and concerns, so journalists can do a better job of covering them.

• To cultivate newspaper readership among young people so they develop an appetite for news.

• To instill an appreciation of First Amendment freedoms in students, who become better citizens and in the process enrich our democracy.

In 1989, the American Society of Newspaper Editors surveyed its membership to find out what community newspapers were doing to help student newspapers. The professional journalists were concerned about three national trends: falling newspaper circulation, a perception that fewer young people are attracted to journalism as a career and the industry's lackluster success in hiring minority journalists.

St. Louis Post-Dispatch Managing Editor David Lipman led the committee that conducted the survey. "I was reasonably pleased that almost 41 percent of newspapers sponsor high school journalism seminars, but a one-day seminar may not be enough. Then I looked at those heavily involved in mentorship, internships, financial aid, and basically only a quarter of the newspapers do that. Once you strip away the metropolitan newspapers, the numbers are even more depressing."

Especially discouraging, Lipman says, is that small newspapers generally don't offer high school programs designed to target young minorities. This is important because small newspapers are where most young journalists get their start. "I think we have a double-double whammy," he says. "We have far too many small newspapers that have no minority staffers, and too many that aren't doing anything to encourage minorities to go into print journalism. If they did that encouragement, maybe the kids would come back to their communities after college and work at those newspapers."

Diane McFarlin, executive editor of the *Sarasota Herald-Tribune,* believes that newspapers need to mount a "rescue mission" to save high school journalism from the onslaught of budget cuts, administrative censorship and weakening support from school officials and the public. "I believe that students who attend high school where there is a strong newspaper — one that is protecting the First Amendment and doing a responsible job of covering the news in the high school and the community — that they go on to become newspaper readers and appreciate the role of newspapers in society."

Journalism: Teaching social issues, civic responsibilities

Sometimes support from the community newspaper takes a different form. Joe Moss, editor of the weekly *Dell Rapids Tribune* (circulation 1,166) and the *Baltic Beacon* (circulation 318) in South Dakota, believes it is important for professional journalists to serve as First Amendment advocates for the students, who may not get such support from their teachers and administrators.

Three local high schools publish their newspapers within the pages of the *Tribune* and *Beacon,* and Moss encourages the student journalists to tackle controversial subjects. "The kids are shying away from controversy [because] this is a fairly protective environment and we're a small community,"

says Moss.

Case in point: St. Mary's High School newspaper, *Cardinal Review,* carried a student editorial bemoaning the lack of school spirit at games and placed some of the blame on the attitude of parents and administrators. "When the students kick the bleachers, the noise annoys the parents, therefore it has become school policy not to kick the bleachers," wrote Christopher Benhoof.

But the editorial angered some parents, who complained to the principal. Two weeks later, the *Cardinal Review* printed an apology to anyone who was offended by the editorial and said that the newspaper did not intend to place "blame on anyone in particu-

lar for the problem concerning the school spirit."

Because all this was unfolding inside the pages of his newspapers, Moss wrote an editorial in defense of the student journalists, who, he said, were simply trying to "open an exchange of ideas" for improving school spirit. "What they got," wrote Moss, "was a slap in the face."

"Journalism," concludes Moss, "can be a great tool to teach social issues and civic responsibilities, and to help prepare [students] for life after they leave the protected confines of high school."

"Some papers have been doing things for many years," says McFarlin, who was the 1992 chair of the American Society of Newspaper Editors Education for Journalism Committee. "But there are too many communities and cities where there probably is not enough support."

To spur on community newspapers, McFarlin's committee produced a "how to" report called *Rescuing High School Journalism.* It recommended five ways for newspapers to get involved:

(1) Conduct a journalism workshop for teens
(2) Publish students' work
(3) Send staff members into the classroom
(4) Start a summer internship for advisers
(5) Sponsor a scholastic press awards program

Proponents say that exciting things happen when professionals and students work together. From the students' point of view, Brenda Neel, a journalism adviser in Canton, Ohio, says that classroom walls get knocked down, textbook lessons get thrown out and students are forced to match wits with the real world. Steve O'Donoghue, adviser of the award-winning *The Green & Gold* at The Media Academy at John C. Fremont High School, an inner-city school in Oakland, Calif., says journalism may be the most perfect teaching tool around. The process stimulates intellectual curiosity and critical analysis. After all, when a student is forced to go down to city hall and interview the mayor, figure out the municipal budget and write about it, that's a real exercise in putting theory to practice.

Add to these benefits the notion that the school newspaper represents a hands-on lesson in civics — an opportunity to participate in the democratic process. Teaching the art and craft of journalism to students not only advances a school's language arts program, but it also imparts the values of democracy

and citizenship, says Roy Peter Clark, an associate director at The Poynter Institute for Media Studies, a non-profit journalism teaching and research center in St. Petersburg, Fla. Clark has spread his love of writing and the values of democracy to hundreds of elementary, middle and high school students who have gone through the institute's summer writers camps.

Just consider, says Clark, what a young person can learn by writing a letter to the editor. "It's a way that a 10-year-old can connect writing to some of the greater purposes of public life and see the relationship between writing and democracy."

The *Free Press* model

This kind of work — propping up the schools, growing young journalists and servicing democracy — doesn't show up in the mission statement of your typical newspaper. To see how it can be done, let's return to the newsroom of the *Detroit Free Press,* specifically the copy desk.

Since copy editors don't start work until midafternoon, expensive computer equipment — equipment that would be the envy of any high school journalism program — is sitting idle for several hours a day. The *Free Press* editors came up with the bright idea of letting students use the copy desk in the mornings.

From this simple idea, the High School Journalism Program was born. It started in 1985 when many high school newspapers in Detroit were dead or dying.

Journalism class students write the stories at their schools under the guidance of their teachers. Then, school-by-school, the teacher and a small team of students go to the *Free Press* newsroom, where they edit the stories and write headlines.

Darlene Harper, left, and her mentor Lori Mathews worked together at the *Detroit Free Press.* The newspaper works with 21 high schools.

One Tuesday each month, a portion of the 21 schools in the program get a full page each in the *Free Press* to print high school news. The special high school edition is almost the same as the regular newspaper, minus some features like stock market listings.

For example, the Tuesday March 24, 1992, edition contains news from eight high schools—Henry Ford, Northwestern, Southwestern, Cooley, Central, Renaissance, Northern and Mumford. This edition is delivered free to the eight schools; so students get to read news not only about their own school, but also about the others as well. And, of course, they get all the news in the *Free Press.* The newspaper also is delivered to the middle schools that feed the high schools.

But there's more: At the end of the school year, the *Free Press* publishes a special section called *We the Students* with each school writing on a specific theme. And each summer, the *Free Press* hires some of the best students as newsroom apprentices. They help reporters do research and interviews, and they get to write their own stories at a salary of $6 an hour. *Free Press* journalists serve as mentors to the students and run Saturday workshops to help them plan for college and fill out scholarship applications.

The efforts are a boon to teachers like Mackenzie High School's Lena Teagarden. "If I had to do the school newspaper without the help of the *Detroit Free Press,* I wouldn't do it," she says. "There's so much hands-on experience in the real world that it sometimes sparks an interest in the students to study journalism. This year I had more students in the ninth grade who wanted to be in journalism simply because they started to send the newspaper to the middle schools."

In fact, each year, two to three dozen *Free Press* proteges go off to college to study journalism.

Neal Shine, *Free Press* publisher, sees future dividends. "The payoff, very selfishly for the paper, will be in finding and nurturing bright young minority high school students," he says. "We don't have a lot of home-grown minorities on the staff. This has been a business that has excluded minorities for too long a time."

The power of mentoring

One of those waiting-in-the-wings journalists is Darlene Harper, an 18-year-old African-American graduate of Detroit's Denby High School, who grew up on Detroit's east side. As a child, her inspiration was Carmen Harlan, a black news broadcaster on Detroit's WDIV-TV. "We had an essay contest in the fourth grade about what we wanted to be," says Harper. "I said journalist and spelled it g-e-r-l-i-s-t."

She got involved in the *Free Press* program in 1990. Her first published article was about Denby's homecoming king and queen. In 1991, the *Free Press* hired her as a summer apprentice. "They taught me so much about how journalism works," Darlene says. "It was totally different from what they taught in school. We wrote articles, we did tours, they taught us more grammar and they critiqued our writing. It was a big turning point in my life as far as journalism. I really, really knew then that I wanted to go into journalism."

Reporter Lori Mathews, a nine-year veteran of the *Free Press,* was asked to work with Darlene as a mentor. Mathews helped Darlene with her stories, with her college applications and talked her through some difficult times. She helped Darlene apply for a journalism workshop at the University of Michigan. In the summer of 1992, thanks to support from the *Free Press,* Darlene also was chosen as one of 15 students to attend the Rainbow Institute, an intensive journalism workshop held at the University of North Carolina at Chapel Hill.

Over the years, Mathews has seen Darlene grow. "You just saw her gradually gaining confidence," she says. "After she came back from the Rainbow Institute, she just seemed like more of a take-charge person."

Darlene says of Mathews, "She is one of the best things that ever happened to me. I'm glad that she came into my life. She's like a big sister to me."

Mathews, who also does volunteer teaching at Denby High, says nothing beats the satisfaction she gets out of working with Darlene and other students. "You go into the schools and because you're a *Free Press* reporter and your name is in the newspaper, they hang onto your every word," she says. "I feel like Norm in *Cheers.* I walk into the classroom and they all yell 'Lori!' "

This is the kind of story that gives *Free Press* Publisher Shine the confidence to declare: "We've reached a point where the kids feel connected to us and they feel connected to journalism through us. We consider this as important as anything we do."

Controversy is part of the job

Darlene Harper graduated from Denby High School in Detroit and is studying journalism at Michigan State University. Here are her reflections on her time as a high school editor.

I learned the hard way that being a high school journalist doesn't necessarily mean you'll be the most popular person around, even where your best friends are concerned.

Controversy was sometimes as big a part of my job as the writing.

At the beginning of the year, as senior class president and editor of my newspaper, I planned to dedicate my first editorial of the year to the senior class. But instead of a positive editorial about the seniors, it ended up being an article criticizing their behavior as role models for the rest of the student body.

The senior class decided to get together at a restaurant in Detroit. We were anticipating about 50 people but 120 showed up instead.

It was big trouble because we had not made reservations for such a large group. After a while the restaurant became very noisy. Some people were jumping from one end of the table to another and when everyone finally left, the restaurant was a mess.

For the rest of the weekend, I thought about what had happened and Monday morning I sat at the computer and wrote about it. I wrote that we — the senior class at a predominantly black school — are often stereotyped about how we conduct ourselves in public.

People often expect the worst. I said we shouldn't live that stereotype and that to be treated like young adults, we had to act like young adults.

I received positive feedback from many teachers, but a lot of negative feedback from students. I even received a letter to the editor, saying I had degraded the senior class and that the seniors had conducted themselves in a very good manner.

As a journalist, I saw it that way and that's the way I wrote it. The letter bothered me a little. But I said what I wanted to say and got my message across. Once again, I learned sometimes people will criticize and cause controversy.

Journalism has taught me so much in the past three years, from the *Free Press* newsroom to the *Denby Log* newsroom.

Educators have told me journalists are idealists, and their mission is to change the world. I know I may not change the world, but I can write about it

How professional newspapers help high schools

Percent who sponsor:

	Yes	No
Mentor program	14%	86%
Internships	25%	75%
Financial aid for projects	18%	82%
High school papers	30%	70%
Minority student scholarships	24%	76%
High school journalism seminars	41%	59%

Source: American Society of Newspaper Editors survey of 234 newspapers

so people can see for themselves what's out there and try to change the negative things and convince others to do the same.

A small newspaper shows the way

Some may say it's easy for a Goliath like the *Free Press* (circulation 636,000 and a member of the Knight-Ridder news chain) to harness the resources to take on a project of this magnitude. The newspaper estimates that the High School Journalism Program costs about $150,000 annually, not including all the volunteer time provided by staff members. The *Free Press* solicits financial support from Ford Motor Co. and other businesses to help pay for the school distribution.

Size and money are important, but more important is commitment. Some small newspapers have extended this "can-do" spirit to help out their local schools.

To see that, go to northeast Ohio, to Canton, home of Timken roller bearings, the Pro Football Hall of Fame and *The Repository,* a 64,000-circulation daily owned by the Thomson Newspapers. Pick up the Monday edition of the paper, pull out the Community section and you'll find *The Student Times.* It's a page of news, photographs and artwork produced by journalism students from six local high schools. *The Student Times* represents a melding of the classroom and the newsroom, and it gives journalism students a chance to do real work for a real newspaper.

The program started in 1990 when Brenda Neel, a journalism teacher and newspaper adviser at Canton's McKinley Senior High School, was trying to find a way to "pump up" her journalism class. "I felt we needed a real punch," says Neel. "I didn't think I was doing justice to the teaching of journalism, even though I had taken a little college journalism." She was interested in getting some kind of tie-in developed with *The Repository.*

Editors liked the idea and assigned Rick Senften, assistant city editor, to work with Neel. Together they developed the idea for *The Student Times.* Senften was chosen because, as the father of two, he had been pestering the newspaper for years to get involved with the schools. "Nobody seemed to be getting the idea that we need to cultivate our readers and that means we had to get into the schools," he explains. "We need better consumers of the news so we can get better at our work."

Senften now spends much of his time working with students. He scoots out of his work cubicle in *The Repository's* newsroom, bounds down the stairs and drives his red pickup out to one of the six participating high schools — McKinley, Timken, Hoover, Sandy Valley, GlenOak, or Minerva. He leads classroom discussions, gives students reporting

tips and works with them on their story ideas.

And the story ideas! They are not the usual run of club events, teacher profiles and student gossip. They are stories of broad interest, substance and even controversial subjects that teachers and principals acknowledge would not have been touched before:

Loretta Davis interviewed a white supremacist on why he advocates racial purity. Karen Motley met one of her idols, Magic Johnson, and wrote about the experience. Greg Siegfried did a story on children who are homeless. Wendy Smith did an expose on how Canton's Amateur Sports Hall of Fame had failed to attract many visitors and failed to file its required non-profit papers with the state Attorney General's office. Robyn Katz investigated the health claims of the so-called "heartsmart" meals offered by some local restaurants.

"The focus is on the audience," says Neel. "Now there's the possibility that 64,000 people will read the story. The students have a real purpose in their writing. The whole world is open. We've canned the textbook exercises."

Chris McCalmont, 18, of Hoover High School says the experience of reporting and writing for *The Repository* has helped with his other studies, given him more self-confidence and convinced him to go into journalism. His dream is to work for a magazine like *Sports Illustrated.* "I want to be able to sit down and interview the most famous athletes in the world."

The newspaper also has allowed the journalism classes, via modem, to tap into the newsroom's computers so students can access news from wire services. In addition, the newspaper has recruited photojournalism students from nearby Kent State University to meet on Sundays with high school students to teach them photography.

The newspaper supports education and literacy in other ways. Like many newspapers, it has a Newspaper in Education (NIE) program to promote the use of the paper in schools and finds businesses and other sponsors to underwrite the costs. Through aggressive marketing, NIE circulation has grown from 47,000 in 1991 to 155,000 in 1992.

"We'd like to be known as the education newspaper," says James McKearny Jr., publisher. "It's part of our commitment to the community. We also have a commitment to the printed word. I'm making sure that it continues. Frankly, I think the broadcast media have fallen down on this. Our kids need to learn. We want to make some contribution to the nation that really is important and fun."

Home-grown solutions

The programs operated by the *Detroit Free Press* and *The Repository* represent intensive efforts to support high school journalism. Other newspapers and

What teens most want covered in daily newspapers

	Very interested	Somewhat interested	Little interest
Local student polls	52%	33%	14%
Local high school sports	48%	29%	22%
Local school news	46%	38%	15%

Source: Gallup, 1991. (Note 1% did not express interests.)

Rick Senften now spends much of his time working with students at one of six high schools participating in a program that produces *The Student Times,* a one-page insert in *The Repository* where Senften is assistant city editor.

journalists have developed their own programs. Some are intended to give schools a helping hand. Some emphasize recruiting and training of young talent. Others help the newspaper produce the kind of stories that will attract young readers. Whatever their scope and mission, there is a congruency in outcome:

• *The Morning Call* in Allentown, Pa., lets journalism classes use its computer, production and graphics equipment to prepare school newspapers for printing. A newspaper staffer serves as an editorial consultant to each school. The School Newspaper Advisory Program began in 1979 with three schools and has grown to 11 schools with about 250 students. An unexpected dividend is that three former SNAP participants now work for the paper.

"We hope that we will keep the students interested in newspapers, that they see the importance of the newspaper and become better, more critical readers," says Siobhan McManus, the newspaper's public relations coordinator and SNAP director.

• The *Dayton Daily News* in Dayton, Ohio, and nearby Antioch University operate a one-week summer workshop for about 25 high school journalism students. The students get a crash course in journalism from their *Daily News* staffers. One year the students covered the "shooting" of a principal — a mock event staged with the cooperation of campus security.

"It's no small feat to keep 16- and 17-year-olds entertained for 24 hours a day," says editorial writer Ellen Belcher. She is working with public television station WPTD on a series of instructional videotapes that will be made available to high school teachers.

• The *Virginian-Pilot & The Ledger-Star* in Norfolk, Va., has recruited and trained nearly 100 teen correspondents from 40 schools to produce stories and provide news tips for the professional staffers.

The teens often develop ideas that the adult reporters would never stumble across, such as Joe Marino's feature on a group of teens who produced 30 low-budget horror films with a video camera. Other writings are intensely personal, like Dee Dee Love's column on a friend who died in an alcohol-related car accident.

"It became increasingly apparent to me that teenagers have a lot to say, that they understand the issues of the day and that they are a lot more intellectual than people give them credit for being," says Lorraine Eaton, the newspaper's high school editor. "Teenagers have a place. I don't know why we have ignored them for so long."

• The *Sun-Sentinel* in Fort Lauderdale, Fla., visited schools to solicit the opinions of teenagers before launching a high school news page. Then the paper recruited 126 students to contribute to the section as writers, photographers and artists. Working under the tutelage of *Sun-Sentinel* staffers, teen journalists write features, movie and music reviews and take photos for about $25 an assignment.

"We want these kids to be reading us," says Gail Bulfin, an assistant city editor. "We want to recruit. We want them to come back and work for us."

• "It sounds as though typical advisers are beaten up, beaten down and bedraggled," says Loren Ghiglione, editor of *The News* in Southbridge, Mass., and former president of the American Society of Newspaper Editors. "We need to go to advisers and invite them to list the ways we can help. Some of these ways may be low cost. In our case, this year we spent $450 on AP stylebooks, manuals and writing guides for the region's high schools. We ran a Saturday morning session for advisers and editors and virtually every adviser in the area came, and it was a simple thing."

• Schools in Richmond, Va. and Washington, D.C., benefitted from the attention of full-time pro-

Where new hires at newspapers land	
Cities of fewer than 100,000 people	64%
Cities with 100,000 to 1 million	25%
Cities with 1 million or more	11%

Source: Dow Jones Newspaper Fund, The Ohio State University; based on 1991 journalism graduates

fessional journalists-in-residence who started working with them during the 1992-93 school year, thanks to funding from journalism organizations.

In Richmond, reporter Steve Row had been volunteering during his lunch hour to help an inexperienced journalism teacher at his daughter's high school. When the two Richmond newspapers merged, he was ready for a change. "I figured I had written every story that could be written in my 24 years as a reporter," he says. He convinced Richmond Newspapers, Inc. to support a more organized outreach program to high school newspapers. He works with 26 high schools, going to each at least once every three weeks to teach what they request, from one-on-one mentoring to help in drafting a student policy statement.

In Washington, Retha Hill, a reporter for *The Washington Post,* spent a year working intensively with 20 public high school journalism programs. Hill, who was also president of the Washington Association of Black Journalists, spent her time finding out what training, advice and supplies they needed, and figuring out ways to provide them.

The Freedom Forum funded Hill's year in the schools with two grants for a total of $115,000, while *The Post* allowed her to take the time away from the newsroom. In October 1993, Hill returned to reporting.

Final lessons

None of this is meant to suggest that newspapers can solve all of the challenges facing our schools, nor should they be expected to. There are practical limits to what a newspaper can do — it can open doors to only so many students, send reporters to so many schools. Nor can journalists replace journalism teachers. And when institutions with dramatically different missions and cultures come together, there's always the chance of disagreement and disharmony.

When the *Los Angeles Times* agreed in 1993 to donate printing for *LA Youth,* an independent youth newspaper, controversy erupted over the first issue. Some sexually explicit language in a story about AIDS and safe sex was deleted at the insistence of the *Times'* community affairs director, who considered it in poor taste.

LA Youth called the action censorship, and said that while it welcomed the *Times'* donation of printing, it was not giving up editorial control in the process.

"It was a red flag to us," says *Times* spokeswoman Laura Morgan. "When you sponsor it [the publication], and your name is on it, it reflects on your image."

Both sides now say the matter is resolved and the *Times* will continue to print *LA Youth* without interference.

"It was a miscommunication problem," says Donna Myrow, executive director of *LA Youth.* "[The decision] was not made by the editorial department at the time. It was made by community affairs. They assumed they had editorial control and they were mistaken. They are now printing the paper and everything is worked out."

Some news organizations could be apprehensive about getting too closely connected to public institutions — the schools — that it must cover in the news. Michael Hanke, editor of *The Repository* in Ohio, acknowledges that the newspaper's involvement with high school journalism classes presents possibilities for ethical concerns. "The purest side of me says not to do it," he says. "The human side of me says this is a great thing we're doing."

Or, as *Free Press* reporter Lori Mathews says of her time with students such as Darlene Harper, "It's the most enjoyable aspect of my job, period. Just think if we could get every newspaper in the country to do this."

Making a difference

Only about eight percent of the journalists working for daily newspapers in the United States are people of color. That statistic has spurred some journalists to develop innovative programs to recruit young people into the profession.

When *The Seattle Times* offered Don Williamson a job in 1989, he asked if he could bring along his pet project, a summer journalism workshop designed to recruit minority students into the business. The newspaper said yes, Williamson got a new job and the *Times* got a passel of budding journalists.

About 20 high school students are picked for the two-week program held at the University of Washington. As many as 60 *Times* staffers rotate as guest instructors, teaching subjects from punctuation to newswriting. The students get story assignments and publish a newspaper at the end of the program.

"We try to give kids a sense of what it's like to be in the business," says Williamson. "We try to pack as much into two weeks as we can, so that all the things that a reporter might experience in a year, they get a taste of. The kids work 12, 13, 15 hours a day."

"I think it's the responsibility of newspapers to run these kinds of programs," says Williamson. "The No. 1 reason is that there are not enough people of color in this business. I don't say that to be philanthropic or because it's a nice thing to do, but because of it, we don't do our job very well. If we don't understand our communities, then we fail to do our job as newspapers."

More than 50 similar workshops exist across the country, run by newspapers, universities and journalism organizations. Many workshops receive

In Iowa, it's common for high schools to print their school newspapers on the "school page" of the local newspaper.

"We are a rural state. There are lots of little weekly newspapers with low budgets," says Mary Arnold, executive director of the Iowa High School Press Association. "They get a page of local news essentially for minimal expense, and the kids get their paper in every single house in the coverage area."

The practice started in the 1950s, sparked by Arnold's predecessor, Lester Benz.

Benz went from town to town, convincing newspapers to adopt the "school page" idea. He told the editors, "school news has the highest readership of all categories in the weekly paper . . . your readers want it and are going to demand it." And to this day more than half the schools in Iowa publish their newspapers on the "school page."

grants from the Dow Jones Newspaper Fund, which started funding minority journalism workshops in 1968.

In the summer of 1992, the American Society of Newspaper Editors launched the Rainbow Institute, a national program aimed at giving an academic, financial and moral boost to some of the top teenage journalists in the country. The Rainbow Institute — the first was held at the School of Journalism and Mass Communication at the University of North Carolina at Chapel Hill — is three weeks of newsroom madness, rather like putting the best young journalists together in one pot and setting it to boil. The project was funded by The Freedom Forum, as a part of the foundation's efforts to promote newsroom diversity.

The Rainbow Institute stands out for several important reasons, including its national scope, its emphasis on multiculturalism and its strong tie-in with newspapers. Each student must be nominated by the editor of a community newspaper. More than 100 students were nominated; 15 were accepted. The first participants truly formed a rainbow. Among them: Binh Ly, an Asian American from Ashland, Ore.; Jessica deSouza, an African American from Utica, N.Y.; Sean Lopez, a Latino from Miami, Fla.; and Bethanne Williams, a white student from Pueblo, Colo.

The project was the brainstorm of David Hawpe, editor of *The* (Louisville) *Courier-Journal,* who was the 1991 chair of ASNE's Minorities Committee. Hawpe and Mervin Aubespin, associate editor of the *Courier-Journal* and a past president of the National Association of Black Journalists, helped teach the workshop.

"It's a special partnership between America's editors and academia," says Hawpe. "I know of no other thing where a major news organization like ASNE has put itself to the task of identifying a group of kids whom they want to support and ultimately subjecting them to the best training that they can find for them in academia."

In developing the project, Hawpe was well aware that many newspapers have been criticized for putting a low priority on diversity and being reluctant about spending money on these programs. That's why he sought out the support of The Freedom Forum, which put up the money for the students' airfare, room and board, instruction and even a $1,000 college scholarship. Instead of money, the editors had to commit to scouting their communities for good candidates and to doing some follow-up mentoring with the students after the program.

"I tried to shame my colleagues in the letter," says Hawpe. "I said all this requires is that you find somebody. It won't cost you a penny, so shame on you if you don't. We tried to eliminate every impediment other than the will to do it."

Justino Aguila, a student at California State University, Long Beach, says he was inspired to go into journalism after a classroom visit by George Ramos of the *Los Angeles Times.*

The importance of role models

One can't underestimate the value of role models. Justino Aguila remembers that he decided to go into journalism as a student at Garfield High School in East Los Angeles. What convinced him was a classroom visit by *Los Angeles Times* staffer George Ramos, a former Garfield student.

"Being that he is Latino and that he is a prominent journalist, it was very inspirational to me," says Aguila, 24, who currently is studying journalism at California State University, Long Beach, and working as a news clerk at the *Press-Telegram* in Long Beach. "It was important to find out that he was once a student there, that he decided to go to college and then he got hired by the *L.A. Times.* Maybe, someday, my dream will be fulfilled. Who knows? I might be working there."

Ramos says he frequently visits schools and colleges to exhort young people to go into journalism. As a Latino journalist, he feels these pep talks are especially important for young people of color who don't see many options in their future.

"I do it because I think that we need more people in journalism," he says. "There was no role model for me when I went through junior high and high school to say, 'You too can be a journalist.' I remember my high school counselors said I'd be good as a mechanic. I'm probably one of the few Mexicans who doesn't know anything about cars. But I liked journalism."

Journalism students learn from the pros at two-week Urban Newspaper Workshop

The Urban Newspaper Workshop was founded in 1990 by Don Williamson, *The Seattle Times'* editorial columnist, in photo at right. Each summer minority students from around Seattle gather at the University of Washington for two weeks of intensive journalism and advertising training, at the end of which they produce a 36-page tabloid. The newspaper is distributed to area high schools in September and to other workshops around the country. In 1993, 26 Asian-American, Latino, Native-American and African-American high school juniors and seniors attended the workshop, which is funded by *The Seattle Times,* the University of Washington, School of Communications and the Dow Jones Newspaper Fund.

Top photo: Yoo-Lee Yea edits copy. Right: Gary Settle, *The Seattle Times'* photo coach, works with Bina Hanchinamani on a class assignment. Above: Showing On, left, and Ben Lee take notes during discussion of a food bank story.

Above: Yoo-Lee Yea, left, with Jeanhee Hong go through the camp's daily news check by reading local newspapers to be prepared to discuss play of stories, editorial content, etc.

Right: Jean Sim, left, with Laila Halhuli look over photographic negatives in the photo lab while Boaz Herzog gets an introduction to Adobe Photoshop by Gary Settle (standing).

Left: Teresa Tamura, left, of *The Seattle Times,* edits photos with Jean Sim.

Below: David Gavino works on the editorial cartoon.

Bottom: *The Seattle Times* Director of News Graphics David Miller helps Showing On with a page layout on a Macintosh personal computer.

Rainbow Institute: The value of a multicultural experience

The Freedom Forum Rainbow Institute, founded in 1992, takes place each summer at the University of North Carolina at Chapel Hill. In 1993, 14 high school students from 13 states and Washington, D.C., spent three weeks at Chapel Hill getting a multicultural education in reporting, news writing and editing. Participants are sponsored by a newspaper editor from their hometowns, where they will receive mentoring once they leave the Institute. Students also receive a $1,000 scholarship for college work in journalism.

Above: UNC-Chapel Hill journalism professor and co-director of The Freedom Forum Rainbow Institute Chuck Stone on steps of the journalism building with students from the Rainbow Institute. Evelyn Hsu, center, a *Washington Post* editor and president of the Asian American Journalists Association, was a guest speaker at the workshop.

Right: Student Michael Lee, right, of Kansas City, takes photos of student Javier Martinez, of Lincoln, Neb. during a visit to Raleigh, N.C.

Left: Carl Andrews, left, of Rochester, N.Y., and Eliseo Amezcua of Santa Ana, Calif., walk on campus.

Below: Merv Aubespin works with student Suzanne Lye of Pembroke Pines, Fla. Aubespin is associate editor of *The* (Louisville) *Courier-Journal.*

Top right: Students take a tour of *The News & Observer* offices during a field trip to the nearby state capitol in Raleigh, N.C. Above: Victoria Lopez, left, of Portland, Texas, and Mimi Moon, from Chandler, Ariz., take a lunch break.

Above: Jan Elliott, left, is an associate professor of journalism at UNC-Chapel Hill and co-director of The Freedom Forum Rainbow Institute, which began due to the urging of David Hawpe, right, editor of *The Courier-Journal.*

Loren Ghiglione: It's a personal issue

Loren Ghiglione may be the strongest ally of student journalism in the newspaper business today.

A former president of the American Society of Newspaper Editors, Ghiglione long has been a vocal supporter of youth journalism, but he has done much more than speak out.

In 1969, at age 28, he bought *The News,* a tiny daily newspaper in Southbridge, Mass., and became the editor. *The News,* with a circulation of 6,349, is a model of how local newspapers can support and promote student journalism in their communities.

The News' involvement with Southbridge schools began in 1976 when Ghiglione wrote a series of articles on the state of local high school newspapers. That lead to training sessions on editorial writing, photography and production. He even brought in someone from the Student Press Law Center in Washington to talk about free press issues.

But perhaps the best example of Ghiglione's uncommon commitment came on Dec. 30, 1992, when he wrote a massive report — four full pages in *The News* — on the student newspapers published

at Southbridge High School since the school opened in 1961. The school spawned five different newspapers and won some awards in the process, but none of the papers lasted more than five years. In fact, Southbridge High has not published a school newspaper for almost two-thirds of the school's existence, including the past 11 years. The story of the school publications' various incarnations, name changes and deaths required extensive interviews with former students and faculty from the different eras of the publications' checkered histories.

"The absence of a student newspaper deprives children of a very important part of their education," says Ghiglione. "It deprives schools of their voice ... of the fresh ideas that come out of a student publication. When a student newspaper folds, we're all worse for it."

It was an intensely personal story for Ghiglione, who is alarmed by the indifference with which many students today view their school newspapers. Few editors would have devoted so much energy, or space, to an article about a high school newspaper. But few editors are as passionate about youth journalism.

"There was a feeling on the part of some people that we devoted too much space to the issue," he says. "On the other hand, a lot of space is a way of saying to your readers, 'Damn it, we think this is very important. Look at it! Take the time to read it. What we're telling you is that this issue is as important as anything we're going to talk about this year.'"

Like so many other print journalists, Ghiglione got his start on his high school paper. But unlike so many others, he has retained the same passion for student journalism that he had back in high school at The McBurney School in New York City.

Part hard-boiled newsman, part wide-eyed idealist, Ghiglione remains passionate about all things journalistic — the role of journalists in society, their responsibility as recorders of history, the protection of the First Amendment and, in particular, the importance of a free and active student press.

"If students want to write, they should have every opportunity. It is extremely important that they have an outlet. That's why newspapers are so crucial.

"I worry because I see so many schools where there is no advocate for [the student press], where there is no one on the faculty who cares enough to say, 'We're going to have a student newspaper.'"

Ghiglione has made a standing offer to every school in his community: Any school with an interest in publishing a student newspaper will get help from *The News* — it could be printing the paper free of charge or working with advisers on editing copy and laying out pages. Just ask.

Rick Senften: "The dynamics of mixing kids from so many backgrounds with a common interest in describing their worlds have been exciting."

Making the connection

Rick Senften is assistant city editor of The Repository *in Canton, Ohio. He has been working with high school students since 1990. Here are his thoughts on high school journalism.*

Always, Sippo Woods was more alluring.

The choice presented itself constantly — a day of drudgery in school or a day of happy hooky with Mother Nature. Well, it was no choice: duck into the woods on the way to school or fake sick and head there after a miraculous recovery.

What would I miss, after all? Reading, writing and arithmetic were unrelated abstractions that had little to do with the real world — or at least the real world as I imagined it in the early 1960s on the rural/suburban outskirts of Canton, Ohio.

Came the mid-1960s and other interests lured me from the woods. Not among these, though, was school.

Today, I am amused by the irony: The kid whose pants you had to staple to his desk seat is a grown man determined to show kids school is important and, yes, neat. As they say these days, "Go figure."

Well, here's what I figure.

I figure a lot of kids are a lot like I was, in need of help to see the relevance of school. So happens that in high school a nun named Sister Cathleen Robinson made me see the relevance by way of journalism. It tied all the subjects together, made them mean something outside the schoolhouse walls.

Wherever she is these days, "Thank you, Sister!"

I wish every kid could have a Sister Cathleen. The introduction she gave to journalism helped me understand that the bone-dry topic of economics meant something down at the F&E Dairy, a mom-and-pop grocery threatened by the fledgling super-markets. It helped me understand that the intimi-dating sciences had something to do with the bloat-ed white fish on the banks of my beloved Sippo Lake, as too much lakeweed and pollution choked them to death.

Discoveries were not always happy, but the real-ization that school makes sense was a happy one for me. It's been a happy one for many students in *The Repository's* school partnership, too.

Many students who had but a marginal interest in school have caught fire. They don't attend any class without imagining stories that relate. Their interest in their connection with their communities and the world is much keener. Local and world his-tories and current events mean something.

The business reason to enter a partnership is obvious: to develop future readers. Many partner-ships have that goal at their heart, and it is a good goal. But better results come from goals that are educational in nature. I have two from which all others follow:

• Understanding that after high school or college the media will be the primary educators for the vast majority of students, teach them to be more demanding of the media. Make them understand what fairness, accuracy, completeness and context are. Teach them to demand it from their future media. This makes them better future citizens and will make us better future messengers.

• Make them understand that their school sub-jects relate to the real world. This is best done by introducing good thinking, research, interview and writing techniques. Whether they become journal-ists is irrelevant. They will become more aware of where to get information, how to use it and how to be confident in the outside world.

Many spinoff benefits are obvious. An important one that might not be is the opportunity to get a better cross-section of kids interested in newspapers, and maybe even becoming involved.

Stark County, where *The Repository* resides, is interesting in its composition: three hard-bitten, inner cities surrounded by booming retail and service sectors surrounded by thriving residential neighborhoods surrounded by working farms. The dynamics of mixing kids from so many backgrounds with a common interest in describing their worlds have been exciting. Consciousness and understanding have been raised among the students, their teachers and the folks here, as we've discussed in depth such topics as multicultural education, the effects of extracurriculars and jobs on athletics and teen aspirations. Everyone involved has been enriched by such efforts and will continue to be as long as the goals are pure. And the goals are the kids themselves — to keep them out of the woods.

An experience to remember

In 1988, Cincinnati was trying to integrate its schools, and the school district was putting together plans for a magnet school program to help achieve that goal.

At the same time, Al Schottelkotte, recently retired from the news desk of a Cincinnati television station, became the president and CEO of the Scripps Howard Foundation and was trying to figure out a way to integrate newsrooms. Armed with the knowledge that many journalists worked on their high school publications, Schottelkotte approached the Cincinnati school district with a timely proposal: Why not open a magnet school in mass communications? The High School for the Communication Professions opened in September 1989.

The school is located in the Hughes Center, a large turn-of-the-century building that now serves as the city's "alternative school center" with other profession-oriented schools.

The building was renovated with money from the school system and a $581,000 donation from the Scripps Howard Foundation. The foundation also enlisted the help of the E. W. Scripps School of Journalism at Ohio University to help with the curriculum and design.

The foundation also offered a generous challenge grant. If Cincinnati's media companies contributed $250,000, Scripps Howard would match it.

Despite the successful start, which included building state-of-the-art television production facilities and buying enough computers to allow one for each student reporter in journalism class, the challenge grant was never met.

Even without the grant, in 1993 communications enrollment at the school was 221. And students throughout the city benefit.

Eleventh graders produce *Cincinnati Youth*

Times, a newspaper distributed via English classes to students throughout the Cincinnati public high schools. Circulation is 11,000, but in school year 1992-93, only three editions were published. The year before, only three editions came out, and the first issue was held up a month by controversy over an editorial cartoon — eventually the cartoon and issue were published. Jene Galvin, dean of the high school, says that in 1994 he hopes to publish monthly. "Our dream down the road is to publish weekly," he says.

The school also publishes *The Hughes Inside Edition,* a newspaper printed in-house, that prepares the students to work on the *Cincinnati Youth Times* when they get older. In 1993-94, the school stopped publishing a yearbook, which turned out to be too time-consuming. In 12th grade, the students leave print journalism and switch to broadcast journalism, when they produce a news show called *Cincinnati Youth News* on cable, a talk show called *Cincinnati Youth Expression* and a several editions of a music video show. In 1992-93, they produced 20 talk shows, six news shows, several music videos and other miscellaneous shows.

Galvin has high praise for Schottelkotte and Scripps Howard. "Scripps does not push into what we're doing. They aren't looking over our shoulder or interfering. There are struggles that we deal with that are, basically, in the nature of inner-city schools. But if I call and ask for a consultation — anything from 'How do we deal with this subject in the paper?' to getting opinions on equipment — they're just ready to help in so many ways."

The Scripps Howard Foundation continues its financial support of the High School for the Communication Professions' programs through student scholarships to several regional universities. Each scholarship is for $2,000 annually, which is matched by $2,000 from the university. By 1993, nine students were offered the scholarship.

The Scripps Howard vision that fuels the school shapes a uniquely intense journalism experience. According to Galvin, journalism classes account for about a third of each student's course load. The school offers no electives, and the majority of classes are college preparatory. All students are exposed to the basic aspects of the business: print, broadcast, advertising, public relations, and photography.

The original Scripps Howard proposal for the school was ambitious: the High School for the Communication Professions ought to be "a distinct and frankly special high school," and they've followed through right down to the wallpaper. At Ohio University, where professors also work closely with the high school's faculty and students, the alumni magazine said of the newly opened school, "the facility resembles a corporate headquarters, except for the rows of lockers." Galvin says the effect is very intentional. "Kids need to experience this atmosphere. It's where they're headed, it's where they should want to go."

Poynter's wide-ranging program

The Poynter Institute for Media Studies and the *St. Petersburg Times* boast two substantial programs that help high school newspapers.

Their High School Production Program serves 16 high schools in the area. Students come to Poynter to use the computer facilities to typeset, design and lay out their newspapers, with some supervision from the staff — all experts in the journalism training that is Poynter's stock in trade.

The Poynter Institute for Media Studies also hires professional journalists to serve as consultants to the 16 newspaper staffs. Each consultant visits a high school about twice a month. They are recruited from the *St. Petersburg Times* and other newspapers in the Tampa Bay area.

Associate Director Roy Peter Clark, a major force behind the development of high school programs at Poynter, says "some newspapers are quite strong, others are much weaker. The determining factor, overall, is the quality of the school adviser and the support that person receives from the principal. We offer tremendous resources, but some people don't take advantage of them."

Poynter's High School Writers Camp runs for five weeks every summer. It took shape in its current form in 1980. About 28 students, most from the area, take part each summer. The program is racially integrated, with an emphasis on minority recruitment. "Because of our demographics on this side of the Bay, that's usually African American," says Clark.

Students are paid $100 per week for successful completion of the program. Seven teachers take part in the program, so there is greater opportunity for working in small groups and individual coaching. An issue of the *Third Street Journal,* a student news-magazine, is published each summer.

"We encourage the students to move from the camp back to their student publications," says Clark. The best students from the program, as they move into college journalism programs, are supported by scholarships of up to $5,000 per year from Poynter. A few of the best students get internships at the *St. Petersburg Times.*

Clark says that 20 to 30 students who started in this pipeline are in "really good shape" and are continuing in journalism education or starting journalism careers.

The Poynter Institute for Media Studies has published a "how to" book on starting a summer writing camp, and offers to visit and consult with any organization that wants to copy what they view as a real success.

By the standards of most media outlets, high school newspapers are a cheap form of expression.

At Munster High School in Munster, Ind., Nancy Hastings requires each staffer on *The Crier* to sell two ads per grading period. In the school year 1992-93, advertising brought in $5,800. In addition, staffers sell *The Crier* in their homerooms for 25 cents a copy.

"I can't imagine going to the principal and having to whine that we're out of money," says Hastings. "Any time the school turns around and gives you money you lose control."

Munster High School is lucky. It's in a community with a strong retail base. It has an energetic journalism adviser and a staff that, by and large, meets the ad-selling requirement. As a result, *The Crier* is one of the country's most successful high school newspapers — financially and editorially.

But *The Crier* is the exception. Finding money to keep publishing regularly is a major preoccupation of many newspaper advisers across the country. Budget cuts take a terrible toll on journalism:

• Lack of money limits how often a newspaper can publish, and the number of pages per issue. Student newspapers that publish only once every few months can't really cover the "news" in the school. Students lose interest.

• The schools that most need to give voice to their students, urban schools, may be most likely to cut funds for student newspapers And often there are not the neighborhood retailers and other advertisers to pick up the slack. Many urban school districts are experiencing budget crises that have made courses outside the core curriculum — such as journalism — particularly vulnerable.

• By relying on schools for the bulk of their funding, newspapers may be more susceptible to control or interference by school officials.

• School officials who see student publications as one more headache can use budget cuts as an excuse to ax the newspaper.

A common lament

Despite differences in their schools, journalism teachers and newspaper advisers have a common lament: A shortage of funds leads to lack of equipment and computers, crowded classrooms, and the emotionally draining effects of being close to the bottom on the educational and financial priority lists of their schools. It seems that only the students' and teachers' enthusiasm and determination keep their newspapers alive.

Three school newspapers, all pinched for money, handle the budget squeeze in different ways:

The West Wing, **Mission High School, San Francisco. Budget: $3,657 for eight issues a year.**

Mission High School in San Francisco has 1,450 students. Situated in the city's heavily Latino Mission District, it is just around the corner from the Mission Dolores, one of the nation's oldest churches, built by Spanish missionaries in the 1700s.

After two decades running *The West Wing,* Katharine Swan still has to fight for basic supplies and equipment. Adjoining her classroom is a small room, containing three computers, a laser printer and wobbly chairs into which students squeeze themselves to put out the newspaper.

"It's a joke," she says.

All the equipment was bought with donations

Chapter 5

Black ink, red ink: Dollars and cents of high school newspapers

from student fundraisers. The 1989 senior class, for example, made a handsome profit, about $2,200, from the annual San Francisco Bay Boat Dance for graduating seniors. They bought two computers with the money.

Printing costs are covered by $1,500 from the school and proceeds from advertisements, which students are required to sell. There's no darkroom, so Swan has photos developed at the local Safeway grocery store.

"It's a rock-bottom operation," Swan says. "I do it on nothing."

The Epic, **Lynbrook High School, San Jose, Calif. Budget: $9,000 for 12 issues a year.**

At Lynbrook High School, situated in an affluent suburb of San Jose, it looks, on the surface at least, as if Arnetta Garcin's newspaper program has won the California lottery.

The 42 students working on *The Epic* have access to five computers, a laser printer, two cameras, and a scanner for photographs and art work. The classroom has three light tables, two of which were built by parents.

The Associated Student Body contributed $2,800 in 1992-93 from sales of student body cards, which it sells for $40 each. The cards give students reduced prices for school events.

The Epic raises more money through advertising and fundraisers, such as Valentine's Day candy and flower sales. Garcin also insists that each journalism student sell subscriptions and $125 in ads each semester.

Yet Garcin has to struggle to keep the program going. Some equipment was bought from donations — a parent's gift of $2,000 bought the scanner, other parents gave money for one of the cameras.

When inspectors found that her darkroom did not meet fire codes, there were no funds to do the necessary alterations. So the newspaper had to manage without a darkroom.

"You want to create the best environment for your students," says Garcin. "But it is a real battle to do it all by yourself, even in an affluent school district like ours," says Garcin.

The PawPrint, **Crow High School, Eugene, Oregon. Budget: $600 for 10 to 11 issues a year.**

The *PawPrint* publishes every three weeks on an annual budget of $600. It's a tiny budget compared to most schools, but adviser Sheree Shown is pleased with it. When she started in 1990, her annual budget was $100. The six to 12 students in the journalism program — out of a total school enrollment of 145 students — put out the 12-page *PawPrint* on 11-by-17 paper, folded in half.

From the journalism classroom, she and her students gaze out on a pasture where cattle graze.

Her principal, she says, has been "very supportive and very encouraging" of the journalism program. Each year her budget has increased. In fall 1993, she made the big leap and purchased 10 textbooks for her class.

Almost all of the $600 budget is spent on film developing and halftones. The newspaper can't rely on ads because the yearbook has a lock on all advertising revenues.

How does she do it? The dozen or so students in the program lay out the paper on Aldus PageMaker software on the one computer in her classroom, and print it out on the laser printer they share with the yearbook staff and the computer lab. Then copies are made on a copier that reproduces photos nicely (total copying time: 35 minutes) and distributed in the school.

When extra computers are needed, students can go to the computer lab or the library where there are three computers. Shown often brings in her own computer from home to help with layout.

"We do things in an odd way, but the paper does look fantastic when it comes out," she says.

To raise the $150 needed to send a student editor to a summer workshop, journalism students run the school store for several weeks. Copying costs are charged to the school's general budget. The yearbook staff donates surplus film.

The financial situation is typical of other rural schools in her area, says Shown. "We're pretty much the norm, a production class with limited funding and having to scramble. If we had more of a town, we'd raise more money from advertising," she says. "But we're a one grocery store town. We don't even have a post office."

Who funds the high school press?

By the standards of most media outlets, high school newspapers are a cheap form of expression. Most of the costs, including teachers' salaries, classroom space and overhead, are paid for by the schools.

No layers of highly paid media executives here. A school newspaper adviser plays all the roles found on a professional newspaper. And even though the journalism teacher's salary is the biggest expense on any newspaper, only a portion goes directly to support journalism. Most teach only one or two journalism classes. The rest of the school day is spent teaching other courses, usually English.

Most newspaper advisers also receive a stipend — typically about $1,000 — for their extra work on the paper. But the stipend seldom compensates fairly for the extra hours an adviser puts in to produce a newspaper.

Equipment typically is pieced together from a variety of sources. A computer or two might be purchased with school funds; additional equipment,

How three school newspapers operated in 1992-93

Suburban school

Irmo High School, Columbia, S.C.

A suburban school with a largely white enrollment in an upper- middle-income neighborhood.

- **Enrollment:** 2,155
- **Newspaper:** *The Stinger*
- **Publication:** 9 issues a year, plus an 8-page promotional issue in September and a 4-page student election issue.
- **Pages per issue:** 16 to 20
- **Circulation:** 2,600
- **Adviser:** Karen Flowers
- **Journalism stipend:** $1,518
- **Experience:** Master's degree in English, 22 years teaching experience, 20 years as an adviser. Karen Flowers teaches journalism half-time and English and creative writing, the other half.

The Stinger
■ Income

Student activity fees	$5,442
Advertising	$6,430
Typesetting and design of parents' newsletter	$700
Typesetting commencement program	$350
Total income	**$12,922**

■ Expenses

Printing	$6,712
Social activities, gifts, supplies	$717
Computer costs (purchase of Macintosh, repairs)	$2,795
Library subscriptions	$197
Mailing	$188
Photography	$461
National journalism organizations	$664*

*Includes critiques of paper by outside reviewers and visit by graphics specialist

Total expenses	**$11,734**
Balance	**$1,188**

In-kind contributions
- Use of classroom space, janitorial services
- Telephone
- School computer lab

Equipment
- 7 Macintosh computers (including 3 SEs)
- 1 laser printer

Karen Flowers: "I feel like I am in heaven. But even though I have a wonderful situation in my school, it does not present a realistic picture of journalism in South Carolina. I want to weep when I hear what other teachers have to put up with."

Urban school

Mission High School, San Francisco

An urban school in a low-income neighborhood with a diverse enrollment: 37.8 percent Hispanic; 47 percent Asian; 11.6 percent black; 3 percent white; .6 percent American Indian.

- **Enrollment:** 1,450
- **Newspaper:** *The West Wing*
- **Publication:** 8 issues a year
- **Pages per issue:** 12 pages for one issue; 8 pages for six issues; 4 pages for one issue.
- **Circulation:** 1,500
- **Adviser:** Katharine Swan
- **Journalism stipend:** $1,100
- **Experience:** Master's degree in English literature, 23 years teaching experience, 20 as an adviser. Katharine Swan spends one-fifth of her time teaching journalism.

The West Wing
■ Income

Advertisements	$1,868
Leftover surplus	$289
School funds for printing	$1,500
Total income	**$3,657**

■ Expenses

Printing	$2,352
Film and developing	$331
Journalism conventions (4 students)	$501
Light table (built by students)	$100
Camera bag	$55
Binding back issues	$116
Camera	$50
Tape recorder	$57
Phone connection for computer	$38
Total expenses	**$3,600**
Balance	**$57**

In-kind contributions
- Classroom space
- Telephone
- Use of school computer lab
- Halftone conversions for photos donated by local newspaper (approximate value: $1,200)
- Laser printer donated by student government
- 2 Macintosh computers bought with funds from senior dance
- 1 Macintosh bought with state grant
- Camera bought with district award money given for improved school attendance

Katharine Swan: "It's a rock-bottom operation. My goals are to come out eight times a year and to break even."

Rural school

Crow High School, Eugene, Ore.

A rural school with a largely white enrollment in a middle-income neighborhood.

- **Enrollment:** 145
- **Newspaper:** *The PawPrint*
- **Publication:** 10 to 11 issues a year
- **Pages per issue:** 12 (11-by-17)
- **Circulation:** 145
- **Adviser:** Sheree Shown
- **Journalism stipend:** None
- **Experience:** 11 years teaching experience, three years as journalism adviser. Sheree Shown teaches one journalism class and the freshman and sophomore English classes.

The PawPrint
■ Income

Funds from school	$450
Profits from school store	$150
Total income	**$600**

■ Expenses

Film processing	$200
Halftone conversions for photos	$250
Summer journalism workshops (for students)	$150
Total expenses	**$600**
Balance	**$0**

In-kind contributions
- Classroom space
- Copying costs, paper contributed by school
- Film from yearbook surplus

Equipment
- 1 computer
- 1 laser printer shared with yearbook and computer lab

Sheree Shown: "I've been very lucky. That's not to say we're a great paper, but we're getting there."

such as cameras and software, might come from donations and advertising. Often, an adviser is responsible for raising money to gradually accumulate equipment.

In addition to the costs of equipment, the ongoing annual operating costs of publishing a newspaper — mainly printing, supplies and film — are minimal by conventional newspaper standards.

Selling ads: Pros and cons

Nancy Hastings' students at Munster High School in Munster, Ind., do more than sell ads for *The Crier.*

Each year one student is designated as a business manager, and another as ad manager. Hastings says students need to know how much it costs when they make a decision such as whether to use a second color in printing (which costs an additional $53 per issue). More important, they need to take responsibility for paying for those decisions.

Hastings says that advertising is vital to students' understanding of the newspaper business.

In the 1992-93 school year, senior Sanjay Paul hit his stride by selling five ads, including one to a fast food outlet and another to a pet hospital. He embraces his entrepreneurial role. "It builds communication skills," he says. "And it helps you deal with other adults." At the school, he says, "most of the adults you come into contact with are your teachers."

Andy Kulas, a junior, is less enthusiastic. He finds trying to sell the ads discouraging, and the numerous rejections he received as he tried to make his quota are still painfully fresh in his memory. "I felt I was wasting my time," he says.

Kim Vargo, a senior who was the previous year's ad manager, proudly describes herself as a Super Pub Geek, meaning she hangs out in the publications room. She has little sympathy for her classmates who resist selling ads. "If students don't sell ads, we can't put out the paper," she explains simply. "We have to pay our bills like anybody else."

Like commercial newspapers, many high school newspapers depend on advertising to stay afloat. Just how much and what kind of advertising, though, is often a hotly debated question. Advertising has been the center of some of the more contentious student press rights battles in recent years. At issue:

• By providing some financial autonomy, does advertising give a school newspaper more editorial autonomy?

• Should students learn as much as possible about all that goes into putting out a newspaper, including the business side?

• Is it unfair to require students to sell ads because journalism is about writing, not ad sales?

• Is it unethical, as it would be on the profession-al level, for reporters and editors to sell ads? Would students at newspapers with McDonald's ads cover stories about working conditions in fast food outlets? Would they write stories critical of SAT preparation courses if they sold the ads to the organizations running those classes?

Some newspapers are unable to sell a significant number of ads because of the economic conditions in their communities. And some don't need to sell ads because they get sufficient income from other sources.

And at one time or another student staffs usually face the decision of whether or not to accept ads from organizations such as those offering pregnancy counseling or from gay and lesbian groups.

Advertising ups and downs

At Cape Coral High School in Florida, Marge Craig's students need to raise money each year to put out the monthly *Seahawk's Eye.* Students typically sell about $6,300 in ads to about 100 different advertisers during the school year. Craig insists that students sell ads, although their efforts do not count toward their grades.

"I think advertising is an important element of newspapering because the students understand that they are responsible for creating a professional product and that this is how the professional world runs," she says. "When you see this timid person come in with an ad and the jubilation that comes with it, then it is worth it."

Advertising can be critical for some newspapers:

• In 1992-93, *The Torch,* the school paper of St. Johns High School in St. Johns, Mich., cut its press run by 20 percent, from 2,000 to 1,600 copies, as the result of a drop in advertising. Bob Holzhei, the newspaper's adviser, says *The Torch* and the yearbook were running into competition from school newspapers and yearbook staffs in surrounding communities. *The Torch* relies solely on advertising.

• Pat McCarthy, at Lake Braddock Secondary School in Burke, Va., outside Washington, D.C., advises *The Bear Facts,* a financially savvy high school newspaper.

"We make money in a number of different ways," says McCarthy. "Our number one way is advertising. Advertising pays the freight. If we don't have advertising, we're dead."

The Bear Facts comes out every other week with 3,200 copies mailed to students' homes. A 1984 staff member did a custom design for advertising software for *The Bear Facts,* enabling billing to be handled efficiently. Just like community newspapers, *The Bear Facts* has a rate sheet and an advertising contract.

Letters go out to old advertisers before school starts in the fall. Thanks to the paper's wide reach, advertisers jockey for page position. "Everybody gets

At a glance

Lake Braddock Secondary School
Burke, Va.

Principal: Jack Dorminey.
Number of students: 3,900.
Publication adviser: Pat McCarthy.
Newspaper: *The Bear Facts,* 3,200 circulation, biweekly, 8 1/2-by-14, 16 pages average; $20,000 annual budget.
Revenue sources: $12,000 advertising; $1,500 school; $1,000 PTA; remainder from sales of printing services.
Staff: 100 in three journalism classes.
Computers: IBM.
Software: WordPerfect and Aldus PageMaker operating under Windows.
Offered for credit: English elective.
Other publication activities: Yearbook as an English elective; literary magazine, extracurricular.

a discount," says McCarthy. "I don't think anybody pays full price. If we make a mistake, no charge. We don't want to penny ante them. The advertiser is usually right."

Prom advertising is "the biggest moneymaker for high school journalism," he says. "Florists, dresses, limousine ads, tux ads. The best selling season." Other strong advertising categories include orthodontists and a local fitness center.

Thanks to ad revenues of about $12,000 per year, McCarthy has been able to purchase some impressive equipment. *The Bear Facts* has its own print shop. It not only prints its own newspaper, but it also receives payment for printing other school newspapers and items for other departments in the school system, such as forms or purchase orders.

• Spring Valley High School in Columbia, S.C., is another example of what can be accomplished through strong advertising sales. Spring Valley students work on a budget of $10,000 a year, of which about $1,500 is donations and subscriptions. Most of the rest comes from advertising.

"The money doesn't just magically appear in an account," says Greg Jones, who runs the journalism program. "They have to work to get it."

Jones gets his students into the right frame of mind each year. "You guys are the ones supporting this publication," he tells them. "If you don't sell the ads, they aren't going to get sold."

Selling ads can bring tough lessons for students. Theresa Boscacci, a senior at Spring Valley, ran the ad department for *The Viking Shield* in 1993. She convinced a pizza outlet to print coupons in her paper. Out of 3,500 copies printed, the pizza restaurant got only two back. "No high school students cut out coupons," she says. "It was terrible." Another real-life lesson in the free enterprise system.

Lack of funds limits diversity

Jonathan Kozol, in his book *Savage Inequalities: Children In America's Schools,* documented the vast disparities between today's urban and suburban schools. The same disparities are evident in high school journalism programs.

The differences among journalism programs are not as clear-cut as in some other academic areas, such as science and biology, because journalism in many schools, whether urban or suburban, is not a high priority in the academic life of the school.

As a result, even a wealthy suburban school is unlikely to invest as much in its journalism program as in core curriculum areas.

But interviews and surveys suggest that the flourishing and well-equipped newspapers are found in suburban areas.

Rather than the absence of a newspaper altogether, the major problems in inner-city schools

appear to be erratic publication schedules, a small number of pages, and inadequate facilities and equipment, all of which set them apart from more affluent suburban schools.

It seems that even those suburban programs that get little financial support from the schools can draw on a richer base — parents from upper-income backgrounds who can donate money and equipment, businesses that can contribute equipment or buy ads, or students who can pay special fees to support the newspaper.

Add to that the fact that the basic costs of pub-

Above: Adviser Pat McCarthy, left, and *Bear Facts* staffer Penelope Crocker, sell ads to Dave Christie, manager of Burke Nautilus.

Below: (From left) McCarthy, students Ryan LaPrade, 18, and Jennifer Posner, 17 prepare negatives for printing in the newspaper's print shop.

lishing the newspaper — film and developing fees, printing — are usually highest in the center of large urban areas.

Few urban districts are able to sell activity cards to students to help support the newspapers. Few parents have money to donate to the newspaper or have the contacts in the business community to find equipment. In addition, many urban schools are located in economically depressed areas where businesses are struggling to survive. Advertising in a high school newspaper is a luxury most of these businesses can't afford.

All of these forces — infrequent publication schedules, inadequate equipment and lack of funds — make recruiting students to journalism at these schools much more difficult.

A 1993 survey of a selected number of inner-city schools nationwide confirms that newspapers in these schools indeed lead a tenuous existence.

Mary Arnold, a program associate at the School of Journalism and Mass Communication at the University of Iowa and the executive director of the Iowa High School Press Association, surveyed 149 inner-city schools around the nation. She found 19

of those schools had stopped publishing within the past 10 years. The main reason for closing the newspapers: no funds for production.

Unless schools can overcome these fiscal inequities that translate into a cheapened journalistic experience for many urban youth, the demographic profile of minorities in the media professions will not change significantly. More than that, the voices of young people who are already marginalized will rarely be heard.

Facing, fixing problems in the cities

The state of high school newspapers in Washington, D.C., gives some idea of the difficulties faced by all urban school districts.

On the surface it looks as if high school journalism is doing well in the nation's capital. The city has set up a fund of $18,000 to pay for printing all high school newspapers in Washington. Out of 20 high schools, 18 have journalism programs, and in the 1992-93 school year, 17 of those put out newspapers.

But approximately $1,000 per school only pays for printing three to four times a year, and most of

How to go about the business of getting advertising

Advertising, even in the high school press, is never charity. It may seem so at first glance, but your school has spending power that any advertiser would love to get. This is as much a business proposition as advertising in the local newspaper.

Be prepared to meet your client. Create an easy-to-read flier (a flat piece of paper is quicker to read than a folded one) with basic information about your newspaper — such as circulation and frequency of publication.

Also include information about the spending habits of the students, information you can collect through a school survey.

Be organized. Create a list of clients by going through the Yellow Pages from A to Z. Write down only the names of companies likely to profit from students' patronage. A new-car dealer probably won't benefit from student patronage, but a used-car dealer might. Create a list of prospect cards with room for the dates of appointments, student who made the sale, and the person spoken to.

When you go to make a sale, bring an advertising rate schedule for your newspaper, saying exactly how much each size ad costs and how much an extra — like a photo — will cost. Sketch a couple of ads. Remember every ad should sell a specific thing to a specific person. Don't try to sell everything in stock.

Establish a newspaper budget to figure out how much to charge. After selling the ad and the contract is signed, keep a careful record to make sure the ad appears in each issue that was contracted.

Source: *The Advertising Survival Kit, A Guide to Advertising in High School Newspapers and Yearbooks* by Larry Lain, published by the Quill and Scroll Foundation.

---

the schools don't publish even that often.

Most schools don't have funds to buy a decent camera and film, so advisers often count on students to use their own cameras. Some schools use color Polaroid cameras, donated by a non-profit organization. The donations are appreciated, but Polaroid photos do not reproduce well. Newspapers get almost no money from advertising, and most have only one computer.

Joseph Pope, the adviser at the D.C. Street Academy, a special school for potential dropouts, has to use a friend's computer to print stories that students write in longhand. He created the journalism program for the first time in the 1992-93 school year, and missed out on a journalism bonanza in 1990 when the District, with the help of a volunteer group of journalism professionals, purchased a color computer, layout software, printer and a scanner for each of the schools.

Extra money was made available to D.C. schools to allow them to add issues to their publishing schedules in 1993-94, or to start publishing, thanks to a Freedom Forum grant based on a yearlong analysis by Retha Hill, a journalist in residence.

All urban schools can profit greatly from focused financial assistance. Take The Media Academy at John C. Fremont High School in Oakland, Calif. It is one of a number of special "academy" programs for at-risk students in California that concentrate on specific careers.

Since 1989, The Media Academy has received a total of $50,000 from the state, local government and school board.

Steve O'Donoghue, the driving force behind the program, has built an impressive operation. The publication facilities, in a modest bungalow in the heart of a low-income, largely Hispanic neighborhood of Oakland, has 30 computers, two laser printers, eight cameras, a darkroom and separate rooms for production of the school newspaper, *The Green & Gold,* and the school magazine.

Other notable sponsors of programs for urban schools include the *Detroit Free Press,* which offers a mentor program and special printing and distribution and Cincinnati's Scripps Howard Foundation,

A full-page ad costs:

$190 — **Lake Braddock Secondary School, Burke, Va.**
$320 — **Irmo High School, Columbia, S.C.**
$500 — **Mission High School, San Francisco**

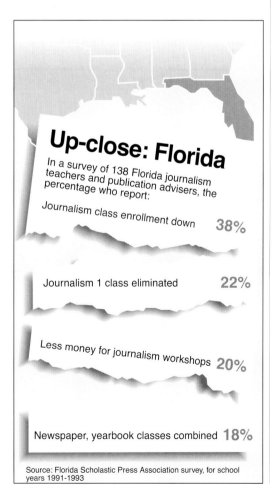

Up-close: Florida

In a survey of 138 Florida journalism teachers and publication advisers, the percentage who report:

Journalism class enrollment down **38%**

Journalism 1 class eliminated **22%**

Less money for journalism workshops **20%**

Newspaper, yearbook classes combined **18%**

Source: Florida Scholastic Press Association survey, for school years 1991-1993

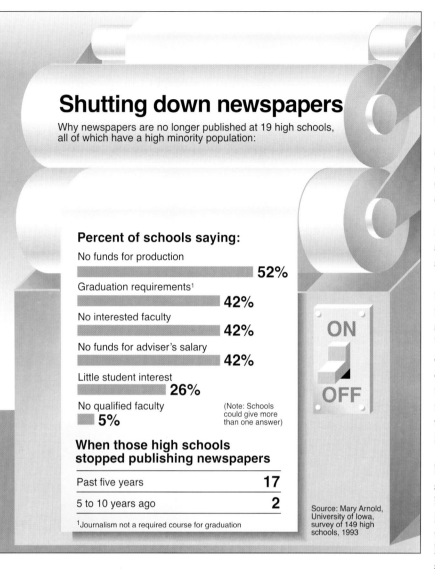

Shutting down newspapers

Why newspapers are no longer published at 19 high schools, all of which have a high minority population:

Percent of schools saying:

No funds for production
52%

Graduation requirements[1]
42%

No interested faculty
42%

No funds for adviser's salary
42%

Little student interest
26%

No qualified faculty
5%

(Note: Schools could give more than one answer)

When those high schools stopped publishing newspapers

Past five years	17
5 to 10 years ago	2

[1]Journalism not a required course for graduation

Source: Mary Arnold, University of Iowa, survey of 149 high schools, 1993

ON

OFF

which funded a magnet high school. Both have made significant changes in the actual newspaper product and in the attention paid to journalism by the school system. These and other newspaper organizations see these efforts as an investment in future talent and diversity for the newspaper business.

Holding the purse strings

The answer to the financial travails of high school newspapers at first seems obvious: Schools need to make newspapers a priority and find the necessary funds to support them.

School newspapers can be a generally inexpensive form of expression.

However, total dependence on a school for funding presents pitfalls as well. That dependency may bring financial stability. But there is also the danger that a student newspaper's editorial independence will be compromised.

John McCartney, adviser to *The Lone Star Dispatch* at James Bowie High School in Austin, Texas, is aware of the dangers. That is why he wants his students to raise money independently. He knows it

will buy them more editorial control.

"He who buys ink by the barrel carries the pistol with the most bullets," he says, only half-jokingly.

The dependence of newspapers on funding from a single source — their own schools — is at the heart of an issue rarely addressed in discussions of the independence of the high school press.

Granting the newspaper free use of space in the school, paying the advisers' salaries, often supplying equipment and sometimes even paying for the costs of printing, can give principals even greater power to control their content.

University of Dayton's Laurence Lain says that newspapers that rely heavily on funding from schools are more likely to be subjected to censorship and editorial control.

"Newspapers which take responsibility for raising the greater part of their operating budgets do seem to enjoy greater latitude in several respects than their administratively subsidized cousins," writes Lain. "Financial self-sufficiency is not the only route to ensuring a free and self-reliant scholastic press, of course, and is not even the most important. But it is time for its importance to be recognized and added to the agendas of those who seek to understand the ways in which the student press can be brought to its full potential."

The fact that the adviser is a school employee can be the source of the most basic, and chilling, editorial control by the administration. An adviser might be reluctant to take on the administration, especially if he or she is a new teacher and does not yet have tenure. And in the close-knit world of the typical high school, even experienced journalism teachers are reluctant to antagonize their supervisors and colleagues.

Both advisers and students who seek free expression through the school newspaper are in a difficult position. Advisers can be reassigned or even lose their jobs. Student journalists publish at the pleasure of teachers and administrators who give them grades, recommendations to colleges, and even permission to stay in school. And the newspaper as an institution risks being starved of financial support. The easy way out is to run a docile newspaper that does not bother the administration, thereby ensuring that it is favorably viewed when it comes time to dole out scarce school funds.

Those who see the school principal as the simple equivalent of the publisher, who logically controls the purse strings, fail to take into account the fact that this publisher also represents the government. The democratic principle of a free press was intended to protect news media from the government.

At the same time, trying to become financially independent also has its drawbacks. When students publish newspapers on their own, often in response to a controversy or crisis at their school, these out-

"Very honestly, I think this paper is going to die"

Mary Wright, journalism teacher and adviser at Oakwood High School in rural Illinois, recounts a tough two years since the Oakwood school board made drastic cuts in all clubs and activities in response to economic hard times.

Until 1992, the school system paid all expenses to publish *The Oakwood Times* on a monthly basis and distribute it to every student and staff member at the high school. No advertising revenues were needed. In fact, expenditures had become more lavish than necessary. "The whole process was absurd," says Wright. "They paid $4,000 to someone to create laser copy, when they refused to buy page design and layout equipment for us."

As of September 1992, all funds to support the newspaper were cut. The newspaper struggled through the year, selling advertising, candy, pizza, flowers at Christmas — and continuing to publish and deliver the newspaper. They even earned enough money to buy a laser printer ($700), inexpensive page layout program ($140), upgrade for their computer ($250) and waxer ($500) so they could save money by designing and laying out the newspaper themselves.

Editors for the 1993-94 school year decided free distribution of the paper was no longer feasible. Subscriptions were sold to students for $5 and mailed to others in the community for $10. About 45 percent of the 350 students subscribed, along with 250 interested individuals in the community. "I think the kids who didn't get the paper wish they did," says Wright.

The future is bleak. While the staff is devoted, and the paper continues to win awards, Wright receives no subsidy for advising the newspaper. "It's considered just an extension of my journalism teaching," she says. "I'm going to retire at the end of this year, and I doubt they'll be able to hire a young person who will be willing to raise $5,000 per year and advise the paper for no money."

The staff went to the school board at the end of the '92-93 school year to ask for the subsidy of $5 per student to help defray the cost of publishing the newspaper. They were turned down.

Wright says that cuts made in 1992 may have been more drastic than necessary: A substantial surplus is expected when the 1993-94 school year ends. There is no talk of reinstating support for the newspaper, however.

"I can name at least three working journalists who came through our program in the last eight years. Three members of last year's staff went to college to major or minor in journalism/communications.

"The obligation of a school is to prepare young people for tomorrow. If I can graduate a student who has some basic skills, and he can go to college and perfect those skills and go out and get a job, then I have more than met my obligation. I feel the journalism program is doing all those things."

of-school papers usually publish a few times and then disappear when the issue that sparked their publication is resolved or forgotten, or when the students graduate.

Where should the balance rest between depending on school-supplied funds and raising money from outside sources? For a school newspaper to survive, it is almost certain that students need to have at least use of a classroom space and a teacher or adviser whose salary is paid for by the school.

The majority of newspapers will have to live uneasily in the cramped space between free expression and administrative control. The best cases will always be those where the administration, advisers, and students cooperate to guarantee adequate financial support along with guarantees of editorial independence.

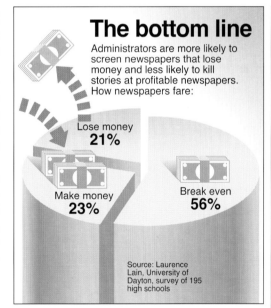

The bottom line

Administrators are more likely to screen newspapers that lose money and less likely to kill stories at profitable newspapers. How newspapers fare:

Lose money
21%

Break even
56%

Make money
23%

Source: Laurence Lain, University of Dayton, survey of 195 high schools

*I*n time the furor over *Captive Voices* calmed down, and journalism educators began to view it as a call for strengthening the high school press.

Chapter 6

"Unless we listen and learn ..." Looking at *Captive Voices* 20 years later

Memory has a way of smoothing out rough spots. When *Captive Voices* is mentioned today, it is with reverence for a seminal work that brought the problems of the high school press to the fore when few were paying attention. This was not the story when it was first published in 1974 by the Robert F. Kennedy Memorial, a Washington, D.C.-based foundation established to continue the pursuit of societal change that marked Kennedy's life.

"High school journalism was given its soundest thrashing ever," wrote John Bowen, now a journalism adviser at Lakewood (Ohio) High School, in *Communication: Journalism Education Today* (since renamed *C:JET*), the magazine of the Journalism Education Association. "This report created a wide and continuing controversy about the status of scholastic journalism, particularly among journalism educators across the country, much of it negative in nature."

Today Bowen recalls the reaction of the late Benjamin Allnutt, then a journalism teacher at Bethesda-Chevy Chase High School in Maryland and a national leader in the Columbia Scholastic Press Advisers Association. "He argued that the commission didn't interview a lot of people with status in scholastic journalism, and therefore they never heard the positive side. He also felt that they found what they wanted to find — and his reaction was typical of a lot of others." Allnutt wrote Bowen: "Nothing I know of in any way substantiates this report — nor has any relationship to it."

For his master's at Kent State University in 1975, Bowen surveyed 43 advisers, 29 principals and 22 student editors, asking them questions relat-

ing to the negative statements made in *Captive Voices* about censorship and journalism education in U.S. high schools. His survey showed that overall *Captive Voices* painted a representative picture of what was happening in the high schools.

Louis Ingelhart, who is the former chairman of the journalism department at Ball State University and an expert on college and high school press rights, commented on *Captive Voices* in a February 1975 article in the *Bulletin* of the National Association of Secondary School Principals: "This was the time of denouement for the so-called radical movements and the romanticized underground press of the college campus and of the secondary school's rather pale imitations. It is not surprising that bright, young persons [the RFK staff members], fresh from the exhilarating scenes of campus liberalism, would assume that high school students would be interested in heavy sociological and political issues and would write perceptively about such matters.

"The high school press, they reasoned, should be filled with articles reflecting these interests and concerns. From the beginning, the one guiding criterion of the inquiry was the assumption that a good high school publication should be a microcosm of depth reporting and socially significant journalism."

There were a few who welcomed the book with open arms. Tom Eveslage was at St. Cloud State University in Minnesota, starting what would become a long career as a college journalism educator/advocate for the high school press. He reviewed the report in the winter 1974 issue of *Journalism Quarterly*, published by the Association for Education in Journalism and Mass Communication. He wrote, " … confirming what have been only suspicions about the state of high school journalism, the commission has made a worthy contribution by clarifying the problems and specifying ways to solve them."

The work and the players

The $65,000 study was carried out over 15 months by a commission of 22 educators, lawyers and civic activists — "the single largest national inquiry into American high school journalism so far conducted," according to the report's introduction, written by the chairman of the commission, Franklin Patterson, who was an English professor at the University of Massachusetts and chairman of the board of trustees of Hampshire College.

John Seigenthaler, then publisher of *The* (Nashville) *Tennessean* and a member of the RFK Memorial board, recalls, "RFK Memorial had bumped into two or three cases of high school journalists being suppressed. The case in South Bend is the one I remember best … that being the young woman who had written the piece on Planned Parenthood that said, 'Babies aren't born under cabbage leaves, and you'd better believe it!' My recollection is that her parents called me and said, 'We've had dozens of letters from all over. This is a national problem.' We worked out a proposal and took it to the board, to hold these hearings across the country."

On March 17, 1973, at the annual Columbia Scholastic Press Association convention, Senator Edward Kennedy announced the plans of the RFK Memorial. "The foundation has launched an independent national commission of inquiry into high school journalism, to be composed of … men and women experienced in the fields of education, journalism and youth affairs. Beginning next week in San Francisco, the commission will hold public hearings and discussions in many different parts of the country designed to produce a comprehensive study of the problems and potential of high school journalism in America."

Kennedy identified three areas of special interest: (1) The serious problem of minority opportunity and access in the field of high school journalism; (2) the scope of free expression in student journalism; the degree, if any, to which school authorities should control the tone and content of high school publications; and (3) an effort to suggest some new directions in the role and function of high school journalism.

"For every school newspaper in which interference with student editors is an issue," Kennedy said, "there are dozens more so dead that controversy would be welcomed as a spark of life, a sign that the publication is alive and well, still relevant to stu-

dents, still raising issues that matter to the school. In this sense, I think there can be a 'new' journalism in high school education, a counterpart to the breakthrough in so many other areas of education in recent years."

The commission decided to focus on four issues: censorship of the high school press, participation of minority students on high school press staffs, secondary school journalism education, and the relationship of professional journalism to high school journalism.

Gathering facts took commission members from coast to coast and included public hearings in Charlotte, N.C., New York, San Antonio, San Francisco, Washington, D.C., and South Bend, Ind. There also were 12 consultative meetings with experts on topics such as electronic media, alternatives to in-school media, and Native-American students. There were four surveys and a content analysis of 293 high school newspapers. A total of 130 students, teachers, administrators and journalists testified at the hearings. More than half of these were students, who often painted a bleak picture of newspapering in America's schools. This is what the commission heard:

• In South Bend, Jann Wesolek, editor in chief of *Liberty Link,* a school newspaper in North Liberty, Ind., testified about the story on Planned Parenthood that had caught John Seigenthaler's attention. She had been told by her adviser, "This isn't going in the paper … it is my paper, and it is not going in." When, after exhausting other avenues, Jann sought a lawyer's advice, the adviser "told me it was like a slap in the face because I was going against her … something about I had agreed to let her censor all articles — which I don't recall — when she selected me to be the editor at the end of last year."

• In San Antonio, Armando Castro, a student at McAllen (Texas) High School, protested the fact that *The Wheel,* the student newspaper, was controlled by Anglos when Chicanos made up about 75 percent of the school's 2,200 student population.

• In Washington, D.C., Ulysses Houston, a journalism adviser, testified "when integration struck" in the 1950s after years of separate school systems in which white students had all the materials, equipment and training, "the whites looked up one day — good God! They took their trophies. They took their equipment. They took their expertise and vanished to the suburbs."

• In New York, Craig Dellemore, editor of the *Black Spectrum,* a teenage newspaper in Harlem funded by *The New York Times,* told the commission about the newspaper in his white-dominated school: "Our newspaper really had nothing to do with us, and just to open it and read it, there was no incentive to work for the paper."

The Commission of Inquiry into High School Journalism

Here are the members of the Commission of Inquiry into High School Journalism *(Captive Voices)*, their jobs and titles in 1974:

Franklin Patterson, commission chairman; Hampshire College board chairman

Msgr. Geno Baroni, president, National Center for Urban Ethnic Affairs, Washington, D.C.

Karen Blank, freshman, University of Kansas

Miguel Berry, teacher, Centro de Servicos Sociales Aztlan

Mae Churchill, director, Urban Policy Research Institute, Beverly Hills, Calif.

Jean Grambs, professor of secondary education, University of Maryland

Sr. Ann Christine Heintz, teacher, St. Mary's Center for Learning, Chicago

Joseph Kuklenski, superintendent of schools, Springfield, Mo.

Charlayne Hunter-Gault, reporter, *The New York Times*

Alan Levine, director, New York Civil Liberties Union

Ida Lewis, editor and publisher of *Encore* magazine

Carl Marburger, former Commissioner of Education, New Jersey

Suzanne Martinez, staff attorney, Youth Law Center, San Francisco

Dorothy McPhillips, teacher and journalism adviser, Maywood, Ill.

Maurine Neuberger, former U.S. Senator, Oregon

Trilla Ramage, freshman, Livingston College, New Jersey

John Seigenthaler, publisher, *The Tennessean,* Nashville, Tenn.

Rev. Douglas Still, former director, Ministries for Educational Justice

Sander Vanocur, former broadcast journalist, WNBC

Tillie Walker, executive director, United Scholarship Services, Inc., Denver

Rufus Washington, freshman, North Carolina Central University

Jules Witcover, reporter, *The Washington Post*

Commission members look back

Dorothy McPhillips, then a journalism teacher and newspaper adviser at Proviso East High School in Maywood, Ill., was pleased to be named to the commission. She had lost her position as adviser at Los Alamitos High School in California because a principal had been disturbed by the paper's coverage of a controversy over class scheduling. She welcomed the unexpected attention to student press rights from the prestigious RFK Memorial.

There were three high school students on the commission as well, and the experience of traveling across the country to hold hearings must have been a heady one. Karen Blank, the former editor of her yearbook and newspaper editorial staff member at Southeast High School in Wichita, Kan., was one of the student commissioners. She is now Karen Lynn Shelor, a lawyer in private practice.

"This was a very remarkable thing for a kid from Wichita. I was probably one of the most fortunate of high school students," she says. "I was in the honors program, which gave lots of flexibility to my schedule." Her journalism teacher, Paula Simons, who was a state director in JEA, paved the way for her selection as a commission member.

She tried to allay any nervousness her parents might have about her traveling alone by assuring them she would be with the adults on the commission. When she told them she would be meeting a nun who was a member of the commission when she changed planes in Chicago, "I didn't tell them what Ann Heintz was like."

In fact, Heintz was a dynamic activist, a nun who didn't wear a habit and seldom was called "Sister." She taught at St. Mary's Center for Learning in Chicago, where she practiced the experiential learning techniques she hoped would revolutionize all of American education. Later Heintz would carry out what she saw as a logical response to *Captive Voices* by starting the first large-circulation, independent, student-run newspaper in the country.

"The meeting that struck me the most was the one at Notre Dame [University in South Bend]," says Shelor. "I was fascinated with the other commission members, especially the lawyers who came as commissioners and, I think, some who came along with students. My eyes were opened a little bit because I came from a pretty white-bread background."

Shelor remembers attending every commission hearing, particularly one in Chicago, where they visited an urban school with Native-American students. "They were very depressing surroundings. The students were not very talkative — not interested in being the focus of all of this. So we mainly talked with all the teachers."

Jack Nelson, then a reporter (now bureau chief) in the Washington bureau of the *Los Angeles Times,* studied 1,725 pages of hearing testimony to write the final report that became *Captive Voices.*

Seigenthaler says, "I recommended Jack Nelson. As I recall, he didn't take much money. It was the work of the Lord, and he knew it."

"I almost didn't take the assignment," Nelson says. "I was right in the middle of covering Watergate, so I hesitated because of my schedule.

"But I'd always had this really strong feeling about the First Amendment and the free press — ever since an experience I had when I was about 14. My father was overseas in World War II, and I was arrested by a Biloxi, Miss., detective who thought I had stolen some jewelry. I was mistreated, threatened, thrown into a cell with a bunch of drunks."

Later, when Nelson got his first newspaper job straight out of high school at *The* (Biloxi) *Daily Herald,* he had a chance to tell the detective, "If I ever see you treat anyone like that again, I'm going to put your name in the paper."

So the searing memory of that experience, plus the fact that in 1963 he had co-authored *The Censors and the Schools* — a book about content and selection of school books — convinced him to take on the job of writing *Captive Voices.*

The findings

Nelson boiled down the hearing transcripts to a hard-hitting, tightly written book. Among its findings were:

• "Censorship and the systematic lack of freedom to engage in open, responsible journalism characterize high school journalism." This censorship was so accepted by administrators, teachers and the students themselves that it had become routine even in the face of laws that prohibited it.

• "The professional news media does not take seriously the First Amendment problems of high school journalists and does little to help protect the free press rights of students."

• "Where a free, vigorous student press does exist, there is a healthy ferment of ideas and opinions with no indication of disruption or negative side effects on the educational experience of the school."

• "Students who are members of racial, cultural and ethnic minorities tend to face special problems in gaining access to high school journalism."

• "Most high school publications analyzed were found to be bland and often served as public relations tools for the schools."

• " … the nation's high schools accord journalism and journalism education low priority … reflected in the elective nature of the courses and assignment of teachers and advisers without special skills in the subject area."

• While "in some school districts electronic media is being effectively utilized to bring minorities into journalism," there was "relatively little exposure of high school-age youth to electronic media instruction or production."

Administrators' reactions

Journalism educators were not the only audience unhappy with the report. Scott Thomson, then associate secretary for research of the National Association of Secondary School Principals, wrote to Dorothy McPhillips, "I simply do not understand the adversary position which you evidently like to identify between principals and those who write and produce the campus newspaper.

"I would not argue that every secondary school principal in the U.S. is tolerant or fair. Some are far too authoritarian … . Most principals, however, are well-educated, reasonable people who are most interested in student projects, [including] the school newspaper. I believe it is highly unjust, as well as the assumption of a false premise, to stereotype the principal as does the commission.

"I would expect that any group, intent on a thorough and fair investigation of secondary school journalism, would include among its membership those persons most intimately involved on a day-to-day basis. … Please understand, I do not question your right to form such a commission. Rather I am questioning the motivations involved. I find it highly probable that the outcome of the commission report was established at the time the commission was appointed, rather than at the time it completed its 'investigation' into the program."

The aftermath

In time the furor over *Captive Voices* calmed down, and journalism educators began to view the report as a legitimate call for strengthening the high school press. John Bowen's carefully written article in the JEA magazine took the report's conclusions, one by one, and tested them against the realities he and others could observe. While noting a few exceptions, he judged most of the findings pretty close to the mark.

"I think it is evident," he wrote, "that *Captive Voices* did make a timely and needed point: that censorship is a problem in high school journalism.

"*Captive Voices* is a beginning, a starting point for reform of scholastic media. Those who say they have never encountered such a problem, therefore it does not exist, are clearly not viewing the total spectrum of high school journalism. Those who say, 'Don't forget the pioneers,' are forgetting that the problem — despite all pioneer efforts — still exists and hampers student growth in the profession of journalism."

Dorothy McPhillips, looking back on her experience as a member of the commission, expresses a similar view: "Overall I was pleased with the book. Why [Jack Nelson] selected certain things and not others, I don't know. But it was good writing, easy to read. I was disappointed that it didn't get more attention. People who could have given it more attention were the professionals, and they didn't."

Captive Voices ended with 47 ambitious recommendations, some of which still apply to high school journalism today. Among the recommendations:

• Established media keep special vigilance to protect First Amendment rights of youth journalists.

• Community-based organizations concerned with minority rights recruit minority youth for in- and out-of-school media.

• Local, state and national scholastic awards programs be revised to include consideration of content as a major criterion in judging youth media.

• Local bar associations form special committees to inquire into the state of First Amendment rights of youth journalists.

Lasting effects

Today, while many of the problems identified in *Captive Voices* still are found in the student press, some of the solutions are in place. Several organizations, for example, were strengthened or started because *Captive Voices* was published. Among them:

1. The Student Press Law Center was founded in 1974 as a direct consequence of *Captive Voices,* within months of its publication. It was a joint project of the Robert F. Kennedy Memorial and the Reporters Committee for Freedom of the Press, a group dedicated to protecting the First Amendment rights of professional journalists. Five years later it became an independent, non-profit corporation, but it still shares an office with the Reporters Committee.

Throughout its 20-year history, the Student Press Law Center has provided high school journalists, advisers and administrators with:

• Free legal opinions and advice over the phone.

• Written opinions.

• *Amicus curiae* briefs on behalf of students in litigation.

• Analysis of cases and legislation.

• Evaluation of existing publications' guidelines and regulations and help in developing new ones.

• Referrals to local lawyers willing to represent students on a *pro bono* basis.

• Publications keeping track of current student press issues.

Each year several law and journalism interns get a baptism in high school press rights issues as they temporarily join the staff to answer phone-in questions and carry out research — unusual exposure for the average lawyer or journalist.

2. The Journalism Education Association of high school journalism teachers, while already in operation at the time of *Captive Voices,* became a higher profile national organization, taking on some of the tasks suggested by the report.

JEA, through *Captive Voices* commission member Dorothy McPhillips, began to form alliances with professional editor and publisher groups. As Seigenthaler remembers it, "The general feeling was that Dorothy McPhillips really used *Captive Voices.* What I think it meant to her was 'People care. They understand right from wrong. The courts are with you, so let's go!' "

• In 1987, JEA published a report on its own extensive study of high school journalism. In part it was a response to the laments of the 1983 *A Nation at Risk* report of the National Commission on Excellence in Education, which said the secondary school curriculum had become "homogenized, diluted, and diffused to the point that they no longer have a central purpose."

• In 1988 JEA, with the support of the Newspaper Association of America and the American Society of Newspaper Editors, sent a resource manual called *Project Outreach* to every state and regional professional press association, listing ways they and their member newspapers could get behind high school newspapers in their areas.

• JEA developed national certification tests for high school journalism teachers, one for Journalism Educators, another for Master Journalism Educators, intended to overcome the reluctance of many state and local school administrators to set their own standards. By November 1993, there were 202 Certified Journalism Educators and 35 Master Journalism Educators — and JEA was looking at ways to analyze the impact of certification on high school journalism.

3. In 1977, Sister Ann Christine Heintz, the member of the *Captive Voices* commission whom Karen Shelor remembers so well, and Craig Trygstad, a former Robert F. Kennedy Memorial fellow involved with *Captive Voices,* began publishing *New Expression* in Chicago. This was the first of what would become a number of independent, big-city "youth-developed media programs in the community," as called for in *Captive Voices.* These newspapers were a new youth medium, destined to have a profound effect on teenage staffers who might never have written or published without them.

Youth Communication: An alternative

A strong conviction that young people have things to say — important questions to ask as well as critical issues to explore — fueled the creation of *New Expression.*

Heintz and Trygstad, although from different generations, both had backgrounds in teaching high school journalism and a visionary respect for teenagers' ability to learn and express themselves, and both were ready to risk their careers to "take a chance that Chicago kids — street kids — would like the idea of running their own citywide newspaper," as Heintz put it — and that there would be some way to raise funds to pay for the enterprise.

What she learned, she said, "is that teenage writers need a refuge from term papers and vocabulary tests. They need a better reason to write than getting an 'A' in English, especially those students who were never fated to compete for A's."

She also learned that "the chance to write for a big community audience is a compelling reason for [young people] to accept the pain of writing well, even for those who come from the city's toughest housing projects." Then, as today, the majority of

teen journalists working on citywide newspapers were from racial and ethnic minority groups — just as *Captive Voices* had prescribed.

Ann Christine Heintz died on Jan. 20, 1989, but her ideas already had taken hold in other urban areas. A string of independent alternative publications, each inspired by the gritty realism of *New Expression* and generally referred to as "Youth Communication" newspapers, exist today in New York, Los Angeles, Washington, D.C., Atlanta, Detroit, Dallas, Hartford and San Francisco. And in Chicago, *New Expression* distributes 70,000 copies monthly during the school year to 80 public and private high schools.

How do they do that?

Each Youth Communication newspaper has been established by a local person with the same determination to give teens a voice. These founders believe alternative newspapers:

• Allow teenage journalists to publish what and when they want, outside the restraints of school issues and administrators.

• Teach journalism through hands-on work and give teenagers a window into the real world of newspapering.

• Give teenagers who want to write, but have no outlet, a chance to do so in cities where high school journalism programs are weak or nonexistent.

• Allow staff members from diverse racial, ethnic and economic groups, who would not normally meet, to work together.

• Give experienced student reporters additional chances to write in less restrictive environments.

• Offer young people a chance for involvement outside of school hours and, especially, during summer vacations.

• Involve professional journalists and mentors, teachers, and role models for staffers.

At the start of an independent newspaper, each founder begins by enlisting other interested adult volunteers. Most form not-for-profit, tax-exempt organizations, rent office space and start recruiting a teenage staff.

Typically, the staff of about 40 meets after school, on weekends and during school vacations. These young journalists become staff writers, photographers, circulation managers and ad sales staff. Students hold most of the key management positions, such as editor in chief and managing editor.

Teenagers almost always work under the close supervision of adult staff. Some newspapers have mentoring relationships with professional reporters and editors. Often advertising executives and local business people volunteer. All of the papers have boards of directors made up of community, business, education and media representatives.

In some cases, teenagers receive school credit for their work and, in a few instances, students in senior positions are paid. At *Teen Track,* a 50,000-circulation Indianapolis newspaper that sprang up outside the Youth Communication network, every teen staffer is paid — from $25 to several hundred dollars per month.

Once the staff is set, each newspaper begins to take on its own personality. Some feature many first-person stories, while others use more traditional journalism.

Citywide coverage

What do teenagers do on these alternative newspapers?

• Consider Maritess Caamic's first photo assignment for *New Expression.* The spirited 18-year-old took a city bus straight from school to cover an abortion rally at Cook County Hospital, where both pro- and anti-abortion groups were expected. Maritess was to shoot photos illustrating a story about the emotional conflict teenagers confront over abortion.

The issue had been simmering in Chicago for days and the rally threatened to turn into a violent confrontation.

Once she reached the rally, the police warned her to be careful. "They said I should stay in between the two groups of demonstrators so that I would not cause any trouble, get hurt or mistakenly arrested."

The scene "was really tense and very strange," but she got her photographs, one of which appeared on the cover of *New Expression,* where it helped dramatize a story with a particular impact on teenagers. It was not the kind of story most high school newspapers would cover.

"My friends are proud of the fact that teenagers are putting out the paper," she says. "I think we do a good job of selecting issues that are relevant to us … . A lot of adults stereotype teenagers as never thinking about 'real' problems. We do."

• *LA Youth* reporter Mitsy Lopez says her paper features writing and issues that she can get nowhere else — from personal stories describing dating violence and offering advice about where teenage victims can turn for help, to special sections about handling money.

"I remember writing about an interracial relationship that I was in. My friends picked it up and as soon as they read it, they talked to me about it. They understood me better and, at the same time, they understood their own interracial dating relationships a little better. I felt like I had accomplished something."

• Andrea Jones, a reporter with *YO!*

in San Francisco, is enthusiastic about everything she has learned at the paper about writing and herself. "We can write anything we want," she says. "In my high school they tried hard to keep us under control. At *YO!* I've really grown and I'm able to figure out who I am." Some of her recent stories have described what it's like being a young feminist of color and explored "why girls fight with other girls."

• In 1987, *NYC* (New Youth Connections) published a special issue about New York teenagers and AIDS. It came at a time when schools across the country were refusing to enroll students known to be infected with the HIV virus.

• *LA Youth* chronicled police abuse of minority teens in the Los Angeles area. The story was picked up by commercial news media (the July 16, 1990, issue of *Time* magazine cited the story in its national examination of police and gangs). Since the incident that prompted the story was not tied to any particular Los Angeles high school and since the story had implications that stretched citywide, *LA Youth* was the only newspaper, youth or otherwise, that felt obliged to go after it.

• In 1983, *New Expression* reporters produced evidence that cocaine was dropping in price and was readily available to Chicago teens: "Cocaine is no

Around the country, independent youth newspapers are a strong presence, including *New Expression* in Chicago, *Young D.C.* in Washington, D.C., *VOX* in Atlanta and *NYC* (New Youth Connections) in New York City.

longer the drug of suburban kids. Now that coke is available at lower prices — as low as ten dollars (dime bag) — the habit is spreading through most Chicago neighborhoods."

The business side

Independence has its price.

While few high school newspapers are awash in dollars, they at least have a guaranteed source of support. The basics — adviser's salary, classroom/workspace and supplies — usually are provided by the schools.

Independent newspapers, however, have to raise all of their funds from outside sources. It is one thing to secure a seed grant from a private foundation, excited about the prospect of a newspaper that will take on tough issues and provide an outlet for expression for disadvantaged teenagers. It is quite another thing to convince the same foundation to provide ongoing support after the first year or two, when the novelty of the project has worn off.

For the people who take on the challenge of raising money to pay the bills and keep these independent newspapers going, the price is often a nerve-racking roller coaster ride.

Susan Herr was named executive director of the Chicago center, where *New Expression* is published, in 1989. Herr is now responsible for raising the financial and in-kind support to keep *New Expression's* doors open.

Her previous job was as a high school teacher in San Antonio. She had no experience as a fundraiser, manager or administrator. She worked at *New Expression* for several months, though, and was bitten by the Youth Communication bug, so she accepted the job as director. In the early days of her tenure, she recalls, "I'd wake up in the middle of the night in a cold sweat just wondering how I was going to make payroll."

An incident during her first year finally put the challenge in context. It was "yet another of the times when it looked like we were going under." She called a meeting of the teenage staffers to tell them the paper was in "serious financial trouble and might not survive."

It was an emotional meeting and she was upset when she left. In the hallway outside her office, Herr was confronted by a teen staffer with the question, " 'Susan, have you ever told us about this situation before?' I said no. She asked, 'Why not?' I said

that I didn't want them to worry about it and, besides, it was my job to raise the money. She looked at me very simply and said, 'But it's not your paper.' "

It was a ringing restatement of the paper's original purpose: to create an independent youth voice by, for and about teenagers. And for Herr, it was "one of the most profound experiences I've ever had here. Everything changed after that. Suddenly, a lot of weight was lifted off my shoulders."

Like everyone charged with raising money for these newspapers, Herr must look to a wide range of local resources to support *New Expression.* Among them: foundation and corporate grants, fund-raising events, individual gifts, in-kind donations, city youth jobs programs and, to a lesser extent than directors often wish, advertising sales.

In a growing number of cities, sponsors are found to help pay for stories or supplements covering particular topics. Health, athletics, teen finances, colleges and multiculturalism are subjects that have been written about courtesy of local corporations and community groups. Buying space almost never influences the editorial copy, however.

While many of the people starting these newspaper hope that local media will be among their strongest funders, that doesn't happen often, at least until they are well-established. One notable exception to this is *Metro Bridge* in Hartford, Conn. *The Hartford Courant* was instrumental in starting this paper, and underwrites printing and circulation throughout Hartford. *Courant* staff members work closely, often one-on-one, with students from across the city. *Courant* advertising sales staff often take teenagers on sales calls.

In California, the *Los Angeles Times* signed on in 1993 to contribute the printing of 100,000 copies of *LA Youth* every other month, and three newspapers in the Bay area print and distribute up to 350,000 copies of *YO!.*

Somehow most of these newspapers manage to stay afloat. With an estimated two readers per copy, they are reaching about 1.5 million young people, their parents and teachers.

Not every enterprise is a success story. Some independent newspapers do not thrive. *The EYE* in Wilmington, Del., for instance, was a vibrant paper that began in the late 1970s just when the city was under a desegregation order. Once the newspaper founders left, however, the paper had difficulty getting a sponsor. It hasn't published since 1992. In Portland, Ore., despite the prestige of a sponsorship by *The Oregonian,* the citywide newspaper *Youth Today's* publication has lapsed since 1993 after its administrative director retired.

Detroit's *Motown Teen* published two issues in the school year 1992-93, then started to fade away due to lack of funds. It was picked up again by the president of its board of directors, who was able to bring in money to get the paper started again.

In school or out of school, depending on the support of a single stalwart leader and dealing with an editorial staff that turns over every two or three years make newspaper longevity an elusive goal.

It is a goal that many adults and teenagers feel is worth reaching for, however. These publications provide much in the way of diversity, freedom of expression and broad coverage that *Captive Voices* found lacking in school newspapers in 1974.

At their best, independent newspapers allow for youth expression in its purest form. In a society where young people are too often the passive recipients of all-encompassing media forms that shape their lives in crucial ways, independent newspapers are rare islands of openness where the young can be themselves and write about themselves — for their peers and for the larger adult community.

The insiders in the journalism education community who felt attacked and misunderstood by *Captive Voices* failed to recognize that even an imperfect report by a commission of outsiders would wake up some people — people who could influence the future of high school journalism. Not the least of these was the RFK Memorial staff and board, who stayed in the fray long enough to establish the Student Press Law Center and help several citywide newspapers get off the ground.

The excitement of *Captive Voices* was based in large part on a 1969 decision by the U.S. Supreme Court, *Tinker vs. Des Moines Independent Community School District,* which gave students strong rights under the First Amendment.

Nineteen years later, a very different Supreme Court would render a very different decision in *Hazelwood School District vs. Kuhlmeier.*

Dorothy McPhillips' sense of purpose

From *Tinker* to *Hazelwood,* from the classroom innovations of the 1960s to the traditions of the 1980s, from *Captive Voices* to *Death By Cheeseburger,* few people have left a larger imprint on high school journalism than Dorothy McPhillips.

Despite her place on the *Captive Voices* commission, despite her four-year presidency of the Journalism Education Association, and despite her unique incursion into the inner workings of commercial newspaper publisher and editor associations, McPhillips, 73, seems curiously surprised at her fame.

She got her start in journalism early. "I was editor of my school paper in junior high and worked on the high school paper and as a stringer for a weekly while in high school."

To hear her tell it, she was always just doing what came naturally — convincing students to write about themselves and protecting their right to publish — when she got into trouble or was cajoled into a student press leadership role. In fact, McPhillips' sense of the larger purpose of teen journalism influenced everything she did and everyone she taught or worked with.

McPhillips, who had taught journalism since 1958, joined the faculty of Los Alamitos High School in California in 1967. The school featured many of the innovations of the day, including "daily demand" flexible scheduling, which allowed students to select classes they wanted to attend.

The Crusader, the school newspaper, reflected that flexibility. Among the available choices in scheduling was the chance for staff members to work on the paper.

But new administrators in spring 1970 forced changes that put in question the future of flexible scheduling.

The uproar from the Los Alamitos students included a threatened walkout and demonstration — "protest activity pretty new at that time," says McPhillips. "We got lots of letters to the editor, and I knew we'd have a problem if we published them." She approached the school superintendent, who favored the innovative scheduling. He said "Print them." The change back to traditional scheduling was stopped, at least temporarily.

McPhillips spent the next year on sabbatical leave, visiting creative journalism programs. When she returned in the fall of 1971, she paid the price for her earlier circumvention of the principal. She was told she could no longer advise the newspaper. She could teach mass media. She could advise the yearbook. But no newspaper. She protested. "It was the only year in my teaching career," she says, "that I did not advise school publications."

When even a grievance procedure failed to get her newspaper adviser's position back, McPhillips moved on to Proviso East High School in Maywood, Ill., near Chicago, where a student body of 3,800, 40 percent black, and a $10,000 budget provided new opportunities. "There was strong involvement of the black students, many of whom were put in the class because counselors didn't know where else to put them. Some got turned on because it was the first time they had been told that they could write."

Attending a JEA convention about that time, she held conversations with two young men, Robert F. Kennedy Memorial fellows, who were looking to see whether there might be a topic worth examining in high school journalism. She soon found herself on the commission that would eventually produce *Captive Voices,* telling her own story of frustration in California and examining the state of the nation's scholastic journalism.

Eventually, McPhillips returned to her home state of Washington to care for sick relatives and

> "It's a continual training program for . . . teachers, administrators, professionals, students. It can't ever be finished. We can never say we've done it. The process goes on."
>
> Dorothy McPhillips

complete her classroom career. She retired early in 1980 after advising the newspaper for seven years at R.A. Long High School in Longview. "There were some things I wanted to do for journalism that I thought I couldn't do if I were still teaching."

"Some things" included being president of JEA from 1983-87, during which she talked several newspaper organizations into funding a study of journalism education that showed that students who served on a school newspaper achieved higher than average scores on college entrance and freshman placement exams. She also began work on what would eventually become JEA's journalism teacher certification process.

During the 1980s, McPhillips became a familiar presence at education committee meetings of the American Society of Newspaper Editors and the American Newspaper Publishers Association (today called the Newspaper Association of America). A cogent five-minute speech here, a pressing suggestion for action there, and she had many editors and publishers taking their first real look at scholastic journalism.

As John Seigenthaler, chairman of The Freedom Forum First Amendment Center and *Captive Voices* commission member, puts it, "When there was very little interest in high school journalism, she forced upon me and other elitists in the American Society of Newspaper Editors a reality that student journalists' rights were being denied."

McPhillips says, "I blundered in. I wasn't always diplomatic. I had no prepared agenda. I responded naturally with what I thought needed to be done. It was a wonderful time — exciting to see things start to happen."

Most recently she led the development of the *Washington State K-12 Journalism Curriculum Guidelines,* a series of comprehensive lesson plans published by the state school system in 1990.

"As I reflect on the current scene," she says, "it's a continual training program for everyone. For journalism teachers and other teachers, for administrators, for professionals as well as students. It can't ever be finished. We can never say we've done it. The process goes on."

Making a dream come true

Craig Trygstad sells himself as a Minnesota country boy, born and reared in Mabel, Minn., population 745. That's been a good ruse for someone who's spent most of the last 20 years in the center cities of Chicago and Washington, D.C., developing a network of sophisticated teen newspapers. Minnesota modesty has gone a long way toward picking up funds and loyal supporters.

Unwavering, "unreasonable" determination hasn't hurt, either.

Trygstad had no idea his life would be devoted to giving teenagers an independent voice when he graduated from the University of Minnesota in 1967. He was headed toward his first year of teaching history at Buffalo Senior High School in Minnesota.

He began to veer off the typical path when he volunteered to start a school newspaper. By the end of the year, *The Bison* was coming out once a month.

In 1969, he took a course that he says "changed my life — it truly did." Sister Ann Christine Heintz (who would later serve on the Robert F. Kennedy Commission of Inquiry into High School Journalism) was teaching a six-week summer course at St. Cloud State University called "Mass Media in the High School Classroom."

"It was actually, 'Teaching as a Subversive Activity,'" says Trygstad. "She introduced me to inductive teaching. She advocated daily newspapers in high school, so kids would learn what it was like to write for a real audience about real issues in schools. When other people were still lecturing, she was talking about experiential learning, learning by doing.

"About 40 teachers were in the class. Twenty of them wanted to leave after the first three days."

Life was different at the high school the next year. The newspaper came out every week. "We started a daily radio program over the PA system that included a lot of newscasting. By the end of the year we had started a monthly news magazine and a rudimentary television program. My idea was to create as many media outlets as possible."

After five years of putting Sister Ann Christine's ideas to work in his classroom, Trygstad was growing restless and longed to test the journalistic potential of teenagers working outside the restrictions of a school environment.

He headed back to the University of Minnesota for a master's degree in journalism and then spent a year as a Robert F. Kennedy Memorial fellow, exploring ways to carry out the recommendations of *Captive Voices.*

In late 1976, Trygstad found himself in Chicago, talking to Sister Ann Christine. St. Mary's Center for Learning, where she had been teaching high school, was closing down. She had an idea, "Let's do a newspaper."

A citywide newspaper! "It seems now such a simple idea," says Trygstad. "Why didn't someone think of it before? But it didn't seem that easy then. People — funders — didn't think it would take off." Two sources came through — The Black United Fund of Chicago and an account executive at the Leo Burnett agency. Total contributions: $3,500.

"That was all we needed to get going," says Trygstad. "In those days that paid for printing the issue and all the supplies and expenses. The initial

organization operated out of Ann's apartment in north Chicago from November through January. In February, we decided we'd make this go or not. We found some office space in the Loop. By now the Chicago Community Trust had offered a $20,000 grant. I'll never forget it. We thought that was it — we'd never heard of such a large amount of money.

"We put out a March 1977 issue of *New Expression.* That proved it could happen."

Trygstad already dreamed bigger dreams. That winter he incorporated the national center of Youth Communication, preparing the way for more newspapers that would spring up in years ahead. "We [a friend, George Pearson] drove down to Springfield in a Chevy Blazer — in an ice storm — we were so determined to save the three weeks that mailing would have taken. We bought each other a mug to commemorate the day."

After 1977, Trygstad worked with other cities. "I traveled. Slept on people's couches, or put them up in Chicago. Told them how Chicago had incorporated, helped them with funding proposals. And just generally tried to help them figure out whether they could do this and really wanted to."

Wilmington, 1978. New York, 1980-81. Philadelphia, tried and failed, 1981-82. Toronto,

1985. Los Angeles, 1986. Others followed. Trygstad moved the "North American" (thanks to Toronto's involvement) office to Washington, D.C., where he continued to talk city newspaper directors through good times and bad, and make contacts to keep them alive. He started the cooperative Youth News Service, pulling news from Youth Communication and high school newspapers together to be published first in a bi-weekly newsletter, now via computer.

Today there is no North American Youth Communication office. The various newspapers have assumed responsibility for maintaining their own informal network and helping others get started. Trygstad continues his work to expand Youth News Service and keeps his hand in *Young D.C.,* one of the newest independent youth newspapers.

Throughout this time he has lived on the personal financial edge, loaning or giving every dime, and sometimes credit card advances, to Youth Communication endeavors.

Why does he keep doing it?

"I learned from Ann something that still drives me: Teenagers are the only people in today's culture that are the true products of that culture. They are the only people who have experienced that and only

Craig Trygstad, with journalists Geeta Valluripalli and Brenna Maloney Sink, managing director of *Young D.C.*

Mark Goodman, executive director of the Student Press Law Center, with Erik Ugland, left, and Christy Mumford, right, at the center where students turn when they need answers to First Amendment questions.

that. They are not burdened by history. The questions that teenagers ask are the purest looks at the problems a society faces. Sometimes those questions are a pleasure, sometimes they're awful." Trygstad, like the teenagers he has devoted his life to, is not ready to stop asking questions.

Mark Goodman, fighting injustice

Mark Goodman recalls what would have been "a great story," one that might have shaken a community, named names and possibly put people in jail.

The story was about prostitution in a small city. But it wasn't written because the writer was afraid that *he* would go to jail.

That writer was Goodman when he was a University of Missouri journalism student in 1981. While reporting for the *Columbia Missourian,* a confidential source told 19-year-old Goodman about the criminal activity. Unsure of what to do with the information, Goodman sought the advice of a faculty member, who said, "Be prepared to be subpoenaed, to turn over your confidential source or to go to jail."

Discouraged, Goodman dropped the story. He never even investigated to see if the story was true.

"Ultimately," he says, "I was intimidated by what the professor told me. I let [the story] languish and my source moved away. We may never know what happened. I very much regret it."

Mark Goodman lost that story. But he found something else: a life work.

After graduating from Missouri, Goodman went to law school at Duke University and took a special interest in First Amendment issues. The story that got away taught him that "no person should let the fear of the law dictate for them what the public has a right to know."

In 1985, Goodman became the executive director of the Student Press Law Center in Washington, D.C. The center was created in 1974 as a direct result of *Captive Voices.* It is the only national organization devoted exclusively to protecting the free press rights of high school and college journalists. It provides free legal advice and information to students and advisers.

About 1,700 calls from colleges, high schools and professionals come into the center each year, Goodman says. "In many cases, they'll call us in extreme frustration, often in times of anger and fear. They are trying to do their jobs as journalists and

Inquiries of the Student Press Law Center

Contacts for legal advice information and comment, Jan. 1 – Dec. 31, 1992

	Censorship	Libel	F.O.I.*	Campus crime	Confidentiality	Copyright	Other	Informational	Comment	Total
Public high school	170	62	12	2	16	33	41	19	8	363
Private high school	5	7	0	0	1	2	2	1	1	19
Public college	203	112	142	110	16	23	96	53	29	784
Private college	61	51	50	34	2	10	52	24	9	293
Professional	22	1	7	6	1	5	7	107	98	254
Total (type of call)	461	233	211	152	36	73	198	204	145	1,713

* Freedom of Information

Source: Student Press Law Center

---

are facing roadblocks."

That's not surprising to First Amendment purist Nat Hentoff, who writes a syndicated column on the subject. Secondary schools, says Hentoff, offer students "little teaching of any worth" about First Amendment freedoms. "Usually students who do understand [a free press] are those who work for student newspapers. And when they get in trouble, they're usually aware of Mark and the center."

"Beyond a doubt," Hentoff says, "Mark's the most important First Amendment figure in the country."

Goodman, who is 34, says that when he was a teenager, he realized that taking a stand on behalf of the rights of others could be a life's work. He also liked writing as a form of expression. It was, he says, a combination of circumstances that brought him to his current position. "Once here, I realized this is where I wanted to be."

Why we must give voice to teens

Sandy Close is executive director of Pacific News Service and founder of YO!, an independent youth newspaper in the San Francisco Bay area. Here is her story.

An hour into my interview with Letitia, a 17-year-old drug dealer from San Francisco's Western Addition, I am ready to call it quits. Either my questions haven't put her at ease or she simply isn't able to articulate her views.

Then: "When did you decide to leave the street life?"

"The night I went up to Omega Boys Club. It was the first time I'd seen black men show love for each other except at a funeral."

Suddenly her words come faster than I can write them down. She speaks of wanting to get away from the city — to go to a black college in the South, to live in a neighborhood where you don't have to

duck every time you hear screeching tires.

At the end of our long conversation, Letitia thanks me. "Until you came I didn't know I had a voice."

We live in a society saturated by media as never before and yet teenagers living in the same city neighborhoods find it easier to kill one another than to talk to one another. That thought haunts me and taunts me, too, as I consider our professional role as communicators, journalists, writers working with so-called "alienated youth."

In part, I believe, we should help those hanging on the edge discover their own voices and bring them into the common experience. To some extent this is already happening — with Oprah, talk radio, rap, video. But we owe it to the kids whose voices we record to preserve the force of their opinions, to keep their voices from becoming merely middle-class entertainment. What kids say to each other is more important than whether their opinions make it into the middle-class media.

The conversations I am thinking of here are not safe: Simi Valley talking to South Central, a street "thug" describing the high of beating someone, a Latina "gangsta girl" screaming at her man not to take his rage out on her, and a Chinese kid methodically plotting his revenge on black tormentors once he becomes an adult. Gang kids eye one another from under black bandannas pulled down to their eyebrows. The point is not getting these kids to like one another. The point is getting them to realize that someone else exists besides themselves.

The other day in a round-table discussion among mostly inner-city youth, a white suburban teen described the most frightening thing that had happened in her life: studying the Holocaust.

"What Holocaust?"

"When the German Nazis killed six million Jews."

"How did you feel?"

Looking back

"Most people got into journalism because they loved to write. I loved to ask questions. And my high school needed someone to do that for a weekly newspaper column. I volunteered. In fact, I was the only volunteer. Other kids saw this as work. I saw it as an opportunity. And it was. I can't imagine any other profession as rewarding as the media."

Nancy Woodhull, a founding editor of USA TODAY, *is president of Nancy Woodhull & Associates. She is a 1963 graduate of Matawan (N.J.) High School, where she wrote a weekly column about her school for the* Perth Amboy Evening News.

"Myself and rage go a long way back"

Editor's note: At the core of the anxiety over the trial of the four police officers accused of beating Rodney King is rage, the rage of young black Americans in particular. Where does this rage come from? And how does one young man, writer Ron Fox of San Francisco's YO! *newspaper, handle it?*

Myself and rage go a long way back. Many times I have felt that the only way I could get my point across was to perpetrate violence. Now I think what difference will violence make? What's the satisfaction of giving in to rage? I'm no longer willing to go to jail for the rest of my life, knowing that while I'm in jail the system remains the same.

My experience with rage started when I got into the system, by which I mean the whole apparatus of criminal justice from cops to juvenile hall. I felt rage cause I felt I didn't deserve to be involved in it at all.

At 13 I couldn't stand cops. Walking down the streets the police would tell me I was nothing but a d-boy (drug dealer), and I would end up like my father in and out of jails. (My father went from juvenile hall to youth authority to county jail to San Quentin by 1990.) I felt even more rage that my pops was doing all this time — even though I knew he had done wrong.

At 14 I was introduced to the wild life of juvenile hall and the anger of being locked up. I had trouble dealing with everybody that was in charge. I saw them as devils cause they treated me like I wasn't worth two cents. They sent me to my room for talking back. I wasn't used to people telling me what to do who weren't related to me. I acted out constantly.

When I was released I had all this rage in me but no way to let it out. Then my older brother got into this big dice game where he had bet his pink slip for his Benz against a so-called buddy's pink slip for a Jeep Cherokee. When my brother won, his friend accused him of cheating, and my brother broke his nose. The guy ran home and got his gun and shot my brother in the back of the head. It took the police forever to come to his rescue. He might still be able to speak clearly if the cops had been on the job.

After that I could have done something terrible to the police for letting my brother suffer. I began this attitude of acting out, like cussing them out and throwing things at them. But each time I acted out things got no better for me. I always dealt with rage by doing things that were only going to hurt me.

Now I've matured to the point where I can look at the larger picture and say, "Every-body isn't honest, everybody ain't fair. It's never been a fair shake with blacks. This ain't anything new. This is the world we live in."

I also learned that it's not just people of European descent who beat up black people. There are black people who do similar things like what was done to Rodney King. After all, it was a black man who killed Malcolm X.

Recently I was coming home from a house party when a black police officer approached me and questioned me about my belongings. He told me that if I didn't leave on the count of 10 he would break a bank window and say I did it. I was mad as hell. I wanted to do something but I didn't know what. But I knew I couldn't give him any reason to do more than what he'd already done.

Just before the Rodney King verdict I overheard a 16-year-old female talk about how we should riot. "Two wrongs don't make a right, but they damn sure make things even," she said. If I ever see her again, I'll tell her by rioting, by fighting, blacks just prove those white people right who say we're ignorant, we're easily provoked, that we can't settle nothing unless we display violence.

Now I can handle rage by writing about it, talking about it. I realize giving in to rage only adds fuel to the fire.

"I had nightmares."

"What kind of nightmares?"

"I dreamt I was walking past my parents' bedroom. I looked inside and it was a concentration camp."

"Why did you make that connection?"

"My parents are Germans and my grandparents — their parents — were Nazis."

"That was deep," a gang kid fresh out of juvenile hall says as he leaves.

A homeless kid, a squatter, defines heaven to a group of young people who live at home: Heaven is sitting around a dining room table with friends.

Isn't it our job as journalists to help these kids plug into each other so they can plug into the rest of us?

Tulani Russell, a k a "the Nob Hill murderer," is 17. On his own since he was nine, Tulani was convicted this spring of the murder of a publisher who was on vacation in San Francisco. In the three months that he's inhabited Block B of San Francisco's juvenile hall awaiting sentencing, Russell has written 42 poems.

"Have you written one about remorse?" I ask.

"My life is remorse, I'm living remorse," he replies.

He hands me a drawing he sketched while we talked. It shows a human mouth, open wide, vomiting images across the page.

The most persistent evidence of hope I have found among the most "irredeemable" young people I have met is this: They have not lost the passion to communicate. If only we as journalists know the right questions to ask.

From the streets to the newsroom

His high school English teacher convinced Ron Fox to trade the streets of San Francisco for the newsroom of *YO!*, an independent teen newspaper published in the San Francisco Bay area by the Pacific News Service (PNS) and the Center for the Integration and Improvement of Journalism at San Francisco State University.

Ron still remembers his teacher's words: "My teacher said I had a 'gift to write.' " Then she introduced him to Sandy Close, executive director of the

Pacific News Service, one of *YO!'s* publishers.

Until then Ron was carving a life for himself on the streets, "doing wild," he says, and getting into trouble. "Growing up, I had a lot of hurt, a lot of pain. It put a lot of hatred in me, especially toward authority figures. I never did respect authority figures whether they were teachers, mothers, fathers or even someone like the counselors inside detention centers."

When the chance to write for *YO!* came along, Ron decided "it wasn't doing me any good to let my anger go into the streets where it was going to get me in more trouble and where my situation would still be the same.

"If there was anything to keep me off the streets and that would help me, that is what I wanted to do. So I just started doing *YO!*"

Writing in a citywide independent newspaper, he says, "gives me peace of mind because it allows me to think things through before I do them. It makes me wiser. It makes me more aware of myself."

"Anything I write about is something I'm going through or something I've been through," Ron says. "And it's from the heart. It's not coerced. Whatever is on my mind, I just write about it."

Where it began ...

Why do teenage — and adult — volunteers spend hundreds of hours producing a newspaper that brings them no pay and little, if any, attention?

Frank Burgos, the first managing editor of the first of these newspapers, remembers how all it worked for him.

Today, a veteran reporter whose career includes reporting stints with the *Dallas Times Herald* and *The Miami Herald,* Burgos is back in Chicago working for the *Sun-Times* covering the city where he grew up.

But he says he will never forget what it was like to be one of the approximately 40 teenagers who created *New Expression.*

There were "all kinds of issues affecting our lives in vital ways that we did not have a chance to talk about," Burgos says. "Most of the teenagers who started our paper felt voiceless and *New Expression* gave us a voice."

It did not take long before "we learned that we could do things through *New Expression* that we couldn't do through our high schools. We learned that the city is a very different beat than a single high school," he says.

Their first issue, published in March 1977, provides a revealing look at the blend of provocative, issue-oriented reporting and hard-hitting editorials that *New Expression* readers would soon come to expect every month. The first issue:

• Offered a tough examination of an Illinois

Institute for Juvenile Research study proclaiming a high incidence of teenage crime.

• Examined the effectiveness of resources for runaways (teen reporters posed as runaways for the story).

• Argued in an editorial that a bill, then before state legislators, to fine teenage smokers represented a hypocritical adult attitude.

This kind of reporting helped Burgos and his colleagues establish a niche for their newspaper in Chicago's media mix. It also brought praise for putting investigation and information in the hands of young people. There had never been a newspaper quite like it anywhere else in the country.

For Burgos, however, there were costs tied to receiving those kinds of accolades and the early success of the paper. He talked to an interviewer about all of that as his year as an editor was ending.

"There were days when the paper was the only thing I thought about from morning until I went to bed. The paper severely interfered with my home life, my social life, my private life. There were days when I would come home late at night and seriously consider the role I was playing, days when I felt the best thing for me to do was quit.

"But I didn't. And the reason I didn't was the special days the [paper] gave me. Days like when [it] was finally done and off the presses and distributed and we could all sit back for awhile and relax and enjoy the feeling that we had done something special, something different and important.

"And, especially, the days when we would get phone calls and letters from teenagers, parents, teachers — either praising us or condemning us, but at least letting us know that we were having an effect on the city.

"And, more privately, the days when the staff, from all parts of the city, would just get together and talk. About everything — what our homes were like, what our different schools were like. All of us came from different parts of the city and if not for [working on the paper together] would probably never have met or learned to respect each other's talents, viewpoints and ways of living."

> "[Young people] have not lost the passion to communicate. If only we as journalists know the right questions to ask.
>
> Sandy Close

YO! puts its own stamp on San Francisco

In the newsroom and on the streets, staff members of *YO!* work to bring a new and different view of San Francisco through their independent youth newspaper.

Above: Sandy Close, founder of *YO!*, in her San Francisco office and, at right, looking over a series of photographs with 21-year-old Jorge Koyama.

Far left: Sandy Close talks on the phone in *YO!* offices while writer/photographer Melinda Busch, left, and editor Nell Bernstein go to work.

Left: Andrea Jones interviews Russell Stanley, a self-described homeless man as he waits for donations on the street near the *YO!* offices. Jones says she has struck up a friendship with Stanley and stops to talk with him often.

Left: *YO!* assistant editor Kevin Weston reads the newspaper as he waits on a San Francisco street.

Above: 20-year-old Andrea Jones working on a *YO!* story in front of a mural depicting the homeless. Above right, while out on assignment, she calls her office on a pay phone.

Left: Jason Horst, 15, Sandy Close and Brian Seales, 17, right, during a weekly news meeting at *YO!*

> ## "I think I've blocked a lot of it out. I didn't realize the significance of the case for years." — Mary Beth Tinker

The Bill of Rights was adopted in 1791. But the First Amendment wouldn't be applied to school newspapers until nearly two centuries later.

It was in 1969 that the U.S. Supreme Court decided the first of two cases that have come to represent the issue of free speech and First Amendment protection for student journalists: *Tinker vs. Des Moines Independent Community School District*. The second case, *Hazelwood School District vs. Kuhlmeier*, was decided in 1988.

The Supreme Court first gave a specific standard for protection of students' First Amendment rights in the *Tinker* case. This grand protector of student press rights didn't involve a student newspaper at all. It dealt instead with high school and junior high school students from Des Moines, Iowa, who wore black armbands to school in protest of the United States' involvement in Vietnam. Still, the Supreme Court's decision in *Tinker* set the legal standard for student free expression rights in newspapers, yearbooks and other publications for the next 19 years.

The *Tinker* tale

Tinker began on a snowy Saturday, Dec. 11, 1965. A large group of students met at the home of Christopher Eckhardt in Des Moines to make plans for a school protest against the Vietnam War. After long discussion, they decided to wear black armbands to school on Thursday, Dec. 16, and to continue wearing them until New Year's Day, 1966.

On Dec. 14, the principals of the Des Moines school system, having learned of the students' plan to wear armbands, adopted a policy that all students wearing armbands to school would be asked to remove them. If they refused, they would be suspended until they were willing to return without the armbands.

Most of the original group of students who had planned to protest backed out when they realized their records and their chances for college entrance and scholarships might be threatened.

On Dec. 16, Christopher Eckhardt, 16, a student at Theodore Roosevelt High, and 13-year-old Mary Beth Tinker, a student at Warren Harding Junior High and family friend, wore their homemade black armbands, complete with peace signs, to school. Mary Beth's 15-year-old brother, John, wore his the following day to North High School.

The three were suspended. They did not return until after New Year's Day, when the planned period for wearing the armbands expired.

More than two decades later, Christopher Eckhardt remembers what happened as if it were yesterday. "I wore the black armband over a camel-colored jacket." There were threats in the hallway. "The captain of the football team attempted to rip it off. I turned myself in to the principal's office, where the vice principal asked if 'I wanted a busted nose.' He said the seniors wouldn't like it. Tears welled up in my eyes because I was afraid of violence.

"He called my mom to get her to ask me to take the armband off." Christopher's parents were peace activists; his mother refused. "Then he called the girls' counselor in. She asked if I wanted to go to college, and said that colleges didn't accept protesters. She said I would probably need to look for a new high school if I didn't take the armband off.

Chapter 7

From *Tinker* to *Hazelwood:* Landmark Supreme Court decisions and how schools deal with them

In February 1993, Mary Beth Tinker, above with her 13-year-old son Lenny, now a pediatric nurse in St. Louis, again was standing up for student free expression rights. She traveled to the state capital of Jefferson City to urge Missouri state lawmakers to pass a bill giving students freedom to control the content of school publications.

Nearly a quarter-century after the decision that made her a teenage celebrity and a pioneer for the cause of student free expression, Tinker says she is now "ready to do whatever I can to give kids a voice. It's interesting that school newspapers are being used a lot now to let kids talk about AIDS, sex education, pregnancy prevention — important topics like that."

"The year before they allowed everyone to wear black armbands to mourn the death of school spirit … but on Dec. 15 the gym coaches said that anyone wearing armbands the next day had better not come to gym class because they'd be considered communist sympathizers.

"My former subversive activities had included being president of the student council in elementary and junior high school, membership in the Boy Scouts, listing on the honor roll, delivering *The Des Moines Register* and shoveling snow for neighbors."

Mary Beth Tinker

Unlike her friend Christopher, Mary Beth Tinker remembers very little about the events of 1965 and the court cases that followed, although she thinks she attended all three court hearings.

"I think I've blocked a lot of it out. I didn't realize the significance of the case for years," she says. "I had just moved to St. Louis when the decision was announced in 1969. I was a high school junior, and I just wanted to fit in, blend in with the crowd. Suddenly, *Newsweek* and *Time* were descending on the school, wanting to take pictures of me.

"Plus we'd gotten a lot of threats [in 1965]. A man who had a radio talk show threatened my father on the air. Red paint was thrown on our house. A woman called on the phone, asked for me by name, and then said, 'I'm going to kill you!'

"I realized how hateful, how irrational people could be. Subconsciously there was a part of me that withdrew. I got a little bit protective of myself and our family."

Winding through the courts

John, Mary Beth and Christopher, the petitioners in the case, filed a lawsuit through their parents in the U.S. District Court of Iowa.

They claimed that by suspending them, their schools had infringed on their First Amendment right to free expression. After an evidentiary hearing, the District Court dismissed the complaint, upholding the constitutionality of the schools' actions, saying that they prevented a disturbance of school discipline.

The case went to the U.S. Court of Appeals for the 8th Circuit, where the judges were split and so the District Court's ruling stood. It finally reached the Supreme Court on Nov. 12, 1968.

On Feb. 24, 1969, the Supreme Court ruled that the Des Moines schools violated the First Amendment rights of the students by suspending them for wearing armbands. But the Court did not say that the schools could never control freedom of expression. It said students are entitled to some First Amendment rights but not necessarily all the First Amendment rights that others would have outside the school context.

The key: "Material and substantial disruption of school activities or invasion of the rights of other students" must be proved if student expression is to be controlled. School officials could censor only when they could show that the expression would disrupt the school environment or invade the rights of other students.

The Supreme Court said this standard had not been met — that by suspending the students for refusing to remove the armbands, the school violated the students' right to free speech. The Court also held that the act of wearing black armbands was "closely akin to 'pure speech'" and, as such, was protected by the First Amendment.

A reflection of the times

Justice Abe Fortas, writing for the majority in *Tinker vs. Des Moines Independent Community School District,* declared, "Neither students nor teachers shed their constitutional rights to freedom of speech or expression at the schoolhouse gate" — thus asserting that students are persons under the Constitution and that states would have to respect their rights in the same way they would citizens in other contexts. This idea became the guiding principle for student free expression rights.

The *Tinker* decision quickly was embraced by free press advocates, but others feared that giving students greater First Amendment rights was setting a dangerous precedent. This concern was particularly relevant in the late 1960s and early 1970s, when student activism and free expression were at their peak.

In 1965, protest in America was coming of age

Why did Mary Beth and John Tinker and Christopher Eckhardt decide to wear black armbands to school in 1965?

It was a sign of the times.

The year 1965 fell in the midst of one of the most tumultuous periods in modern American history. The Cold War with the Soviet Union raged on, and President Lyndon Johnson, having taken office after the assassination of John F. Kennedy two years earlier, was contending with volatile issues both foreign and domestic. Student activism on campus was heading toward its peak. Social protest was becoming a popular form of expression — and law infractions.

A schism between generations was becoming more evident. While their parents held fast to the traditions of the '40s and '50s,

young people chafed under them. Soon free love, drugs and rock and roll would define their culture.

The events of 1965 demonstrated this uncomfortable mixture of the old and new. Winston Churchill died, Malcolm X was assassinated. The Beatles, Elvis Presley and Motown dominated popular music charts, but Frank Sinatra's *September of My Years* took the Grammy Award for Album of the Year. *The Sound of Music* won the Academy Award for Best Picture.

On March 7, 1965, Martin Luther King Jr., disturbed by pathetically low black voter registration in the South, led the now famous Selma, Ala., march. It ended with black people beaten and tear-gassed — all of it televised — and led directly to passage of the Voting

Rights Act that August.

It was also in August of 1965, five months before the Des Moines' students wore their black armbands to school, that the Watts riots broke out in Los Angeles.

And while all this was going on, the U.S. was involved in a military effort in southeast Asia that did not show signs of ending. Antiwar activists, urging a U.S. pullout of Vietnam, staged passionate demonstrations.

In the days to come, the largest and loudest of the anti-war demonstrations often occurred on college campuses. It was here, in the schools, that a generation of students would demand change on issues such as freedom of speech and freedom of the press.

"*Tinker* came out of the Vietnam era, which was a time of great social ferment," says Paul McMasters, executive director of The Freedom Forum First Amendment Center at Vanderbilt University in Nashville, Tenn. "It was all right to question authority and to protest and to state your beliefs loudly and clearly, which is what the students in Des Moines did."

Despite the prevailing climate of free expression in the 1960s, *Tinker* was the first Supreme Court ruling that specifically provided protection for students' First Amendment rights.

"Within a year of the decision we saw dress codes relaxed, hair codes relaxed," says Christopher Eckhardt. "Justice Black was correct in his dissent when he said the decision would usher in a new era of permissiveness."

School press reformers were able to use the *Tinker* decision to bolster high school journalism. Many faculty advisers interpreted *Tinker* as a blueprint for keeping school administrators away from school newspapers. Under the *Tinker* ruling, the advisers believed, students could be prevented from publishing articles in a school newspaper only if the articles were libelous, obscene or "materially and substantially interfered with the requirements of appropriate discipline in the operation of the school."

Newspaper as public forum

In 1969, a U. S. District Court in New York ruled that the principal of New Rochelle High School in New York violated the First Amendment after prohibiting students from accepting a paid advertisement opposing the Vietnam War.

The school contended it could bar the advertisement because of its long-standing policy limiting the content of the paper to "matters pertaining to the high school and its activities." The school also argued that because citizens do not have a right of access to the private press, in a school environment students should not have a right of access to the school paper.

The court rejected those arguments, saying the school paper should be open to free expression of ideas. Even though there were alternate methods of protest, the students must be allowed to use the newspaper as a public forum to express themselves and disseminate ideas.

As the judge in *Zucker vs. Panitz* put it, "It is patently unfair in light of the free speech doctrine to close to the students the forum which they deem effective to present their ideas. It would be both incongruous and dangerous for this court to hold that students who wish to express their views on matters intimately related to them, through traditionally accepted non-disruptive modes of communication, may be precluded from doing so."

The student newspaper as a public forum would become central to the *Hazelwood School District vs. Kuhlmeier* case 19 years later. Indicating that the school newspaper occupied a special place as a means for student expression, the court said, "Clearly a newspaper by its nature is a forum for student expression of ideas and viewpoints. The school cannot realistically argue that this is solely an educational device."

Zucker vs. Panitz was the first in what would be a long line of lower court school newspaper cases

Type of policy schools have for newspaper content

	Northeast	South	Central	West
Open forum for all student expression	3.5%	2.2%	0%	2.2%
Open forum if not libelous, obscene, etc.	63.2%	49.4%	70%	75.3%
Some subject matter not allowed	17.5%	35.2%	21.7%	16.9%
No policy	15.8%	13.2%	8.3%	5.6%

Central

Northeast

West

South

Source: Tom Dickson, Southwest Missouri State University survey of 364 high school newspaper advisers, 1990

between 1969 and 1988. Without exception, when confronted with cases involving censorship of school-sponsored high school newspapers and yearbooks, courts applied the *Tinker* standard. Schools could censor only when they could prove the story at issue would result in a "material and substantial interference with schoolwork or discipline or could result in an invasion of the rights of other students."

"Material and substantial interference with schoolwork or discipline" was typically defined as a physical disruption that directly interfered with the school's primary purpose of educating students. "Invasion of the rights of other students" was usually defined as a legal invasion — libel or invasion of privacy.

Bethel School District vs. Fraser

Bethel School District vs. Fraser, though less than a landmark, was another Supreme Court case that would have an impact on student free expression rights. The central issue in the 1986 case was whether the First Amendment should prevent a school district from disciplining 17-year-old Matthew Fraser, a student at Bethel High School in Washington, who delivered what was considered a lewd election campaign speech at a school assembly.

In front of 600 students, Fraser strung together a list of *double-entendres,* saying the candidate he supported was "... a man who is firm — he's firm in his pants ... in his character ... a man who takes his point and pounds it in ... who will go to the very end — even to the climax, for each and every one of you."

Fraser's candidate won the election. Fraser was suspended for two days.

The Supreme Court said the school did not violate the First Amendment by punishing Fraser for his speech because, unlike that imposed in *Tinker,* the punishment was related to the manner of the speech rather than its content. The Court said the manner of Fraser's speech was disruptive and contrary to the values the school sought to promote. That subtle point, interpreted in a broader sense, would later become a key element of the *Hazelwood* decision.

Bethel sent the first ripple of alarm among student press rights activists, but the *Tinker* interpretation remained the standard for determining students' First Amendment rights on school publications. That would change in 1988, when the Supreme Court decided a case concerning the rights of student editors at a high school newspaper in suburban St. Louis.

Changing the rules

The *Hazelwood* case raised the question of whether the principal of Hazelwood East High School near St. Louis violated the First Amendment rights of his students by deleting two pages of *Spectrum,* the school-sponsored newspaper that was produced in a school journalism course.

The staff of *Spectrum* was supervised by a journalism adviser who submitted each edition to the principal for review prior to publication. In May 1983, a substitute was advising the newspaper because the regular journalism teacher left before the school year ended. After reviewing the May 13 edition of the paper, Principal Robert Reynolds decided that two articles should not be published — one on teenage pregnancy at Hazelwood East and the other on the effects of divorce on students. Reynolds decided to delete the two pages on which they appeared, thus deleting other unobjectionable articles as well.

This is how the story on teen pregnancy in the May 13 issue of the *Spectrum* began:

> *Sixteen-year-old Sue had it all — good looks, good grades, a loving family and a cute boyfriend. She also had a seven pound baby boy. Each year, according to Claire Berman (Readers Digest, May 1983), close to 1.1 million teenagers — more than one out of every 10 teenage girls — become pregnant. In Missouri alone, 8,208 teens under the age of 18 became pregnant in 1980, according to Reproductive Health Services of St. Louis. That number was 7,363 in 1981.*

The article followed with personal accounts of three Hazelwood East students who became pregnant. The names of all three were changed:

Terri: I am five months pregnant and very excited about having my baby. My husband is excited too. We both can't wait until it's born ....

Patti: I didn't think it could happen to me, but I knew I had to start making plans for me and my little one ....

Julie: At first I was shocked. You always think 'It won't happen to me.' I was also scared because I did not know how everyone was going to handle it ....

Principal Reynolds believed the pregnancy article was inappropriate for a school newspaper and its intended audience, and the girls' anonymity was not adequately protected. He also believed that the divorce article, in which a student sharply criticized her father for not spending more time with his family, violated journalistic fairness because the newspaper did not give the girl's father a chance to defend himself. As the journalism class was, in part, designed to teach these notions of fairness, Reynolds asserted that he was acting in the best interests of the school by censoring the material.

Students on the *Spectrum* staff, surprised at finding two pages missing, filed a lawsuit against the school on the grounds that their First Amendment rights had been violated.

Five years later, the final decision came down in *Hazelwood,* the first Supreme Court case to focus specifically on high school student press rights.

On Jan. 13, 1988, the U.S. Supreme Court voted 5-3 to reverse the decision of the U.S. Court of Appeals for the 8th Circuit in St. Louis, which had upheld the rights of the students. The Court ruled that Principal Reynolds had the right to censor articles in the student newspaper that were deemed contrary to the school's educational mission.

Where *Tinker* gave students the power of free expression, *Hazelwood* gave school administrators the power to censor student newspapers.

The Supreme Court began its analysis by citing *Tinker's* basic premise that students "do not shed their constitutional rights to freedom of speech or expression at the schoolhouse gate." But the Court modified this position by citing *Bethel vs. Fraser,* "A school need not tolerate student speech that is inconsistent with its basic educational mission."

The Court said schools could censor any forms of expression deemed "ungrammatical, poorly written, inadequately researched, biased or prejudiced, vulgar or profane, or unsuitable for immature audiences," or any expression that advocates "conduct otherwise inconsistent with the shared values of a civilized social order."

The key: "Educators do not offend the First Amendment by exercising editorial control over the

What kind of newspaper content causes the most conflict

	Northeast	South	Central	West
Potential libel	9.6%	14.3%	11.5%	6.2%
Invasion of privacy	15.4%	26%	21.2%	13.6%
Not fair, balanced	61.5%	54.5%	45.2%	65.4%
Attack on teacher	7.7%	2.6%	13.3%	3.7%
Dirty language	5.8%	2.6%	8.8%	11.1%

Source: Tom Dickson, Southwest Missouri State University 1990 survey of 364 high school newspaper advisers

style and content of student speech in school-sponsored expressive activities so long as their actions are reasonably related to legitimate pedagogical concerns."

The Court found it was "not unreasonable" for Reynolds to have concluded that "frank talk" by students about their sexual histories and the use of birth control, even though their comments were not graphic, was "inappropriate in a school-sponsored publication distributed to 14-year-old freshmen."

Justice Byron White wrote in the Court's majority opinion, "A school must be able to set high standards for the student speech that is disseminated under its auspices — standards that may be higher than those demanded by some newspaper publishers or theatrical producers in the 'real' world — and may refuse to disseminate student speech that does not meet those standards.

"In addition, a school must be able to take into account the emotional maturity of the intended audience in determining whether to disseminate student speech on potentially sensitive topics, which might range from the existence of Santa Claus in an elementary school setting to the particulars of teenage sexual activity in a high school setting."

Justice William Brennan filed the dissenting opinion, which was joined by Justices Thurgood Marshall and Harry Blackmun. In his dissent, Justice Brennan wrote that he found the newspaper at Hazelwood East High School to be a "forum established to give students an opportunity to express their views" and said the Supreme Court should have applied the *Tinker* standard. Justice Brennan characterized the censorship at Hazelwood East as indefensible, saying it "aptly illustrates how readily school officials (and courts) can camouflage view-

Advisers define most important purpose of a high school newspaper

	Northeast	South	Central	West
Promote positive things about the school	3.6%	12%	7.6%	3.4%
Report both the good and bad	23.2%	7.6%	18.6%	12.6%
Publicize school events, activities	7.1%	9.8%	7.6%	5.7%
Means for student expression	48.2%	28.3%	27.1%	32.2%
Students learn skills	17.9%	42.3%	39.1%	46.1%

Central

Northeast

West

South

Source: Tom Dickson, Southwest Missouri State University, 1990 survey of 364 high school newspaper advisers

point discrimination as the 'mere' protection of students from sensitive topics.

"Such unthinking contempt for individual rights is intolerable from any state official," Brennan

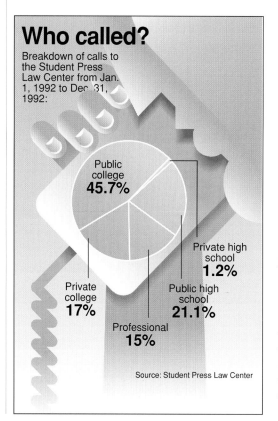

Who called?

Breakdown of calls to the Student Press Law Center from Jan. 1, 1992 to Dec. 31, 1992:

Public college **45.7%**

Private high school **1.2%**

Private college **17%**

Public high school **21.1%**

Professional **15%**

Source: Student Press Law Center

wrote. "It is particularly insidious from one to whom the public entrusts the task of inculcating in its youth an appreciation for the cherished democratic liberties that our Constitution guarantees."

Hazelwood reaction

What has happened in the schools since *Hazelwood*? Not as much as originally feared. First the bad news:

• Many of the 1988 editorials commenting on *Hazelwood* in the professional press almost seemed to mock the students for their arrogance in believing they should be allowed to cover what was important to them. Comparing the principal to a newspaper publisher, they said young people might as well learn early that reporters and editors don't always get their way. Most avoided discussing the principal's unique role as an agent of the government, from which the First Amendment is intended to protect U.S. citizens.

• High school principals who want to control the student press tend to cite *Hazelwood* as a justification for prior review or restricting the subjects students can address in their school publications.

• The Student Press Law Center (SPLC), for years the barometer of student press rights conflicts, has seen the number of requests for assistance from high school journalists rise. In 1992, SPLC received more than 350 calls about high school concerns. That figure does not take into account the censorship cases that go unreported.

The student publications that called SPLC reported censorship of articles, editorials and advertisements that were perceived as controversial or reflecting negatively on the school. Advisers reported threats to their jobs if they refused to follow school officials' orders to censor. And almost all said they attributed the censorship, at least in part, to the *Hazelwood* decision.

• While self-censorship is impossible to measure, there are experts who believe it is more prevalent since the *Hazelwood* decision. Paul McMasters of the First Amendment Center says students — particularly those on newspapers that are cleared by school administrators before publication — try to avoid conflicts and steer clear of potentially sensitive or controversial issues that might not meet with the principal's approval. They fear reprisals from people who can influence the course of their academic careers.

"The student who opposes censorship now is the unique one, not the other way around," McMasters says. "Sometimes the biggest proponents of censorship are fellow students harassing the student journalists. [These students] haven't been taught in their classrooms the benefits and the absolute necessity of a free and open debate and dialogue in our society."

Now for the good news since *Hazelwood*:

The *Tinker* court

Back row, left to right: Abe Fortas, Potter Stewart, Byron R. White, Thurgood Marshall. Front row, left to right: John Marshall Harlan, Hugo L. Black, Earl Warren, William O. Douglas, William J. Brennan

• Research suggests that there was no sudden, sweeping censorship throughout high school newspapers. One year after the ruling, a survey William Click of Winthrop University and Lillian Lodge Kopenhaver of Florida International University showed only 12 percent of advisers had experienced a censorship problem in the previous school year.

• The best evidence may be found in the content of school newspapers. Their pages deal with issues such as crime, drugs, teenage pregnancy, racism, gang violence, homosexuality, AIDS, family dysfunction, child abuse, rape, suicide and school cor-

ruption — not a happy catalog, but certainly not evidence of rigid censorship.

• Five states (California, Massachusetts, Iowa, Colorado and Kansas) have passed student press rights laws, as have a number of local school systems. Similar legislation is stalled in a number of other states, however. Some, Oregon and New Jersey among them, are looking to the wording in their own constitutions to support the rights of student journalists.

• Some individual school newspapers have negotiated with their principals since *Hazelwood* to

The *Hazelwood* court

Back row, left to right: Sandra Day O'Connor, Lewis F. Powell, Jr., John Paul Stevens, Antonin Scalia. Front row, left to right: Thurgood Marshall, William J. Brennan, William H. Rehnquist, Byron R. White, Harry A. Blackmun

101

develop wording that is carried in every issue to the effect that the publication is an "open forum" for students, and that students are fully responsible for its content. While the *Hazelwood* decision muddied the question somewhat about whether the courts would find that such a statement protects student press rights, Mark Goodman of the Student Press Law Center advises that such a policy and practice could "establish a pattern of behavior" in any court case.

• More community newspapers are supporting a free press by offering to print items censored in the student press. In November 1993, for example, a photo of a student smoking off campus was scheduled to run with a front page story about health and school regulation issues related to smoking in *The Bagpipe* at Highland Park High School in Dallas. The student knew the photo was for the school paper and made obvious attempts to move into the range of the camera. His parents threatened suit, and the school superintendent told the newspaper to remove the photo from the front page. He changed his mind when the *Dallas Morning News* said it would run the photo and the censorship story. Paul Watler, a lawyer who counsels the *Dallas Morning News,* assured the school system that he did not believe any newspaper would be subject to legal action for publishing the photograph.

The photo ran as planned in *The Bagpipe.*

• *Hazelwood* may have modified it, but it did not overturn *Tinker.*

But if *Hazelwood* did not negate the solid guidelines that *Tinker* provided for the student press, it certainly blurred them. Tom Eveslage of Temple University explains it this way: "We're in the days now where those of us who like to go by hard and fast rules are frustrated because the *Hazelwood* case has turned all of that to mushiness. It is no longer a case of specific rights to be decided in court. Now everything becomes negotiable."

Or, as Michael Hiestand, attorney for the Student Press Law Center, puts it, "Administrators who are bent on censoring the paper can use *Hazelwood* for that purpose. Those who want to give press rights to students can certainly choose to read *Hazelwood* guidelines that way."

A broader view

The development of policy regarding press rights for students — or for a commercial newspaper — is a process, not a set of static rules. It has changed over the decades through both practice and court decisions. It will keep changing. When advocates on either side of the student press rights debate stand back far enough, they often gain perspective on the issue.

"We are not talking about a conspiracy of high school officials across the land to put a gag on high school students," says McMasters. "Almost without exception, I would dare say, these are good, dedicated and sincere people who have a public trust and are trying to carry it out the best way they can."

School officials approach the free expression issue from the perspective of having to balance responsibilities to the school board, to parents, to teachers, to other administrators and to the community at large. Each school district must find its own balance, so school policies and practices toward student publications vary widely.

Administrators and school board members who want to support student press rights often must face parents and pressure groups that are far less tolerant.

Fay Hartog-Rapp acts as legal counsel to about three dozen school districts in the Chicago area. She says, "It is the responsibility to the entire school community that school officials must consider when they make the difficult decision on censorship."

Hartog-Rapp acknowledges that student journalists can learn valuable lessons from the mistakes they make, but cautions, "One must always question what price [is paid by] those mistakes ... if [they are] to the detriment of other students' personal privacy or their reputation or their view of themselves in the school." She says codes limiting "hate speech" exist for that reason.

"You need to look at it as a lesson not only in civics, but in economics and accountability. The question is, what is our responsibility to the greater community who we serve, and is the educational lesson more important than the harm that might befall the rest of the community."

Eveslage, who debated Hartog-Rapp in a Freedom Forum symposium on high school journalism in May 1992, talked on the subject again in an honors lecture delivered at the August 1993 convention of the Association for Education in Journalism and Mass Communication.

"The *Tinker* Court removed some barriers; the *Hazelwood* Court erected a few," he said. "Both cases altered the school terrain of student journalists, but neither case stopped students from covering the territory. In both rulings, the Court acknowledged the critical-thinking process, and said — in far different language — that the process must be preserved ... .

"After Mary Beth Tinker slipped on her armband that December morning in 1965, she of course went to a much different school [from student journalists today]. But Mary Beth had a lot in common, too, with many of today's student journalists: a sense of concern and caring, a belief that what she had to say was important and worth saying, a feeling that she deserved the chance to tell others what she thought, to make a difference."

Eveslage pointed out that high school journalism textbooks from the *Tinker* era contained almost no

The day was hot; the editorial was hotter

May 10, 1993, was an exceptionally warm spring day in Chicago, 85 degrees.

At Hubbard High School on the city's South Side, the one-day heat wave brought up a long-standing controversy, found the student newspaper editor arrested and landed the school in a free press dispute in the Chicago newspapers and TV news.

On that warm May day several students came to school in shorts and were sent home. The school has a dress code that does not allow shorts.

In 1993, Cynthia Hanifin, a 17-year-old honors student, was editor of the school newspaper, the *Cavalier*. She had been accepted by Medill School of Journalism at Northwestern University and in her final editorial, in the June issue, Cynthia decided to write about that hot May day and the no-shorts rule.

She wrote that other Chicago high schools allow students to wear shorts and that Hubbard students traditionally are allowed to wear shorts during the last week or so of school, a determination made arbitrarily each year by the principal. And she pointed out that the principal's office is air-conditioned and classrooms are not.

Hubbard High School is a racially diverse school of 1,500 with a list of urban school problems — from lack of school funding to gangs, drugs and teen pregnancy. But something in this editorial about wearing shorts to school struck a nerve.

No one disputes the accuracy of Cynthia's facts. What is in dispute is whether she had permission from the newspaper's adviser to publish the column. The adviser, Elayne Sylvester, was in the hospital. Principal Charles Vietzen said Sylvester told Cynthia not to run the column.

"[Ms. Sylvester] was gone for the week before it came out," Cynthia says, "but she did read all the originals and she was there the day it went to the printer and she did approve everything before it went to the printer."

Reaction was swift. Principal Vietzen summoned Cynthia to his office and suspended her for four days, charging her with distributing unauthorized materials and disobeying school personnel. The suspension included the day of the seniors' awards ceremony and Cynthia was slated to receive several school awards.

When she defied the suspension and showed up for the awards ceremony, Vietzen had Cynthia arrested for trespassing on school property. Stories and pictures of the arrest ran in the local dailies and TV news had footage of both the arrest and the principal refusing to be interviewed.

Vietzen, an award-winning principal, cited the *Hazelwood* opinion to back up his decision to suspend Cynthia. "She's trying to make it a free press issue and it's not," he told the Chicago *Sun-Times*. "High school papers don't have that protection. The Supreme Court ruled that. Otherwise you'd have high school kids writing all sorts of things about principals and teachers."

Ironically, the subject of Cynthia's article was moot by the time the newspaper came out. Vietzen had lifted the shorts prohibition three days before the column was published. But the school paper was in production and couldn't be changed.

"The story to me was just trumped-up," Vietzen told the *Chicago Tribune*. "This is a non-issue. It's so silly. Cynthia likes to create issues over nothing. She's a crusader."

Cynthia, who was the editor of the school paper for two years, says the principal had been threatening her with censoring the newspaper since the previous school year when the newspaper ran an editorial criticizing the senior class for tearing down the junior class homecoming decorations.

"I said, 'Listen, this is an editorial,' " Cynthia says. "He kept telling me, 'I have the right to censor the paper. I have the right to do whatever I want to the paper.'

"He just wanted a cute little paper with articles about the basketball team that he could show to the principals of other schools. He didn't want anything controversial in it. He always held it over my head that he could fire me at any time and he could censor the newspaper."

Despite his threats, says Cynthia, Vietzen criticized each issue but never censored anything.

Cynthia's parents sued the principal for $2 million. Because of that suit, neither Vietzen nor Chicago Board of Education representatives would comment for this publication.

references to press rights for students. "Scholastic journalism is far more sophisticated than it was 25 years ago. Substantive student publications have brought the democratic process to life in many high schools. And students today are not just being told, but are discovering for themselves that free speech and a free press are two useful instruments for the struggles of the 21st century."

Gwen Gregory, deputy general counsel for the National School Boards Association, spoke with understanding of both sides' views at a session on student press rights at the fall 1993 convention of the Journalism Education Association.

While she enthusiastically supports the legal reasoning of *Hazelwood*, she said she does not feel that principals should clamp down so hard on student journalists that they're not allowed to write about anything except school events. If agreement can't be reached with the principal, she said "go to the school board to see if you can get more power."

"A lot of schools," Gregory added in a later comment, "don't have the freedom that, as a matter of education, I think they should have. Kids can be helpful in covering a lot of areas — crime, for instance. If they let their feelings be known to the people in power, there might be some changes made."

Perhaps the deepest consideration of the place of freedom of expression in the schools was presented by University of Colorado's Robert Trager and Joseph A. Russomanno in a paper presented at the Association for Education in Journalism and Mass

Hazelwood could have been tougher

The following is reprinted with permission from the fall 1993 Student Press Law Center Report.

While many legal experts and journalism educators were shocked by *Hazelwood* and surprised that the Court would cut back so drastically on the First Amendment rights afforded students, Justice Thurgood Marshall's papers show that the outcome could have been much worse.

The first draft of what would become the majority opinion in *Hazelwood,* written by Justice Byron White and circulated to the Court on Nov. 17, 1987, shows that he would have allowed school officials to censor school-sponsored student expression unless the reason for doing so was "wholly arbitrary."

Under this standard, White indicated that the only time a school official's censorship would violate a student's First Amendment rights was "when school officials g[a]ve no reason whatsoever for refusing to disseminate facially permissible student speech … ."

In a Nov. 20, 1987, letter to White, Justice John Paul Stevens wrote that although he was in "substantial agreement" with White's opinion, he was "troubled by the 'wholly arbitrary' standard … [and found] the use of that term in a First Amendment case … somewhat jarring." He asked that White substitute "something like 'appears to be wholly unrelated to pedagogical concerns' or perhaps, 'appears to have no valid educational purpose' " for the "wholly arbitrary" standard.

Stevens also asked that White change a portion of the draft in which White referred to the newspaper's statement of policy as only an "expression of … students' opinion concerning their First Amendment rights" with which the faculty and administration disagreed. Stevens asked that White alter his opinion to recognize the policy statement's valid role in ensuring "that the administration will not interfere with the students' exercise of those First Amendment rights that attend the publication of a school-sponsored newspaper."

The final version of *Hazelwood* indicates that the decision does not apply to a student publication that has become a "public forum" either by "policy or practice." White's initial characterization of the newspaper's policy as "a mere expression of student opinion" would have made it difficult for any high school student publication to protect itself by establishing its own written publication policy.

"If you make these changes, or ones that will achieve a similar result, you will garner my vote," Stevens wrote.

On Nov. 24, 1987, White circulated a second draft of his opinion that reflected the changes suggested by Stevens. Stevens joined White's opinion later that day.

Stevens' vote appears to have been the crucial one. Justice White's opinion was also joined by Justices William Rehnquist, Sandra Day O'Connor and Antonin Scalia, providing White with the 5-3 majority he needed. Justice William Brennan wrote a dissent joined by Justices Marshall and Harry Blackmun.

Looking back

"My first introduction to journalism was in high school, and I immediately fell in love with it. At our paper we all did everything: advertising, photography, writing, editing. It was a chance to be in a group of people you shared a lot with. That kind of society and shared interest is the thing that keeps a lot of people in this business — because it's certainly not the pay, the hours or the low-stress work environment!"

Sandra Bailey is a senior editor at Sports Illustrated *and a former president of the Associated Press Sports Editors. She is a 1972 graduate of Hillsborough High School in Tampa, Fla., where she was the editor of* The Red & Black.

Communication 1993 convention.

"When free expression is limited in order to instill majoritarian societal values in their schools," the authors wrote, "this turns the First Amendment on its head. Rather … students' expressive rights should be at the core of the societal values that public schools teach — and that schools should allow students to practice.

"The First Amendment is instrumental in providing the foundation for dissent, self-fulfillment, human dignity and liberty — all vital in the realization of both the polity and the individual.

"Every organization, including the school, has a culture, serving to inform its membership about how to interpret and respond to social life … . Schools are societal surrogates for students. The school is one of the few — perhaps the only — institutions with which the pre-adult has contact outside the home.

"By providing structure and standards, the school can bestow a sense of significance to its students, letting them 'know they belong to a functioning and complete society.' Alternatively, a system that distinguishes between what is permitted within the school and outside its door symbolically conveys to students — citizens who are in their politically formative years — that viewpoints can be con-strained based not merely on their content, but also on their location."

A school environment devoid of free expression is not likely to produce an adult ready to support the sentiment attributed to Voltaire: "I disapprove of what you say, but I will defend to the death your right to say it."

W hat needs to be guarded against is censorship on trivial grounds, intended to muzzle legitimate criticism of school officials or stifle expression.

"It can hardly be argued that either students or teachers shed their constitutional rights to freedom of speech or expression at the schoolhouse gate."
— U.S. Supreme Court *Tinker* decision
February 24, 1969

"We hold that educators do not offend the First Amendment by exercising editorial control over the style and content of student speech in school-sponsored expressive activities so long as their actions are reasonably related to legitimate pedagogical concerns."
— U.S. Supreme Court *Hazelwood* decision
January 13, 1988

In civics class students learn about the Bill of Rights. In journalism class they learn that student writers are free to publish well-written and well-researched work — as long as it is not libelous, obscene or disruptive to the school.

But when student journalists try to publish a newspaper relevant to students, they may learn a contradictory lesson — bitter and confusing. For regardless of the protections of the Bill of Rights, student newspapers have little shield against adults who fear controversy and criticism:

• In Manchester, N. H., a principal shut down the student newspaper after an editorial criticized a teacher for refusing to release the vote totals in a student election.

• In Fort Wayne, Ind., a principal censored a report that documented how a tennis coach improperly charged members of the team for court time.

• In Ohio, paramedics were called to the school

when a student, who had been drinking alcohol at a party that morning, passed out from alcohol poisoning. The newspaper was forbidden to write the story.

When student expression is defended, newspapers flourish. Eager young reporters write bold, insightful, sometimes controversial articles that accurately portray life for students and the school. The newspaper gives both news of the school and offers a public forum for ideas.

When student expression is squelched, newspapers fade and become pale imitations of school life. Students may be learning the basics of newspaper production, but they are not learning the principles of journalism.

"Censorship is the fundamental cause of the triviality, innocuousness, and uniformity that characterize the high school press. It has created a high school press that in most places is no more than a house organ for the school administration." These words are from *Captive Voices,* the landmark 1974 report on the state of the high school press.

Two decades later, interviews with teachers, principals and students across the country show that school administrators continue to censor — often on trivial issues such as the "Death By A Cheeseburger" column for which this book is named.

Many school administrators simply do not trust teenagers to publish a newspaper that follows traditional journalistic standards, even when adult advisers are overseeing the newspaper's production. Many school administrators do not want a student newspaper that follows traditional journalistic standards, period.

Chapter 8

You can't print that! Student press rights and responsibilities

105

Ideally, schools should be training grounds for teaching students one of the most distinctive and important dimensions of American democracy: the right to free expression. Instead, students are learning that adults — often the principal — have the right to control, edit and shape what they write in what is often the only official forum for public expression in their schools.

The building blocks of censorship

Censorship can take hold quickly in a school. Any one of these basic elements can lead to possible censorship. More than one assures it:

• Principals insist they have the authority to kill or modify any article in the school paper with which they disagree.

• School administrators believe it is their job to prevent publication of any story that causes embarrassment to them, faculty members or the school.

• Newspaper advisers fear they might upset their colleagues, or be in danger of losing their jobs, if they allow their students too much press freedom.

• Students, advisers and school officials do not understand student journalists' legal rights and even the student journalists rarely challenge censorship.

• Finally, when students have been censored a number of times, they stop writing anything controversial, feeling that whatever they write either won't make it into print or will get them into trouble with school administrators.

Case study: *The Little Green,* **Central High School, Manchester, N.H.**

In the fall of 1990, *The Little Green* found itself without an adviser. Rather than close down the award-winning newspaper, William Burns, the principal, decided to let the student editors have a real journalistic experience and run the newspaper themselves.

"A newspaper is a fragile thing and if you interrupt it, you could make it so disruptive that it might not ever come back," says Burns. "The two student editors urged me to let them run the paper without an official adviser. I would, in essence, be the adviser."

And, by all accounts, the students did an impressive job. The student editors changed the format of the newspaper from a tabloid to a broadsheet and added color pictures. They also arranged for the first issue to come out on the first day of school.

By the third issue, however, they started running into trouble. The editors wanted to cover the results of the freshmen elections. But the teacher who served as the adviser to the freshmen, Salvatore Toscano, would not release the vote totals of those who had run for office. So the students wrote this editorial:

Just A Sham

This year, freshman students entered Central as they have since the closing of the annex. And again, they held elections for leaders to boldly guide this class. And again, the process was flawed to the extent that nothing positive will result from this election.

No freshman running for office was allowed to give a speech to fellow classmates, informing them of goals and plans for the class. Instead, when it came time to vote, the freshmen were expected to make an uninformed decision.

This affords students from Hillside Junior High School an unfair advantage since they form the majority of the class, and therefore frequently win. This year was no exception as all four freshman class officers are from Hillside.

The facts speak for themselves — this election has turned into nothing more than a popularity and poster contest.

In addition, Freshman Class Adviser Salvatore Toscano refused to release the numerical breakdown of votes that were cast.

Is Toscano withholding something from the rest of the school? He claims that he doesn't want to embarrass any of the candidates by releasing the results.

Freedom of information is the backbone of a democracy, and when Toscano fails to release the percentage of votes, he undermines the basic form of government which he is supposed to be upholding.

At a time when democracy is blossoming all over the world, Central High School's freshman class and adviser are taking a giant step backward.

"We wrote the editorial because we wanted to report on the results of the election," says Jeff Brodsky, co-editor in chief of *The Little Green*. "We approached the adviser and asked him if we could have a copy of the results of the election. He would not give them to us. His reason [was] that he didn't want to embarrass any of the candidates. To us that was faulty reasoning. If they didn't want to be embarrassed by the results, they shouldn't have run [for office]. In a democracy when you run, the results are made public."

The principal challenged the accuracy of the article, saying it was his idea, not Toscano's, to withhold the election results. The students say Burns never told them that holding the results was his idea.

"Within a day the principal asked us if we heard the reaction," Jeff recalls. "He said, 'Mr. Toscano is livid. He thinks you slandered him and libeled him and defamed his character.' I said, 'No, not really. We didn't think it was right that he didn't give out

Looking back

"High school journalism was very important to me. I focused on entertainment news, which was as usual for me something completely different. I pushed the limits of our high school press pass by using it to go to things like night club acts and radio interviews. I learned a lot by doing that. When I graduated, I moved home and started the tribal newspaper, *The Sho-Ban News*, in Fort Hall, Idaho, at the age of 17. So I applied my professional skills right away."

Mark Trahant is the executive news editor of The Salt Lake Tribune *in Salt Lake City, Utah. A 1975 graduate of Pasadena (Calif.) High School, he was the features editor of his school paper,* The Chronicle.

As a co-editor in chief of his high school newspaper, Jeff Brodsky ran an editorial criticizing a student body election. The school principal challenged the accuracy of the editorial. The co-editors had to apologize publicly. The incident led to closing down the school newspaper, *The Little Green,* in Manchester, N.H.

the results. It was fair criticism not of him but of his actions.' "

Jeff says the principal called a meeting of the paper's editors and asked them to do something to placate Toscano. "He said that if something isn't done, then you won't be happy with what happens. So we said what does that mean? He said, 'I could shut you down.' He was very serious about the whole thing."

The students decided to draft a letter to Toscano, but Burns demanded they make their apology over the school's PA system. A half-hour before school ended the editors apologized publicly, but Burns said that because many seniors leave school early, they should repeat the apology the following Monday morning.

The editors talked about the incident over the weekend and decided it would be humiliating for the paper to make another apology. Later that day the principal's secretary made a dramatic announcement: *The Little Green* office would be closed at the end of school that day. "Mr. Burns then took the computers, locked them in the school safe, and he locked the door," says Jeff.

The paper published one issue a month later in December, but an adviser who came forward had to step down. In February, another adviser volunteered and the paper started publishing again.

Burns concedes the editorial that led to closing the school paper was rather mild, but he insists there was a lot happening behind the scenes that led to his decision. He calls the editorial "careless reporting" because, although Toscano refused to release the election results, it was under Burns' orders. And he said the editorial stemmed from long-simmering problems between Toscano and Jeff.

"It became a very, very major emotional issue inside the school," Burns says, "especially among the faculty because they knew what was going on."

In retrospect, Burns agrees that the question of releasing student election vote totals is a legitimate subject for a school newspaper editorial. But he says he shut down the newspaper only because the editors broke their promise to publicly apologize for the editorial. He says that it wasn't censorship because he allowed the critical editorial to be published.

"Did we censor that issue? No. I helped [publish] it," he says. "The issue wasn't so much to suppress the issue. The question was whether to continue publishing."

For his part, Toscano believes the principal made the right decision in shutting down the paper: "There's no doubt in my mind that it was a personal attack regardless of what the editors say." In his opinion, "the whole tone of that newspaper for the past two years has been very negative. Kids are kids, and all student organizations need adult supervision. This is a school newspaper. It's not a public paper and they do need advice, guidance and some ground rules."

When told that many adult newspaper advisers who read the editorial saw nothing wrong with it, Toscano says that doesn't matter. "We're talking about a high school newspaper. The Supreme Court has come down in favor of certain types of censorship. High school newspapers are simply not the equal of public publications."

While Burns defends his decision to shut down the school publication until a new adviser could be found, he now says that he agrees with the editorial position the newspaper took. Currently at Central High School, student council election results are provided to the school newspaper if the results are requested.

The Little Green story didn't stay inside the high

school. The Manchester, N.H., newspaper, *The Union Leader,* editorialized against the principal's decision, saying in part: "The purpose of a sanctioned student newspaper is to inform and to enhance learning. What the students have learned from this episode, unfortunately, is that their adult mentors are thin-skinned hypocrites who applaud when the student paper dishes it out to outsiders, but who can't take it when the criticism comes their way."

Burns responds to this broadside by pointing out that if *The Union Leader* Publisher Nackey Loeb doesn't like an editorial by one of the paper's editorial writers or a news story by one of its reporters, she can fire the reporter or shut down the newspaper.

"Who makes those decisions in a regular newspaper?" Burns asks. "The owner does it. If the owner doesn't like it, he can come down and fire them or shut it down. Who is the owner of the school newspaper?"

Ironically, Burns felt he could shut down *The Little Green* even though it is more independent than most school newspapers. The newspaper was not part of any course; it was purely an extracurricular activity. The money for printing it did not come from the school. Even the computers belonged to the newspaper staff. However, the school did provide the space for the newspaper and allowed it to be distributed in the building.

Jeff Brodsky says students on the newspaper staff decided not to challenge *The Little Green's* closing because they didn't have the money or the desire. At that point, says Jeff, most of the students were interested in going to college and feared that challenging school authorities could jeopardize that.

Why principals censor

As in *The Little Green* case, many high school principals argue that they are the publishers of their school newspapers. As publishers, they say, they should have the right to censor news stories in school publications; they are simply exercising the same editorial function as publishers across the country. They point out that schools provide the bulk of the financing of newspapers: salaries of the advisers, equipment, classroom space and, often, printing and distribution costs.

Also, in some cases, newspapers are published in conjunction with a high school journalism class, for which students receive academic credit. Principals argue they have the right and the responsibility to exercise control over school newspapers just as they do over other parts of the school curriculum.

Another argument is that teenage journalists lack the maturity and experience to make decisions that could lead the school and the student journalists into legal difficulties or into controversies that the

young reporters did not intend to provoke.

The view of school officials as publishers with the right to regulate the content of school newspapers has received some support from the mainstream press, which usually is against any kind of censorship. Take the *Chicago Tribune* editorial of Jan. 15, 1988, right after the *Hazelwood* decision. In part it reads:

We now have a decision that says 1st Amendment rights are suspended and censorship allowed when school newspapers are part of the curriculum, are financed by public funds, when the students are below a certain education level and when the court deems that the newspaper is public enough to be considered a "public forum."

What the court should have said is that 1st Amendment rights to expression without censorship do not extend to editor-publisher relationships.

No editors in our history have had a constitutionally guaranteed right to publish something in a newspaper that the publishers did not want in there. Editors who can't agree with publishers have to find a new job or become publishers themselves.

In this case the students and their journalism teacher are, in practice, the editors; the public, through the school board and its agent, the principal, is the publisher.

If the editors don't put out a newspaper with which the publisher agrees, they can express their 1st Amendment rights by producing some newspaper off the publicly owned premises, and for which the school board does not have the ultimate liability.

Why students need breathing room

Advocates of greater freedom for the student press argue that school administrators, while sponsors of the newspapers, are in effect government officials, and intrusive control of student newspapers is exactly the kind of government authority that the First Amendment was designed to blunt.

Student journalists find themselves in the difficult position of covering government officials — the principal, superintendent, school board members — who have the power to be the final editors of stories written about them.

Student advocates say administrators should stay out of content decisions, unless the content is libelous or could disrupt school activities.

And, some argue, once a school gives a faculty adviser the right to oversee publication of a school newspaper, the administration should surrender its role as publisher. As some court decisions have asserted, the state is not the master of everything it creates.

It's easy to tell students that if they don't want to be under the watchful eye of school administrators, they should start their own papers independent of the schools, as suggested by the *Chicago Tribune* in its editorial. In rare instances, students with adult leadership have done just that. But realistically, few students have the resources or the time to run their own papers.

For most students the high school newspaper is the only forum for open expression. For that reason high school newspapers are a special breed of publications. Because of their potentially important role within the culture of a school, and in young people's lives, they can't be directly compared with a professional newspaper whose primary objective is to compete in the commercial marketplace.

Setting policy

Just how much freedom student newspapers should have is a matter of legitimate debate that should be hashed out in every school in the country. A careful debate is needed before there is a fight over censorship between student reporters and their principal. High school journalists and their advisers deserve a carefully crafted school policy that they have drafted with school officials.

Rarely is it the big issues — such as libel — that are questioned in censorship debates.

What needs to be guarded against is censorship on trivial grounds, intended to muzzle legitimate criticism of school officials or stifle young people seeking to express themselves. Unfortunately, many of the examples of editorial intervention cited here fall into this category.

"What we're hearing is that censorship issues are becoming more frequent and more difficult to fight in many places," says Mark Goodman, executive director of the Student Press Law Center in Washington, D.C. Of the legal requests received by the Center from 1990 through 1992, most are about censorship in the nation's public colleges and high schools.

"The people who call us are those usually in extreme situations and in a dire context," says Goodman. "But only those who are knowledgeable enough and courageous enough to fight it usually call. We see only the tip of the iceberg here."

Goodman fears that the amount of censorship will continue to increase, in part because many experienced newspaper advisers are being replaced with teachers who are unfamiliar with freedom of the press and nervous about keeping their teaching positions.

In this atmosphere, Goodman believes that high school principals emboldened by the *Hazelwood* decision will become more involved in school publi-

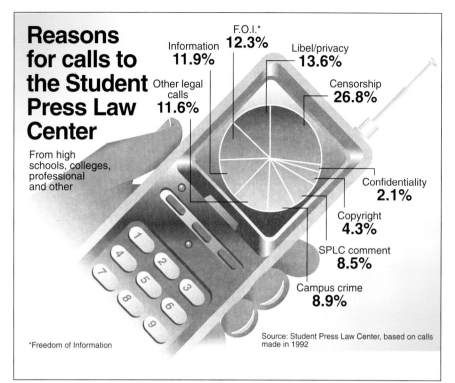

Reasons for calls to the Student Press Law Center

From high schools, colleges, professional and other

F.O.I.* **12.3%**
Information **11.9%**
Other legal calls **11.6%**
Libel/privacy **13.6%**
Censorship **26.8%**
Confidentiality **2.1%**
Copyright **4.3%**
SPLC comment **8.5%**
Campus crime **8.9%**

*Freedom of Information

Source: Student Press Law Center, based on calls made in 1992

cations and exercise censorship more frequently.

Three views of censorship

Some principals, however, believe that the school newspaper is a newspaper and, except in the most controversial or extreme situations, they have a hands-off policy toward the paper. They leave it to the adviser to oversee publication and ensure that nothing libelous, obscene or likely to endanger or disrupt school is published.

Case study: *Trojan Times,* **Johnstown High School, Johnstown, Pa.**

When 15-year-old staffer Becky Smolen became

Mark Goodman runs the Student Press Law Center on an annual budget of $115,000.

pregnant, she began writing a monthly column called "I'm Having My Baby." The column dealt with topics such as how she told her family she was pregnant and how she decided to keep the baby rather than put the baby up for adoption.

Under *Hazelwood*, Frank Garritano, the principal, could have censored the articles, but he didn't. No sanctions were taken against the student, the school newspaper or the adviser. The president of the local school board called the student brave for having shared her experiences. Johnstown High School has been lauded by many student press advocates as a shining example of good journalism where the administration supports a free student press.

In 1990, "the journalism program was in shambles," says Scott McCloud, the newspaper adviser and former professional journalist. "When I agreed to take over I had two stipulations: It would be done my way, and we'll do it first-class."

McCloud said that meant no administrative censorship. "They know it will be responsible, though at times it may be controversial," he says. "But we get it right. We've never had to run a retraction. Our press is probably as free as the local newspaper, and the writing is a lot better."

Principal Garritano disagrees with some of what the school newspaper has written — especially an editorial sharply criticizing him for changing the class schedule. "The principal and I have agreed to disagree," McCloud says. "It helps that the president of the school board has been quoted as saying she is firmly against any high school censorship."

For his part, Garritano supports the U.S. Supreme Court's decision in *Hazelwood*, but he is willing to give McCloud some leeway.

"My standpoint is that as long as Mr. McCloud makes wise decisions about what is printed, he has that autonomy," Garritano explains. "If it gets to the point where I think there needs to be some censorship, I certainly would do that. I don't disagree with the *Hazelwood* decision. I think it is a needed one."

Garritano is concerned that high school publications focus too much on negative things about school, which "I don't think is in the best interests of all of us."

Case study: *The Roaring Lion,* **Central High School, Columbia, Tenn.**

But even at schools with principals who encourage students to write on a wide range of topics, students may still feel administrative control. Students in Dan Bell's journalism class generally put out two newspapers each semester. In recent issues, the students have written on such topics as date rape, a new dress code, fraternity and sorority garb, student parking policy, and new attendance rules.

Thomas Harrison, principal of Central High School, says the students are free to write about whatever topic they choose. He never monitors the newspaper. He says he has never censored an article. "I don't think that's wise," he says. "I think the students take the paper more seriously if they don't view it as some mouthpiece or some public relations effort of the administration. Even students know when they are being manipulated."

Harrison says that, in return for his trust, he expects the students not to write anything irresponsible. "I think if I ever saw or thought there was some irresponsible reporting or libelous kinds of things that occurred, I would deal with it," he says. "But there's no indication of that, so why make a demon out of something that is not a demon?"

Despite his proclamation that the school paper is free of censorship, some students at Central High School still feel hamstrung by explicit and not so explicit restrictions.

In interviews with staff members, most say they feel subtle censorship pressure. Adviser Bell believes the student paper is freer than it has ever been, but concedes he discourages the students from writing some articles he thinks would not please the principal.

In 1992, for example, a teacher's car was stolen by a junior high student. The newspaper dutifully reported the teacher's name and what happened but was encouraged to leave out one relevant detail — the teacher had left her keys in the car.

"I thought it was a very important fact," says Jennifer Wood, a senior. "I wrote the story, but Mr.

Student newspaper staffer Amy Franklin, left, and Executive Principal Jim Neely of Stratford High School, Nashville, Tenn. Neely says that he's never been troubled by anything that appears in the paper.

Bell edited it. I felt a little bit stifled. I think it was Mr. Bell's decision to leave that part out. He didn't want to embarrass her. He's a fellow teacher, and he didn't want to get blamed if she complained, and I think she would have complained."

Bell, a former radio reporter, acknowledges he omitted that fact. He says that while the administration is supportive of his role and that he never has to have a story approved in advance, "there are certain subjects and certain things that I automatically know will not go — like personal gripes about the administration."

Case study: *Spartan Herald,* Stratford High School, Nashville, Tenn.

The *Spartan Herald* was sued in 1988 by a student and her parents who claimed that the student was defamed by a Valentine's Day advertisement in the paper. As a prank, two students quoted song lyrics in the ad implying the girl was a lesbian.

"It was thrown out of court," says Jim Neely, Stratford's executive principal. "We were able to prove that the ad was taken out by other students and who those students were. The judge decided we had done everything in our power and we were not negligent."

Neely says the lawsuit did not bother him, and he has never been troubled by anything that appears in the paper.

"My philosophy on journalism at Stratford High School is that a youngster should be able to learn how to write in the form and style of a basic newspaper reporter, should learn something about layout and should get a general idea how a newspaper is produced," he says. "I simply tell the sponsor, the teacher, that I expect them to make sure to watch out for anything that can be misconstrued in a personal nature as it pertains to other students and to make sure that all students' rights are protected.

"In seven years, I've never killed a story. The only time that I would is if it used explicit sexual overtones or profanity — things that would be completely obnoxious. Even then I don't know if I would kill it. I would just suggest to the writer a way to redo it."

While the school administration believes it is not censoring the student newspaper, the students see the situation differently. On the first day of school in 1990, 19 Stratford students were arrested. According to Beverly Kindall, the newspaper adviser, the incident involved a drug-related fight that started in a neighborhood, continued on the school

Brookline High School's headmaster, Robert Weintraub, above: "We abide by *Tinker.*"

Rebecca Onie, left, a junior and managing editor of *The Sagamore*, and Philip Katz, right, who is the adviser to the student newspaper at Brookline (Mass.) High School, both say the students are responsible for the paper.

bus and then into the school. When student journalists went to Neely to get more facts on the case, he says he told them not to report the story because it was still under investigation by police authorities, and he did not want to jeopardize the investigation. The result was that the student paper did a general editorial about school violence but left out any facts of the incident.

"The local newspapers and television stations covered it," says Kindall. "We could have handled it. We actually had a few more of the facts. But the principal felt we might say something that would jeopardize the case."

Kindall, who had been the newspaper adviser for five years, says that incident, combined with the lawsuit, made her squeamish about having the students deal with anything controversial in the paper.

Kindall was replaced as adviser by Jamye Merritt, who had no previous school newspaper experience.

"Pretty much nobody wanted to [become the newspaper's adviser] because of the liability associated with it," Merritt says. "They have a faculty of more than 70 people and the principal asked everybody, and no one would take it. I took it to get a job teaching here." Merritt has no plans to change the tone of the paper. "When you come off the street you want to make everybody happy. You don't want anybody mad at you."

Sex and other controversial issues

Student reporters often come under fire when covering sensitive issues like AIDS, birth control, drugs or homosexuality — issues that have nothing

to do directly with the school, but are central issues for students. Not surprisingly, these delicate issues have figured prominently in the debate on censorship in high school newspapers.

Case study: *The Sagamore,* **Brookline High School, Brookline, Mass.**

On page 5 of the Jan. 22, 1992, edition of *The Sagamore,* there are two illustrations. The first shows how to use a condom and includes a drawing of an erect penis. The explanation with the picture begins: "Put condom on before entering. Press air out of the condom tip. This leaves room for the cum (semen)."

The second illustration shows how to clean a used syringe, and tells the reader to "rinse twice with bleach and twice with water." Accompanying the illustration are two columns about students with AIDS. Following one of the columns is this editor's note: "We feel it is important to print the graphic below in order to inform those, for their own safety, who do not know how to use a condom properly. This is not meant to shock … but to help" people.

Nevertheless, the article did shock members of the Brookline community. Several local churches reproduced copies of the illustration and handed them out to the congregation, severely chastising the school and the student newspaper. Despite Massachusetts law and school rules prohibiting censorship of high school publications, the school's headmaster demanded that the newspaper adviser apologize and threatened prior review of all future editions of the newspaper.

A year later, the furor died down. A new headmaster was in place at the public high school, and the local school committee overwhelmingly endorsed the student newspaper's approach and called for continuing AIDS education and condom distribution in the school.

"Our advisers are excellent and they never put restrictions on anything," says Rebecca Onie, a junior and *The Sagamore's* managing editor in the school year 1992-93. "They read all the articles only to be aware what is going in the paper. They would never forbid us from putting something in. They make suggestions, but expect us to use our good judgment. We try to use standards of good journalism, what would be acceptable to *The Boston Globe* or *Boston Herald.*

"*The Sagamore* aspires to be a professional newspaper. We look at large newspapers across the country as our role models, and they don't encounter censorship. It would be detrimental to us as young journalists learning the trade if we were censored."

The student handbook of Brookline High School that every student receives at the beginning of the year is quite clear about the role of the student press:

You may express your opinion in publication and other written material as long as it does not violate the foregoing restrictions:

Neither "official" school publications (those financed by school — The Sagamore and Refractions) nor "unofficial" or "underground" publications may be censored by the school administration. (The duty of an adviser to a publication is to advise — not to censor.) You may, however, be sued and brought to court for printing material that is obscene, libelous or violently disruptive.

Philip Katz, adviser to *The Sagamore,* says he totally leaves it up to the students to decide what should go into the newspaper. He agreed with their decision to put the AIDS illustrations in the newspaper, but it would not have made a difference if he objected.

"It's their decision to put it in, not mine," he says. "I either support them or I don't support them and I've never not supported anything. If there came a time where I could not support them, I would make that public and not be a buffer for them. If it were bad enough, I'd step down as adviser."

After the condom and needle illustrations appeared, many members of the Brookline staff, faculty and community harshly criticized Katz and several called for his resignation as adviser. He says the headmaster demanded an apology. "I said I could not apologize and applauded my students for their courage and conviction and I stand behind my students 100 percent." Katz says he ignored the headmaster's threat of prior restraint of future editions of the school newspaper "because I knew he couldn't do it. *Hazelwood* does not apply in Massachusetts."

The current headmaster, Robert Weintraub, spoke to the newspaper staff after the illustrations appeared because of the community reaction. "I think the kids need to understand that they have to be sensitive to the community they serve," he says. "I didn't consider it obscene, but it had to do with sensitivity. They said that this was an important issue to kids. They said it isn't the kids who are offended but the adults who run the school who didn't have to grow up under the specter of AIDS who are offended. I said they weren't being sensitive to the adults, and they said we're not being sensitive to the kids. I thought the editor was quite eloquent on this issue and I respect her a great deal."

As for the issue of censorship, Weintraub says he "has never censored anything. Realistically, I'm not going to censor because I don't preread. We abide by *Tinker.*"

Despite the freedom the student journalists have at Brookline, Katz is worried that there is a tendency by his students to censor themselves, particularly in light of the flap over the condom and syringe articles.

"I'm constantly talking to them about it," he says. "They say 'I don't know whether I should write this or not.' I tell them to 'put in what you think is right, and if I think it is wrong I'll advise you. Don't censor yourself because of what you think someone's response might be.'"

Enterprise stories

Students are most likely to run afoul of administrators when they uncover wrongdoing or controversies in their own school. These are stories that might never have seen the light of day had it not been for the student journalists who are witnesses, or even participants, in the incidents or issues they write about. This kind of reporting is what many principals view as most dangerous.

Thus students may be aware of fights or assaults at school, drug or alcohol use on prom night, teachers who sexually harass students. All these stories are likely to go unreported by the adult press, yet they are central to students' lives. Who will report them?

Case study: *The What's Bruin,* **Northrop High School, Fort Wayne, Ind.**

In the winter of 1990, at one of the biweekly ideas meetings at Northrop High School in Fort Wayne, Ind., "someone suggested the idea of how much money goes into athletics," begins Jeff Lovell, then editor in chief of the newspaper. "I was an athlete and interested in the story, so I decided to write the story myself."

Jeff was a member of the boys' tennis team and another staffer was on the girls' team. She offhandedly told him that the girls' team was currently practicing at an indoor tennis complex at the coach's apartment complex. There was nothing illegal about using such practice sites, and it was February in northern Indiana, too cold to practice outdoors. The staffer told him each member of the team paid $65 to play indoors.

"Doing a quick estimation—there were 22 girls on the tennis team—it sounded like an inordinate amount of money to be paying at an apartment complex where the coach lived," Jeff says.

"The first thing I did was call the apartment complex. I asked how much it cost to rent the tennis court. He said, 'If you play with a member it's free.' I typed up my notes, went over there and had the manager sign my notes to verify the facts."

Jeff then talked to all 22 members of the girls' tennis team. Each player confirmed the amount she paid the coach. "The coach told them he was not making any money on this, that this was just to rent the court," Jeff says.

Word soon leaked out that the school newspaper

was preparing an article on a controversy involving the athletic department. At one point, according to Jeff, the coach called him out of class and wanted to know whether Jeff had a "problem with me." "I said I don't have a problem with you. I'm doing an investigative story and would like to talk to you." Jeff thought the coach was trying to intimidate him. Ultimately, the coach never consented to an interview.

As Jeff researched the article, he told principal H. Douglas Williams "step by step what I was doing and he approved everything I did. He gave me the full go-ahead until I completed the spread."

"I took it to him at which time he said that 'this is well-written, it is factual, it is not libelous. Yet this article will never be printed," says Jeff. "When he told me that it hit me like a ton of bricks. It came from nowhere. I had complete communication with him so this wouldn't happen. The reason he gave me was that it was not in the school's best interest.

"He also told me the reason he let me do my investigation was that he thought I had so little experience I would not come up with anything. I felt like he had belittled the whole journalistic experience by not respecting what I was doing."

Jeff's investigation showed not only that the tennis coach had kept the money from the members of the team, but that the school's athletic adviser had violated school financial rules. "Whenever money is transferred from a student to his team — for example, when a coach makes some T-shirts — the students have to make checks out to the Northrop Athletic Department and not the coach for accounting purposes," Jeff says. "In this case, the athletic director had given the coach full rein to have the checks made out to himself."

For his part, Williams — who no longer is principal but is still an administrator in the school district — is quite laudatory of the job both Jeff and adviser Wendy Kruger did.

"In 12 years as principal, that's the only thing I ever censored and the only thing I came close to censoring," he says. "You had to be there to really understand what was going on. It was a real tough situation."

Williams thought the thrust of the article was going to be on the cost of athletics in general and was surprised when the article simply focused on the tennis coach.

"I don't think in any way Jeff [Lovell] tried to mislead me anymore than I tried to mislead Jeff," Williams says. "It simply was a situation where it became bigger than I thought it would be as time went on. It wasn't something I wanted to have published in a school paper.

"There were some circumstances in the school at the time that I'm not going to get into, but the timing was absolutely ironic and the sensitivities were very pronounced. Had this happened independently of everything else, it would have been a very different matter."

Nonetheless, Jeff and Kruger, his adviser, were shocked the principal killed the story. Kruger wrote to the principal, urging him to reconsider the censorship. He refused. They later learned, says Lovell, that the newspaper article was used in a settlement with the coach.

"I was told by the principal that I was used as a bargaining tool," Jeff says. "The principal took my work, presented it to the central administration. They then asked the coach for his resignation and a restitution of funds, which was given.

"The central administration told the coach that if he were to resign and pay back the money, the story would not be printed. The worst part of the censorship was that there were all sorts of rumors going on around the school and there was never the opportunity to clear them up."

Kruger says Jeff approached the story quite professionally from the beginning. She says only after the story was ready for publication did she learn that the principal agreed to kill the article if the coach paid back the money. According to Kruger, the coach failed to make restitution by the deadline "so we assumed it would go."

The story never ran, according to both Kruger and Jeff, because of the principal's fears that it would exacerbate racial tension at the school. The tennis coach is black. "I realize what Williams was trying to do," Kruger says. "He was trying to prevent Jeff from becoming embroiled in a situation where he would be accused of having a racial motivation. But what he never realized was that the rumors were 1,000 times worse than what Jeff had actually found out. To this day, very few people really know the right story."

Principal Williams cited the *Hazelwood* opinion as his right to censor the newspaper, a decision that both Jeff and Kruger find ironic. "When I was a freshman and *Hazelwood* first came out, our principal met with the staff and said this will never affect Northrop High School," Jeff recalls.

While the article never appeared in the school newspaper, the story was picked up by the local media in June 1990. By the 1992 school board elections, it had become a major issue. Advocates who backed free expression in Fort Wayne's school newspapers won. At the new school board's first meeting in January 1993, these new guidelines were adopted:

The Board of Trustees of the Fort Wayne Community Schools believes that freedom of expression and responsible journalism go hand in hand, and that responsible journalism cannot be taught without freedom of expression. Conse-

quently, student publications should provide a full opportunity for students to inquire, question and exchange ideas, and content should reflect all areas of student interest, including topics about which there may be dissent and controversy.

Williams says under the new guidelines, Jeff's report would be published.

Meanwhile, elsewhere in Fort Wayne

On the same day the Board of Education of Fort Wayne Community Schools passed citywide guidelines establishing press rights, Norma Thiele, a veteran journalism adviser at another Fort Wayne high school, received a jarring phone call in the morning.

William Coats, the superintendent of schools, was on the phone. He was angry about inaccuracies in an article and an editorial in the January 8 edition of *The Northerner,* North Side High School's weekly newspaper, where Thiele is the adviser. The articles suggested Coats was about to do away with honors courses in the Fort Wayne schools. He said he was not.

"I thought the phone was going to melt," Thiele says. The adviser had been out of town and the student editor tried to call Coats, couldn't reach him and, as the deadline loomed, went ahead with the articles.

Thiele, who has been advising *The Northerner* for 40 years (and who was named Distinguished Adviser by the Dow Jones Newspaper Fund in 1989), assured Coats he could respond in the next week's edition — one of the positive points of having a weekly newspaper.

Coats was a driving force behind the proposed press guidelines. In fact, he was in charge of submitting them that night. Would this flare-up jeopardize the vote? Thiele and her students went to the board meeting that night holding their breaths. Coats spoke in support of the guidelines, the vote went through and Fort Wayne ended up with a citywide policy supporting youth expression.

"They needn't have worried," says Coats, who doesn't recall being all that angry. "This was a First Amendment, free press situation. They had the right to publish. I was just pointing out some errors. Actually, it gave them a chance to learn that reporters need to get the details straight."

Censoring from within

Many school newspapers are devoid of aggressive reporting or substantial articles on student life not because principals censor stories but rather because students censor themselves. Often students avoid important issues at their schools because they are afraid they might run afoul of school administrators.

Case study: *West Word,* **Niles West High School, Skokie, Ill.**

During the early 1970s, *West Word's* adviser was a former professional journalist. The philosophy was anything goes as long as it's newsworthy. Many of the student journalists were trained at the summer institute of nearby Northwestern University. The result was a substantial, interesting, and often controversial student newspaper.

For example, one article dealt with the effect of a one-week teachers' strike and included interviews with all the teachers who crossed the picket line. Another article covered a controversial decision by the soccer coach to bar seniors from the junior varsity team. A third dealt with a number of minorities who appeared to have been discriminated against in meting out discipline. Many of the articles angered the administration and some faculty members. Some wrote letters to the editor. But no story was killed and no student disciplined or threatened.

But in the 1990s, following the *Hazelwood* decision, the mood has changed to the point where an editor who had been in trouble for previous pranks was barred from his graduation ceremonies because he wrote that a rival school was "the armpit of Cook County." This is what one of *West Word's* editors, Geoff Dubey, wrote in his farewell column in 1991.

"So here we are, about to leave lovely Niles West, recently proclaimed an 'excellent' school by the U.S. Department of Education. Granted, the award was cheapened by the fact that Niles North, the armpit of Cook County, also won it."

The article went on to make other complaints

Adviser Jerome Orr works with journalism students at Niles West High School in Skokie, Ill., on the student newspaper, *West Word.* **"Right now, the school board attorney comes in and gives a lecture to the staff on libel. ... We also now have a committee of teachers and administrators who read the paper prior to publication, and that had never been the case."**

about the school, some teachers and students. But the "armpit" reference got him in trouble, and it was not Dubey's first run-in with the administration. The previous week, Dubey had been punished for wrongfully inserting comments in the yearbook. The remarks, which the adviser had not seen, were printed in the yearbook. Dubey said the comments got into print by mistake, but faculty adviser Jerome Orr disagreed and came down hard on him. Dubey later admitted he made a mistake and paid for it. He was suspended for five days.

Nevertheless, Orr saw nothing wrong with Dubey's newspaper column. Niles West and Niles North had been district rivals for years. But Niles West principal Donald Ring was not amused. "That afternoon I was called into Dr. Ring's office and informed that the Niles North principal was outraged, and they had students complaining about this and, as a result, I wouldn't be allowed to go to graduation," Dubey recalls. "I was told that I had libeled Niles North and that it was completely out of line. I tried to explain to him that you can't libel Niles North, that you can't libel a building. I tried to explain to him that it wasn't libel, but he insisted it was and said I couldn't go through graduation."

Ring, who has since retired, demanded Dubey apologize to Niles North. "It may have been in jest and there is always some interschool rivalry, but to refer to another school as the armpit of Cook County is not good taste," Ring says. "It shouldn't appear in the school paper."

If the column was the only incident involving Dubey, an apology would have sufficed and it would not have kept him out of graduation, Ring admits. It was because of the yearbook incident that Dubey was barred from graduation.

Orr, an adviser to the student newspaper for 12 years, saw the action taken against Dubey as a way to get back at the student for all the things he had written in the past — including some unflattering remarks about the coaching staff.

"I defended Geoff," Orr says. "I told Ring that it was not a libelous remark whatsoever. I even showed him the book and all the things that constitute libel. Some may consider what he wrote in poor taste but it was not libel." Orr believes that resentment by some teachers about coverage by Dubey, combined with complaints from the Niles North principal and the superintendent, created the confrontation.

The column came out a week before graduation, and Dubey was told he could graduate but not participate in the graduation ceremony or any other festivities. Dubey and his parents went to a federal court seeking a temporary restraining order to allow him to graduate with the other students. Attorneys for Niles West contended Dubey was being barred from the ceremony not just because of his column,

but also because of the earlier yearbook incident.

U.S. District Judge Brian Barnett Duff found on behalf of Dubey.

The judge wrote: "Inasmuch as the punishment leveled by Niles West was in retaliation for the publication of his final column, the court finds that it is a violation of his First Amendment rights. Inasmuch as the punishment was in retaliation for the earlier yearbook incident, the court finds that is a violation of Mr. Dubey's Fourteenth Amendment right to due process, as Mr. Dubey was already punished once for the incident and specifically informed that his punishment would not include prohibition from attending his graduation ceremony."

Attorneys for the school board appealed the decision, but both sides agreed to settle and allow Dubey to graduate if he would make another public apology for the yearbook incident. He did.

Despite the agreement, the dispute has had a lasting effect on the newspaper program.

"Right now, the school board attorney comes in and gives a lecture to the staff on libel," Orr says. "I don't object to that. But what's fair for one should be fair for all. She doesn't have to go to Niles North and give them a lecture. We also now have a committee of teachers and administrators who read the paper prior to publication, and that had never been the case."

The lawyer's view

The lawyer who visits the classroom is Fay Hartog-Rapp, a firm believer in the doctrine expressed in the *Hazelwood* decision. She says it is a mistake to give student journalists the same kinds of First Amendment rights provided to professional reporters.

"*Hazelwood* was a good decision because it recognized the school's authority to recognize what is important," she says. "It's not that students can't learn from the journalism experience and the full experience that a regular private journalist might have. But there are competing interests. Other students have privacy rights to be free from slanderous, libelous comments and to be free from ridicule in the school setting. The rights of student journalists would have to be balanced with the rights of students as a whole."

Hartog-Rapp, who in 1992 represented about three dozen school districts in the Chicago area, says her experience dealing with high school journalists shows that they tend to be irresponsible. She says student journalists, in the guise of investigative reporting, often make allegations that may or may not be true.

School administrators should have the right to censor, she says, because "the school newspaper is a function of the public school district, and the taxpayers' funds and action on the school newspaper can be attached to the school board." Professional newspapers have financial liability if they defame someone, she points out, so professional journalists are schooled in defamation law. If a student defames someone, the school board is responsible.

But Hartog-Rapp, one of the most experienced lawyers in the nation on high school press issues, concedes that she knows of no case where a school board was found liable because of an article that appeared in a school newspaper. In fact, according to Mark Goodman at the Student Press Law Center, there is no known published case of a school newspaper having been successfully sued for libel.

"Best interests of the students"

As in the *Hazelwood* decision, principals sometimes censor stories by saying they wish to protect students from embarrassment, unreasonable public scrutiny, or emotional distress.

Balancing the possible harm to students who are subjects of articles and the rights of student reporters is one of the most difficult dilemmas facing school administrators, and most frustrating for student reporters.

Case study: *The Lion's Roar,* Lincoln High School, Gahanna, Ohio

In late 1992, Scott Stewart, the assistant principal, prevented the school newspaper from printing an article about a specific case of teenage drinking.

Lisa Bigus, a senior and editor of the school newspaper, *The Lion's Roar,* tells the story.

"Our school one day was starting two hours late because of proficiency exams. There was a party at someone's house that morning and there was a junior girl who drank so much alcohol her blood alcohol level was 0.20. [In Ohio a person is considered legally intoxicated if the blood alcohol level is 0.10.]

"She came to school and then dozed off and vomited in math class. They had to call the paramedics, and she was rushed to the hospital. She almost died of alcohol poisoning. A lot of rumors were floating all over the school about what happened.

"We thought it was important to bring out this issue that someone almost died. One of our reporters started talking to other people involved in the party, and they were willing to give quotes and information. They were friends of the girl and thought it was important that the information came out. We never intended to name the girl.

"The girl's parents found out and called the school. They were upset about this being covered and told the principal not to run the story. The assistant principal went to the adviser. He said he spoke to the parents of the girl, and he didn't want a story to run because of her emotional stability. He thought it wasn't appropriate.

"We had never been censored before."

Despite protests by the student editors and the adviser, the assistant principal stood by his decision. He told the editors that if they waited a few issues after the incident died down, they could write a generic story about teenage drinking. The principal also promised the students that if they waited, he would try to convince the parents and the girl to cooperate with the school newspaper. The students agreed to wait, they said, because they felt they had no choice. A general story about teenage drinking ran in April 1993. Another sidebar was planned on the problem of teens coming to school drunk, but it was not written because by then no sources would talk about the incident at the school.

Stewart is convinced he made the right decision. "The reason I felt it was an inappropriate article to write was because it was detrimental to one of our students," he says.

"I don't like to get into censorship. I know what kind of ugly can that opens. But when you negatively impact a student and her family, you have to look out for their benefit. My decision was based on the fact that you have to care about the students in your building and, in my mind, the student has gone through the mud. There's nothing positive that can come out with that kind of scenario being resurfaced."

Dave Weisenburger has been faculty adviser for *The Lion's Roar* for 20 years. This is the first time the newspaper has been prevented from writing something its students thought relevant.

Weisenburger blames the situation, in part, on the *Hazelwood* decision. "When I first started here things were difficult and I had to do a lot of convincing with the administration to let me cover sensitive topics, but I often was able to use the *Tinker* decision in my arguments," he says. "Since *Hazelwood,* things have been more difficult. I think the administration does feel that they have more leeway. Their legal interpretation of what *Hazelwood* stands for tells them different things than what my legal advisers tell me. There's no doubt *Hazelwood* has had a chilling effect on the student press."

John Bowen, the journalism adviser at Lakewood High School in Lakewood, Ohio, and a student press advocate, says what happened with *The Lion's Roar* signals the dangers of censorship for the high school press.

"[Weisenburger's] paper is so good and has won so many awards for its coverage," says Bowen, "you would think from experience they would have no fear of their coverage or how they would cover it."

One difference between the two Ohio high schools is that in Lakewood there is a clear school board policy that the student newspapers are forums for student expression and censorship is not

Looking back

"Hulda Lind was my journalism teacher, and she was really responsible for getting me involved. I was captivated with the idea of sports journalism, and I knew I wasn't going to be a professional athlete, but sports writing was a way to stay close to it. I got so much out of the paper, all of my friends were there and the idea of being able to write about something I love fascinated me."

Bob Giles is the editor and publisher of The Detroit News. *He is a 1951 graduate of John Marshall High School in Cleveland, Ohio, where he was the sports editor of* The Interpreter.

allowed. The school board in Lakewood passed that policy in the wake of the *Hazelwood* decision.

"In the 22 years I've been here, we've never had any hassle or prior review," Bowen says. "In one case, kids were caught drinking on a foreign exchange trip to England, and they were disciplined. We ran a special four-page section and while we didn't name names, the parents read us the riot act. But we worked it out. We explained that the paper is not causing the problem, it is the issue itself that caused the problem."

Censorship from the community

The impetus for censorship does not always come from school officials. Rather, after a story is published, school officials can find themselves under pressure from people in the community — elected officials, clergy, parents. That kind of pressure can lead to censoring future stories.

Case study: *The Harbinger,* **Coconut Creek High School, Coconut Creek, Fla.**

The Harbinger has long tackled controversial issues. Topics for cover stories have ranged from sexually transmitted diseases to teen suicide. In 1992 and 1993, *The Harbinger* won first place from Quill and Scroll and the Florida Scholastic Press Association (FSPA) and was named a medalist from the Columbia Scholastic Press Association. In 1991-92, it was named the best student news magazine in the state by the FSPA.

It was in the Nov. 20, 1991, issue that the staff decided to investigate violence at the school. The main story about violence, written by senior Kristen McCoy, the editor in chief, and junior Orlando Sanchez, begins this way: *"Eighteen arrests as of Oct.*

28 highlight what many see as increased tension at the school."

As part of the project, the newspaper staff also surveyed 250 of the school's approximately 2,500 students. Among the questions asked was whether the students thought there was an increase in tension and whether those tensions were racially motivated. The survey results were reported in sidebars. Here is one of them:

A matter of race?
One of the most popular theories about what is causing tensions on campus is that of racial problems. Sixty-four percent of students surveyed agreed that racism is a main factor in the rising level of violence in school.

"If you even bump into a person of another race in the hallway, they think you are trying to start something," said one white female surveyed.

The racial problem theory stems from the brawl last spring which many believed was racially motivated.

Some students and staff do not find this theory valid.

"When you have two blacks from Pompano fighting, which is what is happening here, there is no way it could be racial," stated school resource office Alma Bosse from the Broward Sheriff's Office.

While many discard the racial theory, the following words "decorate" the walls in one of the girls' restrooms:

"KKK is getting bigger, aren't you sorry you're a nigger."

It was that last line, the graffiti, that brought the notoriety. Adviser Sandi Scaffetti, a former staffer at *The Miami Herald,* received some complaints from parents who said they knew there were racial problems at the school but were upset the school newspaper would print an article about it. They asked Scaffetti why the students did not concentrate on positive issues.

Unknown to the adviser, some community activists and representatives of a local NAACP chapter were outraged that the word "nigger" had been printed in the school newspaper. They called for a meeting of school administrators — a meeting that Scaffetti was not told about and that occurred while she was out of town. Editor in Chief Kristen McCoy was summoned and reprimanded on two counts: for running the article and for having too few minorities on the newspaper staff. (There were three black staffers and one Hispanic staffer out of 20 students on the staff. Black students make up about 20 percent of the students at the school; Hispanic students about 15 percent.)

Sandi Scaffetti, a former *Miami Herald* staffer, now adviser to *The Harbinger,* says the review process is a "logistical nightmare."

Principal Ronald Wilhoit read the controversial article after publication — he had never prereviewed the paper — and "didn't have any problems with it. All that was printed was what was written on the bathroom wall. It wasn't their opinion. It was what was written there."

Nicole Archer, a sophomore and editor at the paper, says those in the community who were upset with the article were misdirecting their anger. "The school has a very serious problem and, unfortunately, the way they want to solve it is to kill the messenger."

After the publication of the article, and even after the meeting with the NAACP, the graffiti remained on the bathroom wall. More than a week later it was finally removed. "These people should have gotten upset that it was on the bathroom wall, not [gotten upset] at *The Harbinger*," Nicole says. "Rather than get it off the wall, their main objective was to stop the newspaper from ever printing again."

Principal Wilhoit was informed that the long-standing Broward County school policy required that he review every article before publication and censor anything he deemed controversial. Wilhoit is uncomfortable with his role as reviewer and potential censor. "If you happen to have a good newspaper sponsor like I do, then you don't worry much about what is going on," he says. "I don't particularly care what they do. In this case I was told to preview it because that was the board policy."

Wilhoit set up a three-member review committee — one white faculty member, one black faculty member and an administrator. Adviser Scaffetti says the review process presents a "logistical nightmare" because it is difficult to get 26 pages of copy reviewed by a committee in a timely fashion.

The students are not happy about it, either. "We are giving the right to censor to a bunch of people who have no journalism background whatsoever," says Nicole. "Ms. Scaffetti was a professional journalist." Adds another editor, sophomore Rachel Warren, "A science teacher has more say over the newspaper now than our journalism adviser."

A different Florida policy

In 1981, Lillian Lodge Kopenhaver, associate dean and professor at Florida International University, helped develop guidelines for Dade County schools calling for freedom of expression in high school publications. A central tenet of those guidelines is that students should make the final determination of what goes into their newspapers and that the adviser is not a censor. Kopenhaver believes that if those guidelines were in place in Broward County, where Coconut Creek is located, the incident never would have occurred.

"There was nothing [the staff of *The Harbinger*]

Although Coconut Creek (Fla.) High School Principal Ronald Wilhoit had never prereviewed *The Harbinger* before, a long-standing county school policy requires that he review every article before publication and censor anything he deems controversial.

did that was wrong at all," she says. "They did everything by the book and they did it legally and responsibly. The worst part of it was that there was community pressure on the principal, but the principal didn't have any strong guidelines to say back to the community that as far as Broward County is concerned, the students have the right to do it."

Wilhoit is hopeful the Broward County School Board will accept a recommendation to change its publication policy, but neither Scaffetti nor Kopenhaver is optimistic. At a recent meeting about new guidelines, the school board attorney objected to any changes in the current policy.

The Harbinger has found an ally in the local professional media, which has covered the case in its news columns and has editorialized in favor of a new policy in Broward County. In a March 1993 editorial, *The Miami Herald* called for a new policy that does not allow prepublication review.

The editorial rejected the notion that reporting about racist graffiti should cause such controversy:

" … as painful as the offending word is, reading it in a serious discussion of racism within a high school is far preferable to reading it on the bathroom wall. If Broward schools are to teach journalism, the school board should provide its journalists the ability to do it well and responsibly."

Going underground

Spurred by a hunger to raise controversial issues and helped along by ever-advancing computer technology, a growing number of teenagers are becoming underground newspaper publishers.

"We hear from teenagers who tell us that they went to an underground newspaper," says Student Press Law Center's Mark Goodman. "They believe there are things they could not say in their officially sponsored school publication."

But, cautions Northwestern University journalism professor Abe Peck, what an underground newspaper gains in liberty it often loses in longevity. "Most underground papers offer a 'message in the bottle,' since when the editor or small group of writers leaves, the paper dies."

The principle of free expression

Ronald E. Hill has been the principal of Richland Northeast High School in Columbia, S.C., since January 1984. Here are his thoughts on a free press.

In the early 1960s, before students knew how to be radical, I was a member of my high school newspaper staff. I was assigned the task of writing an editorial for our two-page school "newspaper." *The Comments* was very provincial stuff. It contained cute "Guess Who?" riddles, crude pictures of the homecoming dance and a listing of the honor roll.

I had a notion that I was going to write something "controversial." Far be it from my mind that I would consider something like American foreign policy in Indochina, or even the school's censorship of *Catcher in the Rye*. I decided to criticize the purchase of artistic prints for the school hallways as an excessive expenditure at a time when there were clearly other needs for the school. (This is ironic considering I recently received the Kennedy Center Outstanding Administrator award for the support of the arts.)

The editorial was not questioned by the faculty adviser and was printed. It hardly received any notice by the students, but the next day I was called to the principal's office — for the first time ever. He calmly explained that the hanging of the prints had been his idea, and that the financing had not come from taxpayers but from some "leftover" funds provided by the school magazine sale. He then tried to justify his attempt to upgrade the aesthetics of the school. That was all there was to our conference. No harsh words, veiled threats or punishment.

This experience had a lasting effect upon me. I was impressed with the mature way that he chose to deal with the problem I had presented to him.

Today as a high school principal of a school twice the size of the one I attended, I realize how dramatically schools have changed. Nevertheless, I still want to give my students the same feeling of maturity and fairness, the same understanding of free expressions and openness that I received from my principal years ago.

High school journalism today can be an extension of collaborative learning, critical thinking and student intellectual growth and it can be a pit full of snakes — student antagonism, community controversy, and legal suits. How does a principal cope with this potential for triumph or doom?

I believe that an outstanding high school has an outstanding school newspaper and video journal that are fully supported by the principal. This means that they are subsidized with any discretionary funds that can be made available. The faculty advisers are qualified and are given the time to teach journalism as well as to supervise the production of the student news vehicles. The journalism programs must also be beneficiaries of scheduling and staff development decisions that are made by the principal. There are so many ways in which support can be given to the program.

High school journalism today should include the latest in computer technology, with desktop publishing, video-editing and video-graphic equipment and library database research capabilities. Students should be taught as if they were in a vocational preparation program for a career in news journalism. Every effort should be made to give them an environment for freedom of expression.

Once this commitment is in place, the principal can proceed to work on avoiding the "snakes." The principal who has invested resources in the program will give it some advance attention. The principal must be viewed as the president of the corporation that "owns" the newspaper or television station as a business. Students must learn that the media are businesses and have responsibilities not only for maintaining freedom of expression, but also for avoiding such things as libel and public indecency.

The faculty adviser should be viewed as the publisher or general manager and the student editor as the editor. The principal, adviser and student editor should meet early in the school year to establish basic editorial policy. Areas of editorial difficulty should be explained and justified.

For example, in our state it is against the law for a school official to counsel a student for an abortion. This means that this topic must be carefully treated in the school media. Although I never get involved in previewing the contents of the media, I trust in the judgment of the adviser to ask my opinion in sensitive or controversial subjects that the students want to pursue.

In the spirit of my own high school principal, I do not fear criticism of administrative policies or decisions. In fact, I personally use the school newspaper not only to gauge the student impact of decisions, but also to explain them. I have been known to write my own letter to the editor.

Some may ask why bother risking controversy by encouraging student freedom of the press. The standard answer is that it teaches responsibility as well as basic citizenship. However, I would like to suggest another good reason for encouraging a strong student media program. I believe that outstanding student journalism enhances the school climate. It can help build a sense of institutional trust and openness that I think is essential for an outstanding learning climate for all students. When students feel they are collaborators with teachers and administrators, more learning takes place. Students are more highly motivated if they perceive that they are allies with the faculty and administration in the battle against ignorance. After all, freedom of the press is our society's battle against ignorance.

Topic:
Censorship

In 1992, Tom Dickson, an associate professor of journalism at Southwest Missouri State University, conducted two surveys about attitudes toward censorship in public schools. He received responses from 323 student newspapers editors and 270 advisers. Then he compared their answers. Dickson's findings:

■ Would editor get into trouble for a controversial story?

	Editor	Adviser
With adviser	12%	12%
With school officials but not adviser	39%	28%
No	49%	60%

■ Is adviser's opinion important to an editor for story selection?

	Editor	Adviser
No/not very	32%	28%
Fairly	47%	48%
Very	21%	24%

■ How much does adviser worry about controversy?

	Editor	Adviser
Not at all	21%	28%
Not much	51%	63%
Fair much/quite a bit	28%	9%

■ How much has an adviser stressed there be no controversy?

	Editor	Adviser
Not at all	45%	49%
Not much	40%	43%
Fairly/quite often	15%	8%

■ Does adviser read story before publication?

	Editor	Adviser
No/not often	5%	5%
Fairly/quite often	13%	6%
Always	82%	89%

■ Does principal read newspaper before publication?

	Editor	Adviser
Never	62%	64%
On occasion	21%	22%
Fairly or quite often/always	17%	14%

■ Has a newspaper failed to run important stories because of subject matter?

	Editor	Adviser
Never	60%	57%
A few times	35%	39%
Fairly/quite often	5%	4%

■ Has adviser withheld a story because of the topic?

	Editor	Adviser
No	74%	65%
Yes	26%	35%

■ Has principal rejected story/required changes?

	Editor	Adviser
No	66%	63%
Yes	34%	37%

Finding common ground for free, responsible student press

Roy Peter Clark is an associate director of The Poynter Institute for Media Studies in St. Petersburg, Fla., which has long run editing and writing programs for newspapers. In 1992, The Poynter Institute began a program on student press rights for local high schools. In an interview, Clark describes the program called "A Free and Responsible Student Press."

"This is a program that is attempting to preserve excellent student journalism in our community in the post-*Hazelwood* environment.

"We've created a summer training program for advisers, two weeks long, focusing on the difficult issues of ethics and law. We really feel the need to help in providing professional development to inexperienced and experienced publications advisers.

"We've developed a number of case studies on difficult or controversial stories — attempting to build those into curriculum material for students, so that students don't have to learn just by stumbling into them. They can get a sense of the history of what's happened in their own county. It includes a workbook with a mission statement on the purpose of the student press — 10 of us are working together to articulate what that mission is and to get people to buy into it.

"There are programs we hope to have for principals. We have interviewed every principal in Pinellas County. We've learned that there is a kind of tension between what some principals say they believe in and how they actually act on issues and questions involving the student press.

"The principals also seem to be more cautious about some of these issues than their boss — the school superintendent — out of worry and out of practical concern. It's easy for the school superintendent to articulate certain kinds of attitudes, but when the phone rings, it will ring on the principal's desk. So the principal is balancing a lot of different issues and values.

"We think one of our jobs is to attempt to create some opportunity for common ground, reconciling some differences and engaging in a conversation with various players so we can identify those shared values that we encourage rather than discourage in the student press. We're going to create a document that will be a blueprint for how a very free and very responsible student press can operate in this county.

"It's going to take some real work. The attorney to the school board has a different perspective on this. He wanted to establish stricter controls. This program is an endorsement that the school system wants to find a way through this farce so that principals won't have to preread every article with an X-acto knife in their hands.

"A lot of us don't believe that this particular generation cares less and is tuned out and illiterate. There are a lot of people I talk to who recognize the potential of student journalism to create laboratories of democratic activity. That's where we rest our hopes for the future: on our ability to inspire this next generation toward participation in journalism and civic life.

"And, in a way, I guess you could argue that all the controversy and debate about student publications and the fact that there has been an unfortunate increase in cases of censorship — that's proof that people care. Even if we think they're doing the wrong thing, I think they're right in recognizing the power of the student press."

"It was over; yet it will never be over"

Franklin McCallie has been principal of Kirkwood High School in Kirkwood, Mo., since 1979. Before that he taught English, coached soccer and track and served as an educational administrator in Baltimore County, Md., Chattanooga, Tenn., Chicago and University City, Mo. Here is his story on encouraging a free press.

If you want the *facade* of an energetic, inquisitive school but a foundation of apathy, establish the student press — then stifle it.

In the short run, is it cheaper, easier and smoother to muzzle the student press or to dissolve it altogether. Why deal with questions that sometimes upset the atmosphere and spotlight shortcomings?

It seems to me that our nation's schools have a love/hate relationship with our students. On the one hand, our public asks for tough schools, tough rules, no-nonsense instruction and a conformity so we may move together to build a strong, monolithic country. On the other hand, our public asks that we produce scholars and thinkers of divergent minds and opinions and empower them with new ideas, new ways to deal with the issues of their generation.

In the fall of 1990, I relished the chance to prove that I mean what I say about the student press when the staff of the Kirkwood High newspaper, *The Call,* accepted an advertisement from the St. Louis chapter of Planned Parenthood. The ad read:

It's not enough to 'just say no.' Say KNOW. Know what you're doing. Know the facts. If you don't know, find out. It's OK to ask questions. Call us. We're part of the oldest and largest family planning organization in the country. We'll give you honest, factual, non-judgmental answers and referrals. You don't have to give your name. And it's free. Now that you know that much, the rest is up to you.

According to an article in the *St. Louis Post-Dispatch, The Call* was one of only eight among the 80 area high schools that accepted the ad. Kirkwood High would eventually receive 300 phone calls, 121 letters and information pickets at meetings of the school board.

Erin Dykstra, left, works with a classmate to find a title of a movie appropriate as a metaphor for an article about the graduating senior class.

Below, teacher Debra Shrout reviews photos from the zoo, made by photography class student Matt Nieman, a senior.

In Kirkwood, Mo., students take *The Call* seriously

A student takes notes from a textbook on color printing. Each student works individually on a final project in photography class.

Linh Do reads a clipping from a local newspaper. Every day, teacher Debra Shrout passes around an example of outstanding photography for students to see.

Above, H.L. Hall looks over a yearbook class as sophomore Margit Toth, left foreground, and Mary Grace McCaskill work on fitting headlines. They are wearing make-up and costumes as part of the initiation rite for new members of the incoming newspaper staff. Hall, a longtime teacher, typically arrives at the school at 6:30 a.m. and leaves at 6:30 p.m. He is both newspaper, *The Call,* and yearbook adviser.

Linh Do, left, with Madeline Hinrichs, Brian Casey and Marion Randall look at a photography book.

> **"Kirkwood High remains strong, while seeking to bring lost supporters back to an understanding of education as a dynamic, uneasy, catalytic process in American students' lives."**
>
> **Franklin McCallie**

Heated statements were delivered in open meetings from normally supportive parents and citizens who were outraged that a journalism teacher, the principal and the superintendent could, in light of the *Hazelwood* decision, so "completely abdicate their administrative responsibility by refusing to overturn the student journalists' decision to run an advertisement from such a controversial and obviously harmful organization."

When the first 10 complaints came in, Tom Keating, the superintendent, asked for a meeting with me, *The Call's* sponsor, H.L. Hall, and the entire *Call* staff. Keating, who had made it clear at the time of the *Hazelwood* decision that he backed a strong student press and journalistic excellence, now told the students that the vociferous opponents — all respected citizens of our community — did not see this as a battle over freedom of the student press, but rather a battle in the war between abortion and anti-abortion foes.

Keating believed the issue was based in journalism and decision-making, but doubted these citizens would ever see it that way. Giving the students a week to ponder, discuss and decide, he told them, "These people will never stop. It will hurt us in the long run. You must make a decision with these new circumstances in mind, and we know you will make the right decision."

In the meantime, letters poured in to the news media and to the school. Phone calls kept the school lines and secretaries busy. To our surprise, now the mail and phone calls ran five to one in support of our stand to support our students' decision-making. It was clear to the vast majority of our taxpayers that this was a question of how far educators should go in aiding students to make meaningful, sometimes controversial, decisions. But a small, organized, well-meaning, narrowly focused, vocal minority can stir a community to angry action.

Superintendent Keating had left the decision to the students. Could he abide by the outcome? Would this school board support him and students if the students voted to keep the ad and Keating backed them?

A week later, *Call* Editor in Chief Michael Griffin, a real hero in this story thanks to his calm and reasoned persistence, asked Keating for several more weeks to study and research the issue through the national student and professional press. Keating granted the delay. The *Call* staff researched. Sponsor Hall and Editor Griffin took the staff for an early December half-day retreat. The staff discussed and voted — 27-0 — to keep the ad.

While a local religious radio station called for pickets before the February school board meeting, speakers now appeared for both sides. Board members were pressed by public opinion for statements on their stands.

At a public meeting to which 400 citizens came, each member of the school board gave a personally written statement of unqualified support for administration-backed, sponsor-guided, genuine student decision-making within a quality journalism program at Kirkwood High School.

It was over — and yet it will never be over. With every school year, with every school election, rumbling is heard about the "Planned Parenthood ad" issue.

The Call continues to run "the ad" and continues to win top journalistic awards on the basis of quality journalism. Michael Griffin is making his mark in college journalism. Superintendent Keating led the district in an overwhelming victory for school bond issues and tax levies. Kirkwood High remains strong, while seeking to bring lost supporters back to an understanding of education as a dynamic, uneasy, catalytic process in American students' lives.

"Computers have made newspapers more fun for the students. It's more of a playground." — Tim Harrower

Video … Cable … Desktop publishing … Electronic bulletin boards … Telecomputing … Multimedia … The electronic age is here, and it belongs to the young.

The price of computers has constantly plummeted. The power of a multimillion-dollar Eniac computer of World War II is now available at Radio Shack for ten dollars. And the three-dimensional graphics system of a mid-1970s Cray supercomputer is now packed inside computer work stations costing $5,000.

The drop in computer equipment prices is permitting high schools to pull onto the new information highway. Student journalists adapt to the technology quickly, creatively.

According to a 1993 survey of 185 schools by the Southern Interscholastic Press Association, 89 percent have desktop publishing systems. These systems give high school journalists the tools to perform advanced layout, composition and production tasks reserved until recently for commercial newspapers. And through alliances with computer networks and universities, high schools already have begun to plug into worldwide research for the price of a local phone call.

Rolling Stone media critic Jon Katz sees a future for media that no generation has yet experienced. In an interview on National Public Radio in November 1993, Katz said, "If you look at the statistics, what we're seeing is media splitting in half. There's one medium for people 45 years and up. There's another medium for people 45 and down. Increasingly, this medium for the young is cable. The young are abandoning news magazines, newspapers

and network news programs in stunning numbers."

Reading today's signposts for tomorrow's media is not easy. Computers already allow print and broadcast to merge. "Right now, the superhighway is a dirt road and the tools we are using are like a Model T," said Donald Brazeal of *The Washington Post*, announcing plans to offer a computerized version of the newspaper in the summer of 1994.

To begin to explore the electronic future of high school journalism, we must consider computers and electronic information exchange.

Designing on an electronic desktop

The (Portland) *Oregonian's* Tim Harrower traveled around the country for five years teaching computer newspaper design to high school newspaper advisers and students. In his travels he made two important observations:

First, he says, "Computers have made newspapers more fun for the students. It's more of a playground. Students can get their hands on the paper, they can play with type and this has made papers a lot more playful than they were 10 years ago." Computers, he says, have breathed new life into student publications that were looking a little dull in the 1970s and early '80s.

Second, he says, computerization is moving so quickly that high schools may blaze the trail toward the electronic newspaper of the future — written, edited, composed and distributed via computer. Harrower says he sees "the most innovative design at the biggest daily papers and secondly at high schools with the most progressive papers."

Beyond how a newspaper looks, computers, says

Chapter 9

The hope and the hardware of tomorrow's news

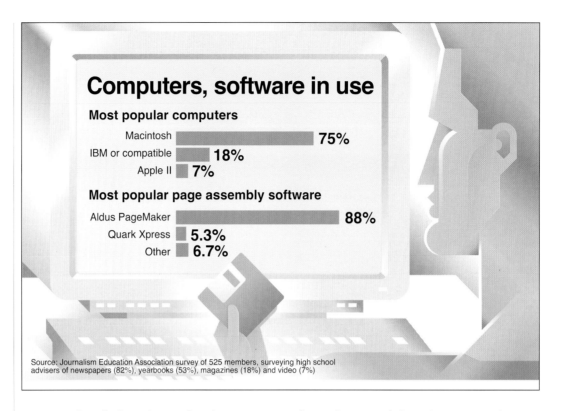

Computers, software in use

Most popular computers

Macintosh	75%
IBM or compatible	18%
Apple II	7%

Most popular page assembly software

Aldus PageMaker	88%
Quark Xpress	5.3%
Other	6.7%

Source: Journalism Education Association survey of 525 members, surveying high school advisers of newspapers (82%), yearbooks (53%), magazines (18%) and video (7%)

Harrower, have had another profound impact on the high school newsroom. The traditional newsroom hierarchy with an editor, managing editor, copy editors and writers is changing. In the past, Harrower says, "there was a clear strata and you could see a story work its way up the ladder." That structure is no longer necessary because each page may have its own editor who designs the page, works with text and might even write the text. It makes a student think in terms of the total journalistic product rather than just in terms of writing or editing or layout.

Computers are changing the face of high school journalism — mostly for the better. In the long run, computers allow students to have more power, give the newspaper a better look and are faster and cheaper than the type-edit-set-paste-up-go-to-printers style of the past. But … there are pitfalls:

• While prices have tumbled, the cost of buying enough computers to satisfy hungry writers, reporters and designers still is beyond most student newspapers.

• Advisers must become computer literate and learn which systems match their schools' needs. Newspaper computer systems definitely are not "one size fits all."

• Students can get so wrapped up in computers that the content of the newspaper suffers.

• Design and page layout may actually be slower on the computer than by hand if equipment is limited and students are constantly experimenting.

• The technology changes constantly.

Newspaper advisers across the country are dealing with a wide range of computer hardware and

software that entered their classrooms in the same way that biology teachers adapted their teaching to microscopes and shop teachers with acetylene torches. Student newspaper advisers cope with the new technology — and its costs — as best they can. Their conversations are filled with words like "want" or "would like" while they dream of The Perfect Computer System.

Irving, Texas: *The Tiger Rag,* Irving High School

Bradley Wilson's students plan to use their computers for full pagination. That means they will use their four Apple Macintosh SE30s and two Macintosh IIsi computers as electronic darkrooms, scanning their photographs on an Apple OneScanner at 300 dpi (dots per inch). Currently, they send each picture to a printer who charges them $5 per halftone and inserts the screened photograph into their layout before printing. They type and edit text with the word processor, Microsoft Word, draw graphics with Aldus FreeHand, an object-oriented drawing program, and design and lay out the paper with Aldus PageMaker.

Once the students can scan the pictures into their computers, they will be able to send the entire newspaper with the nameplate, columns of text, photographs and graphics — all placed correctly on the page — to a phototypesetting device that prints full 11-by-17 pages.

During the school year, Wilson, who is the journalism teacher at Irving High, says his computers are in use "every minute of the day."

Wilson says the computers help students produce a stronger product but the students sometimes become enticed by the computer and forget about the importance of writing solid stories and taking good pictures. He stresses that he's "teaching them journalism, not desktop publishing."

Printing bills run about $300 per issue for 3,000 copies of the paper; the total supplies budget, including film and developing, is about $5,000. Of that, only about $1,100 comes from the school. The rest comes from advertising and sales.

The Tiger Rag's computers are networked using the built-in AppleTalk connections and networking software. The built-in network is slower than other available network programs, but it is very easy to set up. The students keep all the files for the newspaper on one 80mb (megabyte) hard drive. While an 80mb disk provides plenty of storage for the text and layout files of a newspaper, it is not much space for scanned photographs that may occupy more than a megabyte of space each.

Wilson says he instructs students to back up (make electronic copies) important files onto individual floppy disks. If he had unlimited funds, he would get a more efficient backup device, like a removable hard disk or magnetic tape drive to make regular backups of the students' work. Rule of thumb for desktop publishing: The likelihood of something going wrong increases with the approach of any deadline.

Rigby, Idaho: *The Trojanier,* Rigby High School

The student journalists at Rigby High School are using full pagination, an industry technique still unusual at professional newspapers. They scan photographs using an Apple OneScanner into a Mac Classic II with 8mb of RAM (random access memory) and a hard disk. They print on two laser printers using Aldus PageMaker software and run separations to show the printer where to place spot color.

Robert S. Beck, *The Trojanier* adviser, says they converted layout for the newspaper to the Macintosh computer gradually over the past three years. They started by using the computer and laser printer as a typesetter to produce headlines and lines of text that were then cut and pasted into the newspaper format.

He noticed the computer improved the quality of the newspaper. Before computers arrived, Beck says he had a difficult time getting students to revise their work. Word processing makes revisions easy and students don't mind changing a lead or restructuring a written piece.

Before computers, students treated layout as a rushed, last-minute task to make everything fit. Once the page was complete, the students were finished. Now with computer layout, says Beck, his students are more careful about what they are doing

and more willing to experiment with the layout and design of the pages. Beck says the students spend the same amount of time reporting their stories as before computers but up to 40 hours per month, or double the time spent in years past, outside the classroom doing electronic paste-up. In summer 1993, *The Trojanier* acquired 12 new Mac LCs, which is helping the newspaper work flow problems.

Cupertino, Calif.: *El Estoque,* Monta Vista High School

Adviser Terry Cress says his experience with computers is favorable, at least in part because his school won a special grant from the state to put computers in every classroom. The person who maintains the equipment took a special interest in the newspaper and helped Cress and his staff through the transition.

El Estoque uses a number of different models of Apple Macintosh computers. The newspaper design area has only two computers, but there are more than 60 Macintosh computers in the school computer lab.

Grant money to computerize the school has been exhausted, but Cress wants to purchase a printer capable of running 11-by-17 sheets of paper. Currently, they print on three 8.5-by-11 pieces of paper and paste the text together. He says he would "like to shorten up the time it takes to put out the paper, to make more effective use of the students' time."

"I'm trying to have the students learn to communicate better, to write well, to ask good questions and to organize their ideas," Cress says. "The newspaper is just a side effect of the whole thing." In addition, the newspaper is the only academic product seen by the whole student body and that has helped the writing. "If all your peers will see what you write," he explains, "it had better be good."

Coral Gables, Fla.: *Highlights,* Coral Gables Senior High School

Brenda Feldman, a 30-year-veteran journalism teacher and adviser, came to the realization in 1988 that computers were necessary and were going to be a part of the students' lives when they left school. When that happened she "gritted her teeth and ordered the computers."

Her original worry was that the computers would hurt the students' writing and that she would lose control of what she wanted the students to get out of the class. The newspaper, *Highlights,* had won many awards for writing and Feldman saw the machines as a distraction. Feldman says she has overcome those difficulties by stressing that "the purpose of the paper is for students to learn to communicate and to write well and accurately and to have interesting content." In her opinion, if the paper isn't well-written, it doesn't matter how good it looks.

The newspaper currently has 13 IBM PCs and five laser printers. Feldman has the students print minidummies on 8.5-by-11 paper to proof the copy, then print the full-size copy in a tiled format. Their printer strips in the pictures and adds solid color and screened color for added visual effect.

Eugene, Ore.: *The Axe,* South Eugene High School

Journalism teacher Sue Barr says she keeps up with the fast-changing technology "by the seat of my pants." She says her students publish *The Axe* every three weeks during the school year. Students do almost everything on the computer including some informational graphics. The only exceptions are cartoons and photographs, which are screened and then pasted onto the camera-ready copy to be sent to the printer.

"Some of the students are frustrated by the computers and some absolutely love them," she says, "but they are all in a computer world and they accept that." Barr says the students often know more about the computers than she does and a few always seem to know enough to keep things going and trouble-shoot any problems that arise. "I don't think that is something we as advisers should be afraid of," she says. "If we hold them back to everything we know, we are really holding them back."

From the professionals' point of view

"Even though personal computers have been available for over a decade, some schools still send everything out to a printer for assembly," says Randy Stano, the director of editorial art and design for *The Miami Herald,* who gives workshops for advisers and students.

If teachers are not design literate, Stano encourages them to find someone with good design skills from an art or mechanical drawing class to help out. The same goes for those teachers who are not comfortable with computers: The computer will not go away, so teachers must find some means of making the equipment work for them.

Stano says it's important to have someone in charge of limiting extraneous use of type and design, a sort of "design cop." Even though the students may know better, he says, they get carried away with the power of the technology and use too much. In such cases, someone must step in and restrict the overuse of typefaces and graphic elements.

A number of schools are using low-quality laser printers to produce their newspapers, says Stano.

The problem is, the type comes out in a poor quality. A few schools may have the money to send the text through a RIP (Raster Image Processor) that produces high quality camera-ready copy on photo-sensitive paper or film or get access to a higher-quality laser printer. Stano says he is always surprised by the amount of color he finds in high school newspapers, both as spot color in graphic elements and in four-color separations of photographs. But printing in color can be very expensive.

Stano says that some high schools scan black and white pictures into their computers, but working with color photographs on their own computers is rare. The process of separating a color photograph on a desktop computer into CMYK (Cyan, Magenta, Yellow and Key or black) for four different printing screens is difficult and expensive even for professionals.

The (Portland) *Oregonian's* Tim Harrower is the author of *The Newspaper Designer's Handbook.* Harrower says his simple introduction to computer newspaper design has become "very popular at high schools where students and advisers instantly need to know how to fake it." Text is just one of many ways to present information. Harrower emphasizes the shapes on a page, the typography and how to package a story, using main text, graphics, photos and sidebars.

"The technology is socializing the newsroom," says Harrower. The workload has spread in such a way that it defies the traditional traffic flow of stories. That structure, much like an assembly line, is a holdover from the old technology of printing a newspaper that had to have text and images prepared in specific ways. Today, high school newsrooms that publish on desktop computers are finding they form small work groups to write, design and compose different sections of the paper. This tends to democratize the process. Harrower says, "Some advisers are finding that they appoint editors who end up with not much to do because everyone else is busy with the hands-on work of putting out the newspaper."

Computers have raised the level of design savvy needed by the typical newspaper adviser, who can't just hand the text off to a printer anymore. As new technologies like photographic scanners and digital photography become more prevalent and more affordable, students and advisers will have to learn those skills as well.

Ed Sullivan, director of the Columbia Scholastic Press Association, looks at post-computer high school journalism and says, "The biggest problem we have is untrained advisers who continually have to reinvent the wheel."

Sullivan says most high school newspapers go through the same stages when they become computerized:

First, they use desktop publishing for the first year or two as "cheap typesetting," outputting the type from the computer, pasting it up manually, and sending that to the printer with the photos scaled, cropped and marked. Then the printer puts all the pieces together, sends copy back for approval and eventually prints the paper.

The second stage is full pagination of text and some graphics with photographs screened in manually. This is what most school newspapers with computers do today.

Then most student newspapers go through the "desktop distress stage where they are using every piece of type they can possibly put on a page as well as stretching and rotating the fonts." The pages start looking like an advertisement for a collection of typefaces. It's way too busy and hard to read.

Finally, cooler heads prevail. The layout editors start looking at local newspapers and see you can have too much of a good thing. The newspapers choose a few typefaces, set standards for sizes and column widths. The papers become less cluttered.

Photos are still a problem for student papers. High schools with scanners usually use a scanned image for placement and cropping in what is known as "for position only." But in the future, says Sullivan, photographic compact disc technology, which aids in the storage of digital photographs, may make this type of desktop photographic processing a reality for high school newspapers. That will be a boon because "photography is the biggest single production weakness with high school publications," says Sullivan. But that also will be yet one more thing for the adviser to learn.

Traveling the Information Highway

Will high school students travel and talk to each other in cyberspace? Absolutely, according to Everette Dennis, executive director of The Freedom Forum Media Studies Center.

"Electronic publishing is basically an extension of all the same communication impulses that drive people to publish a student newspaper, whether it's refined or primitive," he says. "Publishing by electronic bulletin board, fax newspaper, television or cable, radio, or even experimental media involving virtual reality or some high-tech outlets as yet unimagined, means acquiring information in some systematic way and writing and editing it in a much more visual way. The only question will be how it is disseminated."

Dennis is excited about the possibilities. He predicts that students will talk back to their electronic newspapers — ask questions and get answers. News will be shaped more to accommodate their wishes and needs, based on race, gender, interests or income. Students interested in soccer can order up specific information about the game. They might write their own feature stories on the players, background reports on soccer, and the story of soccer's history at their school.

Material published previously will be easily available. "Anything ever written at that school or other schools might be accessed," Dennis says.

Will the technological revolution worsen the gap between the "haves" and "have-nots" schools in terms of equipment, leaving students at less wealthy schools out of the communications game? Dennis thinks not, at least in the long run. "The equipment's getting cheaper and cheaper, so everyone's going to have something. It might already be available for other use in the school, and could be employed for this. The danger in the short run is that when technologies first come online they are more expensive, so well-heeled schools would have a head start. But other schools will catch up relatively quickly.

"A lot of times, it's more a matter of sophistication of the teachers — knowing what's available and how to apply it," he says.

Jannette Dates, acting dean of the School of Communication at Howard University, is less sanguine about the universal use of new technology. "Students attending schools in the poorer areas of our country don't see technology as a way to help themselves. We need to devise strategies to help poor people see that technology can help them improve their lives and their circumstances. Universal availability of equipment is necessary, but it must be perceived by people as being useful to them."

One way to do this, she says, is to place the equipment where all types of people can use it to access information — in malls, libraries and schools. And make it appealing to those with less sophistication — the information poor as well as the information rich — with icons, graphics, illustrations.

"Beguiling use of the Internet"

Terry Thibodeaux is a former English teacher, journalism adviser and now librarian at Scotlandville Magnet High School in Baton Rouge, La. In 1993, he joined the board of the Louisiana Scholastic Press Association. His job is to explore journalism, telecommunications and electronic innovations, such as electronic reference sources and networking. Thibodeaux says he will determine "how these new electronic means may affect scholastic journalism."

He believes one of the most interesting possibilities for the future may be the Internet — a huge network initially financed in part by the National Science Foundation. Nearly all the major colleges and universities in the United States are on the Internet. While there is no organized national program to get high schools on the Internet, several states, including Texas, New York and Virginia, are

On Jan. 10, 1994, Bell Atlantic Corporation and TCI announced the "largest corporate program ever to link classrooms to the nation's information superhighway."

The "Basic Education Connection" is scheduled to link 26,000 schools — about one-fourth of all elementary and secondary schools in the nation — to the two-way data and video network being developed by the two companies. The Internet will be among the services linked to the schools.

The Internet is an informal connection among thousands of computers in universities and companies. Someone at the keyboard of an individual computer can communicate easily with several dozen others, and each of the others has a simple connection to a further group of computers, resulting finally in a global network. Through the Internet, a student could research data or exchange information with others throughout the world. Few high schools are linked to Internet yet, but there is a High School Scholastic Journalism Bulletin Board, initiated by Eddie Blick at Louisiana Tech University, whose Internet address is:

blick@vm.cc.latech.edu

working to building interest among public schools.

He sees student journalists using the Internet in two ways:

• First, as a pure research tool used in much the same way that journalists use interviews and other references. Internet access may open the door to a bigger, faster and ultimately more useful source of journalistic information. Thibodeaux says his limited experience with the Internet has led him to "White House news releases, new access points to Congress and the Supreme Court and a multitude of other sources of information."

• Second, as a way of networking with other students to improve their skills and learn what other school newspapers are doing. They will be able to ask other students across the nation or around the world about student issues, newspaper content and technical areas from software secrets to computer repairs.

To make things easier for the students, Thibodeaux has put together a kind of road map to the Internet — a brief description and the exact address of different areas on the network. Many adults can't get through the "Internet curtain," he says, because "we are all so caught up with the tool (of the computer) itself that we can't get beyond it." Students, on the other hand, he says, "are incredibly nimble with the transparent but often beguiling use of the Internet."

In addition to the Internet, consumer online services like Prodigy and America Online have a lot of useful information including news stories and the ability to communicate electronically.

What will this mean in the creation of new, alternative opportunities for students in journalism?

Peter Grunwald, longtime industry analyst and California-based developer and marketer of information services, sees a difficult "threshold barrier" to telecommunications in most high school classrooms. After all, most classrooms are not connected electronically and most communication is one way, from teacher to students. But a growing number of journalism classrooms have both computers and dedicated phone lines, so student newspapers could well be the pioneers in school telecommunications.

Ernest Boyer, president of The Carnegie Foundation for the Advancement of Teaching and former commissioner of education during the Carter administration, is distressed that teaching is still primarily lecture-based. "We have not come to grips with a world that has overwhelmed us," he said to a national seminar of education writers. "If we could creatively bring technology into classrooms we would have the best-educated population on the planet by the end of the decade."

Youth News Service

Candace Perkins, a journalism teacher and newspaper adviser at St. Charles (Ill.) High School, is one of the pioneers who is helping students take advantage of new technology and, in the process, create a new kind of youth voice.

In 1988, she joined four other journalism teachers for a weeklong organizing and training session that spurred the electronic version of Youth News Service, an online bulletin board and electronic mail system now operating for student journalists, linked up through the GTE Educational Network Services.

"I was convinced that we were at the beginning of another use of computers that no one in education was bothering to pursue. A lot of people had bought into word processing and were beginning to get into desktop publishing, but not much else," says Perkins, who is president of the Journalism Education Association.

"Everything I read about what the world was going to be like in the year 2000 suggested that we would need to give our students a jump-start on using computer telecommunications if they were going to make it work for us."

YNS offers student journalists in any community in the United States, Europe or Asia the chance to communicate with other school users as well as the YNS national bureau in Washington, D.C., where weekly stories are filed for all subscribers — feature and investigative pieces about teen life in the '90s, as well as news briefs, reviews and editorials. Much of the material is culled from school member publications.

One barrier to subscribing to this or other online services is a less-than-high-tech problem. To communicate, the school newsroom must have a telephone and modem. This is as much a political challenge — "Why should the journalism teacher have a special phone line?" — as a fiscal and technical one of adding a line to the school's system.

The survey by the Southern Interscholastic Press Association in 1993 indicated that 58 percent of journalism advisers responding had a telephone in their classrooms.

Despite obstacles, Perkins believes that the future of telecomputing for student journalism is bright.

"I like it that my students can see, firsthand, that young people across the country are dealing with the same kinds of problems and have the same kinds of concerns that they do."

One of her students agrees. Working with Youth News Service has "helped me realize there's a world outside our small community," says Kirin Kalia, St. Charles High School YNS bureau chief during the 1991-92 school year.

Kirin, the product of an upper-class suburban high school with little racial or ethnic diversity, collaborated via computer with Mai Dang, an editor and reporter at *New Expression* and a student at Von Steuben Metropolitan Science Center, a Chicago city school with a varied ethnic student body. Their story, about the effect that their respective schools' demographics has on teens, won a national award from the Quill and Scroll Society.

An electronic newspaper for students

A project at the University of Missouri School of Journalism takes computer journalism to the next level. The *Digital Missourian* is an electronic newspaper.

Charles Hammer, managing editor of the *Digital Missourian,* says the project is run from the journalism school to about 20 computers located at 14 public schools (elementary, junior, and senior highs) in the area. University students edit copy from news services such as The Associated Press into stories, which are sent by telephone to computers in the schools.

"The beauty of the project is we're able to tailor the content to the school systems. Our distribution costs are nothing … just a phone call," says Hammer.

The system is based on the Optel Newspaper System software that was designed to deliver graphics to local newspapers at the relatively slow transmission rate of 2400 baud. Jock Mirow, who worked on the original project, says the software is easy for the editors and writers who publish on the system and for readers who look at the news. The University of Missouri is successfully using the software today, even though the small company that developed it disbanded because the product was not accepted by the newspaper industry.

Mirow says their goal was to interest young people in reading newspapers. "When you are competing with Nickelodeon and Nintendo you have a difficult time getting kids to read black and white text," says Mirow. "We felt this software system was a viable halfway point between pure entertainment and having news in a computer interface."

When students visit the media center at school, they may call up international, national and local news stories, photographs, graphics and advertisements. Compared with online information services, such as Prodigy and CompuServe, the *Digital Missourian* is quite a lively and cost-effective product.

The *Digital Missourian* is connected electronically to about 20 computers located at 14 public schools in the Columbia, Mo., area. Managing Editor Charles Hammer, above, says "Our distribution costs are nothing … just a phone call."

Student television often plays a more significant role in the life of the school than newspapers. In some cases, TV is the only journalistic outlet.

Chapter 10

Video: Plugged-in journalism

Hidden away in an imposing four-story brick building on Chicago's South Side is a tiny windowless room where students are producing videotapes about their own lives with two low-cost cameras, two videocassette recorders, and a simple editing machine.

There are no white, Asian or Latino students among the 1,200 enrolled here at Paul Robeson High School.

We are watching *Think About the Consequences,* a 10-minute drama about gang life written and produced by Robeson students. The script writer is Maurice Hill, a 17-year-old whose parents are dead. Maurice lives with his grandmother and his 20-month-old son.

"It's the best thing I've done here," Maurice explains. "Television reaches kids. It helps us make sense of our lives."

Maurice says this school, secured at all times by several police officers, is a haven from the dangers that start just beyond the school's front door. This small editing room has given him a home away from home, and his best hope for escaping the gang life we have just witnessed on video. Maurice wants to get a job in television production.

Orchestrating the video class is Markie Hancock, an energetic 33-year-old former film producer, who is officially a history teacher. Hancock, a former divinity school student, and her young producers demonstrate what can be done with minimal equipment and an overflow of energy and enthusiasm. There is no school newspaper here, so the video class is the only outlet for journalistic interests.

Students' productions are shown at lunch time in the cafeteria. Student-made music videos are the most popular. Even the teachers like the videos. "I'm trying to teach them an aesthetic point of view, rather than just techniques of production," says Hancock.

In a similar neighborhood about a mile away stands Hyde Park Career Academy, a magnet school with about 2,200 students. On this day at dismissal time, hundreds of students stream out of the school, between two towering neoclassical Greek columns, and under the watchful eye of police officers in three patrol cars parked nearby.

Edwin Posey has been teaching video production at Hyde Park for almost 10 years. He graduated from the high school in 1981 and came back two years later to help teach the video class. He knows the school, and its students, inside out.

The school's TV studio is basic by professional standards but luxurious in contrast to the facilities at Paul Robeson High. In the late 1980s, Posey's students competed against 20 Chicago high schools at a Chicago video fair. It established Hyde Park's program as one of the best in the city.

In the 1992-93 school year, Posey's video program lost its funding. Just finding the money to buy blank videotapes is difficult. But somehow the program goes on. For unlike print journalism, video programs can manage on little money once the recording and playback equipment is in place. Unlike school newspapers, there are no printing or distribution costs with each edition. A video program can get by with trimmed-down productions, do-it-yourself repairs and reused tapes. Hyde Park students still produce public service announcements

133

Video lures students at Chicago schools

Students from Chicago's tough streets have a chance to express themselves through video journalism and production. Students at Paul Robeson High School find a haven in the video class.

Photo at left: Markie Hancock teaches video production. Above: Marvin Childs, left, and Maurice Hill look at new camera. Right: Nicole Smith, camera, Khanden Howse and Latricia Brown, interview students.

Left: Latoya Evans (camera) and Marvin Childs interview students. Below: Maurice Hill with his son Maurice Jr. watch the anti-gang video he wrote, directed and produced.

Career Academy boasts prize-winning productions

Despite an absence of funding, Edwin Posey, the adviser, continues a program at Hyde Park Career Academy that became known as one of the best in the city during the 1980s.

Left: At Hyde Park Career Academy, Cassandra Bryant and Edwin Posey (kneeling) in video class studio. Below: Ira Rolark looks over yearbook from when his teacher, Edwin Posey was a student.

Edwin Posey repairs aging video equipment.

and commercials as part of the television production class. They also tape football games and school plays.

Video comes of age

Simply put, video is exploding in our schools.

Visits to schools across America and interviews with teachers and media education experts begin to paint a picture of what is happening:

• The content of student television programs tends to be superficial and does not have the investigative edge that some high school newspapers have achieved. In most schools, television and print journalism programs operate separately with little overlap between the two.

• Student-produced television programs often operate without an organized curriculum and are of widely uneven quality. Most programs are operating with minimal equipment and meager budgets, making production of high-quality programs difficult.

• Perhaps because of the lighter content, and because it may be more difficult to monitor, there may be less censorship of broadcast material than of printed material.

• As with student newspapers, high school television programs are grappling with the issue of diversity — how to attract students from diverse racial and ethnic backgrounds to both sides of the camera. There is some evidence that television projects are able to reach students who normally would have enrolled in print journalism classes.

• Video technology is being integrated into the classroom in new ways. Traditional boundaries between video journalism and other parts of the school curriculum are becoming blurred, resulting in a healthier integration of journalism into the academic life of the school.

• Although strong programs do exist, radio is a declining force in schools.

Dearborn, Mich.

In 1980, when Russ Gibb began his television production class at Dearborn High School in Dearborn, Mich., he was an educational oddity in the Detroit area. Now he has been joined by nearly 30 other schools. There are enough teachers to warrant their own organization, Detroit Area Film and Television Educators. In 1993, a video festival sponsored by the Detroit Institute of Arts featured the work of more than 500 students from two dozen high schools.

Broward County, Fla.

In Broward County, Fla., students from 15 high schools in and around Fort Lauderdale produce the monthly *Broward Teen News* for local cable channels. The program started in 1990 with six schools and is sparking growing interest throughout the dis-

trict. To participate, schools must offer television production classes. Since *Broward Teen News* went on the air, a dozen county schools have added their own TV studios.

Alyce Culpepper, a former journalism teacher who heads up the effort, can barely keep up with all the schools that want to get involved. "I physically can't get to all these schools," she says, referring to the sprawling school district. She says it is not uncommon some months to put 1,000 miles on her car driving from school to school. Culpepper offers six classes in television production for teachers at the county schools' Instructional Television Center.

In some schools as many as five television production classes are offered. All high schools in the district publish newspapers, but in some enrollment in television classes exceeds newspaper participation. A large part of the attraction, says Culpepper, is the team approach required in television in contrast to the more solitary work of print journalism.

New York

On the steps outside Middle College High School in New York City, Jessica Roman, an articulate 15 year old, describes how she watches about seven hours of television a day. Sixteen-year-old Bielka Gallegos watches between four and 10 hours a day. Paul Greaves, a sophomore, says a six-hour stint in front of the tube is not unusual for him.

"Nobody likes to read nowadays," says Paul. Newspapers are phony, he says, adding, "Television is our parents."

However, instead of being addicted television consumers, Paul and his classmates are becoming active producers. They are the pumped-up students in Mario Chioldi's video production class in this alternative high school situated in a wing of La Guardia Community College in Queens. The class demonstrates the ability of video to reach students on the margins of the public school system.

Middle College High serves students who were unsuccessful in regular school settings. The goal is to give them a sense of what it is like to be on a college campus in the hope they will approach education with a greater sense of purpose. In addition, the most successful students are given the opportunity to take college courses before they graduate from high school. The program works, and has been replicated in a dozen other communities, including Richmond, Calif., and South Central Los Angeles.

The video program got its start because of the altruism of the school's teaching staff. Every year the school gives each teacher a voucher worth $250 for classroom materials. Instead of spending the money on individual classrooms, Middle College High's teachers pooled their vouchers one year to buy what Chioldi calls a "low-end" video camera.

Chioldi first used video in a psychology class in

which students made short videotapes about their dreams. Chioldi points out that in addition to teaching students the fundamentals of video production, the project also helped students understand basic literary concepts such as symbolism and metaphor.

Today Chioldi's video production class is integrated into the rest of the curriculum. For example, students in video production, English and ecology classes joined forces to make a documentary on a reforestation project in nearby Forest Park. Students in the ecology class did the research, English students wrote the script, and Chioldi's students did the video. The film, *It's About Time,* was so successful, it was shown at a student ecology exhibit at the United Nations.

For another project, Chioldi's students filmed grade school students' reactions to racial insults and redid a famous social science experiment demonstrating that minority children are more likely to view white dolls as more attractive than black dolls. The film is being used by teachers in several elementary schools to help counter negative racial stereotypes.

In the spring of 1993, Chioldi's students began working on a documentary about violence, taking

Jessica Roman, a student at Middle College High School in New York City, says video gives her a chance to perform and to do research.

Mario Chioldi, who teaches video production, says, "The more young people have access to this kind of medium, the less they are likely to be seduced by the slickness of TV."

137

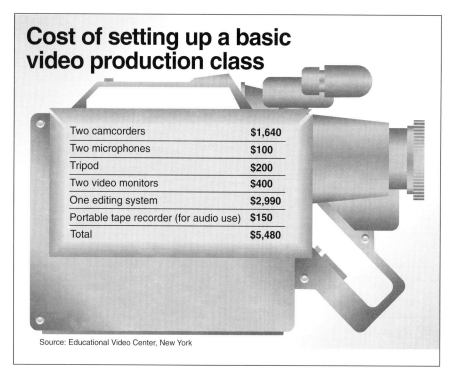

Cost of setting up a basic video production class

Two camcorders	$1,640
Two microphones	$100
Tripod	$200
Two video monitors	$400
One editing system	$2,990
Portable tape recorder (for audio use)	$150
Total	$5,480

Source: Educational Video Center, New York

on issues such as rape, crime, and teenage suicide.

Jessica Roman says working on the documentary on violence fits in perfectly with her career interests to be either an actress or a criminal lawyer by giving her a chance to perform as well as to do research. "This is the most important thing to me," she says, "because violence is something we live every day of our lives."

At any one time, 15 to 20 students out of an enrollment of 500 are in the video class. Most students here never used a video camera before enrolling in the class. Chioldi admits many projects don't end in a finished product. But then, he says, "a lot of Hollywood projects never get finished either."

He says his goal is not journalism in the traditional sense but, rather, to give his students some control over a medium that shapes their lives in fundamental ways. "The more young people have access to this kind of medium, the less they are likely to be seduced by the slickness of TV," he says. By understanding video techniques, the "less likely it is they will think it comes down from the hands of God."

Medium of the young

Television is gaining ground in high schools because TV is the main teenage medium. On average, teenagers watch about 21 hours of television a week, compared to 5.6 hours doing homework and 1.8 hours reading for pleasure, according to a 1992 report by the Carnegie Council on Adolescent Development.

When young people think of going into journalism, they are more likely to think about TV's Con-

nie Chung, Ted Koppel or Tom Brokaw rather than newspaper Pulitzer Prize winners Bob Woodward, Anna Quindlen or Acel Moore.

To most young people, television is tied closely to music, fashion and other dimensions in their lives. Newspapers seem to be local forms of expression, often with little impact within the youth culture. Also many students see the local press as more enemy than friend — too often reporting the bad things that happen in their neighborhoods, ignoring the good.

Aside from television's hold on the youth culture, other forces are driving electronic journalism in the classroom.

Many young people have experience with video equipment before they ever sign up for a broadcasting class; many already have produced their own documentaries.

The low cost of camcorders and videocassette recorders also means that, for a modest investment, high schools can create broadcast production facilities. For about $10,000, schools can purchase a basic video camera, video monitor, and two editing systems. The cost of a fully-equipped television studio, however, could be upward of $100,000.

Once a production facility is established, the cost of running it and producing programs can be minimal compared to the cost of producing a school newspaper, with its ongoing expenditures such as printing, newsprint, and photographic supplies. The main expense is equipment repair and purchase of videocassettes.

The added touch: Advisers find that the conversational, upbeat writing style required for television may be more accessible and less intimidating to young people than the often-stilted style required in many journalism programs. Some teachers, rather than viewing electronic journalism as a threat, use it to attract students who resist signing up for print programs.

Wiring the schools

An unexpected influence has come from Whittle Communications, the producers of Channel One, the controversial in-classroom 12-minute daily newscast, complete with commercials. As of 1993, Channel One was watched by some 8 million junior and senior high school students. To get those viewers Channel One installed video monitors in every classroom of its 12,000 participating schools.

Those Channel One monitors provide a way to communicate instantly with the entire school and are stimulating the emergence of daily or weekly video news-style magazines produced by the students themselves. According to Channel One executives, about 15 percent of participating schools — between 1,500 and 1,800 — are producing their own news shows, using the Channel One system. In some cases, these have taken the place of school newspapers.

Experience counts

There is a substantial pool of professionals who have worked in the video industry — for example, in cable, industrial films or documentaries. And because so many video professionals are accustomed to working on a part-time or free-lance basis, they have been willing to work in the schools as part-time consultants, teaching one or two classes as they are needed. That means in many schools video instructors often have more experience in what they are teaching than newspaper advisers who typically have not worked in daily journalism.

The down side of this arrangement is that many of these video professionals have worked in the production side of the industry, and have strong technical skills rather than strong news or writing skills. This contributes to the major weakness of broadcast journalism programs: the absence of a strong editorial or news focus.

What's on the air

Many high schools have had broadcast journalism programs for years, but these usually involved small numbers of students working primarily on the technical aspects of electronic media. Often the programs took place in the context of a well-established school television studio, where students recorded offerings from, for example, public television and then made them available for classroom use.

Often schools had their own cable channels, which would broadcast these preproduced shows. In some cases, students would produce their own talk shows, tape sports events or school plays. Rarely did the broadcast program attempt any significant news coverage or become a force within the life of the school. However, it played a valuable function in training young people interested in careers in broadcasting.

Today, these early efforts have been overtaken by more ambitious projects. In some cases, students produce their own newscasts, which are broadcast schoolwide. Or they do video documentaries, oral histories, dramas, music videos and other television forms as part of their regular curriculum.

Video education is stretching to meet the needs, demands and interests of students and teachers.

Video freedom

The transient nature of video, within the hectic atmosphere of many high schools, means that for the most part electronic journalism programs have escaped the intense scrutiny to which high school newspapers have been subjected. In part, that's because most school administrators do not regard video productions as the official voice of the school.

Also, administrators and advisers have little legal guidance on how to handle video productions because none of the landmark lawsuits on the high school press deals directly with the electronic media.

That could change if daily broadcasts replace the school newspapers. Also a regular daily newscast broadcast to classrooms — not shown at odd hours on obscure cable channels — is likely to draw more attention from administrators.

If students are allowed to roam freely in a school environment, capturing on videotape incidents that are only impartially and belatedly written about in a school newspaper, video could increasingly come to be viewed as a subversive influence, attracting attention and censorship from school administrators.

So far, however, school officials seem to be most likely to censor language or images they regard as offensive — in song lyrics, music videos and student comments.

But because electronic journalism is still largely unorganized and only just emerging as a force in schools, it has not caught the censor's eye.

Many channels from One

It's 7:30 a.m. and an odd, almost unsettling, silence spreads through the halls of Wheeling Park High School, a long, single-story building perched on an isolated hillside on the outskirts of Wheeling, W. Va.

Instead of settling down to classes, students in every classroom are watching Channel One, the 12-minute program produced by Whittle Communications and broadcast in a growing number of schools around the United States.

The program races by, with quick segments on the Rodney King trial and President Clinton's economic program. It is followed by *What's Up Park,* a short student-produced program.

So what's wrong with this picture? To the horror of many educators, each segment of Channel One is interspersed with commercials pushing products like Mountain Dew and Secret Deodorant.

Whatever the pros and cons of Channel One, it appears to have brought unexpected benefits. Here, as at other schools, the ability to broadcast into each classroom directly has opened up the possibility of home-grown newscasts as a companion to Channel One.

According to Jim Ritts, Whittle's president for network relations, about 15 percent of schools with Channel One are producing some form of auxiliary news program — programs defined as student-based with some faculty involvement — and broadcasting them on Channel One.

Wheeling Park High has 1,800 students, most from solidly middle-income backgrounds. It is the one high school for all of Ohio County. Ninety-five percent of the students are white and almost all the rest are black.

The broadcast program was put together over 15 years by Pat Clutter, who worked closely with WTRF, a local commercial television station.

Channel One "was a good way to get a distribution system in at no cost to us," says Carl Bowman, the school's technology director, who estimates the package was worth $100,000 to the school.

In addition, the school district was able to convince voters to approve a $4.2 million bond measure, mainly for technological improvements in the district's 16 schools.

As a result, the school has been able to expand its broadcast offerings. Three times a week students produce the *Patriot Connection,* a10-minute broadcast. On the other days students broadcast *What's Up Park.*

"Channel One caused the explosion," says the principal, George Krelis. Teachers, he says, are able to use the material in Channel One to stimulate classroom discussion. In addition, teachers can structure classes around special reports on topics such as race relations and AIDS. "There's a very direct link between what is offered on Channel One and what is offered here. It has done nothing but expand the capabilities of classroom teachers."

Students are not required to watch Channel One, and a walk through the school while the program is on reveals that only about half are actually watching. But senior Matt DiLorenzo, who works on the television show, says as soon as the *Patriot Connection* comes on, students pay attention. "I think students watch *Patriot Connection* more than they watch Channel One," DiLorenzo says. "It's about our students."

Melody Worls took over the program in January 1993 when Clutter took a leave of absence. "There's never a dull moment. We work as team. Everyone gets a chance. It doesn't matter how good or bad they are," she says.

Clutter says he designed the program to serve teenagers. "Our audience is not adults," he says. "Throughout this whole effort, kids have a voice and a medium through which they can express themselves."

Mixing media

When computer-savvy people start to talk about "CD-ROMs," they are often discussing the computerized combination of print and video.

South Eugene High School in Eugene, Ore., has been using CD-ROM (Compact Disc-Read Only Memory) since the 1990-91 school year when journalism teacher Sue Barr team-taught with Tom Layton, the school's former computer coordinator, now a teacher. Layton had applied to the Apple computer company and a yearbook publisher for grants to produce a student yearbook on CD-ROM. In the spring of 1991, the vendors gave the school equipment, software and some technical assistance. The disks the students produced would only run on a Macintosh computer.

The Electronic Eugenean, the CD-ROM yearbook of the high school, has been produced for three years. In addition to having photographs of students and staff, various editions of *The Electronic Eugenean* feature an animated map that lets the user "walk" through the school facilities with changing views of the hallways, back issues of the student newspaper, *The Axe,* issues of *South High News,* the informational newsletter published by the school, and short audio clips that play at unexpected moments. The CD-ROM yearbook is an impressive high school journalism project.

Layton says that after spending thousands of hours putting together and publishing a couple of yearbooks on CD-ROM, the students developed a piece of software they call Digital Publisher. It organizes the text, pictures, sound and graphic elements of a multimedia CD-ROM.

In the fall of 1992, the students began working with the Oregon School for the Deaf on a CD-ROM project — a multimedia dictionary of American Sign Language that will let users view a digitized video sequence on the screen of the correct "sign" for each word. This product uses Apple QuickTime to produce the video on the screen.

In 1993 the students also began working with a local newspaper, *The* (Eugene) *Register Guard,* developing a CD-ROM product about old-growth forests incorporating *Register Guard* articles and photographs.

In addition to their grants and gifts of computer equipment and software, the students have been rolling their profits from desktop-publishing projects back into buying the latest computer hardware. Students also train teachers on computers for $10 per hour; the fees come from the teachers' supplies budget. Eventually, says Layton, they may decide to sell their software to a yearbook publisher or to other high schools.

Layton says his students are learning 21st century skills, particularly working in groups on deadline. "In the workplace of the future," Layton says, "people will be put in front of a computer with software they have never used and a project due at the end of the month and we want our students to develop the skills to deal with that situation."

Meeting daily deadlines

The television studios at Connersville High School in Connersville, Ind., are already crowded with students by 9 a.m. It's like this most mornings at this school in a blue-collar neighborhood. The school, with an enrollment of 1,450 students, is situated in a demographically mixed area with farms nestled next to a Ford assembly plant and other factories. Ninety-eight percent of the students are white.

Every day from 9 a.m. to noon the students prepare a live, 20-minute program that broadcasts to every classroom in the school and over a local cable channel as well.

In the pressure of daily deadlines, Joe Glowacki has built one of the most sophisticated high school television production programs in the nation. The facility is divided into two parts. First, there is the studio where the news anchors and student reporters read the news in front of three clunky-looking television cameras. Then there is a much smaller control room crammed full of racks of videocassette recorders, editing consoles, a switching board, and three long tables where students work on the daily production.

A daily hurricane would be a more accurate description. One student, scrawling on a white board with a green marking pen, writes a script for a feature on a student proposal to start graduation with a prayer service — a reaction to a recent Supreme Court decision. Another, the meteorologist for the day, practices his script in front of a camera.

Glowacki, seemingly unperturbed, takes care of a stream of student requests. "Mr. G, should both of these channels be up?" one student yells out, while two others have a more pressing issue on their minds. They discuss their purchase of prom dresses the day before. "I got the magenta one," one says. "It looks so pretty."

Worried by distractions like these, senior Stacy Mengedoht anxiously looks at the clock. "It's 11 o'clock already." Glowacki reassures her. "You have plenty of time." In the middle of the maelstrom, the bell rings, the students leave, and a new group arrives.

The pace quickens as the show's deadline approaches. Two students put up new graphics for the title of the show; old ones have mysteriously disappeared. Another student listens to cassettes to pick out music tracks. Two others lay out the videotapes with each prepackaged segment of the show — 16 of them — on the table in front of the control board.

Minutes before noon, three student anchors take their seats behind the set, as four others wheel the studio cameras into place. A bell rings. "OK, here we are, let's go," student director Julie Long announces in the control booth.

The show, *CHS TODAY*, unfolds seamlessly. Julie issues instructions calmly, and assistant producer Jonathan Raver, doubling as the weatherman, inserts one videotape after the next into a stack of videocassette recorders. Sarah Loyd's story on school prayer comes first, followed by one on the school's

speech team making it into a competition finals, and another piece warning students not to take shortcuts across the courtyard, which has been turned into a muddy swamp by weeks of rain and snow. Another segment covers the latest marketing fad pushing "crystal clear" products ranging from Crystal Clear Pepsi to clear dish washing soap. "You're not only purchasing a product, but buying into the latest marketing craze," the student reporter warns.

Meanwhile, in the classrooms, some students are watching *CHS TODAY* intently while others talk or do homework.

Despite the inattention of some students, the show is a real presence in the school compared to the newspaper. Across the courtyard from the television studio, Debi Cole, in her ninth year as journalism adviser, is struggling to keep the paper afloat.

The lead story in the latest issue of *The Clarion* is a feature article about a nearby steam train that is still running. Other articles are about the school band's participation in the state championships, and an article on the latest school play, *The Nerd*.

Until 1992, the paper was funded out of student activity fees and printed monthly during the school year. But now students must buy subscriptions, and so far only about 300 students have. To make matters worse, Steve Kaiser, the principal, has told the paper it can only print four issues a year.

Cole hints that the newspaper is being picked on for the most trivial mistakes. "You can see our mistakes more easily [than on television]," she says, referring to *CHS TODAY*. "You can't hear typos on video."

She also laments that fewer students seem interested in the newspaper program these days compared to Glowacki's television unit nearby. "We have become a visual society. People don't want to read anymore."

From her perspective, a whole raft of stories are off-limits for coverage by her staff, including stories on abortion, AIDS or teenage pregnancy. However, Kaiser says he has not put any restrictions on what the paper can cover. Rather, he is concerned about superficial coverage of issues. He believes most students don't have the ability to cover complicated issues with the required sensitivity. "We're not here to create sensationalism," he says.

Yet the only time he had concerns about the television show was when it showed a clip from a Madonna video with excessive nudity. He complains about the "shallowness" of some of the reporting he has seen on *CHS TODAY*. But he concedes that he has not watched the program for the past 18 months.

That kind of hands-off attitude has given the 48-year-old Glowacki, who has been running the television program since 1968, a good deal of leeway.

Over five years, he has been able to accumulate equipment, now worth about $100,000.

Glowacki worries that, given the pressure he is under to produce a live show every day, he is unable to spend more time to develop story ideas. "You don't often have kids who are mature enough to function without a whole lot of direction and guidance," he says, "and I don't always have the time to devote the period to working on one story."

In spite of that, some of his students have tackled controversial issues. One notable production was by Misty Ellis, a star student in 1992, who won first place in a statewide contest for her documentary on date rape.

The students in Glowacki's program are among the most academically gifted in the school, and he recognizes that they may not be representative of the entire school. Until recently he had a strict policy of only admitting students with A or B averages. Now he has relaxed that policy somewhat. "I have an inner conflict about putting on a good newscast, and my responsibility to teach kids," he says.

What's clear is that Glowacki has taught students to function successfully in a television environment. It can open doors to students who want to go on in broadcast journalism. "I don't teach this for kids to become professional broadcasters," he says. "I teach it so they will at least be ahead of anyone that they are going to be interviewing against."

As if to prove his point, Misty Ellis, now an 18-year-old freshman at Western Kentucky University in Bowling Green, Ky., drops by to visit. She has already landed a job as an editor at a TV station in Bowling Green.

Where print and video live together

John Coffman, the journalism adviser at Reynoldsburg High School in Reynoldsburg, Ohio, spends a lot of time running from one end of his school to another. At one end is the tiny office housing the eight computers where students put out the *Compass,* the hard-hitting school newspaper.

At the other end is the television studio, where bright orange plastic chairs dot the room and equipment is stacked up in a haphazard pile in a corner near the on-air set. A backdrop reads: "Newscenter 25" in large letters. This is the place where students produce a daily seven-minute newscast called *Newscenter 25.*

Coffman is in charge of both print and electronic broadcast programs. Unlike most high school journalism classes, where television and print classes barely acknowledge each other, Coffman's involvement in both shows the potential of more closely integrating the two.

The school, with more than 1,000 students, has a largely white enrollment, with black students comprising seven percent of the student population.

Coffman says students are from lower-middle to upper-middle class backgrounds.

Some students say they are only interested in either television or print programs. "I love TV," says Craig Daniels, a senior who does mostly weather and sports reports. "I did not care about the newspaper." Other students are loyal to print. Some students are working on both the newspaper and the television program. "If students do a big story for the newspaper, they might do a follow-up on the news show," Craig says.

Curiously, it is rare for students in the broadcasting program to transfer to the print program, although it happens much more frequently the other way around. "The newspaper students seem to have a much more serious attitude," says Craig, as a partial explanation.

Attitude or not, students working on the TV program and the newspaper are often the only ones at the school late at night, jointly ordering pizza as they face looming deadlines. "The relationship [between the staffs] is very good," he says. One indication is that *Newscenter 25* broadcasts public service announcements to recruit students for the newspaper.

After running the print journalism program for eight years, Coffman expanded the curriculum in 1980 to include television. He took some video production classes, and students began producing a weekly half-hour cable television program with the help of the speech and drama teacher. It was a primitive, black-and-white operation.

"A lot of my fellow journalism teachers shy away from broadcasting and say that all they are going to do is print," says Coffman. "We had better pay attention to it, and compete with it."

In 1986, Coffman was able to convince the school superintendent that a poor quality, black-and-white production did not show off the district at its best. He received $32,000 to buy equipment to produce the show in color, an editing system, and two in-studio cameras.

When the school was wired to receive Channel One in 1991, Coffman abandoned the cable show and, instead, began producing a live in-school program during the second period, which was lengthened by seven minutes to accommodate the show.

Coffman helps cover the costs of the program with an ingenious student birthday feature. Students send in photographs of friends and in exchange for $1 the show will broadcast each photo with birthday greetings. Some students send in numerous photos, which means more money for the television coffers.

A 1993 broadcast, for example, carried brief announcements on the Rodney King trial, Yeltsin's problems in Russia, followed by birthday announcements, and a brief feature on three stink bombs that were thrown in the hallways.

Coffman's main concern is that students in the TV program are reluctant to take on substantial or controversial issues. He says his students tell him that kind of coverage would not appeal to their peers.

"We feel hard news is good, but depending on what it is, people are not going to watch it," says Craig. But it is not as if students would have to look very far for a model to emulate. The school's newspaper, the *Compass,* comes out 10 times a year and is an impressive 20-page publication.

"Racism seems to have hit Reynoldsburg High School along with hundreds of other schools across the country," a lead story on race relations began. "And although there has not been much physical violence on campus, students complain of verbal exchanges, threats and ill feelings among the races represented at the school."

The story went on to detail several confrontations between black and white students, and the administration's efforts to ease tensions.

"Stink bombs, physical abuse, verbal abuse, disrespect. All seem to be a part of daily life in high schools across America," began another story on discipline problems at the local junior high school. "They're a part of life for Reynoldsburg Junior High School students and teachers too."

Another issue reported on the conviction of two former Reynoldsburg students, ages 15 and 16, on murder charges, on the resignation of the school's band director for an undisclosed "indiscretion," and how poor magazine sales intended to raise funds for the prom could mean a radical revision of the school's annual extravaganza.

The reluctance to tackle such serious issues on television is even more surprising in light of the hands-off attitude of the administration. The principal reviews each issue of the newspaper before it goes to print, but after previewing the TV program during the first week it aired, he abandoned the practice.

One big constraint is time, Coffman says. Students must produce the daily show during the first period for broadcast at the beginning of the second period. That makes in-depth reporting on TV almost impossible.

Despite these obstacles, Coffman's efforts demonstrate that integrating television and print programs sets up a healthy tension in which young people are exposed to both media, and learn about the opportunities and weaknesses in both.

A new world of possibilities

My name is Millie Reyes. I am a teenager, and I was raised in Harlem and lived in a building with broken windows, garbage, rats and no hot water. This is a film I made with other teenagers about my family, *my neighbors as we struggle to survive under these conditions.*

This is New York, one of the richest, most glamorous cities in the world, a playground for the rich and famous. But there is another side to New York, an ugly side, a side which is ignored by many.

—Opening scene from
2371 Second Avenue: An East Harlem Story

Millie Reyes' documentary about East Harlem dramatically portrays life for young people in poverty. It also presents a model of what is possible for high school students to achieve in terms of the content and quality of production.

Reyes, a high school senior whose family is from Puerto Rico, spent a semester as an intern at the Educational Video Center (EVC) in Manhattan, a non-profit youth training center that is independent of the schools.

Its location in New York gives the center certain advantages — and also makes it difficult to copy elsewhere. For example, New York City gives credit to students for a semester of part-time study. EVC's students are able to receive more intensive training — three hours a day —and produce more ambitious videos and documentaries than would be possible in a regular high school class.

Steven Goodman, EVC's 35-year-old executive director, got his start in documentary journalism while producing an independent documentary on youth gangs in the South Bronx.

He began the non-profit Educational Video Center as a way "to empower inner-city youth through the creative use of media." Most of the funding comes from private foundations.

In an interview in the center's neat offices on the fourth floor of an East Village building in New York City, Goodman explains that his center takes a "Deweyan approach" to working with young people. "Learning by doing," he calls it. And, he says, the video documentary presents "the richest possibilities for learning" because it involves research, reporting, writing, using a camera and editing.

In the spring of 1992, students produced documentaries on cultural stereotypes facing Native-American students. Another group taped community meetings on school violence and conflict resolution. Others did a documentary capturing the complexities of life for recent immigrants from the Dominican Republic.

Then, in an impressive breakthrough for youth-produced television, a documentary titled *Unequal Education: Failing Our Children,* comparing schools serving middle class students and poor students in the Bronx, was broadcast as part of Bill Moyers' *Listening to America* series on public television.

EVC has developed a considerable collection of student-produced videotapes that are listed in an impressive catalog. The tapes are available for purchase or rental. During the fall of 1992, 120 tapes were bought, rented or previewed.

The product is not the most important goal. "We insist that they write and develop critical thinking skills here and that video does not mean the absence of writing," says Goodman. Students are required to keep a portfolio of their work, following highly detailed guidelines developed by Goodman and his staff.

In an age when young people, and adults, are accustomed to seeing polished produced video products, Goodman says the inevitable rough quality of some youth productions could be used to dismiss what young people are saying. As a result, EVC has had some difficulty getting its tapes into some schools.

"If adult gatekeepers feel threatened by the issues being explored, or stories being told, or the people telling them, then they won't allow the tapes in the schools," he says. "People will use the excuse of technical quality."

He cites the case of a documentary on poverty in Tennessee that won several awards and was accepted for use in the New York City public schools. However, a documentary about poverty in New York — the one produced by Millie Reyes — was rejected. Among other things, the film, which won first place in a video film competition in Japan, showed students leading a rent strike in East Harlem. "It pushed the wrong buttons," says Goodman.

Translating EVC's approach to regular schools will not be easy. Advisers are frequently reluctant to allow students free use of the video equipment because of the possibility of damage or theft of equipment. "So many high schools have a static studio-based program where the camera does not leave the tripod, there is no group process, and it is hierarchical and vocational rather than intellectual," says Goodman.

Goodman is trying to extend EVC's approach to school settings perhaps in the New Visions and Coalition Campus schools, new public schools being set up in New York City as part of a major reform initiative. Perhaps, Goodman suggests, video documentary production or media education could be made a graduation requirement in these schools.

Bill Tally works at the Center for Children and Technology at the Education Development Center in New York. He is working with EVC to develop a standard way for teachers to evaluate students' video work, some alternative to the traditional written test.

"We want to show that there is a heck of a lot more that goes into video production than just the product. It is a complex process that involves … research, writing, narration, interviewing as well as a range of technical arts." This could push video production far beyond old models of the little-used school television studio run by adults with minimal involvement of students.

Beyond that, electronic journalism holds out the hope that large numbers of young people can develop a different relationship to television. Rather than being passive consumers, wasting the equivalent of a full day each week in front of a TV set, students can become active participants in the video.

Teaching students to communicate

If you are a talented, aspiring high school journalist in Montgomery, Ala., chances are you will encounter Earlene Hollinger.

Hollinger is mass media instructor and newspaper adviser at Carver Creative and Performing Arts Center (CCPAC), a magnet school for performing arts housed at Carver High School in Montgomery.

The program began in 1982. Before that, Hollinger was teaching English at Jefferson Davis High School in Montgomery and was hosting a public affairs show on the local cable access channel in her spare time. The superintendent of the Montgomery school system saw Hollinger and was so impressed that he offered her a chance to head up the radio-TV curriculum at the new performing arts center.

Since then, Hollinger has been primarily responsible for shaping the CCPAC's comprehensive mass media program — a program that has gained statewide and national attention.

She established the award-winning *Omnibus,* the first high school literary magazine in Montgomery. She single-handedly revived the high school's newspaper, *Wolverine Pride,* after a long absence.

And she produces a monthly news/variety show that is written, edited and performed entirely by the CCPAC students. It airs on a local cable channel.

The TV show won't be mistaken for *60 Minutes,* but it is an informative, 30-minute mix. "We do school news, community news, sports, features, teacher spotlights — a variety of things," says Hollinger. "Sometimes we'll have a book review or an editorial. We throw in a lot of different elements."

One of the most popular elements is the newscast, where student anchors take stories from *Wolverine Pride* and rewrite them in broadcast form, a sort of televised version of the school newspaper. Beyond being informative, the newscast provides practical training for aspiring broadcast students.

Hollinger's students report the stories, write the scripts, read them on the air, run the cameras and edit the videotape. They are responsible, in one way or another, for virtually every aspect of the show.

It wasn't always that way. There have been some technical improvements. In the early years, shows were taped on Beta instead of the current Super

VHS. The students read scripts from cue cards rather than electronic teleprompters. And no one, including Hollinger, had any significant experience in TV production.

Still, the show went on.

"To be honest, we really didn't know how to use all that equipment properly," Hollinger recalls. "We had to learn a lot of the technical things by trial and error, and we jumped right in and had a broadcast in the very first month. I'm not going to say the show was perfect — it was pretty unpolished — but we wanted to get on the air."

"We've come a long way," she says. "Now we're broadcast quality."

Before being accepted into the Carver Creative and Performing Arts Center, students are interviewed, auditioned and asked to write an essay stating their desire to be in the program. Of the roughly 75-80 applications received each year, only about 10 new students are admitted.

Since CCPAC draws students from all four public high schools in Montgomery, as well as private schools, aspiring communications students from all over the city are bused to Carver three times daily. They stay for two-hour blocks and are bused back to their home schools. All take classes with Hollinger, who teaches three classes per day in addi-

tion to her extracurricular workload. What her students receive is a comprehensive curriculum that exposes them to print and broadcast journalism, broadcast production, drama, English and creative writing.

"I had to write my own curriculum, and since that time I've revised it four times," Hollinger says. "I want to teach the skills necessary for students to become good writers, either in print or broadcast journalism."

Although she has no formal training, Hollinger is a firm believer in the benefits of a journalism background. An admitted "lover of language," her appreciation of journalism stems from a lifelong fascination with the beauty and power of the written word — a passion she shares with her students.

"I'm very much aware of the need for students to know how to write and to communicate well," she says. "I tell them that no matter what they do, strong writing skills are the foundation of anything they will do in life."

Hollinger's dedication to journalism is perhaps best exemplified by her successful crusade to revive the high school's newspaper, *Wolverine Pride.* When Hollinger arrived in 1982, the paper had been dormant for six years. No faculty advisers had the time or energy to commit to the newspaper. Worse yet,

Earlene Hollinger, a mass media instructor and newspaper adviser at Carver Creative and Performing Arts Center in Montgomery, Ala., says, "I'm very much aware of the need for students to know how to write and to communicate well."

the students didn't seem to miss it. The prospects for its revival seemed dim.

"I just felt that the students had lost the opportunity to express themselves ... to hear their own voices at school," she says. "A student body needs to be aware of events and issues that are going on within that school or within that community. And those stories should be told by other students."

She showed students and faculty how easy publishing a student newspaper can be. Hollinger enlists English teachers to give story assignments to their students as class projects, and then she selects and edits the best of them. The creative writing teacher, who has computer equipment, puts the articles together in newspaper format and the finished publication is printed on a copier at the school. The result: an eight-page paper every month.

Hollinger doesn't consider herself a crusader for student journalism. She considers herself simply a teacher who enjoys seeing her students express themselves creatively.

"I enjoy showcasing the positive things students do. When students are working on a TV show — or their school newspaper, yearbook or magazine — to me, that's a positive thing."

*T*o chart a course for the future: 12 steps for improving high school journalism programs.

1 Every high school should have a newspaper that publishes at least once a month.

Without a high school newspaper, communication at all levels of the school suffers, endangering the educational process itself. Foundations, professional press groups and scholastic journalism associations should mount a major effort to identify high schools without newspapers and develop action plans to help them get newspapers started.

2 High school newspapers should include racial, ethnic and gender diversity in staffing and coverage to enrich content and broaden students' exposure.

Many high school newspapers are out of step with the social and demographic realities of their schools, communities and society itself. Newspaper staffs and advisers should make special efforts to include racial, ethnic and gender diversity in their coverage of school affairs and in their staffing patterns.

3 Journalism teachers should be well-trained and qualified at the highest level with a thorough grounding in reporting and editing, ethics, First Amendment law and the newspaper business.

University schools of journalism and education should work collaboratively with teachers' scholastic journalism organizations to improve the education and training of journalism teachers through formal academic programs, workshops and publications. They should also work to keep research current regarding trends in high school journalism.

4 Principals, administrators, school boards and parents must recognize the value of student expression for an effective education. High schools need policy guidelines or state laws that allow student journalists to exercise First Amendment press rights responsibly.

Administrative associations, teachers' groups and other interested community groups should be urged through a systematic campaign to make student publications a major vehicle to foster freedom of expression, to assure the flow of information in the school system, and to instill First Amendment values.

5 News media should provide vigorous moral and material support for the practice and teaching of journalism in high schools and independent youth newspapers.

Every newspaper should take responsibility for the existence — and well-being — of school newspapers in its community. State press associations and other groups at the national level, should develop plans to support scholastic journalism, whether this is initiated through individual schools, school systems, or scholastic journalism associations.

6 Students deserve clear teaching regarding the role of free expression within a democratic society and the responsibility of those who have access to the means of expression.

All high school journalism courses should present concepts of freedom of expression and the First Amendment. Textbooks should discuss the history and philosophy surrounding student press rights.

Recommendations

7 The curriculum and training associated with school newspapers should include design, illustration, cartooning, photography, advertising, production and distribution as well as solid teaching in reporting, writing and editing.

Opportunities for people with widely differing talents abound in school and commercial newspapers. Media organizations should encourage high school faculty and students to teach and practice all the skills necessary to produce a good newspaper, including the business management and advertising sales that help finance the enterprise.

8 School newsrooms and journalism classrooms should be well-equipped with computers to attract students, enhance learning and provide tools for producing an attractive newspaper and preparing students for their later work life.

School newspaper staffs and advisers should identify equipment and technology needs and work to get support for adequate facilities through school administrations or with the help of local newspapers and media organizations.

9 Schools must have adequate funding to afford the materials, resources and adviser compensation necessary to produce a good newspaper every month.

Faculty, administration, parents and outside media organizations should work with newspapers to make certain they have enough basic funding to publish on a regular basis.

10 School newspapers should be widely circulated to parents, feeder junior high schools and local communities, cultivating future staff members and creating a strong base for readership and advertising revenue.

School administrations, teacher organizations and local newspapers can help with the broad distribution of high school newspapers.

11 School broadcast media should be integrated with newspapers to serve diverse student interests and talents, and to let electronic media, including broadcast, cable and electronic bulletin boards become a part of high school journalism.

News organizations and schools should recognize the place, and need for support, of all modes of information delivery.

12 Students and teachers should have opportunities to use the services and attend meetings of state and national scholastic press organizations.

Scholastic press organizations should develop aggressive membership campaigns to convince media, educational and civic leaders that student news media are essential to a high school education.

Tinker et al. v. Des Moines Independent Community School District et al.

Argued November 12, 1968
Decided February 24, 1969

Summary

Petitioners, three public school pupils in Des Moines, Iowa, were suspended from school for wearing black armbands to protest the Government's policy in Vietnam. They sought nominal damages and an injunction against a regulation that the respondents had promulgated banning the wearing of armbands. The District Court dismissed the complaint on the ground that the regulation was within the Board's power, despite the absence of any finding of substantial interference with the conduct of school activities. The Court of Appeals, sitting en banc, affirmed by an equally divided court. *Held:*

1. In wearing armbands, the petitioners were quiet and passive. They were not disruptive and did not impinge upon the rights of others. In these circumstances, their conduct was within the protection of the Free Speech Clause of the First Amendment and the Due Process Clause of the Fourteenth.

2. First Amendment Rights are available to teachers and students, subject to application in light of the special characteristics of the school environment.

3. A prohibition against expression of opinion, without any evidence that the rule is necessary to avoid substantial interference with school discipline or the rights of others, is not permissible under the First and Fourteenth Amendments.

Reversed and remanded

Dan L. Johnston argued the cause for the petitioners.

Allan A. Herrick argued the cause for respondents.

Charles Morgan Jr. filed a brief for the United States National Student Association, as *amicus curiae,* urging reversal.

Opinion of the Court

Mr. Justice Fortas delivered the opinion of the Court.

Petitioner John F. Tinker, 15 years old, and petitioner Christopher Eckhardt, 16 years old, attended high schools in Des Moines, Iowa. Petitioner Mary Beth Tinker, John's sister, was a 13-year-old student in junior high school.

In December 1965, a group of adults and students in Des Moines held a meeting at the Eckhardt home. The group determined to publicize their objections to the hostilities in Vietnam and their support for a truce by wearing black armbands during the holiday season and by fasting on December 16 and New Year's Eve. Petitioners and their parents had previously engaged in similar activities, and they decided to participate in the program.

The principals of the Des Moines schools became aware of the plan to wear armbands. On December 14, 1965, they met and adopted a policy that any student wearing an armband to school would be asked to remove it, and if he refused he would be suspended until he returned without the armband. Petitioners were aware of the regulation that the school authorities adopted.

On December 16, Mary Beth and Christopher wore black armbands to their schools. John Tinker wore his armband the next day. They were all sent home and suspended from school until they would come back without their armbands. They did not return to school until after the planned period for wearing armbands had expired — that is, until after New Year's Day.

This complaint was filed in the United States District Court by petitioners, through their fathers, under Section 1983 of Title 42 of the United States Code. It prayed for an injunction restraining the respondent school officials and the respondent members of the board of directors of the school district from disciplining the petitioners, and it sought nominal damages. After an evidentiary hearing the District Court dismissed the complaint. It upheld the constitutionality of the school authorities' action on the ground that it was reasonable in order to prevent disturbance of school discipline. The court referred to but expressly declined to follow the Fifth Circuit's holding in a similar case that the wearing of symbols like the armbands cannot be prohibited unless it "materially and substantially interfere[s] with the requirements of appropriate discipline of the school." (Burnside v. Byars, 1966).

On appeal, the Court of Appeals for the Eighth Circuit considered the case en banc. The court was equally divided, and the District Court's decision was accordingly affirmed, without opinion. We granted certiorari.

I. The District Court recognized that the wearing of an armband for the purpose of expressing certain views is the type of symbolic act that is within the Free Speech Clause of the First Amendment. ... As we shall discuss, the wearing of armbands in the circumstances of this case was entirely divorced from actually or potentially disruptive conduct by those participating in it. It was closely akin to "pure speech" which, we have repeatedly held, is entitled to comprehensive protection under the First Amendment ... .

First Amendment rights, applied in light of the special characteristics of the school environment, are available to teachers and students. It can hardly be argued that either students or teachers shed their constitutional rights to freedom of speech or expression at the schoolhouse gate. This has been the unmistakable holding of this Court for almost 50 years. In *Meyer v. Nebraska* (1923), and *Bartels v. Iowa* (1923), this Court, in opinions by Mr. Justice McReynolds, held that the Due Process Clause of the Fourteenth Amendment prevents States from forbidding the teaching of a foreign language to young students. Statutes to this effect, the Court held, unconstitutionally interfere with the liberty of teacher, student, and parent. ...

In *West Virginia v. Barnette* (1943), this Court held that under the First Amendment, the student in public school may not be compelled to salute the flag. Speaking through Mr. Justice Jackson, the Court said:

"The Fourteenth Amendment, as now applied to the States, protects the citizen against the State itself and all of its creatures — Boards of Education not excepted. These have, of course, important, delicate, and highly discretionary functions, but none that they may not perform within the limits of the Bill of Rights. That they are educating the young for citizenship is reason for scrupulous protection of Constitutional freedoms of the individual, if we are not to strangle the free mind at its source and teach youth to discount important principles of our government as mere platitudes."

On the other hand, the Court has repeatedly emphasized the need for affirming the comprehensive authority of the States and of school officials, consistent with fundamental constitutional safeguards, to prescribe and control conduct in the schools ... . Our problem lies in the area where students in the exercise of First Amendment rights collide with the rules of the school authorities.

II. The problem posed by the present case does not relate to regulation of the length of skirts or the type of clothing, to hair style, or deportment ... . It does not concern aggressive, disruptive action or even group demonstrations. Our problem involves direct, primary First Amendment rights akin to "pure speech."

The school officials banned and sought to punish petitioners for a silent, passive expression of opinion, unaccompanied by any disorder or disturbance on the part of petitioners. There is here no evidence whatever of petitioners' interference, actual or nascent, with the schools' work or of collision with the rights of other students to be secure and to be let alone. Accordingly, this case does not concern speech or action that intrudes upon the work of the schools or the rights of other students.

Only a few of the 18,000 students in the school system wore the black armbands. Only five students were suspended for wearing them. There is no indication that the work of the schools or any class was disrupted. Outside the classrooms, a few students made hostile remarks to the children wearing armbands, but there were no threats or acts of violence on school premises.

The District Court concluded that the action of the school authorities was reasonable because it was based upon their fear of a disturbance from the wearing of the armbands. But, in our system, undifferentiated fear or apprehension of disturbance is not enough to overcome the right to freedom of expression. Any departure from absolute regimentation may cause trouble. Any variation from the majority's opinion may inspire fear. Any word spoken, in class, in the lunchroom, or on the campus, that deviates from the views of another person may start an argument or cause a disturbance. But our Constitution says we must take this risk ... and our history says that it is this sort of hazardous freedom — this kind of openness — that is the basis of our national strength and of the independence and vigor of Americans who grow up and live in this relatively permissive, often disputatious, society.

In order for the State in the person of school officials to justify prohibition of a particular expression of opinion, it must be able to show that its action was caused by something more than a mere desire to avoid the discomfort and unpleasantness that always accompany an unpopular viewpoint. Certainly where there is no finding and no showing that engaging in the forbidden conduct would "materially and substantially interfere with the requirements of appropriate discipline in the operation of the school," the prohibition cannot be sustained. (Burnside v. Byars).

In the present case, the District Court made no such finding, and our independent examination of the record fails to yield evidence that the school authorities had reason to anticipate that the wearing of the armbands would substantially interfere with the work of the school or impinge upon the rights of other students. Even an official memorandum prepared after the suspension that listed the reasons for the ban on wearing the armbands made no reference to the anticipation of such disruption.

On the contrary, the action of the school authorities appears to have been based upon an urgent wish to avoid the controversy which might result from the expression, even by the silent symbol of armbands, of opposition to this Nation's part in the conflagration in Vietnam. It is revealing, in this respect, that the meeting at which the school principals decided to issue the contested regulation was called in response to a student's statement to the journalism teacher in one of the schools that he wanted to write an article on Vietnam and have it published in the school paper. (The student was dissuaded.)

It is also relevant that the school authorities did not purport to prohibit the wearing of all symbols of political or controversial significance. The record shows that students in some of the schools wore buttons relating to national political campaigns, and some even wore the Iron Cross, traditionally a symbol of Nazism. The order prohibiting the wearing of armbands did not extend to these. Instead, a particular symbol — black armbands worn to exhibit opposition to this Nation's involvement in Vietnam — was singled out for prohibition. Clearly, the prohibition of expression of one particular opinion, at least without evidence that it is necessary to avoid material and substantial interference with schoolwork or discipline, is not constitutionally permissible.

In our system, state-operated schools may not be enclaves of totalitarianism. School officials do not possess absolute authority over their students. Students in school as well as out of school are "persons" under our Constitution. They are possessed of fundamental rights which the State must respect, just as they themselves must respect their obligations to the State. In our system, students may not be regarded as closed-circuit recipients of only that which the State chooses to communicate. They may not be confined to the expression of those sentiments that are officially approved. In the absence of a specific showing of constitutionally valid reasons to regulate their speech, students are entitled to freedom of expression of their views. As Judge Gewin, speaking for the Fifth Circuit, said, school

officials cannot suppress "expressions of feelings with which they do not wish to contend." *(Burnside v. Byars).*

In *Meyer v. Nebraska,* Mr. Justice McReynolds expressed this Nation's repudiation of the principle that a State might so conduct its schools as to "foster a homogeneous people." He said:

"In order to submerge the individual and develop ideal citizens, Sparta assembled the males at seven into barracks and intrusted their subsequent education and training to official guardians. Although such measures have been deliberately approved by men of great genius, their ideas touching the relation between individual and State were wholly different from those upon which our institutions rest; and it hardly will be affirmed that any legislature could impose such restrictions upon the people of a State without doing violence to both letter and spirit of the Constitution."

This principle has been repeated by this Court on numerous occasions during the intervening years. In *Keyishian v. Board of Regents,* Mr. Justice Brennan, speaking for the Court, said:

" 'The vigilant protection of constitutional freedoms is nowhere more vital than in the community of American schools.' *(Shelton v. Tucker).* The classroom is peculiarly the 'marketplace of ideas.' The Nation's future depends upon leaders trained through wide exposure to that robust exchange of ideas which discovers truth 'out of a multitude of tongues, [rather] than through any kind of authoritative selection.' "

The principle of these cases is not confined to the supervised and ordained discussion which takes place in the classroom. The principal use to which the schools are dedicated is to accommodate students during prescribed hours for the purpose of certain types of activities. Among those activities is personal intercommunication among the students. This is not only an inevitable part of the process of attending school; it is also an important part of the educational process. A student's rights, therefore, do not embrace merely the classroom hours. When he is in the cafeteria, or in the recess period, or on the way to or from class, or

on the playing field, or on the campus during the authorized hours, he may express his opinions, even on controversial subjects like the conflict in Vietnam, if he does so without "materially and substantially interfer[ing] with the requirements of appropriate discipline in the operation of the school" and without colliding with the rights of others. *(Burnside v. Byars)* But conduct by the student, in class or out of it, which for any reason — whether it stems from time, place, or type of behavior — materially disrupts classwork or involves substantial disorder or invasion of the rights of others is, of course, not immunized by the constitutional guarantee of freedom of speech … .

Under our Constitution, free speech is not a right that is given only to be so circumscribed that it exists in principle but not in fact. Freedom of expression would not truly exist if the right could be exercised only in an area that a benevolent government has provided as a safe haven for crackpots. The Constitution says that Congress (and the States) may not abridge the right to free speech. This provision means what it says. We properly read it to permit reasonable regulation of speech-connected activities in carefully restricted circumstances. But we do not confine the permissible exercise of First Amendment rights to a telephone booth or the four corners of a pamphlet, or to supervised and ordained discussion in a school classroom.

If a regulation were adopted by school officials forbidding discussion of the Vietnam conflict, or the expression by any student of opposition to it anywhere on school property except as part of a prescribed classroom exercise, it would be obvious that the regulation would violate the constitutional rights of students, at least if it could not be justified by a showing that the students' activities would materially and substantially disrupt the work and discipline of the school … . In the circumstances of the present case, the prohibition of the silent, passive "witness of the armbands," as one of the children called it, is no less offensive to the Constitution's guarantees.

As we have discussed, the record does not demonstrate any facts which might reasonably have led school authorities to forecast substantial disruption of or material interference with school activities, and no disturbances or disorders on the school premises in fact occurred. These petitioners merely went about their ordained rounds in school. Their deviation consisted only in wearing on their sleeve a band of black cloth, not more than two inch-es wide. They wore it to exhibit their disapproval of the Vietnam hostilities and their advocacy of a truce, to make their views known, and, by their example, to influence others to adopt them. They neither interrupted school activities nor sought to intrude in the school affairs or the lives of others. They caused discussion outside of the classrooms, but no interference with work and no disorder. In the circumstances, our Constitution does not permit officials of the State to deny their form of expression.

We express no opinion as to the form of relief which should be granted, this being a matter for the lower courts to determine. We reverse and remand for further proceedings consistent with this opinion.

Reversed and remanded

Mr. Justice Stewart, concurring

Although I agree with much of what is said in the Court's opinion, and with its judgment in this case, I cannot share the Court's uncritical assumption that, school discipline aside, the First Amendment rights of children are co-extensive with those of adults. Indeed, I had thought the Court decided otherwise just last Term in *Ginsberg v. New York.* I continue to hold the view I expressed in that case: "[A] State may permissibly determine that, at least in some precisely delineated areas, a child — like someone in a captive audience — is not possessed of that full capacity for individual choice which is the presupposition of First Amendment guarantees."…

Mr. Justice White, concurring

While I join the Court's opinion, I deem it appropriate to note, first, that the Court continues to recognize a distinction between communicating by words and communicating by acts or conduct which sufficiently impinges on some valid state interest; and, second, that I do not subscribe to everything the Court of Appeals said about free speech in its opinion in *Burnside v. Byars,* a case relied upon by the Court in the matter now before us.

Mr. Justice Black, dissenting

The Court's holding in this case ushers in what I deem to be an entirely new era in which the power to control pupils by the elected "officials of state supported public schools …" in the United States is in ultimate effect transferred to the Supreme Court. The Court brought this particular case here on a petition for certiorari urging that the First and

Fourteenth Amendments protect the right of school pupils to express their political views all the way "from kindergarten through high school." Here the constitutional right to "political expression" asserted was a right to wear black armbands during school hours and at classes in order to demonstrate to the other students that the petitioners were mourning because of the death of United States soldiers in Vietnam and to protest that war which they were against. Ordered to refrain from wearing the armbands in school by the elected school officials and the teachers vested with state authority to do so, apparently only seven out of the school system's 18,000 pupils deliberately refused to obey the order. One defying pupil was Paul Tinker, 8 years old, who was in the second grade; another, Hope Tinker, was 11 years old and in the fifth grade; a third member of the Tinker family was 13, in the eighth grade; and a fourth member of the same family was John Tinker, 15 years old, an 11th grade high school pupil. Their father, a Methodist minister without a church, is paid a salary by the American Friends Service Committee. Another student who defied the school order and insisted on wearing an armband in school was Christopher Eckhardt, an 11th grade pupil and a petitioner in this case. His mother is an official in the Women's International League for Peace and Freedom.

As I read the Court's opinion it relies upon the following grounds for holding unconstitutional the judgment of the Des Moines school officials and the two courts below. First, the Court concludes that the wearing of armbands is "symbolic speech" which is "akin to 'pure speech' " and therefore protected by the First and Fourteenth Amendments. Secondly, the Court decides that the public schools are an appropriate place to exercise "symbolic speech" as long as normal school functions are not "unreasonably" disrupted. Finally, the Court arrogates to itself, rather than to the State's elected officials charged with running the schools, the decision as to which school disciplinary regulations are "reasonable."

Assuming that the Court is correct in holding that the conduct of wearing armbands for the purpose of conveying political ideas is protected by the First Amendment … the crucial remaining questions are whether students and teachers may use the schools at their whim as a platform for the exercise of free speech — "symbolic" or "pure" — and whether the courts will allocate to themselves

the function of deciding how the pupils' school day will be spent. While I have always believed that under the First and Fourteenth Amendments neither the State nor the Federal Government has any authority to regulate or censor the content of speech, I have never believed that any person has a right to give speeches or engage in demonstrations where he pleases and when he pleases. The Court has already rejected such a notion. In *Cox v. Louisiana* (1965), for example, the Court clearly stated that the rights of free speech and assembly "do not mean that everyone with opinions or beliefs to express may address a group at any public place and at any time."

While the record does not show that any of these armband students shouted, used profane language, or were violent in any manner, detailed testimony by some of them shows their armbands caused comments, warnings by other students, the poking of fun at them, and a warning by an older football player that other, nonprotesting students had better let them alone. There is also evidence that a teacher of mathematics had his lesson period practically "wrecked" chiefly by disputes with Mary Beth Tinker, who wore her armband for her "demonstration." Even a casual reading of the record shows that this armband did divert students' minds from their regular lessons, and that talk, comments, etc., made John Tinker "self-conscious" in attending school with his armband. While the absence of obscene remarks or boisterous and loud disorder perhaps justifies the Court's statement that the few armband students did not actually "disrupt" the classwork, I think the record overwhelmingly shows that the armbands did exactly what the elected school officials and principals foresaw they would, that is, took the students' minds off their classwork and diverted them to thoughts about the highly emotional subject of the Vietnam war. And I repeat that if the time has come when pupils of state-supported schools, kindergartens, grammar schools, or high schools, can defy and flout orders of school officials to keep their minds on their own schoolwork, it is the beginning of a new revolutionary era of permissiveness in this country fostered by the judiciary. The next logical step, it appears to me, would be to hold unconstitutional laws that bar pupils under 21 or 18 from voting, or from being elected members of the boards of education.

The United States District Court refused to hold that the state school order violated the First and Fourteenth Amendments. Holding that the protest was akin to speech, which is protected by the First and Fourteenth Amendments, that court held that the school order was "reasonable" and hence constitutional. There was at one time a line of cases holding "reasonableness" as the court saw it to be the test of a "due process" violation. Two cases upon which the Court today heavily relies for striking down this school order used this test of reasonableness, *Meyer v. Nebraska* (1923), and *Bartels v. Iowa* (1923). The opinions in both cases were written by Mr. Justice McReynolds; Mr. Justice Holmes, who opposed this reasonableness test, dissented from the holdings as did Mr. Justice Sutherland. This constitutional test of reasonableness prevailed in this Court for a season. It was this test that brought on President Franklin Roosevelt's well-known Court fight. His proposed legislation did not pass, but the fight left the "reasonableness" constitutional test dead on the battlefield, so much so that this Court in *Ferguson v. Skrupa,* after a thorough review of the old cases, was able to conclude in 1963:

"There was a time when the Due Process Clause was used by this Court to strike down laws which were thought unreasonable, that is, unwise or incompatible with some particular economic or social philosophy … .

"The doctrine that prevailed in *Lochner, Coppage, Adkins, Burns,* and like cases — that due process authorizes courts to hold laws unconstitutional when they believe the legislature has acted unwisely — has long since been discarded."

The *Ferguson* case totally repudiated the old reasonableness-due process test, the doctrine that judges have the power to hold laws unconstitutional upon the belief of judges that they "shock the conscience" or that they are "unreasonable," "arbitrary," "irrational," "contrary to fundamental 'decency,' " or some other such flexible term without precise boundaries. I have many times expressed my opposition to that concept on the ground that it gives judges power to strike down any law they do not like. If the majority of the Court today, by agreeing to the opinion of my Brother Fortas, is resurrecting that old reasonableness-due process test, I think the constitutional change should be plainly, unequivocally, and forthrightly stated for the benefit of the bench and bar. It will be a sad day for the country, I believe, when the present-day Court returns to the McReynolds due process concept. Other cases cited by the Court do not, as implied, follow the McReynolds reasonableness doctrine. *West Virginia v. Barnette,* clearly rejecting the "reasonableness" test, held that the Fourteenth Amendment made the First applicable to the States, and that the two forbade a State to *compel* little schoolchildren to salute the United States flag when they had religious scruples against doing so. Neither *Thornhill v. Alabama; Stromberg v. California; Edwards v. South Carolina;* nor *Brown v. Louisiana,* related to schoolchildren at all, and none of these cases embraced Mr. Justice McReynolds' reasonableness test; and *Thornhill, Edwards,* and *Brown* relied on the vagueness of state statutes under scrutiny to hold them unconstitutional. *Cox v. Louisiana* and *Adderley v. Florida,* cited by the Court as a "compare," indicating, I suppose, that these two cases are no longer the law, were not rested to the slightest extent on the *Meyer* and *Bartels* "reasonableness-due process-McReynolds" constitutional test.

I deny, therefore, that it has been the "unmistakable holding of this Court for almost 50 years" that "students" and "teachers" take with them into the "schoolhouse gate" constitutional rights to "freedom of speech or expression." Even *Meyer* did not hold that. It makes no reference to "symbolic speech" at all; what it did was to strike down as "unreasonable" and therefore unconstitutional a Nebraska law barring the teaching of the German language before the children reached the eighth grade. One can well agree with Mr. Justice Holmes and Mr. Justice Sutherland, as I do, that such a law was no more unreasonable than it would be to bar the teaching of Latin and Greek to pupils who have not reached the eighth grade. In fact, I think the majority's reason for invalidating the Nebraska law was that it did not like it or in legal jargon that it "shocked the Court's conscience," "offended its sense of justice," or was "contrary to fundamental concepts of the English-speaking world," as the Court has sometimes said … . The truth is that a teacher of kindergarten, grammar school, or high school pupils no more carries into a school with him a complete right to freedom of speech and expression than an anti-Catholic or anti-Semite carries with him a complete freedom of speech and religion into a Catholic church or Jewish synagogue. Nor does a person carry with him into the United States Senate or House, or into the Supreme Court, or any other court, a complete constitutional right to go into those places contrary to their rules and speak his mind on any subject he pleases. It is a myth to say that any person has a constitutional right to say what he pleases, where he pleases, and when he pleases. Our Court has decided precisely the opposite … .

In my view, teachers in state-controlled public schools are hired to teach there. Although Mr. Justice McReynolds may have intimated to the contrary in *Meyer v. Nebraska,* certainly a teacher is not paid to go into school and teach subjects the State does not hire him to teach as a part of its selected curriculum. Nor are public school students sent to the schools at public expense to broadcast political or any other views to educate and inform the public. The original idea of schools, which I do not believe is yet abandoned as worthless or out of date, was that children had not yet reached the point of experience and wisdom which enabled them to teach all of their elders. It may be that the Nation has outworn the old-fashioned slogan that "children are to be seen and not heard," but one may, I hope, be permitted to harbor the thought that taxpayers send children to school on the premise that at their age they need to learn, not teach.

The true principles on this whole subject were in my judgment spoken by Mr. Justice McKenna for the Court in *Waugh v. Mississippi University.* The State had there passed a law barring students from peaceably assembling in Greek letter fraternities and providing that students who joined them could be expelled from school. This law would appear on the surface to run afoul of the First Amendment's freedom of assembly clause. The law was attacked as violative of due process and of the privileges and immunities clause and as a deprivation of property and of liberty, under the Fourteenth Amendment. It was argued that the fraternity made its members more moral, taught discipline, and inspired its members to study harder and to obey better the rules of discipline and order. This Court rejected all the "fervid" pleas of the fraternities' advocates and decided unanimously against these Fourteenth Amendment arguments. The Court in its next to the last paragraph made this statement which has complete relevance for us today:

"It is said that the fraternity to which complainant belongs is a moral and of itself a disciplinary force. This need not be denied. But whether such membership makes against discipline was for the State of Mississippi to determine. It is to be remembered that the University was established by the State and is under the control of the State, and the enactment of the statute may have been induced by the opinion that *membership in the prohibited societies divided the attention of the students and distracted from that singleness of purpose which the State desired to exist in its public educational institutions.* It is not for us to entertain conjectures in opposition to the views of the State and annul its regulations upon disputable considerations of their wisdom or necessity." (Emphasis supplied.)

It was on the foregoing argument that this Court sustained the power of Mississippi to curtail the First Amendment's right of peaceable assembly. And the same reasons are equally applicable to curtailing in the States' public schools the right to complete freedom of expression. Iowa's public schools, like Mississippi's university, are operated to give students an opportunity to learn, not to talk politics by actual speech, or by "symbolic" speech. And, as I have pointed out before, the record amply shows that public protest in the school classes against the Vietnam war "distracted from that singleness of purpose which the State [here Iowa] desired to exist in its public educational institutions." Here the Court should accord Iowa educational institutions the same right to determine for themselves to what extent free expression should be allowed in its schools as it accorded Mississippi with reference to freedom of assembly. But even if the record were silent as to protests against the Vietnam war distracting students from their assigned class work, members of this Court, like all other citizens, know, without being told, that the disputes over the wisdom of the Vietnam war have disrupted and divided this country as few other issues ever have. Of course students, like other people, cannot concentrate on lesser issues when black armbands are being ostentatiously displayed in their presence to call attention to the wounded and dead of the war, some of the wounded and the dead being their friends and neighbors. It was, of course, to distract the attention of other students that some students insisted up to the very point of their own suspension from school that they were determined to sit in school with their symbol-ic armbands.

Change has been said to be truly the law of life but sometimes the old and the tried and true are worth holding. The schools of this Nation have undoubtedly contributed to giving us tranquility and to making us a more law-abiding people. Uncontrolled and uncontrollable liberty is an enemy to domestic peace. We cannot close our eyes to the fact that some of the country's greatest problems are crimes committed by the youth, too many of school age. School discipline, like parental discipline, is an integral and important part of training our children to be good citizens — to be better citizens. Here a very small number of students have crisply and summarily refused to obey a school order designed to give pupils who want to learn the opportunity to do so. One does not need to be a prophet or the son of a prophet to know that after the Court's holding today some students in Iowa schools and indeed in all schools will be ready, able, and willing to defy their teachers on practically all orders. This is the more unfortunate for the schools since groups of students all over the land are already running loose, conducting break-ins, sit-ins, lie-ins, and smash-ins. Many of these student groups, as is all too familiar to all who read the newspapers and watch the television news programs, have already engaged in rioting, property seizures, and destruction. They have picketed schools to force students not to cross their picket lines and have too often violently attacked earnest but frightened students who wanted an education that the pickets did not want them to get. Students engaged in such activities are apparently confident that they know far more about how to operate public school systems than do their parents, teachers, and elected school officials. It is no answer to say that the particular students here have not yet reached such high points in their demands to attend classes in order to exercise their political pressures. Turned loose with lawsuits for damages and injunctions against their teachers as they are here, it is nothing but wishful thinking to imagine that young, immature students will not soon believe it is their right to control the schools rather than the right of the States that collect the taxes to hire the teachers for the benefit of the pupils. This case, therefore, wholly without constitutional reasons in my judgment, subjects all the public schools in the country to the whims and caprices of their loudest-mouthed, but maybe not their brightest, students. I, for one, am not fully persuaded that school pupils are wise enough, even

with this Court's expert help from Washington, to run the 23,390 public school systems in our 50 States. I wish, therefore, wholly to disclaim any purpose on my part to hold that the Federal Constitution compels the teachers, parents, and elected school officials to surrender control of the American public school system to public school students. I dissent.

Mr. Justice Harlan, dissenting

I certainly agree that state public school authorities in the discharge of their responsibilities are not wholly exempt from the requirements of the Fourteenth Amendment respecting the freedoms of expression and association. At the same time I am reluctant to believe that there is any disagreement between the majority and myself on the proposition that school officials should be accorded the widest authority in maintaining discipline and good order in their institutions. To translate that proposition into a workable constitutional rule, I would, in cases like this, cast upon those complaining the burden of showing that a particular school measure was motivated by other than legitimate school concerns — for example, a desire to prohibit the expression of an unpopular point of view, while permitting expression of the dominant opinion.

Finding nothing in this record which impugns the good faith of respondents in promulgating the armband regulation, I would affirm the judgment below.

Hazelwood School District, et al., Petitioners v. Kuhlmeier et al.

Argued October 13, 1987
Decided January 13, 1988

Summary

Respondents, former high school students who were staff members of the school's newspaper, filed suit in Federal District Court against petitioners, the school district and school officials, alleging that respondents' First Amendment rights were violated by the deletion from a certain issue of the paper of two pages that included an article describing school students' experiences with pregnancy and another article discussing the impact of divorce on students at the school. The newspaper was written and edited by a journalism class, as part of the school's curriculum. Pursuant to the school's practice, the teacher in charge of the paper submitted page proofs to the school's principal, who objected to the pregnancy story because the pregnant students, although not named, might be identified from the text, and because he believed that the article's references to sexual activity and birth control were inappropriate for some of the younger students. The principal objected to the divorce article because the page proofs he was furnished identified by name (deleted by the teacher from the final version) a student who complained of her father's conduct, and the principal believed that the student's parents should have been given an opportunity to respond to the remarks or to consent to their publication. Believing that there was no time to make necessary changes in the articles if the paper was to be issued before the end of the school year, the principal directed that the pages on which they appeared be withheld from publication even though other, unobjectionable articles were included on such pages. The District Court held that no First Amendment violation had occurred. The Court of Appeals reversed.

Held: Respondents' First Amendment rights were not violated.

(a) First Amendment rights of students in the public schools are not automatically coextensive with the rights of adults in other settings, and must be applied in light of the special characteristics of the school environment. A school need not tolerate student speech that is inconsistent with its basic educational mission, even though the government could not censor similar speech outside the school.

(b) The school newspaper here cannot be characterized as a forum for public expression. School facilities may be deemed to be public forums only if school authorities have by policy or by practice opened the facilities for indiscriminate use by the general public, or by some segment of the public, such as student organizations. If the facilities have instead been reserved for other intended purposes, communicative or otherwise, then no public forum has been created, and school officials may impose reasonable restrictions on the speech of students, teachers, and other members of the school community. The school officials in this case did not deviate from their policy that the newspaper's production was to be part of the educational curriculum and a

regular classroom activity under the journalism teacher's control as to almost every aspect of publication. The officials did not evince any intent to open the paper's pages to indiscriminate use by its student reporters and editors, or by the student body generally. Accordingly, school officials were entitled to regulate the paper's contents in any reasonable manner.

(c) The standard for determining when a school may punish student expression that happens to occur on school premises is not the standard for determining when a school may refuse to lend its name and resources to the dissemination of student expression. *(Tinker v. Des Moines Independent Community School Dist.).* Educators do not offend the First Amendment by exercising editorial control over the style and content of student speech in school-sponsored expressive activities so long as their actions are reasonably related to legitimate pedagogical concerns.

(d) The school principal acted reasonably in this case in requiring the deletion of the pregnancy article, the divorce article, and the other articles that were to appear on the same pages of the newspaper.

Reversed

Robert P. Baine Jr. argued the cause for petitioners.

Leslie D. Edwards argued the cause and filed a brief for respondents.

Opinion of the Court

Justice White delivered the opinion of the Court.

This case concerns the extent to which educators may exercise editorial control over the contents of a high school newspaper produced as part of the school's journalism curriculum.

I. Petitioners are the Hazelwood School District in St. Louis County, Missouri; various school officials; Robert Eugene Reynolds, the principal of Hazelwood East High School; and Howard Emerson, a teacher in the school district. Respondents are three former Hazelwood East students who were former staff members of *Spectrum,* the school newspaper. They contend that school officials violated their First Amendment rights by deleting two pages of articles from the May 13, 1983, issue of *Spectrum.*

Spectrum was written and edited by the Journalism II class at Hazelwood East. The newspaper was published every three weeks or so during the 1982-1983 school year. More

than 4,500 copies of the newspaper were distributed during that year to students, school personnel, and members of the community.

The Board of Education allocated funds from its annual budget for the printing of *Spectrum.* These funds were supplemented by proceeds from sales of the newspaper. The printing expenses during the 1982-1983 school year totaled $4,668.50; revenue from sales was $1,166.84. The other costs associated with the newspaper — such as supplies, textbooks, and a portion of the journalism teacher's salary — were borne entirely by the Board.

The Journalism II course was taught by Robert Stergos for most of the 1982-1983 academic year. Stergos left Hazelwood East to take a job in private industry on April 29, 1983, when the May 13 edition of *Spectrum* was nearing completion, and petitioner Emerson took his place as newspaper adviser for the remaining weeks of the term.

The practice at Hazelwood East during the spring 1983 semester was for the journalism teacher to submit page proofs of each *Spectrum* issue to Principal Reynolds for his review prior to publication. On May 10, Emerson delivered the proofs of the May 13 edition to Reynolds, who objected to two of the articles scheduled to appear in that edition. One of the stories described three Hazelwood East students' experiences with pregnancy; the other discussed the impact of divorce on students at the school.

Reynolds was concerned that, although the pregnancy story used false names "to keep the identity of these girls a secret," the pregnant students still might be identifiable from the text. He also believed that the article's references to sexual activity and birth control were inappropriate for some of the younger students at the school. In addition, Reynolds was concerned that a student identified by name in the divorce story had complained that her father "wasn't spending enough time with my mom, my sister and I" prior to the divorce, "was always out of town on business or out late playing cards with the guys," and "always argued about everything" with her mother. Reynolds believed that the student's parents should have been given an opportunity to respond to these remarks or to consent to their publication. He was unaware that Emerson had deleted the student's name from the final version of the article.

Reynolds believed that there was no time to make the necessary changes in the stories before the scheduled press run and that the newspaper would not appear before the end of the school year if printing were delayed to any significant extent. He concluded that his only options under the circumstances were to publish a four-page newspaper instead of the planned six-page newspaper, eliminating the two pages on which the offending stories appeared, or publish no newspaper at all. Accordingly, he directed Emerson to withhold from publication the two pages containing the stories on pregnancy and divorce. He informed his superiors of the decision, and they concurred.

Respondents subsequently commenced this action in the United States District Court for the Eastern District of Missouri seeking a declaration that their First Amendment rights had been violated, injunctive relief, and monetary damages. After a bench trial, the District Court denied an injunction, holding that no First Amendment violation had occurred.

The District Court concluded that school officials may impose restraints on students' speech in activities that are " 'an integral part of the school's educational function' " — including the publication of a school-sponsored newspaper by a journalism class — so long as their decision has "'a substantial and reasonable basis.' " (quoting *Frasca v. Andrews,* EDNY 1979). The court found that Principal Reynolds' concern that the pregnant students' anonymity would be lost and their privacy invaded was "legitimate and reasonable," given "the small number of pregnant students at Hazelwood East and several identifying characteristics that were disclosed in the article." The court held that Reynolds' action was also justified "to avoid the impression that [the school] endorses the sexual norms of the subjects" and to shield younger students from exposure to unsuitable material. The deletion of the article on divorce was seen by the court as a reasonable response to the invasion of privacy concerns raised by the named student's remarks. Because the article did not indicate that the student's parents had been offered an opportunity to respond to her allegations, said the court, there was cause for "serious doubt that the article complied with the rules of fairness which are standard in the field of journalism and which were covered in the textbook used in the Journalism II class." Furthermore, the court concluded that Reynolds was justified in deleting two full pages of the newspaper, instead of deleting only the pregnancy and divorce stories or requiring that those stories be modified to address his concerns, based on his "reasonable

belief that he had to make an immediate decision and that there was no time to make modifications to the articles in question."

The Court of Appeals for the Eighth Circuit reversed. The court held at outset that *Spectrum* was not only "a part of the school adopted curriculum," but also a public forum, because the newspaper was "intended to be and operated as a conduit for student viewpoint." The court then concluded that *Spectrum's* status as a public forum precluded school officials from censoring its contents except when "'necessary to avoid material and substantial interference with school work or discipline … or the rights of others.' " (quoting *Tinker v. Des Moines Independent Community School Dist.,* 1969).

The Court of Appeals found "no evidence in the record that the principal could have reasonably forecast that the censored articles or any materials in the censored articles would have materially disrupted classwork or given rise to substantial disorder in the school." School officials were entitled to censor the articles on the ground that they invaded the rights of others, according to the court, only if publication of the articles could have resulted in tort liability to the school. The court concluded that no tort action for libel or invasion of privacy could have been maintained against the school by the subjects of two of the articles or by their families. Accordingly, the court held that school officials had violated respondents' First Amendment rights by deleting the two pages of the newspaper.

We granted *certiorari,* and we now reverse.

II. Students in the public schools do not "shed their constitutional rights to freedom of speech or expression at the schoolhouse gate." *(Tinker).* They cannot be punished merely for expressing their personal views on the school premises — whether "in the cafeteria, or on the playing field, or on the campus during the authorized hours" — unless school authorities have reason to believe that such expression will "substantially interfere with the work of the school or impinge upon the rights of other students." *(Tinker).*

We have nonetheless recognized that the First Amendment rights of students in the public schools "are not automatically coextensive with the rights of adults in other settings," *(Bethel School District No. 403 v. Fraser, 1986),* and must be "applied in the light of the special characteristics of the school environment." *(Tinker).* A school need not toler-

ate student speech that is inconsistent with its "basic educational mission," *(Fraser),* even though the government could not censor similar speech outside the school. Accordingly, we held in *Fraser* that a student could be disciplined for having delivered a speech that was "sexually explicit" but not legally obscene at an official school assembly, because the school was entitled to "disassociate itself" from the speech in a manner that would demonstrate to others that such vulgarity is "wholly inconsistent with the 'fundamental values' of public school education." We thus recognized that "[t]he determination of what manner of speech in the classroom or in school assembly is inappropriate properly rests with the school board," rather than with the federal courts. It is in this context that respondents' First Amendment claims must be considered.

A. We deal first with the question whether *Spectrum* may appropriately be characterized as a forum for public expression. The public schools do not possess all of the attributes of streets, parks, and other traditional public forums that "time out of mind, have been used for purposes of assembly, communicating thoughts between citizens, and discussing public questions." *(Hague v. CIO, 1939).* Hence, school facilities may be deemed to be public forums only if school authorities have "by policy or by practice" opened those facilities "for indiscriminate use by the general public," *(Perry Education Assn. v. Perry Local Educators' Assn., 1983),* or by some segment of the public, such as student organizations. If the facilities have instead been reserved for other intended purposes, "communicative or otherwise," then no public forum has been created, and school officials may impose reasonable restrictions on the speech of students, teachers, and other members of the school community. "The government does not create a public forum by inaction or by permitting limited discourse, but only by intentionally opening a nontraditional forum for public discourse." *(Cornelius v. NAACP Legal Defense & Educational Fund, Inc., 1985).*

The policy of school officials toward *Spectrum* was reflected in Hazelwood School Board Policy 348.51 and the Hazelwood East Curriculum Guide. Board Policy 348.51 provided that "[s]chool sponsored publications are developed within the adopted curriculum and its educational implications in regular classroom activities." The Hazelwood East Curriculum Guide described the Journalism

II course as a "laboratory situation in which the students publish the school newspaper applying skills they have learned in Journalism I." The lessons that were to be learned from the Journalism II course, according to the Curriculum Guide, included development of journalistic skills under deadline pressure, "the legal, moral, and ethical restrictions imposed upon journalists within the school community," and "responsibility and acceptance of criticism for articles of opinion." Journalism II was taught by a faculty member during regular class hours. Students received grades and academic credit for their performance in the course.

School officials did not deviate in practice from their policy that production of *Spectrum* was to be part of the educational curriculum and a "regular classroom activit[y]." The District Court found that Robert Stergos, the journalism teacher during most of the 1982-1983 school year, "both had the authority to exercise and in fact exercised a great deal of control over *Spectrum.*" For example, Stergos selected the editors of the newspaper, scheduled publication dates, decided the number of pages for each issue, assigned story ideas to class members, advised students on the development of their stories, reviewed the use of quotations, edited stories, selected and edited the letters to the editor, and dealt with the printing company. Many of these decisions were made without consultation with the Journalism II students. The District Court thus found it "clear that Mr. Stergos was the final authority with respect to almost every aspect of the production and publication of *Spectrum,* including its content." Moreover, after each *Spectrum* issue had been finally approved by Stergos or his successor, the issue still had to be reviewed by Principal Reynolds prior to publication. Respondents' assertion that they had believed that they could publish "practically anything" in *Spectrum* was therefore dismissed by the District Court as simply "not credible." These factual findings are amply supported by the record, and were not rejected as clearly erroneous by the Court of Appeals.

The evidence relied upon by the Court of Appeals in finding *Spectrum* to be a public forum is equivocal at best. For example, Board Policy 348.51, which stated in part that "[s]chool sponsored student publications will not restrict free expression or diverse viewpoints within the rules of responsible journalism," also stated that such publications were "developed within the adopted curriculum and its educational implications." One might reasonably infer from the full text of Policy 348.51 that school officials retained ultimate control over what constituted "responsible journalism" in a school-sponsored newspaper. Although the Statement of Policy published in the September 14, 1982, issue of *Spectrum* declared that *"Spectrum,* as a student-press publication, accepts all rights implied by the First Amendment," this statement, understood in the context of the paper's role in the school's curriculum, suggests at most that the administration will not interfere with the students' exercise of those First Amendment rights that attend the publication of a school-sponsored newspaper. It does not reflect an intent to expand those rights by converting a curricular newspaper into a public forum. Finally, that students were permitted to exercise some authority over the contents of *Spectrum* was fully consistent with the Curriculum Guide objective of teaching the Journalism II students "leadership responsibilities as issue and page editors." A decision to teach leadership skills in the context of a classroom activity hardly implies a decision to relinquish school control over that activity. In sum, the evidence relied upon by the Court of Appeals fails to demonstrate the "clear intent to create a public forum," *(Cornelius,* that existed in cases in which we found public forums to have been created … . School officials did not evince either "by policy or by practice," *(Perry Education Assn.),* any intent to open the pages of Spectrum to "indiscriminate use," *(Perry Education Assn.),* by its student reporters and editors, or by the student body generally. Instead, they "reserve[d] the forum for its intended purpos[e]," as a supervised learning experience for journalism students. Accordingly, school officials were entitled to regulate the contents of *Spectrum* in any reasonable manner. It is this standard, rather than our decision in *Tinker,* that governs this case.

B. The question whether the First Amendment requires a school to tolerate particular student speech — the question that we addressed in *Tinker* — is different from the question whether the First Amendment requires a school affirmatively to promote particular student speech. The former question addresses educators' ability to silence a student's personal expression that happens to occur on the school premises. The latter question concerns educators' authority over school-sponsored publications, theatrical productions, and other expressive activities that students, parents, and members of the public might reasonably perceive to bear the imprimatur of the school. These activities may fairly be characterized as part of the school curriculum, whether or not they occur in a traditional classroom setting, so long as they are supervised by faculty members and designed to impart particular knowledge or skills to student participants and audiences.

Educators are entitled to exercise greater control over this second form of student expression to assure that participants learn whatever lessons the activity is designed to teach, that readers or listeners are not exposed to material that may be inappropriate for their level of maturity, and that the views of the individual speaker are not erroneously attributed to the school. Hence, a school may in its capacity as publisher of a school newspaper or producer of a school play "disassociate itself," *(Fraser),* not only from speech that would "substantially interfere with [its] work … or impinge upon the rights of other students," *(Tinker),* but also from speech that is, for example, ungrammatical, poorly written, inadequately researched, biased or prejudiced, vulgar or profane, or unsuitable for immature audiences. A school must be able to set high standards for the student speech that is disseminated under its auspices — standards that may be higher than those demanded by some newspaper publishers or theatrical producers in the "real" world — and may refuse to disseminate student speech that does not meet those standards. In addition, a school must be able to take into account the emotional maturity of the intended audience in determining whether to disseminate student speech on potentially sensitive topics, which might range from the existence of Santa Claus in an elementary school setting to the particulars of teenage sexual activity in a high school setting. A school must also retain the authority to refuse to sponsor student speech that might reasonably be perceived to advocate drug or alcohol use, irresponsible sex, or conduct otherwise inconsistent with "the shared values of a civilized social order," *(Fraser),* or to associate the school with any position other than neutrality on matters of political controversy. Otherwise, the schools would be unduly constrained from fulfilling their role as "a principal instrument in awakening the child to cultural values, in preparing him for later professional training, and in helping him to adjust normally to his environment." *(Brown v. Board of Education,* 1954).

Accordingly, we conclude that the standard articulated in *Tinker* for determining when a school may punish student expression need not also be the standard for determining when a school may refuse to lend its name and resources to the dissemination of student expression. Instead, we hold that educators do not offend the First Amendment by exercising editorial control over the style and content of student speech in school-sponsored expressive activities so long as their actions are reasonably related to legitimate pedagogical concerns.

This standard is consistent with our oft-expressed view that the education of the Nation's youth is primarily the responsibility of parents, teachers, and state and local officials, and not of federal judges … . It is only when the decision to censor a school-sponsored publication, theatrical production, or other vehicle of student expression has no valid educational purpose that the First Amendment is so "directly and sharply implicate[d]," as to require judicial intervention to protect students' constitutional rights.

III. We also conclude that Principal Reynolds acted reasonably in requiring the deletion from the May 13 issue of *Spectrum* of the pregnancy article, the divorce article, and the remaining articles that were to appear on the same pages of the newspaper.

The initial paragraph of the pregnancy article declared that "[a]ll names have been changed to keep the identity of these girls a secret." The principal concluded that the students' anonymity was not adequately protected, however, given the other identifying information in the article and the small number of pregnant students at the school. Indeed, a teacher at the school credibly testified that she could positively identify at least one of the girls and possibly all three. It is likely that many students at Hazelwood East would have been at least as successful in identifying the girls. Reynolds therefore could reasonably have feared that the article violated whatever pledge of anonymity had been given to the pregnant students. In addition, he could reasonably have been concerned that the article was not sufficiently sensitive to the privacy interests of the students' boyfriends and parents, who were discussed in the article but who were given no opportunity to consent to its publication or to offer a response. The article did not contain graphic accounts of sexual activity. The girls did comment in the article, however, concerning their sexual histories and

their use or nonuse of birth control. It was not unreasonable for the principal to have concluded that such frank talk was inappropriate in a school-sponsored publication distributed to 14-year-old freshmen and presumably taken home to be read by students' even younger brothers and sisters.

The student who was quoted by name in the version of the divorce article seen by Principal Reynolds made comments sharply critical of her father. The principal could reasonably have concluded that an individual publicly identified as an inattentive parent — indeed, as one who chose "playing cards with the guys" over home and family — was entitled to an opportunity to defend himself as a matter of journalistic fairness. These concerns were shared by both of *Spectrum's* faculty advisers for the 1982-1983 school year, who testified that they would not have allowed the article to be printed without the deletion of the student's name.

Principal Reynolds testified credibly at trial that, at the time that he reviewed the proofs of the May 13 issue during an extended telephone conversation with Emerson, he believed that there was no time to make any changes in the articles, and that the newspaper had to be printed immediately or not at all. It is true that Reynolds did not verify whether the necessary modifications could still have been made in the articles, and that Emerson did not volunteer the information that printing could be delayed until the changes were made. We nonetheless agree with the District Court that the decision to excise the two pages containing the problematic articles was reasonable given the particular circumstances of this case. These circumstances included the very recent replacement of Stergos by Emerson, who may not have been entirely familiar with *Spectrum* editorial and production procedures, and the pressure felt by Reynolds to make an immediate decision so that students would not be deprived of their newspaper altogether.

In sum, we cannot reject as unreasonable Principal Reynolds' conclusion that neither the pregnancy article nor the divorce article was suitable for publication in *Spectrum*. Reynolds could reasonably have concluded that the students who had written and edited these articles had not sufficiently mastered those portions of the Journalism II curriculum that pertained to the treatment of controversial issues and personal attacks, the need to protect the privacy of individuals whose most intimate concerns are to be revealed in

the newspaper, and "the legal, moral, and ethical restrictions imposed upon journalists within [a] school community" that includes adolescent subjects and readers. Finally, we conclude that the principal's decision to delete two pages of *Spectrum*, rather than to delete only the offending articles or to require that they be modified, was reasonable under the circumstances as he understood them. Accordingly, no violation of First Amendment rights occurred.

The judgment of the Court of Appeals for the Eighth Circuit is therefore

Reversed

Justice Brennan, with whom Justice Marshall and Justice Blackmun join, dissenting.

When the young men and women of Hazelwood East High School registered for Journalism II, they expected a civics lesson. *Spectrum*, the newspaper they were to publish, "was not just a class exercise in which students learned to prepare papers and hone writing skills, it was a … forum established to give students an opportunity to express their views while gaining an appreciation of their rights and responsibilities under the First Amendment to the United States Constitution … . [A]t the beginning of each school year," the student journalists published a Statement of Policy — tacitly approved each year by school authorities — announcing their expectation that "*Spectrum*, as a student-press publication, accepts all rights implied by the First Amendment … . Only speech that 'materially and substantially interferes with the requirements of appropriate discipline' can be found unacceptable and therefore prohibited." (quoting *Tinker v. Des Moines Independent Community School Dist.*, 1969). The school board itself affirmatively guaranteed the students of Journalism II an atmosphere conducive to fostering such an appreciation and exercising the full panoply of rights associated with a free student press. "School sponsored student publications," it vowed, "will not restrict free expression or diverse viewpoints within the rules of responsible journalism."

This case arose when the Hazelwood East administration breached its own promise, dashing its students' expectations. The school principal, without prior consultation or explanation, excised six articles — comprising two full pages — of the May 13, 1983, issue of *Spectrum*. He did so not because any of the articles would "materially and substantially interfere with the requirements of appropriate discipline," but simply because he considered two of the six "inappropriate, personal, sensitive, and unsuitable" for student consumption.

In my view the principal broke more than just a promise. He violated the First Amendment's prohibitions against censorship of any student expression that neither disrupts classwork nor invades the rights of others, and against any censorship that is not narrowly tailored to serve its purpose.

I. Public education serves vital national interests in preparing the Nation's youth for life in our increasingly complex society and for the duties of citizenship in our democratic Republic... . The public school conveys to our young the information and tools required not merely to survive in, but to contribute to, civilized society. It also inculcates in tomorrow's leaders the "fundamental values necessary to the maintenance of a democratic political system... ." *(Ambach v. Norwick, 1979).* All the while, the public educator nurtures students' social and moral development by transmitting to them an official dogma of "community values." *(Board of Education v. Pico, 1982).*

The public educator's task is weighty and delicate indeed. It demands particularized and supremely subjective choices among diverse curricula, moral values, and political stances to teach or inculcate in students, and among various methodologies for doing so. Accordingly, we have traditionally reserved the "daily operation of school systems" to the States and their local school boards. *(Epperson v. Arkansas, 1968).* We have not, however, hesitated to intervene where their decisions run afoul of the Constitution... .

Free student expression undoubtedly sometimes interferes with the effectiveness of the school's pedagogical functions. Some brands of student expression do so by directly preventing the school from pursuing its pedagogical mission: The young polemic who stands on a soapbox during calculus class to deliver an eloquent political diatribe interferes with the legitimate teaching of calculus. And the student who delivers a lewd endorsement of a student-government candidate might so extremely distract an impressionable high school audience as to interfere with the orderly operation of the school... . Other student speech, however, frustrates the school's legitimate pedagogical purposes merely by expressing a message that conflicts with the school's, without directly interfering with the school's expression of its message: A student who responds to a political science teacher's question with a retort, "socialism is good," subverts the school's inculcation of the message that capitalism is better. Even the maverick who sits in class passively sporting a symbol of protest against a government policy ... or the gossip who sits in the student commons swapping stories of sexual escapade could readily muddle a clear official message condoning the government policy or condemning teenage sex. Likewise, the student newspaper that, like *Spectrum,* conveys a moral position at odds with the school's official stance might subvert the administration's legitimate inculcation of its own perception of community values.

If mere incompatibility with the school's pedagogical message were a constitutionally sufficient justification for the suppression of student speech, school officials could censor each of the students or student organizations in the foregoing hypotheticals, converting our public schools into "enclaves of totalitarianism" that "strangle the free mind at its source," *(West Virginia Board of Education v. Barnette, 1943).* The First Amendment permits no such blanket censorship authority. While the "constitutional rights of students in public schools are not automatically coextensive with the rights of adults in other settings," *(Fraser),* students in the public schools do not "shed their constitutional rights to freedom of speech or expression at the schoolhouse gate." *(Tinker).* Just as the public on the street corner must, in the interest of fostering "enlightened opinion," *(Cantwell v. Connecticut,* 1940), tolerate speech that "tempt[s] [the listener] to throw [the speaker] off the street," *(Cantwell v. Connecticut),* public educators must accommodate some student expression even if it offends them or offers views or values that contradict those the school wishes to inculcate.

In *Tinker,* this Court struck the balance. We held that official censorship of student expression — there the suspension of several students until they removed their armbands protesting the Vietnam war — is unconstitutional unless the speech "materially disrupts classwork or involves substantial disorder or invasion of the rights of others ... ." School officials may not suppress "silent, passive expression of opinion, unaccompanied by any disorder or disturbance on the part of" the speaker. The "mere desire to avoid the discomfort and unpleasantness that always accompany an unpopular viewpoint," or an unsavory subject, *Fraser,* does not justify official suppression of student speech in the high school.

This Court applied the *Tinker* test just a Term ago in *Fraser,* upholding an official decision to discipline a student for delivering a lewd speech in support of a student-government candidate. The Court today casts no doubt on *Tinker's* vitality. Instead it erects a taxonomy of school censorship, concluding that *Tinker* applies to one category and not another. On the one hand is censorship "to silence a student's personal expression that happens to occur on the school premises." On the other hand is censorship of expression that arises in the context of "school-sponsored ... expressive activities that students, parents, and members of the public might reasonably perceive to bear the imprimatur of the school."

The Court does not, for it cannot, purport to discern from our precedents the distinction it creates. One could, I suppose, readily characterize the students' symbolic speech in *Tinker* as "personal expression that happens to [have] occur[red] on school premises," although *Tinker* did not even hint that the personal nature of the speech was of any (much less dispositive) relevance. But that same description could not by any stretch of the imagination fit Fraser's speech. He did not just "happen" to deliver his lewd speech to an ad hoc gathering on the playground. As the second paragraph of *Fraser* evinces, if ever a forum for student expression was "school-sponsored," Fraser's was:

"Fraser ... delivered a speech nominating a fellow student for student elective office. Approximately 600 high school students ... attended the assembly. Students were required to attend the assembly or to report to the study hall. The assembly was part of a *school-sponsored* educational program in self-government." (Emphasis added).

Yet, from the first sentence of its analysis, *Fraser* faithfully applied *Tinker.*

Nor has this Court ever intimated a distinction between personal and school-sponsored speech in any other context. Particularly telling is this Court's heavy reliance on *Tinker* in two cases of First Amendment infringement on state college campuses. See *Papish v. University of Missouri Board of Curators* (1973); *Healy v. James* (1972). One involved the expulsion of a student for lewd expression in a newspaper that she sold on campus pursuant to university authorization, and the other involved the denial of university recognition and concomitant benefits to a political student organization. Tracking *Tinker's* analysis, the Court found each act of suppression unconstitutional. In neither case did this Court suggest the distinction, which the Court today finds dispositive, between school-sponsored and incidental student expression.

II. Even if we were writing on a clean slate, I would reject the Court's rationale for abandoning *Tinker* in this case. The Court offers no more than an obscure tangle of three excuses to afford educators "greater control" over school-sponsored speech than the *Tinker* test would permit: the public educator's prerogative to control curriculum; the pedagogical interest in shielding the high school audience from objectionable viewpoints and sensitive topics; and the school's need to dissociate itself from student expression. None of the excuses, once disentangled, supports the distinction that the Court draws. *Tinker* fully addresses the first concern; the second is illegitimate; and the third is readily achievable through less oppressive means.

A. The Court is certainly correct that the First Amendment permits educators "to assure that participants learn whatever lessons the activity is designed to teach ... ." That is, however, the essence of the *Tinker* test, not an excuse to abandon it. Under *Tinker*, school officials may censor only such student speech as would "materially disrup[t]" a legitimate curricular function. Manifestly, student speech is more likely to disrupt a curricular function when it arises in the context of a curricular activity — one that "is designed to teach" something — than when it arises in the context of a noncurricular activity. Thus, under *Tinker*, the school may constitutionally punish the budding political orator if he disrupts calculus class but not if he holds his tongue for the cafeteria... .That is not because some more stringent standard applies in the curricular context. (After all, this Court applied the same standard whether the students in *Tinker* wore their armbands to the "classroom" or the "cafeteria.") It is because student speech in the noncurricular context is less likely to disrupt materially any legitimate pedagogical purpose.

I fully agree with the Court that the First Amendment should afford an educator the

prerogative not to sponsor the publication of a newspaper article that is "ungrammatical, poorly written, inadequately researched, biased or prejudiced," or that falls short of the "high standards for ... student speech that is disseminated under [the school's] auspices. ... " But we need not abandon *Tinker* to reach that conclusion; we need only apply it. The enumerated criteria reflect the skills that the curricular newspaper "is designed to teach." The educator may, under *Tinker,* constitutionally "censor" poor grammar, writing, or research because to reward such expression would "materially disrup[t]" the newspaper's curricular purpose.

The same cannot be said of official censorship designed to shield the *audience* or dissociate the *sponsor* from the expression. Censorship so motivated might well serve (although, as I demonstrate *infra,* cannot legitimately serve) some other school purpose. But it in no way furthers the curricular purposes of a student *newspaper,* unless one believes that the purpose of the school newspaper is to teach students that the press ought never report bad news, express unpopular views, or print a thought that might upset its sponsors. Unsurprisingly, Hazelwood East claims no such pedagogical purpose.

The Court relies on bits of testimony to portray the principal's conduct as a pedagogical lesson to Journalism II students who "had not sufficiently mastered those portions of the ... curriculum that pertained to the treatment of controversial issues and personal attacks, the need to protect the privacy of individuals ... , and 'the legal, moral, and ethical restrictions imposed upon journalists ... .' " In that regard, the Court attempts to justify censorship of the article on teenage pregnancy on the basis of the principal's judgment that (1) "the [pregnant] students' anonymity was not adequately protected," despite the article's use of aliases; and (2) the judgment that "the article was not sufficiently sensitive to the privacy interests of the students' boyfriends and parents ... ." Similarly, the Court finds in the principal's decision to censor the divorce article a journalistic lesson that the author should have given the father of one student an "opportunity to defend himself" against her charge that (in the Court's words) he "chose 'playing cards with the guys' over home and family ... ."

But the principal never consulted the students before censoring their work. "[T]hey learned of the deletions when the paper was released ... ." Further, he explained the dele-

tions only in the broadest of generalities. In one meeting called at the behest of seven protesting *Spectrum* staff members (presumably a fraction of the full class), he characterized the articles as " 'too sensitive' for 'our immature audience of readers,' " and in a later meeting he deemed them simply "inappropriate, personal, sensitive and unsuitable for the newspaper." The Court's supposition that the principal intended (or the protesters understood) those generalities as a lesson on the nuances of journalistic responsibility is utterly incredible. If he did, a fact that neither the District Court nor the Court of Appeals found, the lesson was lost on all but the psychic Spectrum staffer.

B. The Court's second excuse for deviating from precedent is the school's interest in shielding an impressionable high school audience from material whose substance is "unsuitable for immature audiences." Specifically, the majority decrees that we must afford educators authority to shield high school students from exposure to "potentially sensitive topics" (like "the particulars of teenage sexual activity") or unacceptable social viewpoints (like the advocacy of "irresponsible se[x] or conduct otherwise inconsistent with 'the shared values of a civilized social order'") through school-sponsored student activities.

Tinker teaches us that the state educator's undeniable, and undeniably vital, mandate to inculcate moral and political values is not a general warrant to act as "thought police" stifling discussion of all but state-approved topics and advocacy of all but the official position ... . Otherwise educators could transform students into "closed-circuit recipients of only that which the State chooses to communicate," *(Tinker),* and cast a perverse and impermissible "pall of orthodoxy over the classroom" *(Keyishian v. Board of Regents,* 1967). Thus, the State cannot constitutionally prohibit its high school students from recounting in the locker room "the particulars of [their] teen-age sexual activity," nor even from advocating "irresponsible se[x]" or other presumed abominations of "the shared values of a civilized social order." Even in its capacity as educator the State may not assume an Orwellian "guardianship of the public mind" *(Thomas v. Collins,* 1945).

The mere fact of school sponsorship does not, as the Court suggests, license such thought control in the high school, whether through school suppression of disfavored viewpoints or through official assessment of topic sensitivity. The former would constitute unabashed and unconstitutional viewpoint discrimination ... as well as an impermissible infringement of the students' " 'right to receive information and ideas'" ... . Just as a school board may not purge its state-funded library of all books that "'offen[d] [its] social, political, and moral tastes,' " (*Board of Education v. Pico*), school officials may not, out of like motivation, discriminatorily excise objectionable ideas from a student publication. The State's prerogative to dissolve the student newspaper entirely (or to limit its subject matter) no more entitles it to dictate which viewpoints students may express on its pages, than the State's prerogative to close down the schoolhouse entitles it to prohibit the nondisruptive expression of antiwar sentiment within its gates.

Official censorship of student speech on the ground that it addresses "potentially sensitive topics" is, for related reasons, equally impermissible. I would not begrudge an educator the authority to limit the substantive scope of a school-sponsored publication to a certain, objectively definable topic, such as literary criticism, school sports, or an overview of the school year. Unlike those determinate limitations, "potential topic sensitivity" is a vaporous nonstandard — like " 'public welfare, peace, safety, health, decency, good order, morals or convenience,' " *(Shuttlesworth v. Birmingham,* 1969), or " 'general welfare of citizens,' " *(Staub v. Baxley,* 1958) — that invites manipulation to achieve ends that cannot permissibly be achieved through blatant viewpoint discrimination and chills student speech to which school officials might not object. In part because of those dangers, this Court has consistently condemned any scheme allowing a state official boundless discretion in licensing speech from a particular forum ... .

The case before us aptly illustrates how readily school officials (and courts) can camouflage viewpoint discrimination as the "mere" protection of students from sensitive topics. Among the grounds that the Court advances to uphold the principal's censorship of one of the articles was the potential sensitivity of "teenage sexual activity." Yet the District Court specifically found that the principal "did not, as a matter of principle, oppose discussion of said topi[c] in *Spectrum.*" That much is also clear from the same principal's approval of the "squeal law" article on the same page, dealing forthrightly with "teenage sexuality," "the use of contraceptives by teenagers," and "teenage pregnancy." If topic

sensitivity were the true basis of the principal's decision, the two articles should have been equally objectionable. It is much more likely that the objectionable article was objectionable because of the viewpoint it expressed: It might have been read (as the majority apparently does) to advocate "irresponsible sex."

C. The sole concomitant of school sponsorship that might conceivably justify the distinction that the Court draws between sponsored and nonsponsored student expression is the risk "that the views of the individual speaker [might be] erroneously attributed to the school." Of course, the risk of erroneous attribution inheres in any student expression, including "personal expression" that, like the armbands in *Tinker,* "happens to occur on the school premises." Nevertheless, the majority is certainly correct that indicia of school sponsorship increase the likelihood of such attribution, and that state educators may therefore have a legitimate interest in dissociating themselves from student speech.

But " '[e]ven though the governmental purpose be legitimate and substantial, that purpose cannot be pursued by means that broadly stifle fundamental personal liberties when the end can be more narrowly achieved.' " *(Keyishian v. Board of Regents* [quoting *Shelton v. Tucker,* 1960]). Dissociative means short of censorship are available to the school. It could, for example, require the student activity to publish a disclaimer, such as the "Statement of Policy" that *Spectrum* published each school year announcing that "[a]ll ... editorials appearing in this newspaper reflect the opinions of the *Spectrum* staff, which are not necessarily shared by the administrators or faculty of Hazelwood East"; or it could simply issue its own response clarifying the official position on the matter and explaining why the student position is wrong. Yet, without so much as acknowledging the less oppressive alternatives, the Court approves of brutal censorship.

III. Since the censorship served no legitimate pedagogical purpose, it cannot by any stretch of the imagination have been designed to prevent "materia[l] disrup[tion of] classwork." *(Tinker).* Nor did the censorship fall within the category that *Tinker* described as necessary to prevent student expression from "inva[ding] the rights of others." If that term is to have any content, it must be limited to rights that are protected by law. "Any yardstick less exacting than [that] could result in

school officials curtailing speech at the slightest fear of disturbance," a prospect that would be completely at odds with this Court's pronouncement that the "undifferentiated fear or apprehension of disturbance is not enough [even in the public school context] to overcome the right to freedom of expression." *(Tinker).* And, as the Court of Appeals correctly reasoned, whatever journalistic impropriety these articles may have contained, they could not conceivably be tortious, much less criminal ... .

Finally, even if the majority were correct that the principal could constitutionally have censored the objectionable material, I would emphatically object to the brutal manner in which he did so. Where "[t]he separation of legitimate from illegitimate speech calls for more sensitive tools," *(Speiser v. Randall,* 1958), the principal used a paper shredder. He objected to some material in two articles, but excised six entire articles. He did not so much as inquire into obvious alternatives, such as precise deletions or additions (one of which had already been made), rearranging the layout, or delaying publication. Such unthinking contempt for individual rights is intolerable from any state official. It is particularly insidious from one to whom the public entrusts the task of inculcating in its youth an appreciation for the cherished democratic liberties that our Constitution guarantees.

IV. The Court opens its analysis in this case by purporting to reaffirm *Tinker's* time-tested proposition that public school students "do not 'shed their constitutional rights to freedom of speech or expression at the schoolhouse gate.' " That is an ironic introduction to an opinion that denudes high school students of much of the First Amendment protection that *Tinker* itself prescribed. Instead of "teach[ing] children to respect the diversity of ideas that is fundamental to the American system," *(Board of Education v. Pico),* and "that our Constitution is a living reality, not parchment preserved under glass," *(Shanley v. Northeast Independent School Dist., Bexar Cty., Tex.,* CA5 1972), the Court today "teach[es] youth to discount important principles of our government as mere platitudes." *(West Virginia Board of Education v. Barnette).* The young men and women of Hazelwood East expected a civics lesson, but not the one the Court teaches them today.

I dissent.

State and local laws

California Education Code, Section 48907, "Student Exercise of Free Expression."

Students of the public schools shall have the right to exercise freedom of speech and of the press including, but not limited to, the use of bulletin boards, the distribution of printed materials or petitions, the wearing of buttons, badges, and other insignia, and the right of expression in official publications, whether or not such publications or other means of expression are supported financially by the school or by use of school facilities, except that expression shall be prohibited which is obscene, libelous, or slanderous. Also prohibited shall be material which so incites students as to create a clear and present danger of the commission of unlawful acts on school premises or the violation of lawful school regulations, or the substantial disruption of the orderly operation of the school.

Each governing board of a school district and each county board of education shall adopt rules and regulations in the form of a written publications code, which shall include reasonable provisions for the time, place, and manner of conducting such activities within its respective jurisdiction.

Student editors of official school publications shall be responsible for assigning and editing the news, editorial, and feature content of their publications subject to the limitations of this section. However, it shall be the responsibility of a journalism adviser or advisers of student publications within each school to supervise the production of the student staff, to maintain professional standards of English and journalism, and to maintain the provisions of this section.

There shall be no prior restraint of material prepared for official school publications except insofar as it violates this section. School officials shall have the burden of showing justification without undue delay prior to any limitation of student expression under this section.

"Official school publications" refers to material produced by students in the journalism, newspaper, yearbook, or writing classes and distributed to the student body either free or for a fee.

Nothing in this section shall prohibit or prevent any governing board of a school district from adopting otherwise valid rules and regulations relating to oral communication by students upon the premises of each school.

Reprinted with permission from West's Annotated California Codes, Education Code, © 1993 by West Publishing Company.

Colorado

Colorado Revised Statues Annotated, Section 22-1-120, "Rights of free expression for public school students."

(1) The general assembly declares that students of the public schools shall have the right to exercise freedom of speech and of the press, and no expression contained in a student publication, whether or not such publication is school-sponsored, shall be subject to prior restraint except for the types of expression described in subsection (3) of this section. This section shall not prevent the adviser from encouraging expression which is consistent with high standards of English and journalism.

(2) If a publication written substantially by students is made generally available throughout a public school, it shall be a public forum for students of such school.

(3) Nothing in this section shall be interpreted to authorize the publication or distribution by students of the following:

(a) Expression which is obscene;

(b) Expression which is libelous, slanderous, or defamatory under state law;

(c) Expression which is false as to any person who is not a public figure or involved in a matter of public concern; or

(d) Expression which creates a clear and present danger of the commission of unlawful acts, the violation of lawful school regulations, or the material and substantial disruption of the orderly operation of the school or which violates the rights of others to privacy.

(4) The board of education of each school district shall adopt a written publications code, which shall be consistent with the terms of this section, C.R.S., and shall include reasonable provisions for the time, place, and manner of conducting free expression within the school district's jurisdiction. Said publications code shall be distributed, posted, or otherwise made available to all students and teachers at the beginning of the 1991-92 school year and at the beginning of each school year thereafter.

(5) (a) Student editors of school-spon-sored student publications shall be responsible for determining the news, opinion, and advertising content of their publications subject to the limitations of this section. It shall be the responsibility of the publications adviser of school-sponsored student publications within each school to supervise the production of such publications and to teach and encourage free and responsible expression and professional standards for English and journalism.

(b) For the purposes of this section, "publications adviser" means a person whose duties include the supervision of school-sponsored student publications.

(6) If participation in a school-sponsored publication is part of a school class or activity for which grades or school credits are given, the provisions of this section shall not be interpreted to interfere with the authority of the publications adviser for such school-sponsored publication to establish or limit writing assignments for the students working with the publication and to otherwise direct and control the learning experience that the publication is intended to provide.

(7) No expression made by students in the exercise of freedom of speech or freedom of the press shall be deemed to be an expression of school policy, and no school district or employee, or parent, or legal guardian, or official of such school district shall be held liable in any civil or criminal action for any expression made or published by students.

(8) Nothing in this section shall be construed to limit the promulgation or enforcement of lawful school regulations designed to control gangs. For the purpose of this section, the definition of "gang" shall be the definition found in section

19-2-1111(2)(d)(II), C.R.S.

Reprinted with permission from West's Colorado Revised Statutes Annotated.

Dade County, Fla.

"Guideline #26: Student Publications," from the Dade County, Florida, *Procedures for Promoting and Maintaining a Safe Learning Environment,* 1992.

Current Practices and Procedures

It is the policy of Dade County Public Schools that students are protected in their exercise of freedom of expression by the First

Amendment to the Constitution of the United States: "Congress shall make no law ... abridging the freedom of speech or of the press."

There are three classifications of speech that are prohibited by law or not protected by the First Amendment. Following publication, these types of materials may be subject to legal and/or official action:

1. material that is "obscene for minors"
2. material that is defined as "libelous"
3. material that will cause "a material and substantial disruption of school activities"

Procedures

A. School-sponsored publications

1. Students who work on official student publications will:

a. rewrite material, as required by the faculty advisers, in order to improve sentence structure, grammar, spelling, and punctuation

b. check and verify the accuracy of all facts and quotations

c. provide space in the same issue of the newspaper, when feasible, for rebuttal and opinions in case of news articles, editorials, or letters to the editor concerning controversial issues

d. determine the content of the student publication

e. consult with legal resources, local and national, in any case where the legality of content is questioned

2. Advisers to official school publications will:

a. serve primarily as teachers whose chief responsibility is to guide students to an understanding of the nature, function, and ethics of a free press and of student publications, not acting as censors

b. encourage the staff toward editing an intelligent publication that presents a complete and unbiased report and that reflects accurate reporting and editorial opinion based upon facts

c. function as liaison between officials and students to ensure full communication of administrative guidelines to:

(1) students — advising of their right to print without censorship or prior restraint

(2) school officials — advising that it is the duty of the institution to allow full and vigorous freedom of expression

d. ensure that guidelines for the staffing and operation of scholastic publications are developed in concert with the publication's current staff and furnished to administrators

3. School administrators will:

a. communicate to the adviser and student editors any district guidelines that may affect student publications

b. be aware of the most current of court rulings as they relate to free expression

c. support the First Amendment rights of students and the efforts of publication advisers to guarantee those rights in their daily work with publications; communicate to other members of the school community the rights of student journalists to question, inquire, and express themselves through student publications

d. consult with the Board attorney and/or other legal resources when an editor, adviser, and/or principal are in disagreement over the legality of content. Final decision regarding content should be solely based upon its legality

e. not terminate, transfer, or remove a person from his/her advisership for failure to exercise editorial control over student publications or otherwise suppress the rights of free expression of student journalists

f. not impose academic disciplinary action upon students, except in cases involving violations of unprotected speech

B. Literature not sponsored by school

1. Publication

a. Students should have the right to publish on their own, to possess, and to distribute on school grounds printed material not sponsored by the school when it is consistent with distribution policies of the school and the content is such that it will not create disruption in the conduct of school activities.

b. Students publishing material not sponsored by the school may not use the school's name when soliciting advertisers. Those who do will be subject to the disciplinary action of the school.

c. Students who publish such literature should be made aware of the legal responsibilities for libelous or obscene material.

2. Distribution

a. Each school should establish reasonable regulations regarding the time, place, and manner of distribution of all student publications.

b. Distribution should be conducted in a manner that does not interfere with the normal flow of traffic, both within the school and at exit doors.

c. Distribution should be conducted in a manner that prevents undue noise that interferes with normal classroom activities.

d. Students distributing literature should not interfere with the rights of others to accept or reject such literature.

e. Students who distribute material not sponsored by the school are responsible for the removal of litter created or for the cost of having such litter removed.

f. There should be no other regulation of the distribution process except, as with other modes of expression, where such activity directly causes, or is clearly likely to cause, physical harm or the substantial and material disruption of the educational process.

C. Bulletin boards

1. Ample bulletin board space should be provided for the use of students and student organizations, including an area for notices relating to out-of-school activities or matters of general interest to students.

2. Regulations should require that notices or other communications be dated before posting and that such material be removed after a prescribed, reasonable time to ensure full access to bulletin boards.

3. School authorities may restrict the use of certain bulletin boards to official school announcements.

D. Definitions — unprotected speech

There are three classifications of speech that are prohibited by law or not protected by the First Amendment. Following publication, use of these types of speech may be subject to legal and/or official school action.

1. The first classification is material that is "obscene as to minors." Obscene as to minors is defined as follows:

a. The average person, applying contemporary community standards, would find that the publication, taken as a whole, appeals to a minor's prurient interest in sex.

b. The publication depicts or describes, in a patently offensive way, sexual conduct such as the ultimate sexual act (normal or perverted), masturbation, excretory functions, and lewd exhibition of genitalia.

c. The work, taken as a whole, lacks serious literary, artistic, political, or scientific value.

d. "Minor" means any person under the age of eighteen.

2. The second classification is libel, which is defined as a "false and unprivileged statement about a specific individual that injures the individual's reputation in the communi-

ty."

If the allegedly libeled individual is a "public figure" or "public official," as defined below, then school officials must show that the false statement was published "with actual malice," i.e., that the student journalists knew that the statement was false, or that they published the statement with reckless disregard for the truth without trying to verify the truthfulness of the statement.

a. A public official is a person who holds an elected or appointed public office.

b. A public figure is a person who either seeks the public's attention or is well-known because of personal achievements.

c. School employees are to be considered public officials or public figures in articles concerning their school-related activities.

d. When an allegedly libelous statement concerns a private individual, school officials must show that the false statement was published willingly or negligently, i.e., the student journalist failed to exercise the care that a reasonably prudent person would exercise.

e. Under the "fair comment rule," a student is free to express an opinion on matters of public interest. Specifically, a student enjoys the privilege of criticizing the performance of teachers, administrators, school officials, and other school employees.

3. The third classification is material that will cause "a material and substantial disruption of school activities."

a. Disruption is defined as student rioting; unlawful seizures of property; destruction of property; widespread shouting or boisterous conduct; or substantial student participation in a school boycott, sit-in, stand-in, walk-out, or other related form of activity. Material that stimulates heated discussion or debate does not constitute the type of disruption prohibited.

b. In order for a student publication to be considered disruptive, there must exist specific facts upon which it would be reasonable to predict that a clear and present likelihood of an immediate, substantial, material disruption of normal school activity would occur if the material were distributed. Mere undifferentiated fear or apprehension of disturbance is not enough; school administrators must be able to present substantial facts which reasonably support a prediction of likely disruption.

c. In determining whether a student publication is disruptive, consideration must be given to the context of the distribution as well as the content of the material. In this regard, consideration should be given to past experience in the school with similar material, past experience in the school in dealing with and supervising the students, current events influencing student attitudes and behavior, and whether there have been any instances of actual or threatened disruption prior to or contemporaneously with the dissemination of the student publication in question.

d. School officials must act to protect the safety of advocates of unpopular viewpoints.

Reprinted with permission from Procedures for Promoting and Maintaining a Safe Learning Environment © *1992, from the Dade County Superintendent of Schools.*

Iowa

Iowa Code Annotated Section 280.22, "Student Exercise of Free Expression."

1. Except as limited by this section, students of the public schools have the right to exercise freedom of speech, including the right of expression in official school publications.

2. Students shall not express, publish, or distribute any of the following:

a. Materials which are obscene.

b. Materials which are libelous or slanderous under chapter 659.

c. Materials which encourage students to do any of the following:

(1) Commit unlawful acts.

(2) Violate lawful school regulations.

(3) Cause the material and substantial disruption of the orderly operation of the school.

3. There shall be no prior restraint of material prepared for official school publications except when the material violates this section.

4. Each board of directors of a public school shall adopt rules in the form of a written publications code, which shall include reasonable provisions for the time, place, and manner of conducting such activities within its jurisdiction. The board shall make the code available to the students and their parents.

5. Student editors of official school publications shall assign and edit the news, editorial, and feature content of their publications subject to the limitations of this section. Journalism advisers of students producing official school publications shall supervise the production of the student staff, to maintain professional standards of English and journalism, and to comply with this section.

6. Any expression made by students in the exercise of free speech, including student expression in official school publications, shall not be deemed to be an expression of school policy, and the public school district and school employees or officials shall not be liable in any civil or criminal action for any student expression made or published by students, unless the school employees or officials have interfered with or altered the content of the student speech or expression, and then only to the extent of the interference or alteration of the speech or expression.

7. "Official school publications" means material produced by students in the journalism, newspaper, yearbook, or writing classes and distributed to the student body either free or for a fee.

8. This section does not prohibit a board of directors of a public school from adopting otherwise valid rules relating to oral communications by students upon the premises of each school.

Reprinted with permission from Iowa Code Annotated, © *1991 by West Publishing Company.*

Kansas

Kansas Statutes Annotated, Sections 72-1504 et seq., "The Student Publications Act."

Section 1. This act shall be known and may be cited as the student publications act.

Section 2. **Definitions:** As used in this act:

(a) "School district" means any public school district organized and operating under the laws of this state.

(b) "Student publication" means any matter which is prepared, substantially written, or published by students, which is distributed or generally made available, either free of charge or for a fee, to members of the student body, and which is prepared under the direction of a certified employee.

Section 3.

(a) The liberty of the press in student publications shall be protected. School employees may regulate the number, length, frequency, distribution and format of student publications. Material shall not be suppressed solely because it involves political or controversial subject matter.

(b) Review of material prepared for student publications and encouragement of the expression of such material in a manner that is consistent with high standards of English and journalism shall not be deemed to be or construed as a restraint on publication of the material or an abridgment of the right to freedom of expression in student publications.

(c) Publication or other expression that is libelous, slanderous or obscene or matter that commands, requests, induces, encourages, commends or promotes conduct that is defined by law as a crime or conduct that constitutes a ground or grounds for the suspension or expulsion of students as enumerated in K.S.A. 72-8901, and amendments thereto, or which creates a material or substantial disruption of the normal school activity is not protected by this act.

(d) Subject to the limitations imposed by this section, student editors of student publications are responsible for determining the news, opinion, and advertising content of such publications. Student publication advisers and other certified employees who supervise or direct the preparation of material for expression in student publications are responsible for teaching and encouraging free and responsible expression of material and high standards of English and journalism. No such adviser or employee shall be terminated from employment, transferred, or relieved of duties imposed under this subsection for refusal to abridge or infringe upon the right to freedom of expression conferred by this act.

(e) No publication or other expression of matter by students in the exercise of rights under this act shall be deemed to be an expression of school district policy. No school district, member of the board of education or employee thereof, shall be held responsible in any civil or criminal action for any publication or other expression of matter by students in the exercise of rights under this act. Student editors and other students of a school district, if such student editors and other students have attained the age of majority, shall be held liable in any civil or criminal action for matter expressed in student publications to the extent of any such student editor's or other student's responsibility for an involvement in the preparation and publication of such matter.

Reprinted with permission of the Revisor of Statutes of the State of Kansas from Kansas Statutes Annotated, 1993.

Massachusetts

Massachusetts General Laws Annotated, Chapter 71, Section 82, "Public secondary schools; right of students to freedom of expression; limitations; definitions."

The right of students to freedom of expression in the public schools of the commonwealth shall not be abridged, provided that such right shall not cause any disruption or disorder within the school. Freedom of expression shall include without limitation, the rights and responsibilities of students, collectively and individually, (a) to express their views through speech and symbols, (b) to write, publish and disseminate their views, (c) to assemble peaceably on school property for the purpose of expressing their opinions. Any assembly planned by students during regularly scheduled school hours shall be held only at a time and place approved in advance by the school principal or his designee.

No expression made by students in the exercise of such rights shall be deemed to be an expression of school policy and no school officials shall be held responsible in any civil or criminal action for any expression made or published by the students.

For the purposes of this section and sections eighty-three to eighty-five, inclusive, the word student shall mean any person attending a public secondary school in the commonwealth. The word school official shall mean any member or employee of the local school committee.

Reprinted with permission from Massachusetts General Laws Annotated, © 1992 by West Publishing Company.

SPLC model guidelines for student publications

Preamble: The following guidelines are based on state and federal court decisions that have determined the First Amendment rights of students, including the Supreme Court's decision in *Hazelwood School District v. Kuhlmeier* (1988). These guidelines do not provide a legal basis for school officials or employees to exercise prior restraint or prior review of student publications. The Student Press Law Center cautions that court rulings indicate that policies which provide for prior review and restraint and meet constitutional requirements of precision, narrow scope and protection of speech are almost impossible to develop for forum publications.

In addition, schools that adopt a prior review and/or prior restraint policy assume legal liability for the content of the publications, whether they are school-sponsored or non-school-sponsored. Court decisions indicate that a school likely will be protected from liability if by written policy it rejects prior review and prior restraint.

I. Statement of policy

It is undeniable that students are protected in their exercise of freedom of expression by the First Amendment to the Constitution of the United States. Accordingly, school officials are responsible for ensuring freedom of expression for all students.

It is the policy of the _____ Board of Education that (newspaper), (yearbook) and (literary magazine), the official, school-sponsored publications of _____ High School have been established as forums for student expression and as voices in the uninhibited, robust, free and open discussion of issues. Each publication should provide a full opportunity for students to inquire, question and exchange ideas. Content should reflect all areas of student interest, including topics about which there may be dissent or controversy.

It is the policy of the _____ Board of Education that student journalists shall have the right to determine the content of official student publications. Accordingly, the following guidelines relate only to establishing grounds for disciplinary actions subsequent to publication.

II. Official school publications

A. Responsibilities of student journalists

Students who work on official student publications determine the content of those publications and are responsible for that content. These students should:

1. Determine the content of the student publication;

2. Strive to produce a publication based upon professional standards of accuracy, objectivity and fair play;

3. Review material to improve sentence structure, grammar, spelling and punctuation;

4. Check and verify all facts and verify the accuracy of all quotations; and

5. In the case of editorials or letters to the editor concerning controversial issues, determine the need for rebuttal comments and opinions and provide space therefore if appropriate.

B. Prohibited material

1. Students cannot publish or distribute material that is "obscene as to minors." "Minor" means any person under the age of 18. Obscene as to minors is defined as material that meets all three of the following requirements:

(a) The average person, applying contemporary community standards, would find that the publication, taken as a whole, appeals to a minor's prurient interest in sex; and

(b) The publication depicts or describes, in a patently offensive way, sexual conduct such as ultimate sexual acts (normal or perverted), masturbation and lewd exhibition of the genitals; and

(c) The work, taken as a whole, lacks serious literary, artistic, political or scientific value.

Indecent or vulgar language is not obscene.

{Note: Many statues exist defining what is "obscene as to minors." If such a statue is in force in your state, it should be substituted in place of Section II (B) (1).}

2. Students cannot publish or distribute libelous material. Libelous statements are provably false and unprivileged statements that do demonstrated injury to an individual's or business's reputation in the community. If the allegedly libeled party is a "public figure" or "public official" as defined below, then school officials must show that the false statement was published "with actual malice," i.e.,

that the student journalists knew that the statement was false or that they published it with reckless disregard for the truth — without trying to verify the truthfulness of the statement.

(a) A public official is a person who holds an elected or appointed public office.

(b) A public figure either seeks the public's attention or is well known because of personal achievements.

(c) School employees are public officials or public figures in articles concerning their school-related activities.

(d) When an allegedly libelous statement concerns a private individual, school officials must show that the false statement was published willfully or negligently, i.e., the student journalist who wrote or published the statement has failed to exercise reasonably prudent care.

(e) Under the "fair comment rule," a student is free to express an opinion on a matter of public interest. Specifically, a student may criticize school policy or the performance of teachers, administrators, school officials and other school employees.

3. Students cannot publish or distribute material that will cause "a material and substantial disruption of school activities."

(a) Disruption is defined as student rioting; unlawful seizures of property; destruction of property; or substantial student participation in a school boycott, sit-in, walk-out or other related form of activity. Material such as racial, religious or ethnic slurs, however distasteful, are not in and of themselves disruptive under these guidelines. Threats of violence are not materially disruptive without some act in furtherance of that threat or a reasonable belief and expectation that the author of the threat has the capability and intent of carrying through on that threat in a fashion not permitting acts other than suppression of speech to mitigate the threat in a timely manner. Material that stimulates heated discussions or debate does not constitute the type of disruption prohibited.

(b) For a student publication to be considered disruptive, specific facts must exist upon which one could reasonably forecast that a likelihood of immediate, substantial material disruption to normal school activity would occur if the material were further distributed or has occurred as a result of the material's distribution. Mere undifferentiated fear or apprehension of disturbance is not enough; school administrators must be able affirmatively to show substantial facts that reasonably support a forecast of likely disruption.

(c) In determining whether a student publication is disruptive, consideration must be given to the context of this distribution as well as the content of the material. In this regard, consideration should be given to past experience in the school with similar material, past experience in the school dealing with and supervising the students in the school, current events influencing student attitudes and behavior and whether there have been any instances of actual or threatened disruption prior to or contemporaneously with the dissemination of the student publication in question.

(d) School officials must protect advocates of unpopular viewpoints.

(e) "School activity" means educational student activity sponsored by the school and includes, by way of example and not by way of limitation, classroom work, library activities, physical education classes, official assemblies and other similar gatherings, school athletic contests, band concerts, school plays and scheduled in-school lunch periods.

C. Legal advice

1. If, in the opinion of student editor, student editorial staff or faculty adviser, material proposed for publication may be "obscene," "libelous" or would cause an "immediate, material and substantial disruption of school activities," the legal opinion of a practicing attorney should be sought. The services of the attorney for the local newspaper or the free legal services of the Student Press Law Center (202-466-5242) are recommended.

2. Legal fees charged in connection with the consultation will be paid by the board of education.

3. The final decision of whether the material is to be published will be left to the student editor or student editorial staff.

III. Non-school-sponsored publications

School officials may not ban the distribution of non-school-sponsored publications on school grounds. However, students who violate any rule listed under II(B) may be disciplined after distribution.

1. School officials may regulate the time, place and manner of distribution.

(a) Non-school-sponsored publications will have the same rights of distribution as

official school publications;

(b) "Distribution" means dissemination of a publication to students at a time and place of normal school activity, or immediately prior or subsequent thereto, by means of handing out free copies, selling or offering copies for sale, accepting donations for copies of the publication in areas of the school which are generally frequented by students.

2. School officials cannot:

(a) Prohibit the distribution of anonymous literature or require that literature bear the name of the sponsoring organization or author;

(b) Ban the distribution of literature because it contains advertising;

(c) Ban the sale of literature; or

(d) Create regulations that discriminate against non-school-sponsored publications or interfere with the effective distribution of sponsored or non-sponsored publications.

IV. Protected speech

School officials cannot:

1. Ban speech solely because it is controversial, takes extreme, "fringe" or minority opinions, or is distasteful, unpopular or unpleasant;

2. Ban the publication or distribution of material relating to sexual issues including, but not limited to, virginity, birth control and sexually-transmitted diseases (including AIDS);

3. Censor or punish the occasional use of indecent, vulgar or so called "four-letter" words in student publications;

4. Prohibit criticism of the policies, practices or performance of teachers, school officials, the school itself or of any public officials;

5. Cut off funds to official student publications because of disagreement over editorial policy;

6. Ban speech that merely advocates illegal conduct without proving that such speech is directed toward and will actually cause imminent unlawful action;

7. Ban the publication or distribution of material written by non-students;

8. Prohibit the school newspaper from accepting advertising; or

9. Prohibit the endorsement of candidates for student office or for public office at any level.

V. Commercial speech

Advertising is a constitutionally protected expression. School publications may accept advertising. Acceptance or rejection of adver-

tising is within the purview of the publication staff, who may accept any ads except for those for products or services that are illegal for all students. Political ads may be accepted. The publication should not accept ads only on one side of an issue of election.

VI. Adviser job security

The adviser is not a censor. No teacher who advises a student publication will be fired, transferred or removed from the advisership by reason of his or her refusal to exercise editorial control over the student publication or to otherwise suppress the protected free expression of student journalists.

VII. Prior restraint

No student publication, whether non-school-sponsored or official, will be reviewed by school administrators prior to distribution or withheld from distribution. The school assumes no liability for the content of any student publication, and urges all student journalists to recognize that with editorial control comes responsibility, including the responsibility to follow professional journalism standards.

VIII. Circulation

These guidelines will be included in the handbook on student rights and responsibilities and circulated to all students.

Student newspapers analyzed in the study

Newspaper	School	City, State
The Aggie Journal	Jackson	Jackson, Ala.
The Imprint	Grissom	Huntsville, Ala.
The Willcox Word	Willcox	Willcox, Ariz.
The Cardinal's Scream	Camden Fairview	Camden, Ark.
Blue Print	Yosemite	Oakhurst, Calif.
The Charger	Bullard	Fresno, Calif.
The Charger Account	Leland	San Jose, Calif.
The Cry of the Cougar	Crenshaw	Los Angeles, Calif.
Dragon's Tale	Sonoma Valley	Sonoma, Calif.
El Estoque	Monta Vista	Cupertino, Calif.
The Epic	Lynbrook	San Jose, Calif.
The Epitaph	Homestead	Cupertino, Calif.
The Forge	Santa Barbara	Santa Barbara, Calif.
The Franklin Press	Benjamin Franklin	Los Angeles, Calif.
The Green & Gold	Narbonne	Harbor City, Calif.
The Green & Gold	John C. Fremont	Oakland, Calif.
Mt. Carmel Sun	Mt. Carmel	San Diego, Calif.
The Panther Tales	Perris	Perris, Calif.
Pathfinder	John C. Fremont	Los Angeles, Calif.
Prospector	Cupertino	Cupertino, Calif.
Sword and Shield	South	Torrance, Calif.
The Talon	Los Altos	Los Altos, Calif.
Ukiahilite	Ukiah	Ukiah, Calif.
The Union Street Journal	Cherry Creek	Englewood, Calif.
Gateway Medallion	Gateway	Aurora, Colo.
Horizon Profile	Horizon	Brighton, Colo.
Lions' Roar	Littleton	Littleton, Colo.
South Confederate	South	Denver, Colo.
Tenderfoot Times	Salida	Salida, Colo.
The Voice	Thompson Valley	Loveland, Colo.
The WHS Rodeo	West	Denver, Colo.
The Beacon	Woodrow Wilson	Washington, D.C.
Brighter Days	M.M. Washington Career	Washington, D.C.
The Ellington Express	Duke Ellington School of the Arts	Washington, D.C.
The Indian Post	Anacostia Senior	Washington, D.C.
The Rainbow	Bell Multicultural	Washington, D.C.
Train of Thought	Benjamin Banneker Academic	Washington, D.C.
Highlights	Coral Gables Sr.	Coral Gables, Fla.
in flight	Lake Howell	Winter Park, Fla.
The Paw Street Journal	Dr. Phillips	Orlando, Fla.
Bulldog Bark	Thomson	Thomson, Ga.
The Bulldog Bulletin	Thomasville	Thomasville, Ga.
Chant	North Cobb	Kennesaw, Ga.
The Chariot	Coffee	Douglas, Ga.
The Galleon	Stone Mountain	Stone Mountain, Ga.
McIntosh Trail	McIntosh	Peachtree City, Ga.
The Panther Press	Lakeside	Evans, Ga.
The Sentinel	Brookwood	Snellville, Ga.
The Southerner	Henry W. Grady	Atlanta, Ga.
The Trojanier	Rigby	Rigby, Idaho
the Blueprint	Downers Grove South	Downers Grove, Ill.
Deerprints	Deerfield	Deerfield, Ill.
Echo	Glenbard East	Lombard, Ill.
Green & Gold	St. Patrick	Chicago, Ill.
The Lion	Lyons Township	LaGrange, Ill.
Panther Press	DuSable	Chicago, Ill.
Southwords	Maine South	Park Ridge, Ill.
X-Ray	St. Charles	St. Charles, Ill.
York-hi	York Community	Elmhurst, Ill.
The Hi-Lite	Carmel	Carmel, Ind.
The Hyphen	Jeffersonville	Jeffersonville, Ind.
The Mirror	Merrillville	Merrillville, Ind.
The Northerner	North Side	Fort Wayne, Ind.
Pantherette	Corydon Central	Corydon, Ind.
Paw Print	Hagerstown	Hagerstown, Ind.
Pow Wow	Portage	Portage, Ind.
Raiders Riot	South Ripley	Versailles, Ind.
Southport Journal	Southport	Indianapolis, Ind.
Beak 'n Eye	West	Davenport, Iowa
The Blackhawk	Central	Davenport, Iowa
The Echoes	Abraham Lincoln	Council Bluffs, Iowa
The Hi-Breeze	Storm Lake	Storm Lake, Iowa
JHS in Black & White	Johnston	Johnston, Iowa
Little Dodger	Fort Dodge Senior	Fort Dodge, Iowa
Little Hawk	City	Iowa City, Iowa
Outlook	Jefferson	Cedar Rapids, Iowa
The Purple & Gray	Burlington Community	Burlington, Iowa
Ram News	Dubuque Senior	Dubuque, Iowa
The Spartan Shield	Pleasant Valley Comm.	Pleasant Valley, Iowa
Spotlight	Valley West	Des Moines, Iowa
The Surveyor	George Washington Senior	Cedar Rapids, Iowa
Web	Ames Senior	Ames, Iowa
The Academician	Sumner Academy of Arts and Science	Kansas City, Kan.
Bearcat	Ellsworth	Ellsworth, Kan.
The Booster	Pittsburg	Pittsburg, Kan.
The Booster	Turner	Kansas City, Kan.
The Budget	Lawrence	Lawrence, Kan.
The Charger Courier	Burrton	Burrton, Kan.
Chaparral Hi-Lites	Chaparral	Anthony, Kan.
Cheyenne Indian News	St. Francis Community	St. Francis, Kan.
The Crusader	Buhler	Buhler, Kan.
Cub Tracks	Humboldt	Humboldt, Kan.
The Dickinsonian	Chapman	Chapman, Kan.
The Dodger	Dodge City	Dodge City, Kan.
The Eagle	Olathe North	Olathe, Kan.
The Echo	Emporia	Emporia, Kan.
Express	Basehor-Linwood	Basehor, Kan.
Express	Maize	Maize, Kan.
The Holtonian	Holton	Holton, Kan.
The Mentor	Manhattan	Manhattan, Kan.
The Newtonian	Newton	Newton, Kan.
Northeast Viking	Northeast	Arma, Kan.
The Northwest Passage	Shawnee Mission Northwest	Shawnee, Kan.
Paladin	Kapaun Mt. Carmel	Wichita, Kan.
The Panther Pause	Phillipsburg	Phillipsburg, Kan.
Sugar Beet	Garden City	Garden City, Kan.
Trail Blazer	Council Grove	Council Grove, Kan.
Trailblazer	Gardner Edgerton	Gardner, Kan.
Tripodium	Salina South	Salina, Kan.
Newtonite	Newton North	Newtonville, Mass.
Sagamore	Brookline	Brookline, Mass.
The Aquila	Columbia Central	Brooklyn, Mich.
The Arrow	Utica	Utica, Mich.
The Blazer	Flushing	Flushing, Mich.
Blue and White	Petoskey	Petoskey, Mich.
Buckaneer	Pine River	LeRoy, Mich.
The Catalyst	Harrison	Farmington Hills, Mich.
Comets' Tail	Grand Ledge	Grand Ledge, Mich.
The Easterner	Lansing Eastern	Lansing, Mich.
The Emissary	Hillsdale	Hillsdale, Mich.
Fitz-Herald	Fitzgerald	Warren, Mich.
Focus	Midland	Midland, Mich.
Generation	Wayne State/ Detroit Public Schools Advanced Studies Program	Detroit, Mich.
The Informer	Laingsburg	Laingsburg, Mich.
Lancer	South Lake	St. Clair Shores, Mich.
The Purple Pride	Gladstone	Gladstone, Mich.
RamPage	Lamphere	Madison Heights, Mich.
Reflector News	Jackson	Jackson, Mich.
Sailors Log	Mona Shores	Muskegon, Mich.
The Scarlet Letter	Athens	Troy, Mich.
Shamrock	East Detroit	Eastpointe, Mich.
Spectrum	West Bloomfield	West Bloomfield, Mich.
The Tower	Grosse Pointe South	Grosse Pointe Farms, Mich.
The Trojan Torch	Plainwell	Plainwell, Mich.
The Vanguard	Adlai E. Stevenson	Sterling Heights, Mich.
The Ahlahasa	Albert Lea	Albert Lea, Minn.
The Charger	Oxford	Oxford, Miss.
The Charger Flash	Southaven	Southaven, Miss.
Echoes	Natchez	Natchez, Miss.
The Emphasis	Oak Hill Academy	West Point, Miss.
Hi-Flashes	Hattiesburg	Hattiesburg, Miss.
Hi-Times	Union	Union, Miss.
Highlander	Ripley	Ripley, Miss.
The Maroon Tribune	Horn Lake	Horn Lake, Miss.
The Northwestern	Northwest Rankin Attendance Center	Brandon, Miss.
Student Press	George County	Lucedale, Miss.
The Wildcat	Meridian	Meridian, Miss.
The Kirkwood Call	Kirkwood	Kirkwood, Mo.
The Torch	John F. Kennedy	Manchester, Mo.
Kodiak	Billings West	Billings, Mont.
Stampede	Charles M. Russell	Great Falls, Mont.
Bear Tracks	Blair	Blair, Neb.
Miner Detail	Bishop Manogue	Reno, Nev.
Hi's Eye	Westfield	Westfield, N.J.
Pawprint	Manzano	Albuquerque, N.M.
The Spectator	Stuyvesant	New York, N.Y.
The Voice of King	Martin Luther King Jr	New York, N.Y.
The Eagle Times	Western Harnett	Lillington, N.C.
Falcon's Cry	Jordan	Durham, N.C.
Green & White	Durham Academy	Durham, N.C.
Hi-Zette	Ralph L. Fike	Wilson, N.C.
Pine Whispers	R.J. Reynolds	Winston-Salem, N.C.
The Proconian	Chapel Hill	Chapel Hill, N.C.
The Raider Review	Southern Vance	Henderson N.C.
The Rambler	Greene County Central	Snow Hill, N.C.
The Round Table	Northern	Durham, N.C.
Viking Ventures	South Granville	Creedmoor, N.C.
Wavelengths	Ashbrook	Gastonia, N.C.
Wingspan	West Henderson	Hendersonville, N.C.
Arlingtonian	Upper Arlington	Upper Arlington, Ohio
The Bulldog Bulletin	Lakeview	Cortland, Ohio
The Catalyst	Sylvania Southview	Sylvania, Ohio
Compendium	Newark	Newark, Ohio
The Cougar's Roar	Van Wert	Van Wert, Ohio
The Courier	Solon	Solon, Ohio
The Devil's Tale	Tallmadge	Tallmadge, Ohio
Harding Herald	Marion Harding	Marion, Ohio
Insights	Pickerington	Pickerington, Ohio
The Lakewood Times	Lakewood	Lakewood, Ohio
Lebanon Light	Lebanon	Lebanon, Ohio
The Ramble	Whitehall-Yearling	Whitehall, Ohio

The Ravine	Worthington Kilbourne	West Worthington Ohio
The Searchlight	North	Eastlake, Ohio
The Torch	Bexley	Bexley, Ohio
The Visor	Archbishop Hoban	Akron, Ohio
The Wildcat	Hilliard	Hilliard, Ohio
Blueline	Guthrie	Guthrie, Okla.
CHS Times and Democrat	Checotah	Checotah, Okla.
The Demon Pitchfork	Duncan	Duncan, Okla.
Excelsior	Stillwater	Stillwater, Okla.
The Fourth Estate	Bartlesville	Bartlesville, Okla.
North Star	Putnam City North	Oklahoma City, Okla.
The Pirate	Locust Grove	Locust Grove, Okla.
Ruff Draft Magazine	Edmond Memorial	Edmond, Okla.
The Sentinel	Tulsa Memorial	Tulsa, Okla.
Tatler	Lawton	Lawton, Okla.
Tatler	Claremore	Claremore, Okla.
The Axe	South Eugene	Eugene, Ore.
Crescent Crier	Crescent Valley	Corvallis, Ore.
Crimson Times	Glencoe	Hillsboro, Ore.
The Expression	Yamhill-Carlton Union	Yamhill, Ore.
Franklin Post	Franklin	Portland, Ore.
Hi-Times	North Medford	Medford, Ore.
Jeffersonian	Jefferson	Portland, Ore.
The Ma-Hi Times	Marshfield Senior	Coos Bay, Ore.
Maroon and Gold	Junction City	Junction City, Ore.
Current Waves	N. Myrtle Beach	Little River, S.C.
The Odyssey	James Island	Charleston, S.C.
Palmetto Leaf	Camden	Camden, S.C.
The Tribal Tribune	Wando	Mt. Pleasant, S.C.
The Roaring Lion	Central	Columbia, Tenn.
The Antler	Deer Park	Deer Park, Texas
The Colt	Arlington	Arlington, Texas
Cricket Chirps	Seguin	Seguin, Texas
Eagle Eye	DeSoto	DeSoto, Texas
The Fang	Lake Highlands	Dallas, Texas
The Gavel	Holmes	San Antonio, Texas
Hillcrest Hurricane	Hillcrest	Dallas, Texas
Hoof Beat	Bellville	Bellville, Texas
Image	Haltom	Ft. Worth, Texas
Mane Event	Taylor	Katy, Texas
The Pioneer	Tascosa	Amarillo, Texas
Pride	South San Antonio	San Antonio, Texas
Radar	John H. Reagan	Austin, Texas
The Raider Echo	North Garland	Garland, Texas
Southern Accent	Robert E. Lee	Tyler, Texas
Trailblazer	McNeil	Austin, Texas
Westlake Featherduster	Westlake	Austin, Texas
tjToday	Thomas Jefferson	Fairfax County, Va.
The Peninsula Outlook	Peninsula	Gig Harbor, Wash.
Sandstorm	Richland	Richland, Wash.
Troy In Voice	Auburn	Auburn, Wash.
The View	Mountain View	Vancouver, Wash.

Scholastic press associations

The city, state, regional and national scholastic press associations listed here offer a variety of services. Though different associations focus on different people and services, a basic list of help available from them includes: critiques and contests for school publications, conferences and summer workshops for students and teachers, magazines/newsletters and special topic publications.

School and publication memberships in scholastic press associations are reasonably priced. Sponsored activities and products usually require an additional fee.

If you're a teacher, you and your students can get assistance and ideas as well as win awards for your newspaper. If you're a professional newspaper publisher or editor, the local scholastic press association is an excellent first stop on the way to getting teens involved in your publication and helping them with theirs. If you're a college administrator, the scholastic press association gives you access to tomorrow's journalism majors.

No scholastic press association in your area? Start one! Contact a state association close to you, or one of the national groups, for pointers and assistance. Many state press associations are located on college campuses; perhaps a university in your area could house your new organization.

National associations

Jennifer McGill
Executive Director
Association for Education in Journalism and Mass Communication
Also contact for Scholastic Journalism Division, AEJMC
1621 College St.
University of South Carolina
Columbia, S.C. 29208-0251
803-777-2005

Edmund Sullivan
Director
Columbia Scholastic Press Association
Columbia University
Box 11, Central Mail Room
New York, N.Y. 10027
212-854-9400

Linda Puntney
Executive Director
Journalism Education Association
Kansas State University
103 Kedzie Hall

Manhattan, Kan. 66506-1505
913-532-5532

Tom Rolnicki
Executive Director
National Scholastic Press Association
University of Minnesota
620 Rarig Center
330 21st Avenue South
Minneapolis, Minn. 55455
612-625-8335

Richard Johns
Executive Director
Quill and Scroll Society
School of Journalism and Mass Communication
University of Iowa
Iowa City, Iowa 52242-1528
319-335-5795

Regional associations

Robert Baram
Director
New England Scholastic Press Association
Boston University
College of Communication
640 Commonwealth Avenue
Boston, Mass. 02215
617-353-3485

Nancy Gallinger
Executive Director
Yankee Press Education Network (Yankee PEN)
School of Journalism
Northeastern University
102 Lake Hall
Boston, Mass. 02115
617-373-3221

Barbara Hines
Coordinator
Capital Area Youth Journalism Exchange
P.O. Box 3036
Silver Spring, Md. 20918
301-593-4416

Linda Fritz Glomski
Coordinator
Great Lakes Interscholastic Press Association
School of Mass Communication
302 West Hall
Bowling Green State University
Bowling Green, Ohio 43403-0237
419-372-8725

Beth Dickey
Associate Director
Southern Interscholastic Press Association
College of Journalism and
    Mass Communications
University of South Carolina
Columbia, S.C. 29208
803-777-6284

Young Dan Inyang
Director
Southern Regional Press Institute
P.O. Box 20634
Savannah State College
Savannah, Ga. 31404
912-356-2169 or 912-356-2287

Debra Belluomini
Director
United Press Association
W. Page Pitt School of Journalism and
    Mass Communication
Marshall University
400 Hal Greer Blvd.
Huntington, W.V. 25755
304-696-2736

Alabama
Kathy Lawrence
Director
Alabama Scholastic Press Association
P.O. Box 031609
Tuscaloosa, Ala. 35403
205-348-7257

Alaska
Lael Morgan
Alaska Journalism Teachers
Department of Journalism and Broadcasting
University of Alaska
106 Bunnell Building
P.O. Box 756120
Fairbanks, Alaska 99775-6120
907-474-7995

Arizona
Kerry Benson
President
Arizona Interscholastic Press Association
Chandler
6250 N. Arizona Avenue
Chandler, Ariz. 85224
602-786-7140

Arkansas
William D. Downs Jr.
Director
Arkansas Press Association

P.O. Box 3761
Ouachita Baptist University
Arkadelphia, Ark. 71998
501-245-5207

California
Jay Berman
Board Member
California Scholastic Press Association
2005 Faymont Avenue
Manhattan Beach, Calif. 90266
310-374-5186

Hilda Walker
Treasurer
JEA of Northern California
3055 W. Princeton
Stockton, Calif. 95204
209-465-0584

Greg Lewis
Executive Director
San Joaquin Valley Scholastic
    Press Association
California State University, Fresno
Department of Mass Communication
    and Journalism
2225 E. San Ramon
Fresno, Calif. 93740
209-278-2087

Dwight Bustrum
President
Southern California JEA
Santa Fe
10400 Orr and Day Road
Santa Fe Springs, Calif. 90670
310-698-8121, ext. 8509

Gil Chesterton
Director
California Scholastic Press Association
Beverly Hills
241 Moreno Drive
Beverly Hills, Calif. 90212
310-201-0661, ext. 410

Colorado
Don Ridgway
Executive Director
Colorado Press Association
Campus Box 287
School of Journalism and Mass
    Communication
University of Colorado
Boulder, Colo. 80309
303-492-5045

Florida
Julie Dodd
Executive Director
Florida Scholastic Press Association, Inc.
2077 Weimer Hall
College of Journalism and Communication
University of Florida
Gainesville, Fla. 32611-2084
904-392-0460

Georgia
Margaret M. Johnston
Coordinator
Georgia Scholastic Press Association
College of Journalism and Mass Communication
University of Georgia
Athens, Ga. 30602-3018
706-542-5022

Hawaii
Barry Masuo
President
Hawaii Schools Publications Association
Kaimuki
2705 Kaimuki Avenue
Honolulu, Hawaii 96816
808-732-7711

Idaho
Dan Prinzing
Past President
Idaho Journalism Advisers Association
3421 S. Crosspoint
Boise, Idaho 83706
208-336-9896

Illinois
James Tidwell
Director
Eastern Illinois Press Association
Journalism Department
Eastern Illinois University
Charleston, Ill. 61920
217-581-2812

James Tidwell
Executive Secretary
Illinois JEA
Journalism Department
Eastern Illinois University
Charleston, Ill. 61920
217-581-2812

Dana Ewell
Director
Illinois State Press Association
Journalism Department
University of Illinois
119 Gregory Hall
810 S. Wright
Urbana, Ill. 61801
217-333-1508, ext. 0709

Ted Heiser
Treasurer
Northern Illinois School Press Association
Glenbrook South
4000 W. Lake Avenue
Glenview, Ill. 60025
708-729-2000, ext. 4497 or 708-486-4497

Herman Albers
Chairman
Southern Illinois School Press Association
Coulterville
Box 386
Coulterville, Ill. 62237
618-758-2338

Indiana
Dennis Cripe
Director
Indiana Press Association
Franklin College
Shirk Hall
501 E. Monroe Street
Franklin, Ind. 46131
317-738-8198

Iowa
Mary Arnold
Executive Director
Iowa High School Press Association
303 Communications Center
University of Iowa
Iowa City, Iowa 52242
319-335-5833

Kansas
John Hudnall
Executive Director
Kansas Scholastic Press Association
2063 Dole Center
University of Kansas
Lawrence, Kan. 66045
913-864-0605

Kentucky
Ms. Maria Braden
Coordinator
Kentucky Journalism Day

School of Journalism and
    Telecommunications
University of Kentucky
218 Grehan Building
Lexington, Ky. 40506-0042
606-257-4361

Gail Henson
Executive Director
Greater Louisville Press Association
Bellarmine College
2001 Newburg Road
Louisville, Ky. 40205-0671
502-452-8223

Louisiana
Phil Ward
Executive Director
Louisiana Scholastic Press Association
Manship School of Mass Communications
Louisiana State University
Baton Rouge, La. 70803-7202
504-388-2336

Maryland
Christopher Callahan
Executive Director
Maryland Scholastic Press Association
College of Journalism
University of Maryland
College Park, Md. 20742-7111
301-405-2391

Michigan
Cheryl Pell
Executive Director
Michigan Interscholastic Press Association
School of Journalism
Michigan State University
305 Communication Arts and Sciences Bldg.
East Lansing, Mich. 48824-1212
517-353-6761

Minnesota
Brent Norlem
Director
Journalism Advisers of Minnesota
St. Cloud State University
Department of Mass Communications
720 Fourth Avenue S.
St. Cloud, Minn. 56301-4498
612-255-4202

Don Reeder
Executive Director
Minnesota Press Association
University of Minnesota
620 Rarig Center

330 21st Avenue S.
Minneapolis, Minn. 55455
612-625-8335

Mississippi
Robin Street
Director
Mississippi Scholastic Press Association
Department of Journalism
University of Mississippi
331 Farley Hall
University, Miss. 38677
601-232-7146

Missouri
Ann M. Brill
Executive Director
Missouri Interscholastic Press Association
University of Missouri
School of Journalism
P.O. Box 838
Columbia, Mo. 65205-0838
314-882-2380

Sandy Newcomer
President
Missouri JEA
Mt. Vernon
Mt. Vernon, Mo. 65712
417-466-7526

Karen Ray
President
Ozark Publications Advisers
Glendale High School
2727 Ingram Mill
Springfield, Mo. 65804
417-887-0653

Curtis Kenner
President
Sponsors of School Publications of
    Greater St. Louis
1129 Buckley Road
St. Louis, Mo. 63125
314-892-6747

Karen Black
President
Journalism Educators of Metropolitan
    Kansas City
Hickman Mills
9010 Old Santa Fe Road
Kansas City, Mo. 64138
816-763-8374

Montana

Patty Reksten
Director
Montana Interscholastic Press Association
School of Journalism
University of Montana
Missoula, Mont. 59812
406-243-2191

Nebraska

Mike Lederer
UNL Liaison
Nebraska Press Association
College of Journalism and Mass
   Communications
University of Nebraska at Lincoln
206 Avery Hall
Lincoln, Neb. 68588-0127
402-472-3042

Nevada

V. LaVerne Forest
President
Nevada JEA
563 Penny Way
Sparks, Nev. 89431
702-358-2762

New Jersey

Sherry Haklik
President
Garden State Scholastic Press Association
411 Tappan Avenue
North Plain Field, N.J. 07063
908-755-3961

New Mexico

Pat Graff
President
New Mexico Scholastic Press Association
La Cueva
7801 Wilshire N.E.
Albuquerque, N.M. 87122
505-823-2327

New York

Marshall Matlock
Director
Empire State School Press Association
School of Public Communications
Syracuse University
215 University Place
Syracuse, N.Y. 13244-2100
315-443-3300

Regina Vogel
President
New York City Scholastic Press Association

Department of Journalism
New York University
10 Washington Place, Fifth Floor
New York, N.Y. 10003
212-998-7980

Penelope Deakin
Director
Western New York School Press Association
Hendrix Hall
SUNY - Fredonia
Fredonia, N.Y. 14063
716-673-3550

North Carolina

Richard Beckman
Director
North Carolina Scholastic Press Association
14 Howell Hall
University of North Carolina
School of Journalism and
   Mass Communication
Campus Box 3365
Chapel Hill, N.C. 27599
919-962-1204

North Dakota

Robin Bergstrom
Director
Northern Interscholastic Press Association
School of Communications
University of North Dakota
Box 7169
Grand Forks, N.D. 58202
701-777-2159

Ohio

Sarah Ortman
Executive Director
Journalism Association of Ohio Schools
Ohio State University
School of Journalism
242 W. 18th Avenue
Columbus, Ohio 43210
614-292-9240

William Sledzik
Executive Director
Northeastern Ohio Press Association
130 Taylor Hall
Kent State University
School of Journalism and
   Mass Communications
Kent, Ohio 44242
216-672-2572

Oklahoma

Laura Schaub

Executive Director
Oklahoma Interscholastic Press Association
P.O. Box 5539
Norman, Okla. 73070
405-325-2453

Oregon

Carla Harris
Director
Northwest Scholastic Press
1947 N.E. Estate Drive
Hillsboro, Ore. 97124
503-648-7415

Carla Day
President
Oregon JEA
Dallas High School
901 Southeast Ash
Dallas, Oregon 97338
503-623-8336

Jennifer King
Director
Oregon Scholastic Press Association
School of Journalism and Communication
University of Oregon
Eugene, Ore. 97403-1275
503-346-5847

Pennsylvania

Kathleen Zwiebel
Treasurer
Pennsylvania School Press Association
Pottsville Area High School
16th and Elk Avenue
Pottsville, Penn. 17901
717-621-2974

South Carolina

Mr. Bruce Konkle
Director
South Carolina Scholastic Press Association
College of Journalism and
   Mass Communications
University of South Carolina
Columbia, S.C. 29208
803-777-6284

John Lopiccolo
Director
South Carolina Scholastic Broadcasters
   Association
College of Journalism and
   Mass Communication
University of South Carolina
Columbia, S.C. 29208
803-777-3324

South Dakota
Doris Giago
Director
South Dakota High School Press Association
Department of Journalism
South Dakota State University
Brookings, S.D. 57007
605-688-4171

Tennessee
Bonnie Hufford
Director
Tennessee Press Association
University of Tennessee
330 Communications Building
Knoxville, Tenn. 37996-0330
615-974-5155

Texas
Bobby Hawthorne
Director
Interscholastic League Press Conference
P.O. Box 8028
UT Station
Austin, Texas 78713-8028
512-471-5883

Pat Brittain
Executive Director
Texas Association of Journalism Educators
P.O. Box 23202
Waco, Texas 76702-3202
817-755-9517

Billy Smith
Director
Panhandle Press Association
Box 747, WT Station
Canyon, Texas 79016
806-656-2414

Merlin Mann
Executive Director
Texas Press Association
Abilene Christian University
Department of Journalism and
    Mass Communication
ACU Box 7892
Abilene, Texas 79699
915-674-2019

Mark Murray
President
Association of Texas Photography Instructors
P.O. Box 121092
Arlington, Texas 76012
817-459-8354

Utah
DeAnn Evans
Faculty Liaison
Utah Journalism Educators Association
301 LCB
Department of Communication
University of Utah
Salt Lake City, Utah 84112
801-581-5847

Virginia
Linda Mercer
Virginia Association of Journalism
    Teachers and Advisers
P.O. Box 914
Halifax, Va. 24558
804-476-7947

Ken Tilley
Programs Supervisor
Virginia High School League, Inc.
1642 State Farm Blvd.
Charlottesville, Va. 22901-8809
804-977-8475

Washington
Lu Flannery
Treasurer
Washington JEA
2802 N.W. 92nd Street
Seattle, Wash. 98117
206-784-9167

West Virginia
Pamela Yagle
W.Va. High School Journalism Teachers
    Association
West Virginia University
P.I. Reed School of Journalism
Martin Hall
Box 6010
Morgantown, W.Va. 26506-6010
304-293-3505

Nan Cayton
West Virginia Scholastic Press Association
Fairmont Senior
Loop Park
Fairmont, W.Va. 26554
304-367-2150

Wisconsin
Richard Gustafson
Wisconsin Chippewa Valley
    School Press Association
Hudson High School
1501 Vine Street
Hudson, Wis. 54016
715-386-4226

Mark Thompson
President, Board of Directors
Kettle Moraine Press Association
Continuing Education Services
University of Wisconsin at Whitewater
Whitewater, Wis. 53190
708-395-1421

Leroy "Skip" Zacher
Director
N.E. Wisconsin Scholastic Press Association
Department of Journalism
University of Wisconsin at Oshkosh
Oshkosh, Wis. 54901-8696
414-424-1042

Rose Richard
Coordinator
The Connection
Marquette University
1131 W. Wisconsin Avenue
Milwaukee, Wis. 53233
414-288-3448

Wyoming
Rita Isabell
Executive Director
Wyoming Press Association
Shoshoni High School
Box 327
Shoshoni, Wyo. 82649
307-876-2576

Biographies

Writing and editing

Zita Arocha is a bilingual free-lance journalist with 15 years' experience as a reporter for *The Washington Post, The Miami Herald, The Miami News, El Miami Herald and Tampa Times*. In 1993, she was named interim executive director of the National Association of Hispanic Journalists. She was a contributing writer to *Death By Cheeseburger* and the main author of Chapter 2.

Gelareh Asayesh is a free-lance writer who has covered education for *The* (Baltimore) *Sun* and *The Miami Herald*. Born in Tehran, Iran, she is fluent in several languages. She has won investigative reporting awards from the Washington-Baltimore Newspaper Guild and the Maryland chapter of the Society for Professional Journalists. She was the main author of Chapter 1.

Jacqueline Blais is an editor at *USA TODAY*, where, among other duties, she began *USA TODAY's* Best-Selling Book List in 1993. She was the copy editor for *The USA TODAY Weather Book*, which was published in 1992. Before joining *USA TODAY*, she was the features editor and a columnist for the *Norwich Bulletin* in Connecticut. In 1971, she started a weekly community newspaper, *The Poquonnock Bridge Times*, in Groton, Conn. She was the copy editor for *Death By Cheeseburger*.

Alice Bonner is the director of journalism education for The Freedom Forum. She originated the concept of *Death By Cheeseburger* and oversaw its development. Her 20 years in journalism include reporting and editing at *The Washington Post* and *USA TODAY*, and recruiting journalists for Gannett Co., Inc., newspapers. She was Howard University's first journalism graduate and a 1978 Nieman Fellow at Harvard University. She received the Robert P. Knight Multicultural Recruitment Award of the AEJMC Scholastic Journalism Division in 1993.

Mike Brodie is a reporter for Paramount Publishing Co.'s *Catonsville Times* and edits the jazz magazine, *The Music*. He is the author of *Created Equal: The Lives and Ideas of Black American Innovators* and has been a senior writer of *Black Issues in Higher Education*. A University of Colorado graduate, he

has written for *Black Collegian, California Gazelle* and the *NABJ Journal*. He was a contributing writer for Chapter 3.

Sara Cormeny spent nine months as a journalism education research assistant at The Freedom Forum, working on *Death By Cheeseburger*. She was circulation manager and mentor program coordinator for *Youth Communication*. She has written articles for *Communication: Journalism Education Today*, Youth News Service and *The Newbury Street Guide*. She graduated magna cum laude from Brandeis University in 1991. She was a contributing writer for Chapter 3.

Louis Freedberg, a Washington correspondent for the *San Francisco Chronicle*, has covered higher education and race relations. He is a Yale graduate and an anthropologist with a Ph.D. from the University of Califonia at Berkeley. He founded Youth News, an Oakland, Calif., program that trains teens as radio news reporters and was a founder of Pacific Youth Press, a project of Pacific News Service that trains teenagers to be reporters. He has worked in the public schools running programs for at-risk minority youth. In 1991, he was a John S. Knight Professional Journalism Fellow at Stanford University. He was a primary writer of *Death By Cheeseburger* and the main author of Chapter 10.

Jon Funabiki is the founding director of the Center for Integration and Improvement of Journalism at San Francisco State University, where he also is a lecturer in the journalism department. The Center was created in 1990 to develop model programs at the university and to recruit and train ethnic minorities for careers in journalism and to promote improved news coverage of ethnic communities and issues. A journalist for 20 years, he spent 16 years as a writer and editor at *The San Diego Union*. He was a John S. Knight Professional Journalism Fellow at Stanford University in 1985 and a Jefferson Fellow at the East-West Center in 1989. He was a primary writer of *Death By Cheeseburger* and the main author of Chapter 4.

Leonard Hall is coordinator of journalism education for The Freedom Forum, where he assists in directing programs for youth and college journalists and administers The Freedom Forum Sports Journalism Institute. Hall was a reporter at *The Virginian-Pilot & The Ledger-Star* in Norfolk, Va., where he covered

college and community sports and was sports editor of the *Clipper*, a tri-weekly tabloid edition of the newspapers. He has worked at *The Washington Post*, the *Daily Press* in Newport News, Va., and Black Entertainment Television. He graduated cum laude from Howard University in 1985. He was a contributing writer for Chapter 3 and Chapter 10, and the main author of Chapter 7.

Retha Hill is a reporter for *The Washington Post* with extensive experience covering government, social and urban issues. She spent 12 months in 1992-93 as The Freedom Forum's Journalist-in-Residence for Washington, D.C., public schools, evaluating and developing high school journalism programs in the nation's capital. She worked directly with students, newspaper advisers and administrators. Hill is former president of the Washington Association of Black Journalists. She has worked at *The Charlotte Observer, Detroit Free Press, New York Newsday* and *The* (Detroit) *Metro Times*. She was a contributing writer to *Death By Cheeseburger*.

Judith Hines is the Journalism Education Program Officer at The Freedom Forum. She was project director and the principal writer of *Death By Cheeseburger*. From 1979 to 1990, she served as executive vice president of the American Newspaper Publishers Association (now Newspaper Association of America). A former junior high school English teacher, she was president of the First Amendment Congress from 1984-88. She was honored by the Journalism Education Association in 1989 for outstanding service to scholastic journalism and served as vice chair of the board of directors of Youth Communication until 1993.

Joel Kaplan is an assistant professor at Syracuse University's Newhouse School of Public Communications. He was an investigative reporter for 12 years at the Chicago Tribune and *The* (Nashville) *Tennessean*. He has been a Nieman Fellow at Harvard University and a Journalism Fellow at Yale Law School. His national honors include the Sigma Delta Chi Green Eyeshade Award (1985) and a National Headliner Award (1984). He is co-author of *Murder of Innocence: The Tragic Life and Final Rampage of Laurie Dann*. He was the main author of Chapter 8.

Carol Knopes, the editor of *Death By Cheeseburger,* has worked on daily newspapers since 1968. She is a Special Projects editor at *USA TODAY* and has worked at *The Philadelphia Inquirer, The* (Bergen) *Record* and *Detroit Free Press.* She was the editor of *The USA TODAY Weather Book,* which was published in 1992. She majored in journalism at the University of Detroit Mercy. She is also a former staffer of *The Leprechaun Lookout* at St. Patrick's High School in Wyandotte, Mich.

Anne Lewis is a former newspaper reporter and past editor of *Education USA,* a weekly newsletter of the National School Public Relations Association. She now works with Education Writers of America, writing and editing reports on educational issues. She has extensive knowledge about the people, programs and trends in the field of public education. She was an advisory editor and contributing writer to *Death By Cheeseburger.*

Shinji Morokuma is the chief writer in The Freedom Forum Publications Department. He joined The Freedom Forum (then the Gannett Foundation) in 1989 as media relations coordinator in the Communications Department. He was an assistant director of public relations at the University of Rochester, where he also was editor of the official newspaper of the university and staff writer for its flagship magazine. He was a contributing writer to *Death By Cheeseburger.*

Sheila Owens is publications coordinator of The Freedom Forum. She was a newsletter editor at the International Food Information Council, a Washington, D.C.-based nonprofit association. A former public affairs specialist for Gannett Co., Inc., she is a journalism graduate of the University of Maryland. She was a contributing writer to *Death By Cheeseburger.*

Michael E. Phelps is the managing principal of Phelps, Cutler and Associates, a newspaper consulting group. He has worked in the newspaper business since 1971. He was president and publisher of the Weekly Group, Newspapers of New England and managing editor of *The Enterprise* in Falmouth, Mass. He is an adjunct associate professor and acting director of the Communication Industries Management Program at Emerson College. He has lectured at Michigan State University and the University of North Carolina. He was

a contributing writer for Chapter 5.

Adam Clayton Powell III has served as a consultant and lecturer at The Freedom Forum Media Studies Center since 1985, focusing on unanticipated consequences of technological innovation in news organizations. He is project coordinator for an exchange of American and South African journalists, a joint project of The Freedom Forum and the National Association of Black Journalists. He has been a journalist for nearly three decades, working at National Public Radio, CBS News and for Quincy Jones Entertainment. He was a contributing writer to *Death By Cheeseburger.*

Larry Sanders, the founder of L& D Information Services of Falls Church, Va., is a Special Projects editor at *USA TODAY,* where he began the database journalism department in 1989. He has worked for newspapers for more than 25 years. He is an instructor of computer-assisted journalism at the University of Maryland. He analyzed the *Death By Cheeseburger* content survey of 233 high school newspapers.

Mark Thalhimer is technology manager at The Freedom Forum Media Studies Center, where he runs the Technology Lab. He was most recently associate editor for NYNEX Information Systems and sales team leader for Harris/3M Document Products Inc. He was also an announcer and training director for WCWM-FM in Williamsburg, Va. He is a graduate of the College of William and Mary and has a master's degree from New York University. He has written articles about communications and computer technologies included in *The People's Right to Know: Media, Democracy and the Information Highway* and *The Media Studies Journal.* He was the main author of Chapter 9.

Craig W. Trygstad is co-founder of Youth Communication, the former Washington D.C.- based youth journalism organization that spawned a national group of independent citywide newspapers He founded Youth News Service, the only national news service operated by teenagers. A former journalism teacher at the university and high school level, he is recognized as a national leader in journalism education and alternative youth media. He was a fellow at the Robert F. Kennedy Memorial, where he worked to implement the recommendations of *Captive Voices.* He wrote about independent youth

newspapers in Chapter 6.

Ed Wiley III is former associate managing editor of *Black Issues in Higher Education.* He has written for *Education Daily,* was a reporter for *The Fresno Bee,* and has published articles in many newspapers, including *The Washington Post,* the Atlanta *Constitution* and the *Philadelphia Daily News.* He has been listed in Who's Who Among Black Americans and has won awards for his work from the Education Press Writers Association and the California Press Association. He was a contributing writer for Chapter 3.

Design and photography

Jim Brown is a Nashville, Tenn.-based free-lance photographer.

Mike Clemmer is a free-lance photographer based in Chelsea, Ala.

Richard Curtis is a founding editor and the designer of *USA TODAY* and its managing editor for graphics and photography. He is a founder of the Society of Newspaper Design and founder and editor for several years of *Design,* the society's quarterly journal. With Jim Dooley of *Newsday,* he founded the annual Eastern European seminar in photojournalism. Among other awards, he has won the J.C. Penney-Missouri award for best features section. A design consultant and lecturer in the U.S. and Europe, he has a degree in design from the School of Design, N.C. State University and was named the Outstanding Alumnus in 1993. He designed and produced *Death By Cheeseburger.*

Jeff Dionise is art director at Knight-Ridder Tribune Graphics in Washington, D.C. He has worked as an informational graphics specialist for *USA TODAY* and is an active free-lancer. His clients include the American Bar Association, *Consumer's Digest, Weekly Reader* and *KidSports* magazine. He has won three silver awards and twelve awards of excellence from the Society of Newspaper Design. He did the informational graphics for *Death By Cheeseburger.*

Richard Dole is a free-lancer best known as a sports photographer who specializes in covering the auto racing and golf circuits. His work has appeared in editorial publications throughout the United States and Europe, including *Automobile, Golf, L'Equipe, Newsweek, Sports Illustrated* and *USA*

TODAY. He is based in Charlotte, N.C.

Steven M. Falk is a contributing photographer for Gamma Liaison and a free-lancer for Reuters, *USA TODAY* and the *Los Angeles Times.* His work frequently appears in the corporate publications of Phillip Morris and Frito Lay. He has won more than 100 state and regional awards. He is a past director of the National Press Photographers Association and is a member of the American Society of Media Photographers.

Rick Friedman has been a photographer for more than 20 years. He is based in Boston. His work appears in *Time, Newsweek, U.S. News & World Report, The New York Times, USA TODAY, Stern, Discover* and other publications. His first book on Hillary Clinton was published in 1993 and his second book on the American infrastructure is to be published in 1994. His work has won National Press Photographers Association and American Society of Media Photographers awards.

John Glenn is director of photography for the Ft. Lauderdale *Sun-Sentinel* and a free-lance photographer.

Acey Harper is a photographer and picture editor based in Tiburon, Calif. He was a founder of *USA TODAY* as a photo editor and photographer. He has free-lanced since 1986, working for *USA TODAY, Fortune, National Geographic, People* and *Sports Illustrated,* among other publications. He is a University of Florida graduate.

Joe Kennedy has worked as a free-lance photographer in the Detroit area for 13 years. His clients include The Associated Press, *USA TODAY, The New York Times, Sports Illustrated,* Gamma Liaison, *Time,* HBO, Showtime, MTV, *Interior Design* and others. He also works in product photography, fashion, composites and children's photographs.

Ernie Leyba has worked as a free-lance photographer based in Denver for more than 12 years. Before then, he was a staff photographer for *The Denver Post.* At *The Denver Post,* he won numerous awards, including first place in the Pro Football Hall of Fame contest and special recognition in the World Understanding Through Photography contest presented by Nikon and the University of Missouri School of Journalism.

Scott Maclay is a Boston native who attended Mercer University in Macon, Ga. He was a photographer at *Florida Today,* photography director at the *Clarion-Ledger* of Jackson, Miss., and a photo editor at Gannett Co., Inc. He joined The Freedom Forum in 1991 as photo editor.

M.L. Miller is a free-lance photographer based in Columbia, S.C.

David Rees has taught photojournalism at the University of Missouri, Columbia since 1986 and has been director of the College Photographer of the Year competitions since 1987. He has served as lecturer and contest judge for professional photojournalism and design organizations throughout the Midwest and actively free-lances photographs and stories to clients including *Fortune, Farm Journal, Harrowsmith* magazine, *American Lawyer, National Hog Farmer, World Book Encyclopedia, USA TODAY, The Hartford Courant, The Los Angeles Times* and the United States Information Agency.

Jeff Reinking is a free-lance photographer based in Seattle, Wash.

Barbara Ries, a free-lance photographer based in Alexandria, Va., previously was a staff photographer for *USA TODAY.*

Bob Riha Jr. has been a free-lance/contract photographer with *USA TODAY* since 1983 and is a contributing photographer with the Gamma Liaison Agency. He has worked with Reuters, The Associated Press, United Press International, *U.S. News & World Report, Time* and the Long Beach, Calif., *Press Telegram.* He has been named president of the California Press Photographers Association for the 1993-94 term.

Shawn Spence, a free-lance photographer in Indianapolis, began his newspaper career at age 13, working as a reporter and photographer for his hometown newspaper in Princeton, Ind. He worked his way through college at Indiana University as a stringer for The Associated Press then joined the *Chronicle-Tribune* in Marion, Ind., as a photographer. He has worked for *Florida Today* and the Gannett News Service.

Karen Tam was a photographer for *The News & Observer* in Raleigh, N.C., for 14 years before beginning her free-lance career.

Her news clients include *USA TODAY,* The Associated Press, *The New York Times* and the Atlanta *Journal and Constitution.* She is a graduate in photography of Ohio University.

Bruce Zake is a free-lance photographer based in Cleveland. His clients include *Forbes, Sports Illustrated, Time* and *USA TODAY.* He has worked with companies such as Goodyear, General Motors, Society Corporation and IBM.

John Zich is a free-lance photographer based in Chicago.

About this book ...

Design and layout were done on a Macintosh Centris 650 personal computer using the latest available desktop publishing technology. The computer was equipped with 40 megabytes of random access memory, a 230-megabyte hard drive, a multi-session compact disk drive and was connected to a Super-Match 20-inch color monitor accelerated by a SuperMac 24 PDQ Plus accelerator card. A 44mb Syquest removable cartridge hard disk drive was used for storage and for transporting files. For low-resolution proofing the system was connected to an Apple LaserWriter Pro 600 printer with 8 megabytes of memory.

The manuscript was written by a number of people in different areas of the country using a variety of personal computers and software. The edited manuscript was transferred to the Macintosh by several methods: (1) Saving the files on a floppy disk as ASCII text-only files, which were then translated for the Macintosh using Apple File Exhange software; (2) transferring the files electronically through America Online electronic mail; or (3) rekeyboarding.

Layout software was Quark Xpress. The graphics were created using Aldus FreeHand.

Photographs were shot on 35mm transparency and color negative film. The images were edited and then scanned onto a Kodak Photo CD at five different resolutions per image.

Low-resolution images were used for preliminary layouts. For final output, high-resolution versions of the Kodak Photo CD scans were color corrected, cropped, sized, resampled and separated using Adobe Photoshop. These files were output as DCS (Desktop Computer Separations) files. DCS outputs five separate files — high-resolution Encapsulated PostScript (EPS) files of one each for

Cyan, Magenta, Yellow and Key (or Black), plus one, low-resolution TIFF (Tagged Image File Format) file that was used to replace the low-resolution file within the Quark Xpress document. For final output to high-resolution filmsetters, the low-resolution TIFF files were replaced with the high-resolution files.

All files were transferred to Hagerstown (Md.) Bookbinding & Printing on Syquest 44mb removable cartridges. Color proofs were produced on a Fuji Colorart system. The book was printed by Hagerstown (Md.) Bookbinding and Printing on a five-color Heidelberg Speedmaster press using 70-pound recycled matte white paper with a 12-point cover stock. The book was bound on an 18-station Muller-Martini Panda Perfect-binder.

The text type is Adobe Garamond in 10-point setting on 12-point leading. Headlines are 24-point Garamond with captions in 8-point Helvetica. The original Garamond typeface was designed by Claude Garamond, a noted French type founder of the mid-1500s.

Credits ...

Page	Credit
i	Barbara Ries
vi	From left: Jeff Reinking, David Rees, Joe Kennedy, Barbara Ries
xi	Clockwise, from top: John Zich, Bob Riha Jr., David Rees, Steven M. Falk, Joe Kennedy
3	Scott Maclay (3)
4, 5, 7	Jeff Dionise
9	Karen Tam
10	Top: David Rees; bottom: Mike Clemmer
12	Joe Kennedy
13	Bruce Zake
15	M.L. Miller
16	Top: Richard Dole; bottom: Jeff Dionise
18	Jeff Dionise
19, 20	Barbara Ries
21	Shawn Spence (2)
22, 23	Jeff Dionise
24	Barbara Ries
26	Jeff Dionise
33	Barbara Ries
34	Top: Jeff Dionise; bottom: Ernie Leyba
35	Jeff Dionise
36	Steven M. Falk
37	Mike Clemmer (2)
39	Shawn Spence
40, 41	Jeff Dionise
42, 46	Barbara Ries
50	Jeff Dionise
52	Joe Kennedy
53, 54	Jeff Dionise
55	Top: Bruce Zake; bottom: Jeff Dionise
57	Bob Riha Jr.
58, 59	Jeff Reinking (9)
60, 61	Karen Tam (7)
62	Rick Friedman
63	Bruce Zake
69	Jeff Dionise
71	Barbara Ries (2)
72	M.L. Miller
73-75	Jeff Dionise
82, 87, 88	Barbara Ries
89	Jeff Dionise
92-93	Acey Harper (8)
96	David Rees
98-100	Jeff Dionise
101	Top: Collection of the Supreme Court of the United States; bottom: *National Geographic,* Collection of the Supreme Court of the United States.
107	David Rees
109	Top: Jeff Dionise; bottom: Barbara Ries
110	Jim Brown
111, 112	Rick Friedman
115	John Zich
118, 119	John Glenn
121	Jeff Dionise
123	David Rees (6)
126	Jeff Dionise
131	David Rees
134-135	John Zich (8)
137	Steven M. Falk (2)
138	Jeff Dionise
145	Mike Clemmer

Index